T0272467

We'll Play till We Die

We'll Play till We Die

JOURNEYS ACROSS A DECADE OF
REVOLUTIONARY MUSIC IN
THE MUSLIM WORLD

Mark LeVine

UNIVERSITY OF CALIFORNIA PRESS

University of California Press
Oakland, California

© 2022 by Mark LeVine

Library of Congress Cataloging-in-Publication Data

Names: LeVine, Mark, 1966– author.
Title: We'll play till we die : journeys across a decade of revolutionary music in
  the Muslim world / Mark LeVine.
Description: Oakland, California : University of California Press, [2022] |
  Includes bibliographical references and index.
Identifiers: LCCN 2022000507 (print) | LCCN 2022000508 (ebook) |
  ISBN 9780520350762 (hardback) | ISBN 9780520975859 (ebook)
Subjects: LCSH: Popular music—Social aspects—Islamic countries. |
  Popular music—Social aspects—Middle East.
Classification: LCC ML3918.P67 L483 2022 (print) | LCC ML3918.P67 (ebook) |
  DDC 782.4216/3—dc23
LC record available at https://lccn.loc.gov/2022000507
LC ebook record available at https://lccn.loc.gov/2022000508

Manufactured in the United States of America

31 30 29 28 27 26 25 24 23 22
10 9 8 7 6 5 4 3 2 1

For Alessandro and Francesca

And if one of our instruments breaks, it doesn't matter.
We have fallen into the place where everything is music.
—RUMI, *"Where Everything Is Music"*

Talent has no race; there simply exists a race of musicians.

—MANU DIBANGO

It is the role of the artist to make the revolution irresistible.

—TONI CADE BAMBARA

I broke the law?
No, the law broke me.
Enough, enough, gentlemen.
I was born here, my grandparents too.
You will not sever me from my roots.

—DAM, *"Born Here"*

CONTENTS

ILLUSTRATIONS

AUTHOR'S NOTE

REVOLUTIONARY AURAS AND PHANTASMS

WAKING UP ON FEBRUARY 30

I began writing this author's note in the midst of the tenth anniversary of the Egyptian Uprising and its momentarily successful denouement, when President Hosni Mubarak was finally removed from power. Those two and a half weeks, along with the month before and months after them, constituted the world's most transformative moment since the fall of Communism.

I couldn't help feeling vindicated back on that beautiful Friday evening, standing in Midan Tahrir with some musician friends I'd first met half a decade earlier while researching *Heavy Metal Islam,* the book whose journeys across the Arab and larger Muslim world are continued here, with some additional stops along the way. After all, hadn't that book predicted—with equal measures of confidence and caution—that the ascendant generation of artists, intellectuals, activists, and other cultural and political "creatives" and fugitive explorers across the Arab and broader Muslim world contained within it the political and aesthetic energy, impatience, and vision to push assertively for substantive change across the region?

But even then I also was more than a bit nervous, certainly more so than when *Heavy Metal Islam* was first published two and a half years before. As a historian of revolutions and political violence as well as of music and social movements, I knew well that crowds could be fickle, turning on the very people they had previously cheered, even on the people who had first brought them together, without much warning or reason. Moreover, while Mubarak had been forced from power, the Egyptian *nizam*—the deeply corrupt military-led authoritarian political system that had ruled Egypt for over half a century—wasn't going to give up power without a vicious fight, one that it was unlikely to lose without inflicting a heavy and tragic toll upon Egyptian society. I did not yet comprehend, on that glorious evening in Tahrir, just how powerful and widespread was the energy that young people across the region were then unleashing. Nor could I imagine just how murderously repressive the responses from most governments would be, or the complicity of their powerful patrons, in that violence when it was unleashed. If nothing else, the dozen years since the publication of *Heavy Metal Islam* in 2008 reminds us how much history can fit into the space of a decade.

FROM POTENTIAL TO POWER

In its review of *Heavy Metal Islam* the *New York Times* advocated for a "Marshall Amp Plan" for the region to ensure enough support for democracy to overcome the half-century and more of US- and Western-backed authoritarianism and violence across the region. That certainly sounded like a good idea to me, and with the book out it was time to figure out just what such a plan would look like. My first priority was to release an album featuring many of the artists I'd come to know and love, which was achieved with the release of *Flowers in the Desert* with EMI Arabia in 2009 (the title taken from an Iranian metalhead's description of what the arrival of metal in Iran felt like). My second goal was to find someone to film a documentary based on the book, which happened when Oscar-nominated, Emmy-winning filmmaker Jed Rothstein agreed to direct it, resulting in the award-winning documentary *Before the Spring, after the Fall,* released in 2013.

Like flowers blooming after a desert rain, the media was increasingly interested in the hardcore and extreme music of the Middle East and North Africa (MENA) region. The Austin-based festival South by Southwest (SXSW) invited me to curate a "Heavy Metal Islam" night for their 2009 edition, which featured some of the artists from the book (including Lazy Wall and Palestinian Rapperz), only to screw us by announcing a "secret" Metallica show a few blocks away the same night (it's not hard to imagine which event most attendees at SXSW went to). While I rushed to finish *Flowers in the Desert,* NPR did a special report on how "heavy metal is working its way into Islam." Suddenly, a lot of people seemed to understand that the kids and the music I'd been studying meant something more than the sound, angst, and fury they represented, and they wanted a piece of the story. A decade later, the Indonesian, female, hijab-wearing metal band

FIGURE I. Fans during first metal concert in central Cairo in many years, December 2008. Still image from the documentary *Before the Spring, after the Fall,* Jed Rothstein, dir., Tom Hurwitz, DP.

Voice of Baceprot is the newest NPR darling, as we'll see in the epilogue to this book.

What a dozen years ago was written as a hopeful paean to the future has now become a book of history, one chronicling the first stage of the coming-of-age of a unique generation. In the years since *Heavy Metal Islam*'s publication, that generation moved from the subcultural margins to the countercultural center and the revolutionary avant-garde, only to wind up largely pushed to the margins again, with too many people either crushed or pushed right out of their homelands into exile, if not into prison or even far too early graves. *Heavy Metal Islam* argued for the potential for large-scale, youth-inspired (if not youth-led) revolution; but neither I nor any of the artists or fans I knew had any idea of when, where, or how an explosion of activism and protests might come. During the Muhammad Mahmoud rebellion of November 2011, a young musician activist who was in charge of a group of tents outside the mugamma' (the giant government building in Tahrir that symbolizes the fearsome power of Egyptian bureaucracy) put it best when explaining to me the name he'd given his "neighborhood": "I named it 'February 30' because the chances of our revolution actually succeeding are about as likely as waking up on February 30." Ten years on, there's been more than a few February 29s, but the thirtieth remains as elusive as ever, at least politically.

As we'll see, culturally the story has been much more optimistic in most places much of the time. But music and politics are hardly separable, in the MENA or anywhere else for that matter. The title of this book is a testament to that fact, and was uttered by Zakaria Ibrahim, the founder of the renowned Egyptian folklore group El Tanbura, late one night as we stood at the edge of the shore staring out into the Mediterranean along the shore of his hometown, Port Said, after the group's weekly performance. Reflecting on the political, musical, and financial struggles his band has had to endure over several decades to continue to play their music, he simply said, "We'll play until we die." That drive, determination, and urge to perform, regardless of the risk, remuneration, or reward, perfectly encapsulate the attitudes of most every musician we will encounter in the pages that follow, whether they're teenagers just beginning their musical journey or pushing seventy like Zakaria. Indeed, as the grandma giving the metal horns on the cover of this book, by the Moroccan graffiti and graphic artist D'Et, makes clear, it might be young people who are driving the potentially and sometimes actually revolutionary change across the region, but you're never too old to rock, or to fight for change, as the presence of everyone from five-year-old kindergartners to eighty-five-year-old grandmothers in the protests that shook the MENA region a decade ago—and before and since then everywhere from the boulevards and squares of Arab capitals to the front lines of the Occupied Territories—has made abundantly clear. Sadly, you're still never too young to die fighting for your rights as well.

"RACE," VOICE, AND AUTHORSHIP IN THE ERA OF SOCIAL MEDIA

The manner in which people write about the artists and fans associated with heavy metal, hip hop, punk, and other sonically "extreme" youth music (hereafter, EYM) scenes has certainly changed significantly since the publication of *Heavy Metal Islam*. While the clear political themes and implications of hip hop and punk led academics and journalists to focus attention on them not long after they emerged, the political salience of heavy metal was far less foregrounded until recently, except as they referred to supposed ties between the music and violence, depression, suicide, Satanism, and its kissing cousin, teenage rebellion.

As a quorum of trained scholars with deep historical, sociological, and, as important, musical knowledge of and appreciation for metal began to coalesce in the 2000s, "metal studies" began to solidify as a clearly definable discipline. Not coincidentally (at least in hindsight), the first dedicated "metal studies" conference took place the year of *Heavy Metal Islam*'s original publication, in 2008. Since that time there has been a significant expansion of conferences, dedicated journals, research, and publications on metal (the first academic journal devoted to metal, *Metal Music Studies*, was conceived around the conference in 2008). Punk and hip hop, already far better represented in the scholarly literature and also with their own specialized journals and book series, have developed apace, to the point where leading punk scholars are exploring Indigenous (aboriginal) research methodologies and hip hop dissertations are being delivered as full-fledged rap albums rather than as prose writing.

Today, academic research on heavy metal in all its aspects is fast becoming as robust as hip hop or punk studies. One can find in-depth and highly original analyses of metal across the world, from Scandinavia to Africa, from Latin America to China. Equally deep debates on theory and methodology, including the role of engaged intellectuals in the larger metal communities they study—what one scholar inventively refers to as "metallectuals"—are also becoming more frequent. Even more important from my perspective, the spread of scholarship on metal and other forms of extreme music in the Middle East and broader Muslim world has coincided with an even more profound change in the positionality of the young people who constitute the majority of artists and fans.

Quite simply, the voices of musicians and fans from the Global South have become more amplified, more sophisticated, more politicized, and more accessible to the outside world than ever before. As the way scholars study metal and other forms of EYM developed, the subjects of such research—the musicians and fans—acquired the means to narrate, curate, and broadcast their stories and music themselves in an unmediated fashion and in unprecedented ways. This dynamic was already apparent as I wrote *Heavy Metal Islam,* and led me to try to act, as much as possible, as a facilitator and amplifier of the stories of the voices I encountered rather than attempting to mediate, interpret, or "translate" their experiences for a broader—read, Euro-American—audience.

Today these dynamics have only intensified; the role of scholars of and commentators—locals as much as foreigners—on these scenes is far less important or even necessary than before. The ubiquity and sheer wattage of social media, whether commercialized or semiprivate, are unprecedented, enabling artists to tell their own stories in their voices in innumerable ways. Yet even here, and now, there is no such thing as unmediated (or, increasingly, unsurveilled) circulation and consumption of their art. This raises, at least for me, profound questions on the role of the scholar or even comrade and collaborator across the region, especially as so many countries have reentered a dark era of authoritarian governance, surveillance, censorship, and repression in which a larger number of artists than ever before has left the MENA and moved to Europe and North America.

To be sure, simply being "local" does not guarantee greater trust, access, or insight into a particular group, scene, or subculture, or sympathy for and cooperation with musicians or artists. If anything, the more artists interact with people outside their scenes, the more suspicious they become of outsiders "studying" or otherwise writing about them. Cameroonian world music legend Manu Dibango put it best in his autobiography *Three Kilos of Coffee* when speaking of his fellow musical artists: "Talent has no race; there simply exists a race of musicians. To be part of it, you have to have knowledge." Like other artists, musicians are a breed apart. You can meet a musician from the opposite side of the world and become "family" in the space of a song, "shar[ing] a worldview and emotional knowledge," as the critical theorist Lauren Berlant described it, derived from "broadly common . . . experience." That common experience creating, sharing, and consuming art enables the creation of what she terms "intimate publics." Such communities share worldviews and emotional knowledge as well as common experiences; while they are normally as "tenuous and fragile" as a pop song, if they mix both beauty and political power with just the right balance, as Barry Shank has well shown in his *The Political Force of Musical Beauty,* mass counter and even revolutionary publics become possible.

Such publics, and the relationships and sound that shape them, are only possible if one brings a depth of knowledge, as Dibango put it, that demonstrates true respect for the people and history one is engaging and the music one is creating. In this regard one can be culturally outside—e.g., a "foreigner" in a musical community—yet "racially" inside, as a fellow musician. In scenes where many of the members are alienated and estranged from their broader cultures and societies, the transnational "imagined communities," with their common languages and aesthetic vernaculars (which characterize metal, punk, hip hop, and other EYM scenes), create powerful solidarities among musicians and fans across cultures and even continents.

As Iron Maiden manager Rod Smallwood explained to me not long after the band's Dubai Desert Rock show in 2007—their first ever in the Arab world—Maiden fans everywhere are like one big family, regardless of their country or creed (something that's obvious to anyone who's attended a Maiden show, and many other metal shows for that matter). Because of this, studying and participating in these scenes as an insider to the music enable a kind of insider status in local scenes even as one remains, at best, an intimate outsider within their broader societies. In the same manner, however, those who enter subcultural (never mind countercultural) scenes like metal, punk, or hip hop as "poseurs"—in the words of Egyptian anthropologist Mona Abaza, "academic tourists"—will be met with condescension and hostility as soon as they're sniffed out.

It's clear then that any thought of telling someone else's story or explaining their experiences and struggles to the outside world is far less tenable than it was before. It's far more important to amplify, with the least remixing or mastering possible, different voices, sounds, styles, and experiences that already are quite capable of representing, recording, and producing themselves, of telling their own stories, in unique ways based on their own tastes and experiences, if not allowed to do so.

Indeed, had I begun the journey that produced *Heavy Metal Islam* today, it probably would not wind up as a traditional book, certainly not one with a single author. At least that was my view as I sat down to write what I thought would be an updated edition of the original. And so I imagined new and far more innovative, interactive, and polyphonic ways of engaging these artists and scenes in a context where artists themselves would be able to articulate their own stories more eloquently and authentically, in English and to an international audience, than any foreign member of the "race" could hope to do.

If we translate Manu Dibango's conception of the race of musicians into "profession," anthropologists have been grappling with the similar issue of doing ethnographic research on themselves and their peers, including on "native" scholars who, unlike in previous eras when the subjects of research tended to have far less schooling and knowledge of the outside world, were highly educated, were fluent in the ethnographer's (usually European) language, and likely knew as much about the ethnographer's culture as he or she knew about theirs, if not more so.

Today, with the rise and now ubiquity of social media, with much higher levels of education even among the poor in the Global South, and with

English solidified as a global lingua franca among musicians, this reality is even more important, calling for what anthropologists describe as a collaborative or "para-ethnography," which proceeds in a far more humble and self-reflexive relationship with the people with whom one engages in research. Such a methodology achieves two crucial goals. First, as political scientist Lisa Wedeen has demonstrated with respect to political artists in Syria, it forces scholars to treat the artists with whom we work as "political theorists in their own right," whose art possesses the power to expand "the space of interpretive encounter in order to diagnose (and see ways out of) the impasses—collectively." Wedeen describes such artists as "interlocutors" rather than "informants"; I would describe them, even more, as collaborators and cocreators.

Second, this approach moves beyond an outsider/insider dichotomy, reflecting the kinds of collaborative relationships that, for example, one has to develop with fellow artists in order to write about them in ways that allow their visions and voices to speak as originally and powerfully as possible. In Kevin Dwyer's book *Moroccan Dialogues*, published in 1982, one of the first and still most imaginative attempts at collaborative ethnographic writing between an anthropologist and the main "subject" of research, Dwyer's "interlocutor," a *faqir* (devout Sufi) named Muhammad, explains as they decide what parts of their conversations need to be edited out of the book that "this is all a question of trust. . . . There is trust between us—we've been through a lot together. But as for others—you can't have trust in them whether they're Muslims or Christians. If someone you don't know comes and gets the book he can use it to do something bad for us, even if we haven't done anything wrong."

For Dwyer (and presumably Faqir Muhammad as well, although we can't know for sure), intimacy, vulnerability, and integrity all must be at the core of the cross-or transcultural ethnographic collaboration and be visible to readers in the same manner that they were visible to the collaborators. Such an attitude, he explains, is the sine qua non for preventing the kinds of distortions, misrepresentations, and misunderstandings that normally plague anthropological reflections on "other" cultures. There can be no aura of authenticity, in other words, without a level of openness of interaction that is as important for ethnographic as for musical—or political—collaboration.

As a musician, the attitudes and interactions advocated by Dwyer and Faqir Muhammad are the (hoped-for) normal order of business when collaborating: everyone brings in their particular sounds, melodies, rhythms, and ideas, and, if it's working, something new and powerful is created when you count in the song or hit the record button. But this is much harder to do in the form of a traditional print book, especially when, as opposed to the majority of "collaborations" that take place between professional scholars and nonprofessional "interlocutors" or "subjects," many of my collaborators are as experienced and skilled at music, activism, research, and related pursuits as am I, if not more so. Yet it has never been more important, or possible, to engage in this kind of collaborative creativity with artists and communities globally, or more urgent given the common threats we face and the realities that our own governments are almost always working together to frustrate, coopt, or crush any attempt at solidarity or joint struggle.

In that context, it quickly became clear when I returned to *Heavy Metal Islam* almost ten years after it was first published that it did not require significant revision or updating, but rather should stand as it is, as a historical archive of a particular liminal moment, one that moved in many different directions in the ensuing years, depending on where one was situated. So much has happened in the ensuing decade that not only was a new book warranted, but new ways of writing that book needed to be envisioned as well, or at least new ways of collaborating and composing the narrative that would underlie it. For me, there were two obvious models to emulate in proceeding with this enterprise. The first was composing, arranging, recording, and producing an album with a group of fellow musicians and artists. And so, in this volume I have tried specifically to highlight and, in some cases, cowrite with the artists and critics who I believe have the most perceptive views of the current dynamics in their countries, almost a decade into the uprisings' era—they are, in effect, cowriters, arrangers, orchestrators, and coproducers of the chapters on which we collaborated. As for me, besides being the writer or cowriter on all the chapters that follow, perhaps my most important role is that of "producer," making sure the stories have a consistent sound and flow and tell an overall story that lives up to the sonic force of the music. The second model was the practice of "culture jamming" that I'd helped develop beyond its initial imagining as "jamming" subversive messages into consumer or political advertising, turning it into the far more positive and original practice of bringing artists, activists, and scholars together—within and, increasingly in the context of globalization, between cultures—to create art at the highest possible intersection of aesthetic, political, and intellectual creativity. Only that level of virtuosity could hope to educate, motivate, and ultimately transform subcultures into counter- and revolutionary cultures, as well as move broader publics toward progressive change, especially in societies, from America to Egypt, plagued by such strong and often crippling ideological trauma.

PHANTASMS, AURAS, AND THE SOUL OF MUSIC; OR, WOULD ADORNO HEADBANG?

One of the central claims of both *Heavy Metal Islam* and this volume is that youth music, and particularly its less "pop" and more extreme and (at least initially) underground forms in the Middle East and broader Muslim world, offers an incredibly rich and still underutilized source of knowledge about the lives, dreams, fears, and challenges of young people across the region. By extreme I mean music that has several of the following elements: harsher, louder, more distorted or lo-fi, politically/lyrically and/or aesthetically/sonically dark, and often, although by no means always, political in its referents, narrative, or intentions, compared with other forms of popular music. EYM is concentrated in "extreme" forms of metal, gangsta rap and its subgenres and offshoots, and hardcore punk. Sonically "softer" styles, such as free jazz, electronic music, or funk, can be extreme, depending on their overall sonic characteristics and energy, affective power, and lyrical content. By the same token, I don't consider more mainstream forms of metal, hip hop, and punk to be EYM just because they possess one or more "extreme" sonic or musical elements; nor would simply having political lyrics or context automatically classify music as EYM.

Underground forms of EYM in the MENA offer an incredibly rich yet still underutilized source of knowledge about the lives, dreams, fears, and challenges of young people across the region. As important, through studying the scenes and those participating in them we can gain a deeper understanding of the broader political, economic, and cultural struggles experienced by their societies. This knowledge is particularly powerful because the music is not just a repository of experience; it's equally a weapon in the ongoing struggles against the still-dominant patriarchal, authoritarian, corrupt, and violent political and cultural orders across the region.

In other words, the music we're exploring has been central to the construction, imagination, and operation of the subcultures and later countercultures that offered such a powerful challenge to the systems in the last decade. While I have written this book for a broad audience as well as scholars and specialists in the societies and musics of the Muslim-majority world, a discussion of certain key arguments and terms of art deployed by critical scholars of culture will provide the conceptual skeleture around which we can build the analyses of musical creation and performance, and of the way that music becomes aesthetically embedded—to utilize Philip Bohlman's powerful but underutilized term—with and in larger social and political struggles.

It should not be surprising that among the most important approaches to studying the intersection of politics and cultural creativity are those by the Italian Marxist thinker Antonio Gramsci and the founding members of the Frankfurt School. Their signal contributions were made in the period between the two world wars, when, as Gramsci described it, "the old world [wa]s dying and the new world struggling to be born" (is there any surprise that their analyses would be so relevant in the strikingly similar situation of today?). Both were inspired by Marx's focus on the material grounding of historical economic and political processes yet equally understood the need to understand the powerful role of culture in creating, sustaining, and potentially dismantling oppressive systems.

For Gramsci it is in the cultural arena rather than the economic base of society that the most important struggles for political and ideological power—as he termed it, "hegemony"—took place. Struggles for hegemony are long and painstaking, a kind of political and cultural trench warfare—in Gramsci's words, a "war of position"—that required every weapon in the cultural as well as political-economic arsenal to succeed. But how to weaponize culture, and specifically artistic production? In his view politically powerful art begins as a particularly powerful "phantasm" in the minds of a small vanguard of individuals—in our terminology, a subculture—that is successfully "externalized, objectified, and historicized" to the point that it serves as a conduit for the energy necessary to sustain and potentially convert the war of position into a more fluid and directly political "war of maneuver." That is, the subculture becomes a counterculture and even, potentially, a revolutionary culture capable of leading a direct assault on the state.

It is this power of art to serve as a sociopolitical conductor par excellence that enables it to crystalize and amplify political events, desires, visions, and drives. Music in this regard has, potentially, what performance theorist Bryan Reynolds terms "viscerallectric" power: that is, it's visceral and emotional, intellectual and electric at the same time. If the ideas carried by this energy become aesthetically embedded into a large enough share of society—through the production of what Bryan and I term "em*u*rgent" art (that is, both stylistically innovative and produced in moments of societal urgency)—then, in the words of Toni Cade Bambara, artists can "make revolution irresistible," or at least, as a start, imaginable and desirable. George Lipsitz's work in *Dangerous Crossroads* has shown how jazz musicians "offer an alternative to the atomized individualism" of contemporary neoliberal culture and politics, trying to "change life, to make an audience move, rather than" focusing merely on their own talent or technique. Today more than ever, the same can be said of EYM in its various forms, especially when done with the originality and power of the artists we will encounter in the pages that follow.

At the same time that Gramsci was developing his views of the role of art in political "praxis" (theoretically grounded politically motivated action), some seven hundred kilometers to the north the members of the Institute for Social Research, soon to be known to the world as the "Frankfurt School" because of its original location, were debating the power of art to mobilize— or, as important, demobilize—people. Two of the School's heavyweights, Walter Benjamin and Theodor Adorno, located a similar phantasmagoric energy in what Benjamin, in his groundbreaking "The Work of Art in the Age of Mechanical Reproduction," first termed the "aura" that surrounded great works of art. Put briefly, Benjamin believed that with modern mass— what he terms "mechanical" or "technological"—production and circulation of art, "the aura" that previously had given great works of art their singular aesthetic, and thus social, power was for all practical purposes lost. For Benjamin this was a positive development because it enabled art to exist outside of the ownership and patronage of the powerful—the Church and wealthy elites. Thus liberated from its aura, art could be experienced and even created by the masses, and in so doing enable new and even revolutionary visions of the future to be put forth.

Benjamin's good friend Theodor Adorno was far less sanguine about how and how much the new technologies of production, distribution, and consumption would change art for the better. Rather, he felt that in the industrial era art's quasi-religious aura would simply be replaced by an aura of "style" that had even more power to numb or discipline people to unquestioningly follow the rules of the system. Adorno (in)famously felt that most music—including most classical and, later, jazz and rock as well—had little liberatory potential because of the mechanical, industrial, and commercialized conditions of their creation, circulation, and consumption. Only art that was so dissonant and "aesthetically deviant" that it couldn't possibly be commodified (or even conventionally understood or enjoyed) would have the power to create the kind of critical, transversal aura that could, first, help listeners see through the profoundly alienating nature of modern capitalist cultures and politics; second, remain steadfastly critical and uncoopted in the face of the impossibility of overcoming them in the near term; and, third, ultimately inspire strategies for winning a drawn-out war of position (to bring Gramsci back into the conversation).

If we jump ahead six decades to when I first met the Moroccan OG metal musician Reda Zine, his declaration that "we play heavy metal because our lives *are* heavy metal," which graced the back cover of *Heavy Metal Islam,* illuminated just how metal and other extreme forms of youth music expressed what Adorno described as the "truths behind reality's masks": in this case the masks of neocolonialism, neoliberalism, neopatriarchy, and the violence of contemporary capitalism that sustain all three. Indeed, in many ways the extreme metal beloved by most "metaliens" of the MENA was aesthetically quite similar to Adorno's beloved modern and largely dissonant and atonal classical music.

The way cultural and political energy are generated, focused, directed, distributed, and either absorbed or reflected by artists can from this perspective be understood as offering an important and often overlooked roadmap of how ruling social and political systems maintain or lose their hegemony and power, and thus how the "sound of music" can function as a powerful sonic-ideological weapon against or supporting the state, depending on its frequencies, amplitudes, and phase. This perspective also helps us to understand how artists (and the art and scenes they produce) reshape, reinforce, redirect, or break down existing networks and channels of political and societal power. Essentially, if society is like a forty-eight-track recording, exploring the various forms of art produced within it—especially those seemingly buried in the mix—goes a long way to providing the track-by-track architecture of social, cultural, and political power and how the whole order can be, as it were, remixed, if not rerecorded.

Such a roadmap for understanding the hegemonic mix of a society is particularly crucial in the era of hyperneoliberal—what I term necroliberal and even necrocapitalist—globalization in which we live today. This book argues that contemporary EYM has the cultural, political, and ideological voltage and, under the right circumstances, the amperage to help shake ostensibly rock solid political systems. And its (potential) political wattage is owed in good measure to fundamental changes in the political, technological, and aesthetic economies of music. While in many ways disastrous for musicians from the standpoint of earning a living from their art, these changes have opened new ways to circulate culture virally and widely with political effectivity.

In this regard, too few scholars have explored how the same technological foundations of neoliberal globalization that make it so virulently toxic (that is, the revolutionary acceleration of computer, communications, and transportation technologies beginning in the 1960s) also fostered the emergence of inexpensive digital music and video production technologies and the Internet, which exponentially augmented their power and reach. These in turn enabled unlimited and unprecedentedly inexpensive and even free production, distribution, and consumption of music by anyone anywhere at any time. In fundamental ways the very opposite of the era of commodified mechanical/industrial production, distribution, and consumption investigated by Benjamin and Adorno, this new paradigm of cultural production profoundly changed the nature of political art and its potential power as a means of amplifying and transmitting political critiques and visions of the future.

Suddenly, the kind of harsh and dissonant-sounding music that, in Adorno's day, was the preserve of the (largely German and American and often Jewish) intellectual elite was being recorded, performed, and circulated among growing subcultures who, by the time *Heavy Metal Islam* was published, were on the way to becoming true countercultures and, with the uprisings that began in late 2010, revolutionary cultures. The affective—that is, embodied, highly emotive, and pulsating—power of metal, hip hop, punk, and other forms of EYM was helping to reshape the social and political discourses, and with them power, flowing through their societies, opening new channels for communication, and challenging previously hegemonic or at least dominant social and political imaginaries.

Quite simply, the aura had returned to the work of art, but this time with an unmediated, highly political potential that was profoundly different from the predigital technological environment that existed in Adorno's day. From the Tunisian singer Emel Mathlouthi to the Egyptian "singer of the Revolution" Ramy Essam to Palestinian hip hop pioneers DAM and dozens of other groups from Morocco to Indonesia (and in the Muslim diasporas of Europe as well), music, to update Fela Kuti's famous prediction, had become the "weapon" of the present.

Indeed, it is indisputable today that music created, circulated, and consumed by the young people of the MENA reflected and even played an important role in the rise of the protest movements and ultimately uprisings across the region, something I argued was a strong possibility in *Heavy Metal Islam*. The music that precipitated, accompanied, and broadcast the region-wide uprisings that began in Iran in 2009 and exploded across the Arab world and then Turkey from late 2010 through 2013 "bleeds history" (as Benjamin scholar Carsten Strathausen so eloquently describes art's auratic power), laying bare the disconnect between the promises of authoritarian states like Ben Ali's Tunisia or Mubarak's Egypt and the dystopian realities these leaders worked so hard to conceal. Though Adorno probably wouldn't be headbanging to the likes of Egypt's death metal icons Scarab, Tunisian metal pioneers Myrath, or Egyptian OG hip hop crew Arabian Knightz, philosopher Roger Behrens did describe him as the "very first punk rocker." At the very least, he'd have a hard time arguing that the EYM we'll encounter in the pages to follow wasn't playing the kind of directly political role that he had long ago given up on.

STATES OF AMBIVALENCE, POSSIBILITY, AND ULTIMATELY EXCLUSION

In writing *Heavy Metal Islam* I tried to approach politics indirectly and even obliquely through the music, to let the music point to political processes, conditions, and possibilities that would not necessarily be apparent if approached more directly through traditional scholarly approaches. My goal, riffing on—and, to a certain extent, distorting—the writings of one of Adorno's most adroit students and then colleague, Herbert Marcuse, was to understand how what he described as "repressive tolerance" functioned to constrain dissent while increasingly characterizing the intolerance of the "new generation" for the broken promises and outright lies that characterized the authoritarian bargains implicitly maintained by their parents' generation and the governments that seemed to rule over them without end. In turn, Marcuse's most celebrated student, Angela Davis, brought Marcuse to bear on the great female blues singers of the jazz age, zeroing in on a "historicized and collectivized" remix of his argument that "the political potential of art lies only in its own aesthetic dimension." In their telling, art doesn't just "transcend its social determination and emancipate itself from the given universe"; it has the power to subvert hegemonic experience and reveal the suppressed, clandestine, and politically dangerous experiences that were always there beneath the surface. This same dynamic is evident in the utter disdain shown toward Ben Ali, Mubarak, Ghaddafi, Assad, and other dictators by the musicians, fans, and activists we'll encounter in this book, particularly in their refusal to tolerate the brutality, incompetence, and innumerable failures to bring the benefits of the emerging globalized system to their peoples.

The by turns poignant and outraged lyrics of the EYM artists discussed in the book provided an entry point to the political psychology behind such tolerance for repression on a mass scale by the societies in which the artists and scenes exist, the costs that their desire to refuse to tolerate such a situation would have on their mental health, and the power of their art to heal, however incompletely, the suffering it produces. "We are all mentally ill," the phrase more than a few metalheads would say to me over the years, did not merely refer to an illness of the psyche or soul, but more so to the costs of living in societies dominated by violence, corruption, and a lack of hope. That's why, as one Iranian metalhead put it, "a music about death" was so crucial to giving his generation hope.

What was also clear when *Heavy Metal Islam* was published, and has been borne out by events of the last dozen years, was that the returned aura would only achieve a transformative level of social and political power if the music and the people participating in it were able to move from the digital to the material/physical realm. Just as my friends in the Egyptian activist group Kefaya joked in 2006 that Facebook likes translated at very low ratios into physical presence at demonstrations, so too their power to effect politics directly depended on the possibility of people gathering together in the same physical space. That's why the clandestine or secret metal shows, whether in north Tehran basements or desert villas outside Cairo, were so important for the survival and development of the scenes, holding both the collective memory of a generation in the making and possibilities for new imaginaries. Indeed, Jacques Attali powerfully described music as a sonoric code that "orders power, privilege, and difference within society," and in this way the music chronicled in *Heavy Metal Islam* and now this volume constitutes a counter-*dis*order, a kind of antiauthoritarian creative destruction that, to borrow a phrase from the Zapatistas, helps people imagine "a world where other worlds are possible."

FROM HUNGRY TO RESONANT LISTENING

Female musicians and fans have always been a relatively small (or smaller) but still crucial component of metal, and similarly hip hop, punk, and other EYM scenes, globally since the birth of these genres half a century ago. The situation in the MENA region is broadly similar—as the cover of *Heavy Metal Islam* and the discussion of various female groups across the region hopefully indicated. Yet despite the symbolic importance and significant participation of girls and women in the MENA scenes, there can be no doubt that, as occurs globally, MENA music scenes suffer from their share of misogyny, prejudice, and harassment. (In just the latest incident demonstrating the intersecting imbalances of patriarchy, nationalism, and religious conservatism, as I write these lines in early March 2021, Palestine's premier techno DJ, the internationally renowned Sama Abdulhadi, was arrested and detained for a week by Palestinian authorities after religious conservatives stormed the Nabi Musa heritage site where she was filming a video, accusing her of blasphemy and violating Islam and insulting the Palestinian nation.)

Even if the scenes are for the most part much better than their larger societies in treating women with respect, the challenges faced by Arab/Muslim women who play metal or rap or are fans of the genres are crucial to acknowledge and learn from. Their heightened sensitivity to the violence and proclivity toward strongmen exhibited by so many of their compatriots, women as much as men, was no doubt why they and other female members of the metal scene who were on the streets during the uprisings of 2011–13, and then again in some countries beginning in 2018, were far less sanguine and even pessimistic about the future than most of their male counterparts. Indeed, from Egypt to Iran, some of the most important female voices we first met in *Heavy Metal Islam* have left their home countries for Europe and North America, risking the loss of their fan base back home in order to live in a more liberal culture, even as their closest musical collaborators continue to feel that the cost of leaving their musical cultures behind outweighs the benefit of not being harassed daily or not living under an oppressive regime, while in Morocco, Pakistan, and Indonesia (among other countries) a new generation of female artists are redefining the societal imagination of women as singers, rappers, and musicians. This calculus between musical, political, and personal resources, freedoms, and constraints by women—and, as we'll see across the chapters that follow, increasingly LGBTQ+ artists as well— produces some of the most important equations for understanding the evolution of EYM across the MENA and wider Muslim world today.

Another valuable and till now largely underutilized perspective (as well as the approaches derived from it) is inspired by how Indigenous and first nations scholars and activists research, produce, and engage public knowledge about their communities, which remain some of the world's most marginalized. Even compared with formally postcolonial societies, which too often suffer under regimes that are colonial in all but name, Indigenous peoples have been exploited, lied to, abused, stolen from, and even massacred by (former) colonizers and present-day rulers, while their treatment by the mostly Western scholars—and musicians—who have long studied and even collaborated with them has often been marked by avarice, appropriation, and even prejudice. Dylan Robinson, a xwélmexw (Stó:lō) scholar from what is today British Columbia, uses the evocative term "hungry listening" to describe the attitude of too many non-Indigenous scholars and artists when encountering—and too often appropriating—Indigenous music. That is, they listen the way starving white settlers once approached and too often appropriated Indigenous food and, soon after, territory, customs, people, and sovereignty. Robinson and like-minded scholars call for the decolonization of music studies by moving beyond "hungry" and appropriative listening toward the far more grounded and holistic "resonant listening" strategies practiced by Indigenous communities. Such listening is crucial to enabling art to have its own agency, born out of its deep roots in the history of those who create and perform it.

Indigenous Australians have notions of how art and particularly music can be most powerfully and authentically produced very similar to those of their American First Nations counterparts. They use the notion of songlines, and, even more powerfully, songspirals and "sand talk," to describe the processes through which, in the words of the Indigenous Australian novelist Tyson Yunkaporta, creators and performers channel the creative phantasms that become art through dialogic and auratic visual and aural systems, rather than mere words. In so doing, a far broader and more holistic and healing vision of the future can be imagined and pursued (as opposed to merely resourcing Indigenous musics at the service of other projects and narratives). While Yunkaporta focuses on the visual component of the actual lines drawn in the sand by Indigenous Australians to convey knowledge to the community, we can similarly understand and explore the sonic symbols drawn in the vibrations written into the air by music in order to better hear, and indeed amplify, its auratic power.

Of course, there is a risk that "Indigenous theory" or "Indigenous methodologies" themselves become appropriated by non-Indigenous (mostly but not only Euro-American) scholars who do not appreciate their radical foundation or consequences, much as otherwise not particularly innovative or progressive theories or arguments can be labeled "feminist" or "postcolonial" to boost their appeal. But if there's one thing true metaliens, punks, and hip hop heads can spot a mile away, it's a poseur; at least in the EYM scenes of the MENA and broader Muslim world, such attempts rarely succeed. Indeed, quite the opposite is the case.

What's more, the scenes in this book reveal that as music becomes indigenized, it breaks free from the traps of merely assimilating globally dominant styles, which have rightly prompted accusations of cultural imperialism, or simply adding local "traditional" styles to a Euro-American or global mix (literally and figuratively). These kinds of sonic resistance, however powerful and meaningful in their own right, are better at inspiring and supporting what the sociologist Manuel Castells has termed "resistance identities" than the "project identities" that inspire revolutionary imaginaries and, with them, radical action. Costa Rican composer and musicologist Susan Campos Fonseca best explains the kind of positive musical imaginaries and their impact on political activism, or praxis, in describing the potentially decisive power of experimental music in the Global South: "Experimentalism becomes a decolonizing tool that breaks with the way in which a subaltern identity . . . is built, and that idea that we're always the heirs of something that's made in another place, which is the colonial format." Put simply, EYM, like more formal styles of experimental music, is equally a weapon of resistance and an instrument of hope and imagination for a generation with increasingly little room for either.

It's worth noting here that for all their insights, Gramsci's discussions of hegemony and praxis have not produced either theories or strategies of cultural action that could overcome the sheer force of authoritarian or neoliberal ideologies and violence. Within the Frankfurt School, Adorno and Horkheimer disagreed intensely with Marcuse over whether theory and praxis could or even should, in Marcuse's terminology, be "unified."

Adorno and Horkheimer argue that any attempt by theory to "catch up to capitalism" is not merely futile, but weakens the necessarily dialectical—in practical terms, opposed and even confrontational—relationship between them. In two decades of research and activism in over two dozen countries, it has become clear to me, first, that, as Horkheimer and Adorno warned, most attempts to bring together theory and praxis wind up distorting both; second, that nevertheless the need to create a holistic and mutually informative theory/praxis synthesis has never been greater; and third, that art—in particular, the more radical and extreme forms of music discussed in the pages that follow—is in fact the arena where such a synthesis could most powerfully occur.

Here as in so many areas of life in this era of what E. P. Thompson termed "exterminist" capitalism, it is from the work of Indigenous scholars and activists that we can find the most deeply rooted yet avant-garde approaches to such a synthesis. Northern Irish punk studies scholar and musician Jim Donaghey's innovative research into punk cultures in Northern Ireland and Indonesia provides a good example of how non-Indigenous scholars and musicians can respectfully and effectively utilize Indigenous approaches to research to locate intersections of theory and practice that might be missed, or misinterpreted by less sensitive and nuanced approaches. He utilizes the work of Linda Tuhiwai Smith and other Indigenous and first nations scholars to develop research methodologies and designs grounded in the narratives, needs, and understandings of the artists with whom he works as to what is important to preserve and share with those outside the community. Donaghey's positionality as a punk, anarchist, musician, and scholar enables a relationship with Indonesian punks that mirrors and informs the relationship with his own community of punks in the Six Counties, in the process highlighting the reality that Indigenous methods are highly effective and beneficial when applied to Indigenous and non-Indigenous communities alike, because they ensure that the people whose lives, experiences, and music we're studying help design, shape, and perform our research agendas.

I return to Indigenous theories and methodologies in the epilogue, in the context of offering a decolonial approach to studying EYM that breaks down the still operative if no longer quite so dominant modernist and colonial frameworks that shape the way scholars study music and its multifarious impacts on Arab/Muslim societies. What should be clear here, and will I hope be even more so by the time our journey is complete, is that adopting such perspectives are key to ensuring that the voices of the artists, fans, and communities encountered in the pages to follow—and, with and through them, the aura of the music—are most powerfully and authentically conveyed to the reader.

Needless to say, if you're trying to convey the music, experiences, and imaginations of hundreds of musicians from a dozen countries during more than a decade of protests, uprisings, revolutions, and (civil) wars, the need for a deeply rooted, resonant, and collaboratively created narrative couldn't be more clear. However, the responsibility for whether this endeavor succeeds or falls short, produces treacly harmonies or rich and evocative dissonances, remains mine as the primary "arranger," "orchestrator," and "producer" of this book. One thing I know for sure is that its aura shines brighter the louder

FIGURE 2. Egyptian Death Metal icon Troll reenacting the first time he sang brutally, Giza, December 2008. Still image from *Before the Spring, after the Fall,* original trailer, Jed Rothstein, dir., Tom Hurwitz, DP.

you play the music. Without this aura, there'd be no story, and a far darker and duller future for most everyone we will meet in the pages ahead.

As I finished this author's note, a colleague posted a link on Facebook to a short story by the Egyptian writer Sherif Saleh. Titled "Living in Songs," it offered a magical realist account of the day in 1997 when upward of one hundred metalheads were arrested by Egyptian security forces, many of them jailed and even beaten, and threatened with prison and even death as apostates. The story's protagonist, a young metalhead risen from a deep sleep by his father, surrounded by security forces, on that fateful morning, can never quite process why everyone seems to misunderstand, if not outright hate, him and his fellow metaliens. As he explains to the reader, "They wouldn't believe me if I told them I didn't live in reality like them, but instead I lived in songs. I liberated myself from my dreary room, from our apartment, from the entire world, and I traveled. Don't we all travel with music for a few moments? Let it take us to another world?" As Rumi put it nearly eight centuries ago, some of us "have fallen into the place where everything is music"—or at least we wish we could.

The story is simultaneously poignant, tender, and frightening. But its end rings a bit less true: upon his release from jail on the condition that all his records, posters, and belongings relating to metal be taken away, the protagonist returns home and overdoses, losing consciousness for the last time while the music he loves plays in his head—and, presumably, his soul. As it happened, however, whatever fear, helplessness, and depression they suffered after the Muslim World's worst "Satanic Metal" affair, none of the Egyptian metal fans arrested in that raid committed suicide after their release. Instead, most metaliens I know responded the way Black Panther activist Denise Oliver-Velez described the role of music in the late 1960s—as a wave carrying activists forward rather than an ocean into which they disappear: "We were making a complete and total commitment. It was like going to war and we were propelled on a wave of music."

And so, while some fans quit the scene and the rest went more or less underground into the new millennium, Egyptian metalheads, like their bullied and beaten-down counterparts across the region, continued listening to and playing metal in bedrooms, basements, parties, and abandoned villas, until conditions improved enough for the scene to resurface, musically stronger than ever. And as we'll see in chapter 2, many became journalists, activists, and coders and acquired other skills and professions that would prove highly useful as the youth-led countercultural movements against the system developed.

Metal, as well as EYM more broadly, was always more than just a subcultural salve or a vehicle for escaping from the world. It was also a countercultural tool and a revolutionary weapon—to educate, motivate, and mobilize a rising generation, or at least a certain kind of avant-garde for the wars of position and ultimately maneuver that were approaching ever closer on the horizon. As the chapters that follow make clear, no matter how dark the hour has become, the music and the drive for freedom it represents remain undiminished; their message of angry and even joyful rebellion is still as powerful today as it was before a decade of coups, counterrevolutions, civil wars, and stunted transitions turned EYM from cathartic fantasy into documentary reality for millions of musicians and fans, from North Africa to Southeast Asia.

ACKNOWLEDGMENTS

First and foremost I would like to thank my coauthors, Sameh Zakout (Saz), Abed Hathout, Jackson Allers, Salome MC, Haniya Aslam, Mekaal Hasan, Pierre Hecker, Nahid Siamdoust, Jeremy Wallach, and the two anonymous Egyptian coauthors of chapter 2, for their invaluable insights, criticisms, and contributions not just to the chapters to which they contributed, but to the book as a whole. I would also like to thank my editor, Niels Hooper, as well as Naja Pulliam Collins, Julie Van Pelt, and Robert Demke for their encouragement, support, insightful comments, editing, and organizational help along the way of completing the book.

No part of this book could have been researched, never mind written or even imagined, without the generosity, support, insights, and openness of all the musicians and artists I discuss in these pages, as well as so many others whose music and stories I could not include. Dear friends, colleagues, comrades, and family who went beyond the call of duty to inspire various journeys, read multiple parts of the manuscript, help me track down artists and information, smooth out rough translations from various languages, correct misinterpretations or mistakes concerning music, lyrics, events, and dynamics operating across the various countries include (an asterisk indicates people who read major parts of the manuscript): Mona Abaza, Alaa Abd el-Fattah, Anders Ackfeldt, Teddy A., Hisham Aidi, Cristina Moreno Almeida,* Cherine Amr, Muhammad Antar, Reza Aslan, Arieb Azhar,* Ali Azhari, Hicham Bahou and the entire Boulevard family, Zeb Bangash, Sean Barlow, Armada Bizerte, Sherif Boraie, Elodie Bouffard, Kerim Bouzouita, Dominique Caubet,* Adrian Cheesley, all the kids at Chicoco Music & Radio, Port Harcourt (plus Ana Bonaldo and Michael Uwemedimo, the biggest kids of all), Laryssa Chomiak, Mario Choueiry, John Collins, Lanny

Cordola and the Miraculous Love Kids for unreasonable courage and faith in humanity, Leyla Dakhli, Bassem Deaibess, Donatella Della Ratta, Omar Dewachi, Sam Dunn, Nusrat Durrani, Hossam el-Hamalawy, Maha ElNabawi, Sammia Errazouki, Wael Eskandar, Ramy Essam, Sheikh Anwar al-Ethari, Banning Eyre, Erra Gal, Martin Goldschmidt, Farzad Golpayegani, JP Haddad (RIP), Mahmod Hamasi, Amine Hamma, Rema Hammami, Moe Hamzeh,* Sune Haugbølle, Titus Hjelm, Brian Hickam, Tom Hurwitz, Zakaria Ibrahim, Gameela Ismael, Jif, Furat al-Jamil, Mahmoud Jrere, Keith Kahn-Harris, Deborah Kapchan, Nadeem Karkabi,* Lina Khatib, Carmel Kooros,* Marie Korpe, the Kuti Family and everyone at Felabration, Michael Lerner, Maria Malmstrom, Mohammed Matter (Abu Yazan), Toni Matti-Karjalainen, Ayman Mghamis, Nancy Mounir, Suhel Nafar, Tamer Nafar, Ahmer Naqvi, Noor Ayman Nour, Shady Ayman Nour, Jonas Otterbeck, Robert Parks, Oday Rasheed, Mahmoud Refaat, Ole Reitov, Bryan Reynolds, Paola Rivetti, Andi Rohde, Christina Rothman, Jed Rothstein, Karim Rush, Frank Rynne and everyone in Joujouka, Jackie Reem Salloum, Niall Scott, Tarek Shalaby, Bahia Shehab, Osama Shomar, Shayna Silverstein, Pierre Sioufi, Rod Smallwood and the Iron Maiden family, Lucia Sorbera,* Darci Sprengel, Leif Stenberg and everyone at the Center for Middle East Studies at Lund University, Martin Stokes, Ted Swedenburg,* the Tamimi family and the entire village of Nabi Saleh, Eric Trovalla, Ulrika Trovalla, Treynor Tumwa, Karin van Nieuwkerk, Hakan Vreskala, Deena Weinstein, Rami Younis, Lola and the kids for giving me the space and time to travel, Layla Zubaidi and Armando Salvatore for kickstarting this never-ending journey late one evening at our favorite Beirut bar, and Reda Zine for hitting the record button the next morning . . .

NOTE ON TRANSLITERATION

In transliterating Arabic, Persian, and Turkish words that don't have common English spellings, I have chosen a simplified version of the IJMES transliteration format, except where the local dialect strongly predominates when pronouncing specific letters (e.g., the hard *g* for *j* in Egyptian Arabic), in which case I transliterate the word as commonly pronounced by local speakers. When discussing song lyrics, I have included transliterations of the Arabic, Persian, and Turkish original when the lyrics are open to multiple interpretations and translations.

Introduction

FROM UPRISINGS TO PLAGUES

THERE IS LITTLE DOUBT that when historians reflect on the first two decades of the twenty-first century in the Middle East and North Africa, the revolutionary artists of this era will take their place besides the Dadaists of Zurich, the Beats of Greenwich Village, the metal pioneers of Birmingham, the Plastic People of Prague, the reggae artists of Trench Town, the "citizens" of Fela Kuti's Kalakuta Republic, and the B-Boys and MCs building a new art form in the Bronx and Compton, as artists and scenes that simultaneously forced societies to look at themselves more honestly and, in so doing, pushed them forward—even if it was ultimately further than they were then willing or able to go. Indeed, the chapters that follow demonstrate how the conditions produced by the often horribly violent counterrevolutions have in fact inspired a new generation of countercultures and their attendant musics, which are each playing important roles and offering unique insights into the culturally as well as politically revolutionary eruptions across the Muslim-majority world.

Along with January 14, 2011, when Tunisian dictator Zine El Abidine Ben Ali unceremoniously decamped to Saudi Arabia, ending his inglorious twenty-four-year rule, the removal of Egypt's "Pharaoh," Hosni Mubarak, on February 11 marked the culmination of a process of politicization of a new generation of Egyptians that had begun a decade earlier, in the year between the eruption of the al-Aqsa intifada in September 2000 and the attacks of September 11, 2001. Unfortunately, March 14, 2011, in the Bahraini capital of Manama, some twenty-five hundred kilometers to the east (and a bit south), marked the beginning of a new and much darker phase in the relationship between young people and the governments that ruled over them across the MENA. It was then, as I stood near a music store with members of one of Bahrain's OG metal bands, Motör Militia, that I observed the fantastical sight of American-made Saudi tanks, driven by South Asian mercenary soldiers and festooned with images of Bahrain's King on their turrets, roll by as they entered the country to crush that country's prodemocracy uprising.

When looking back, it's hard to miss just how prescient were the songs on Motör Militia's then forthcoming album, *Cloaked in Darkness*. Tracks like "Flames of Oppression," "Cries of the Innocent," and "al-Nakba" ("The Disaster," the term applied to the expulsion of three-quarters of a million Palestinians from their homeland in 1948) perfectly captured the sense of foreboding and even impending doom I'd felt a few hours before the tanks rumbled by as I walked through the soon-to-be-destroyed "Pearl," where protesters were camped out Tahrir-style, chanting for the downfall of the brutal minority-Sunni monarchy and its replacement with a multisectarian democratic system. Metal might not have provided the soundtrack most people think of when they look back on the Arab uprisings that were igniting like brush fires all across the MENA in the winter (and not, in fact, spring) of 2011. But for anyone who was listening, it both narrated the prehistory of the region-wide protests and foreshadowed how most would turn out. Floating slightly above the historical ground, heavy metal and its sister forms of alternative and extreme youth music such as hip hop, punk, and hardcore in all their various subgenres were among the most aesthetically embedded forms of cultural production and performance in the societies of the MENA and broader Muslim world, deeply shaped by and shaping the larger cultural and political landscapes of the societies in which they are embedded.

But things weren't always so foreboding and dark. When *Heavy Metal Islam* was published in July 2008, the situation actually seemed to be improving. Certainly the region was livening and even lightening up—at least culturally—at an ever-quickening pace. Four months after its publication, MTV Arabia, the regional franchise of the music television giant, aired a wonderfully funny promo video set in a bygone era (circa 1958) in Cairo, Baghdad, or perhaps Beirut. The clip began with a performance by a male crooner with a traditional orchestra of the era (think the Arab equivalent of Sinatra's or Count Basie's big bands), when suddenly the 'oud player stops playing the mellow "conversation music" *maqam* that's barely holding the audience's attention, the 'oud's sound changes from acoustic lute to brutally distorted guitar, and he starts shredding like he's playing a Gibson Flying V through a Marshall stack. The perfectly attired and coiffed, thin-mustachioed crooner adjusts his collar and tries to keep up with his suddenly berserk side man, but fails miserably; as the shredding grows more intense a bejeweled

FIGURE 3. Still for a commercial for MTV Arabia from 2008 featuring metal-themed parody of 1950s Arab cabaret scene. Anonymous 'oud shredder unknown, never identified.

woman in an evening gown swoons. After a solo that would make Steve Vai proud, the portly shredder smashes his 'oud, flashes the metal horns, and stage dives into the shocked audience as the swooning woman faints.

The commercial was certainly a long way from the days of the Satanic Metal affairs that had rocked the region, including the Gulf (where the ad was produced), during the previous decade. Not long after the video premiered, and by no means unrelated, Brad Pitt and Angelina Jolie spent a lovely weekend in Damascus with Syria's equally young and telegenic First Family, Bashar and Asma al-Assad, later recounted by Mrs. Assad for a *Vogue* feature. Among the takeaways of the profile was how shocked (and, we can presume, jealous) America's then First Celebrity Couple was at how the al-Assads could move around in public without—allegedly—any security detail, something, needless to say, Brangelina simply couldn't do. In their minds, it seems, this was clearly a sign of the high regard with which the Syrian people held their president and first lady, as well as the relative normalcy of their life (references to Scandinavian royals and prime ministers biking to the office were hard not to conjure). The two fashionably dressed power couples also shared stories of their mutual humanitarianism.

It goes without saying that the profile was removed from the website after Bashar started murdering his people en masse in the spring of 2011.

Less than a year after the Brangelina-Assad matinée, Damon Albarn, the Britpop icon and leader of Blur, came to Damascus to collaborate with the National Orchestra for Arab Music for the third Gorillaz album; he departed with a lush string and percussion arrangement that would highlight one of *Plastic Beach*'s standout tracks, "White Flag" (a plea for peace in the Middle East), which provided a two-minute book-ending on either side of the three-minute-and-forty-three-second track, perfectly setting off the typically minimalist funky body of the song. So enthused was Albarn with the collaboration that he brought the full band—now featuring live as well as virtual members—back to Damascus in July 2010 for a historic concert at the Damascus Citadel. National Public Radio covered the concert and declared—with some ignorance of other recent collaborations—that it "marked what we can only hope is a new era of music in the Middle East."

Today the metal, rap, punk, hardcore, and other youth-oriented music scenes in the Middle East, North Africa, and the rest of the Muslim-majority world exist in a contradictory state. On the one hand, except for pockets of extreme conservatism, most artists and fans have the ability to perform and listen to these forms of music more or less freely, as long as they are not overly political or antireligious. This represents a sea change in the politics of music whose impact on musicians was impossible to overstate. Even Saudi Arabia and Iran have seen greater tolerance for the music and certain variable and changing conditions. There has also been greater professionalization of the scenes, and the third generation of artists across this vast region has more opportunities for spreading its music and, through it, its culture than ever before.

Indeed, before the coronavirus pandemic closed down the world in early 2020 it had become de rigueur for rock and metal festivals across Europe to include one or more artists from the region, and the idea of metal from the region is no longer eyebrow raising. On the other hand, the idea of hijab-wearing women being a crucial part of the scenes still has the power to surprise if not shock people in the Arab/Muslim world as much as abroad, pointing to the ongoing centrality of gender as a marker of contestation and mystification surrounding Arab/Muslim identities, in and outside the region.

If the MTV Arabia video described above was funny precisely to the extent that the idea of Arab metal was still hard to fathom for the average television viewer in the Arab world, today metal and hip hop and rock more broadly have become far more normalized parts of the sonic landscape. This raises a fascinating question about what happens to scenes that begin deep underground when they are no longer so politically and socially marginalized and in fact are increasingly accepted by the rest of society. During the last thirty years the EYM scenes created spaces where some of the most creative and committed young people, and particularly those outside the highly constricted societies, could gather together to create communities and attempt not merely to survive but also to imagine positive futures for themselves in environments that seemed otherwise devoid of hope. Once sub- or countercultural scenes move more into the open and are tolerated by mainstream society (and those in power) they often lose their subversive, never mind transversal and transformative, power. It's not yet clear whether these scenes will retain their hold on the young people who were previously drawn to them, especially if, when, or as they become more accepted and even, at least for hip hop and its offshoots (like trap or Egyptian *mahraganat,* which we'll meet in chapter 2), commercially viable. In countries like Morocco, many of its biggest hip hop stars are already tied to the King, much as Egypt's biggest pop stars were closely aligned with Mubarak during his reign.

As is the case everywhere else on the planet, the kind of (comparatively) extreme—or at least brutal—metal that characterizes many of the scenes in the MENA and larger Muslim world does not have the same wide commercial potential that hip hop does. When it comes to women-fronted metal groups, like female rappers their very existence points to the emergence of a more open and moderate culture in the society at large. The royal subvention of the female thrash band Mystik Moods in Morocco over a decade ago and the widespread coverage of the all-female metal band Voice of Baceprot (VoB) in Indonesia today attest to the symbolic power and value—in very different ways from the inside and outside—of female artists in patriarchal cultures, especially in genres that are traditionally dominated by and associated with men. Even more so when, as is the case with VoB, the band members all wear hijab while shredding, screaming, or blasting out beats, or, in the case of a few rappers, spitting out rhymes. Of course, what the hijab actually means in the context of the female musicians wearing it onstage, how much it represents something essential about the band or whether it's been overdetermined or even has changed over time, and whether it would actually "mean" anything to anyone outside the band and a limited number of fans if their music wasn't tied strongly to videos that establish their bona fides as seemingly "religious young female metal musicians" (because they're wearing hijab) all beg for answers.

What is clear is that at the same moment these genres have the unprecedented freedom to be recorded, performed, and listened to from Morocco to

Indonesia, the political and economic conditions that inspired and infused them (the same "structural adjustment" of economies great and small that first inspired the sound and lyrics of metal, hip hop, and punk starting in the later 1960s) are more salient than ever. Whether in a context of greater cultural freedom these scenes retain their subversive, subcultural, and countercultural values and sensibilities, which are often but not always coupled with increased political repression and economic marginalization, remains to be seen. The last decade has seen momentous changes not just to the peoples, societies, and music explored by *Heavy Metal Islam* and now this book, but also to the ways all are, or at least should be, studied. Equally important, the approaches and theories we use to study metal and other forms of hardcore music, and the people who inhabit these scenes, have been deeply impacted.

Unfortunately, in the last decade governments across the region have learned how to surveil, utilize, master, bypass, syphon off, or render inutile the power of the digital modes of cultural production, circulation, and consumption that helped enable the uprisings in the first place. Indeed, the defeat was doubly severe: not only were the streets reclaimed by governments and those supporting them through a combination of brute force and ideological manipulation; there was no longer the possibility of retreating to a still-inchoate Internet outside governments' watchful eyes, as existed before the uprisings era.

And so today most of the musicians who rose to prominence from 2009 to 2013 have been either silenced by various means, imprisoned, exiled, or, in some cases, coopted. Several musical and other artists have been murdered by governments or ultraconservative forces. It remains unclear whether the various societies of the MENA have descended permanently from the liminal moment between the old and the new, authoritarianism and democracy, patriarchy and racism and true equality, extreme divergences in wealth and sustainable societies back into the patriarchal and authoritarian norms that long defined them. Or perhaps the majority of citizens remain stuck, unable to function with the status quo but unable to pass over to new ways of thinking, being, and relating to one another. Nor is it clear what role the hardcore music scenes that helped spawn the generation of 2009–13 might play in the forging of a new generation of subcultural and potentially countercultural voices across the MENA, one that has grown up in a very different sonic as much as political environment than their elders.

What I hope is clear from the author's note and this introduction is that we can look at the metal, rap, and other musical artists, graffiti artists, guerrilla filmmakers, 'zine makers, and all the other subversive and street artists as what in the spirit of Nietzsche we can term "cultural physicians," uniquely placed to help diagnose and at least help begin to heal the pathologies of their societies. Egyptian revolutionary singer Ramy Essam succinctly explained it in April 2011 as we walked from a protest in front of the Syrian Embassy in Cairo to a nearby recording studio: "As a singer my job is to take in all feelings and sentiments and ideas of the people, and reflect these back to them in a more condensed and amplified form." Since he explained this to me I've seen artists play a similar role, with the same level of self-consciousness, from the garbage-strewn streets of Beirut to the candle-lit vigils in Hong Kong and the mountains of Chiapas, where the Zapatista movement hosted several "CompArte" festivals that brought artists and activists together from across the world to teach and share their experiences and knowledge with one another (if ever there's been the kind of synthesis of theory and praxis debated within the Frankfurt School, as discussed in the author's note, it was there).

The music and artists featured in this book emerged at a unique moment in the history of authoritarian rule. The "authoritarian bargain," in which these governments in the previous quarter century delivered significant improvements in social and economic development in return for acquiescence to their undemocratic rule, had broken down with the rise of neoliberal capitalism as it was imposed on the MENA and other regions of the Global South. By the 1990s and then the 2000s, increasing numbers of people not merely were forced to live at the economic margins of society but were becoming literally superfluous—of little or no value to systems that were devising new rationales and technologies for deploying violence to maintain order once the authoritarian bargain no longer held and growing to resemble the immensely corrupt and even criminal rackets scholars like Frankfurt School founder Max Horkheimer and sociologist Charles Tilly so expertly diagnosed them to be decades earlier.

Indeed, citizens of countries like Egypt and Tunisia, as well as large parts of Morocco, Syria, and so many other countries, were being treated far more like colonial subjects than as citizens. And so it wasn't surprising that an Egyptian activist (and metalhead) I met during the eighteen-day uprising, when questioned by me as to why he was wearing an "End the [Israeli] Occupation" T-shirt, replied without hesitation that "because we're occupied too." If one thinks about the cauldron in which millions of young people across the MENA came of age in the late 1980s, 1990s, and 2000s—the repression of authoritarian rule, the violence of war, the increasingly hemmed-in and often-superfluous existence imposed by a consolidated and corrupt neoliberal order, with the twin bogeymen of Western neocolonial ideologies and violent political Islamism added in for good measure—the roots of extreme music across the region are clear.

MIGRATING MUSIC

If *Heavy Metal Islam* served as a historical archive of sorts for the prehistory of the first great, and all too predictably tragic, revolutionary era of the twenty-first century, then the uprisings era proper constitutes the canvas upon which the history recounted in this book is painted. Together, they point to many possible avenues for future research on the MENA and larger Muslim world, the role of music in its and other youth cultures, and why young people engaged in creative expression, no matter how "extreme" it might sound, look, or read, are quite possibly shining a light onto the most pressing problems facing their societies. One issue that was important yet not central in 2008 was that of migration, and particularly its experience through exile and as refugees. The story of Reda Zine, one of the main interlocutors of *Heavy Metal Islam,* was emblematic of the move of millions of people from the southern and eastern Mediterranean to Europe. For well-educated young Arabs (and Turks, Iranians, and Pakistanis as well), fluent in one or more European languages, the move often involved attending university or graduate school in a European country and then ultimately making a life there. Thus Reda, fluent in French and Italian, attended the Sorbonne and ultimately moved to Italy, where he still lives, now as an Italian citizen who regularly returns home to Morocco. For the majority of young migrants, without high levels of education or significant economic means, however, the journey was "illegal" and thus clandestine, perilous and too often tragically deadly. For millions the situation has meant long periods of more or less hiding in plain sight in Europe while waiting for the chance—most often through a job or marriage—to obtain working or residency papers.

To the experience of economically, educationally, or artistically motivated migration, however, has now been (once again) added those of political exile in Europe. If Europe and North America have long exerted a strong pull factor on young artists, activists, and cultural creatives more broadly, the push factor of escaping political repression and even threats to their lives, never mind freedom, has the foremost consideration for this generation of artists, as it has for their compatriots of all stripes since 2011. For the millions of refugees joining today's political exiles from war-torn Libya, Syria, Yemen, and Iraq, the situation was even worse, as their migration came with little warning and far more precarious routes and circumstances.

The number of artists I came to know in the last twenty years who were forced to leave their home countries is, if not shocking, still equally surprising and disheartening/demoralizing. Those who left in the period between 2007 and 2014 did so for economic, career, or political reasons, with political concerns becoming more important after 2011 (in Iran after 2009). Those who left beginning in 2015 did so to escape the immediacy of war. In scenes across the region, in Europe, and in North America, these artists are now re-creating their lives and creating new music as migrants, exiles, and refugees (and, in some cases, all three), having to cope not only with living in new countries with far fewer connections to every aspect of life than they had at home, but also with navigating new arenas of sound and aesthetic economies, as well as artistic and economic hierarchies. And they must do this as they struggle both to maintain relevance in their home cultures (even when a good share of that culture is in the diaspora because of war) and to fit in and stand out in their host societies.

THE PANDEMIC AND THE FUTURE

As he did to close chapter 2 of *Heavy Metal Islam,* Egyptian metal guitar legend Marz perfectly summed up the enduring power not merely of metal but of the communities it, more than perhaps any other genre, creates and sustains. As we stood on his balcony overlooking the school where he was teaching in 2019, smoking cigarettes and talking about the life and career trajectories of some of the first- and second-generation metaliens (as many Egyptian metalheads call themselves), he reminisced about that beautiful weekend in February 2007 (recounted in the epilogue of *Heavy Metal Islam*) when he and I attended Dubai Desert Rock together and Iron Maiden rocked the foundations of our world while offering a blueprint for a collective future:

> The experience of Dubai Desert Rocks, and especially the Maiden concert, really showed me that what we had was a true movement: that is, it makes you move. Maiden was giving us a gift. When hearts collide in a moment and space like that Maiden show, you feel like your world is being destroyed and then re-created. Even if you have to go through the darkness, it's okay.

In fact, Marz's band Scarab traveled this very road in Dubai the following two years: competing in but losing the festival's "battle of the bands" in 2008, only to win the competition and perform on the main stage during the festival in 2009. Since then they have released two albums and had been preparing new material as we spoke.

Despite all the political, economic and occasional cultural challenges they continued to face, many of the rock, metal, hip hop, punk, techno, and other music artists across the MENA region and broader Muslim world were in the early winter of 2020 deep into planning their annual concerts and tours, whether across their own countries, the MENA region, or, most important, the increasingly open European festival circuit. And then the coronavirus pandemic hit, bringing 2020 to a screeching halt, at least for musicians who depended—whether financially or more often emotionally and spiritually—on live performances to survive.

Yet however traumatic (certainly to the camaraderie of the scenes explored in this book), because they have always been DIY and rarely produced artists who could earn a decent living just off their music, the closing down of live music did not provoke an existential crisis the way it did for Western artists who lived off touring. To be sure, musicians like everyone else suffered significant psychological trauma from the need to remain largely in their homes and avoid regular contact with friends, which in subcultural scenes are at the core of the bonding and even survival process. But when most of what you're doing is "bedroom music," being cooped up in your bedroom isn't necessarily a new or disheartening experience, and many artists have told me that the pandemic period was also productive, at least in terms of writing and recording (if not finishing) new music.

Scarab front man Sammy Sayed summed up the optimism that a few felt: "Right now we are in the process of recording an EP and a new full length album. So far, it's much grander and more experimental than anything we've done before. Let's see where the tides will take us." Given that their previous release, *Martyrs of the Storm,* released in 2019, presciently dealt with plagues and other natural crises, we can understand how the last two years could be a source of inspiration rather than desperation for them and other extreme metal bands.

Similarly, JP Haddad of the Lebanese death metal group Kimaera explained in a World Metal Congress podcast in November 2020 that "when the pandemic hit we were like, 'Let's take advantage of the situation and record an album.'" Indeed, from Tehran to Lahore, Cairo to LA, guitarists started collaborating on long-form solo tracks, where someone would put up a groove or song form and other musicians would download and record themselves soloing over it, after which someone would edit all the solos together into a mix and put the resulting composite video online. Similar collaborations occurred with hip hop and electronica, which have for two decades been produced through online collaborations. Some leading guitarists, such as Pakistani virtuosi Mekaal Hasan and Faraz Anwar, created video master classes, accessible via sites like Patreon for a small fee, in which they break down and teach budding shredders the secrets behind their best-known solos and songs. While not a major source of sustainable income, musicians did continue to perform live in cities like Beirut and Cairo in between—and, truth be told, even during—lockdowns, but at nothing like the regularity of live music that was possible before.

A few well-established artists moved into the business side of music. Suhel Nafar, cofounder of the most important group in the history of Arab hip hop, DAM, left the stage to become the head of Spotify's Middle East and North Africa division for two years, before joining the independent label and distributor EMPIRE as vice president of Strategy & Market during the pandemic. The Kordz lead singer Moe Hamzeh became the head of Warner Music's Middle East division, overseeing a major expansion of activities. Karim Rush of Egypt's Arabian Knightz continued building his own independent label and digital distribution hub for Arab rappers as well as creating YouTube videos recounting the history of hip hop for an Arabic-speaking audience. Salome MC continued with her own film and music productions. While few women penetrated the upper echelons of the MENA music business (similar to the sad state of representation in the business globally), many female artists saw their music reach an ever-wider audience as YouTube and Spotify streams rose precipitously during lockdowns.

How much money all the increased views, plays, and streams have earned anyone is a different question. Without the press attention and opportunity to reach new fans through touring, the already-small number of albums or downloads sold by metal bands has definitely dropped for most artists, even as rappers have seen their fortunes rise. One million YouTube views can earn someone several thousand to several tens of thousands of dollars, depending on if, where, and what kind of ads are inserted into the video. Get close to one hundred million and it could reach $50,000. This is not a huge amount for a major American or British artist, but for Moroccan or Egyptian rappers, for example, it represents immediate entrée to the upper class, and also leads to the potential for commercial endorsements, ring tone downloads, and other forms of remuneration—as long as they leave politics at their bedroom door.

But access to wealth/money is only part of what's necessary for the artists we'll encounter in the chapters that follow to survive and achieve a meaningful level of success. In twenty years of research on music at and beyond the edge of social and political conflict in the Middle East and larger Muslim world, it has become clear that the music and scenes that become culturally, and potentially politically, salient share at least two of the following three characteristics beyond the general aesthetic quality or originality of the music: first, the music represents a powerful new style that nevertheless is linked to and continues to engage the larger musical sonisystem or soniscape from which it emerged; second, the musicians have a high enough level of charisma, personality, and originality to grab and hold fans' and the broader society's attention; and third, there is enough political as well as cultural space—underground/subcultural at first, but ultimately increasingly public in the fullest and most political sense of the term—to enable the radical sonic or lyrical message of the music to be heard. That the normal path of EYM scene formation (as elaborated by Jeremy Wallach and Alexandra Levine) closely parallels this transformation makes such a trajectory less difficult to imagine.

NB: For the most part, the fieldwork upon which the chapters that follow are based began in 2008 and ended in 2021. What remains clear a year later is that the artists that shine throughout this book, and no doubt a new generation that is still under the radar (if not underground), will emerge from the pandemic era with even more material to challenge, criticize, and even scandalize their governments and broader societies. Willingly or not, many will once again be at the forefront of the struggles for cultural, artistic, and ultimately political freedom from Morocco to Pakistan, and indeed globally. Their music, and their courage, have much to teach us.

ONE

Morocco

FINDING HARMONIES IN A LAND OF DISSIDENCE

Wake up, sleepers!
Look at the Egyptian people!
Look at the Tunisian people!
You are the one who tell you that Morocco is an exception.

—L7A9D

SO RAPPED L7A9D—THE ARABIC chat spelling of El Haqed (The Enraged One), born Mouad Belghouat—one of the Arab world's most important dissident rappers. For decades the "Moroccan exception" had been the veritable slogan of the brand of Morocco, the image sold by the Makhzen, or "ruling system," to the outside world that depicted the country as uniquely stable while progressing at a moderate pace toward a purposefully hazy definition of a liberal future. That image was always tendentious at best; the "years of lead" *(sanawat ar-ruṣaṣ* or *années de plomb),* the 1960s through 1980s, during which Mohammed's father, Hassan II, violently repressed most every hint of democracy, had barely faded into the background when the Satanic Metal scare in 2003 warned a new generation that his successor might be following far more closely in his father's footsteps than most had hoped. Nevertheless, the image of cultural openness, religious toleration, and at least an inchoate political pluralism continued to characterize public perceptions of Morocco outside the kingdom most of the time, especially compared to the harsh conservatism and full-throttled authoritarianism of so many other Arab regimes.

Not surprisingly, however, the uprisings had upset the idea of Moroccan exceptionalism. Echoing the exhortations of revolutionaries the world over, l7a9d reminded his fellow Moroccans that ultimately it was they who allowed the Makhzen to play off of the idea of exceptionality, and who excused the corruption, violence, and repression that went along with it. Like Rage Against the Machine's "Wake Up!" but with a far more subdued delivery (l7a9d rarely if ever raises his voice or emotion during songs), l7a9d used the

FIGURE 4. Mouad Belghouat, aka El Haqed/l7a9d, publicity photo. Photo by Lucas Dragone.

still-fresh uprisings across North Africa to jar Moroccans out of their political slumber and move toward a fundamental transformation in the political life of the country. It was a hope, and a wager, that would cost him several years of his life in jail and, as of 2021, exile in Belgium.

I first met l7a9d in Amman in 2012, at an Arab bloggers summit, about a year after he wrote these words and only a short while after his first stint in prison, which would total eighteen months over three years from September 2011 through September 2014. The "Arab Spring" was still hopeful, if increasingly troubled. Libya and Syria were quickly becoming seemingly intractable nightmares and Bahraini government repression was brutal if not particularly deadly. But Tunisia and, perhaps most important, Egypt were still considered success stories while Yemen was still up for grabs. Morocco too seemed back on the path of "reform" and political liberalization after King Mohammed had adroitly maneuvered in front of the country's February 20 movement, sponsoring a constitutional reform referendum that was approved by around 95 percent of the population.

Indeed, if there was a country that seemed best poised to make a transition toward a vaguely liberal political system at the start of the uprisings era, it was Morocco. Each year since the infamous Satanic affair in 2003 had seen a greater level of cultural openness, while the emerging political system under the still-young king was, if not quite democratic, at least less authoritarian. But history rarely follows its assigned trajectory.

Nonetheless, this narrative of a youthful-yet-steady hand guiding the country toward what sociologist Asef Bayat termed a "refolution" (a much more deliberate, state-led reform process than full-on revolution, in the guise of systematic change) was a façade. While the initial protests were met with a relatively light response while the Makhzen sorted out who was who and what was what, not long after King Mohammed's televised speech announcing the constitutional referendum state violence picked up steam and demonstrations began to be met with harsh repression, including beatings, arrests, and even killings of marchers. Despite this, upward of sixty thousand people were still marching regularly by the time the constitutional referendum took place in June.

L7a9d was, not surprisingly, having none of it. As he wrote in his lyrics notebook shortly before beginning his second stint in prison:

> As long as the power remains in the hands of one person,
> I will be indignant.
> The constitution and the political parties are only a decoration:
> They are waiting for all the driver's orders.
> Long live the people!
> Have you noticed that the king is mentioned sixty-one times in the constitution;
> While the people only once?
> O people, why this humiliation!

In many ways l7a9d's is the story par excellence of the transformations in musical subcultures, countercultures, and revolutionary cultures in the period leading up to and throughout the Arab uprisings era of 2010–16. If heavy metal captured the angst, anger, disillusionment, and lack of hope for the future of the generation that came of age in the first decade of the new millennium, hip hop grabbed the brass ring of politicized artistic production and, along with *chaabi* (popular) music, became the soundtrack of the protests, uprisings, and revolutions. L7a9d was the paradigmatic Arab rapper: working class and from the 'hood, extremely intelligent yet poorly educated thanks to underfunded and authoritarian school systems. And similar to the Tunisian revolutionary rapper El Général (né Hamada Ben Amor, discussed in the epilogue), he was not very well known before his arrest. "Enraged" and fearless, he was blessed with a powerful ability to capture and convey the seething anger of his peers, and with the Internet and social media, a set of new technologies of distribution and consumption that reached an unprecedented number of people broadly outside government control. L7a9d might not have reached that many of them when he began, but the channels were there for him to have an impact once he'd become better known.

METAL CEDES THE STAGE: THE POLITICIZATION OF MOROCCAN HIP HOP

In surveying the musical and political scenes across the MENA during the last decade, one of the main questions that have preoccupied me has been why it was hip hop rather than (and, less often, along with) metal that became the voice for the revolutionary generation. While each country has its own story, and will be discussed in turn, the Moroccan case seems fairly typical: an increasingly sophisticated and successful metal scene was producing ever-more inventive and original music. But the very characteristics that made the music so powerful—heavy instruments played by full bands of well-trained musicians, brutal singing that was nearly impossible to decipher, beats that were rarely amenable to marching or chanting along with—also made it very hard to adopt and adapt the music for street protests and widespread communal camaraderie and solidarity. As Moroccan metal pioneer Reda Zine explains, "We just don't speak the language of the people—literally. Of course, that was never the point of metal. Even in Italy, if I go to my Moroccan barber he's got Moroccan hip hop on; he'd never play metal."

Hip hop, on the other hand, is spoken in the language of everyday life—that was what made it so powerful and even shocking when artists like Don Bigg and H-Kayne first hit the scene. It's perfect for the street because it's from the street, perfect for the protest, and perfect for sharing messages as far and wide as possible. It's thus not surprising that despite being home to some of the most innovative metal anywhere, the Moroccan scene was largely silent in the lead-up to February 20, 2011, when the Arab Spring officially arrived on the western shores of North Africa.

Indeed, what is most striking about the role of youth music during the last decade in Morocco is that metal, which had led the fight for almost a generation, during which hip hop was just becoming established in the Kingdom, has since 2008 retreated to a largely apolitical stance. Part of this might well be economic and generational. Metal artists are increasingly from middle- and upper-income families with more to lose and brighter prospects because of better educational opportunities. At the same time, many if not most rappers, and a large share of fans, come from poorer areas (H-Kayne and Don Bigg being two exceptions to this trend), which have felt the brunt of Morocco's economic travails. So if metal was the perfect subcultural and even countercultural music for the generation that came of age in the 1990s, hip hop was a far better match for protest and countercultural activism, or praxis. But could it stand toe to toe with the Makhzen?

The Arab/Middle Eastern revolutionary wave was always going to hit rocky shores when it arrived at Morocco. The idea of the "deep state" might have originated in Turkey and become popular in the US after the election of Donald Trump, but it's been a reality across the MENA for much of the postcolonial era, particularly once formerly socialist systems (whether "Arab socialist," "Nasserist," "Ba'athist," or "Kemalist") began the inevitable transformation toward inherently criminal neoliberal political economies in the 1970s. With its centuries-long existence the Moroccan Makhzen is the deepest of deep states; rather than being weakened or even destroyed by French colonization in the period between 1912 and 1956, it was modernized and strengthened, its penetrative, organizing, disciplinary, and coercive power made far stronger when the country emerged from colonial rule as a modern monarchy than when it was forced into the protectorate.

In more overtly authoritarian countries like post-2013 Egypt and Turkey, one can say that the deep state has become "the only state" (as *Politico* described it); any semblance of representative politics has been progressively stripped away. The Makhzen, however, has survived for centuries by knowing how to adjust and intimately calibrate its deployment of political, social, economic, and coercive power so as to rarely lose control of the Moroccan people for very long, as King Mohammed's adroit handling of the February 20 movement attests.

This isn't to say that the stability of the system is very firm, even if it does permeate deep into society. As demonstrated by the antigovernment protests in the Rif Mountains of northern Morocco in 2019, large sections of Morocco—its territory and its people—have long been and to a certain degree remain part of the *Bled es-siba,* the Land of Dissidence: that part of Morocco that traditionally was not under direct control of the sultan and that paid at best nominal allegiance to him. (The land under direct control has long been termed the *Bled el-Makhzen* [the Land of the Makhzen], and is primarily the main cities and their hinterlands along and near the coast.) Today, "going into *siba*," a phrase one might periodically hear activists use, means becoming a dissident, directly opposing the state in some fundamental way.

Morocco has lived on the rhythm of Makhzen and *siba*, stability and dissent, for centuries. Indeed, we can argue that the Makhzen, by its very nature, requires—or at least creates or is cogenerative with—its opposite, the forces of resistance or *siba*. The Morocco chapter in *Heavy Metal Islam* did not emphasize enough the nature and dynamics of the two "blads," Makhzen and *siba*, as guiding forces in the performance of political power in Morocco for well-nigh a millennium. The last decades shows why that was a gap needing to be filled. But to do so, we first need to understand another part of the larger mosaic of Moroccan politics and culture that I didn't focus on in the original chapter (in good measure because it wasn't referred to with any frequency by people in the scenes): namely, the larger scene known as *nayda*, which helped define the rapid stylistic innovations of the first decade of the century.

Meaning "rise up" in Darija, the name *nayda* was adopted from the Spanish *movida* movement of popular music, which flourished after the death of the long-reigning fascist Spanish dictator Francisco Franco in 1976. For young Moroccans *nayda* represented the hope for a similar cultural-musical movement toward greater openness and even democracy that would coincide with a weakening of government/Makhzen control over political, economic, and even social life. So important was this development in popular musical culture that only months before the eruption of the Arab uprisings no less than *Foreign Policy* labeled *nayda* a "musical revolution" resulting from "one of the biggest changes brought by the arrival of the 'youth king of youth'... Mohamed VI to power."

The problem with such optimism was, however, that there was no agreement among those involved in Moroccan youth music about whether the term was ever used by people in the scenes it describes or whether it was anything other than an invention by industry people seeking to capture and so more easily market a broader cultural movement (as was the case with "world music" a generation before). Although such a semantic debate might seem like "Inside Baseball" (or cricket or football), it points to the confusion over the roots of the protest culture that fully emerged in 2011 and also doesn't take into account why at this particular time the term emerged into public consciousness, regardless of its roots. But this doesn't gainsay the impetus and movement represented by *nayda*, as depicted in the main image/

logo of the 2008 iteration of the Boulevard (a music festival discussed below), which showed an old Mercedes taxi bursting with funky-looking young people with instruments flying à la *Back to the Future* above the desert toward a gleaming modern city on the horizon.

The moment when *nayda* reached its peak, in the mid-2000s, was also when metal was at its most provocative and progressive (in the wake of the victory overturning of the verdicts and the success of the Boulevard), and hip hop was just breaking into the mainstream. Not surprisingly, it was also when, like a major label swooping in to sign bands from the hottest new scene before they become too powerful and autonomous, the Makhzen, led by the "youth" King, knew to harness and (re)direct the power of the emerging music scenes toward narratives and ends that wouldn't fundamentally challenge the system, and would even, when the time came, support it.

FROM THE BOULEVARD TO THE STREET: THE "GOLDEN YEARS" OF MUSIC AND PROTEST IN MOROCCO

In the summer of 2008, I was back at the Boulevard performing with Lazywall, whom I first encountered at the 2006 edition. The band was in top form and I was excited to be invited to perform and record with them, a project that would continue on and off for another half a decade, including a wild appearance together at SXSW the next year. It is one thing to experience a festival like the Boulevard from the audience and quite another to look out over 30,000 screaming fans from the stage with one of the headlining acts. The feeling was even more intense than that of performing with Farzad Golpayegani the year before at the Barişa Rock for Peace Festival in Istanbul; if it was a largely Iranian band that was exulting in the rare freedom to rock with abandon in then liberal Turkey (one of the few countries Iranians could travel to without a visa), the exuberance at the Boulevard was even more intense, like Eastern European metal fans going to see their favorite rock or metal band right after the Wall had fallen and everything seemed possible.

The organizers of the Boulevard, particularly founders Momo Merhari and Hicham Bahou, seemed to have worked overtime to return the activist spirit to the festival for 2008. In fact, they had worked so hard and had been so understaffed (having relinquished the more lucrative corporate

FIGURE 5. Lazywall with Mark LeVine, l'Boulevard, Casablanca, 2008. Photo by Abderrahmane Marzoug.

sponsorships that would provide a lot more production staff) that Momo had a heart attack only weeks before the festival. He somehow recovered enough to supervise the whole production, which included the festival program, which offered a retrospective of Les Variations, a Fes-based Jewish prog rock group, the composers of the original "Moroccan Roll" in 1974 (the phrase inspired Hoba Hoba Spirit's classic "El Caïd Motorhead," with its refrain "I want Marockan Roll, my rock 'n roll"). Along with the Gnaoua-rock group Nass El Ghiwane, they helped put Moroccan rock on the map inside Morocco as well as on the world stage. But while Ghiwane has remained popular to the present day in their home country, the more Francophone Les Variations soon moved to France, becoming one of the unheralded progenitors of European prog rock.

Making Les Variations's story the centerpiece of the program wasn't just a way to highlight a lost chapter in the larger history of Moroccan rock (and, by extension, Moroccan culture); as Hicham and Momo both explained to me at the time, it was a direct declaration of tolerance and openness to festival attendees at a time in Morocco and across the Maghreb when religious extremism was becoming a major concern. Of course, the fact that one of the King's main advisors, André Azoulay, is Jewish and the Kingdom considers

FIGURE 6. Fans at the 2008 l'Boulevard Festival, Casablanca. Photo by Mark LeVine.

its relationship to Moroccan Jews in France and Israel strategically important didn't hurt.

In retrospect, however genuinely felt by me and so many fans and musicians with whom I spoke at the festival, the activist sentiment was at least to some degree naïve. Yes, kids in kilts and goth makeup could now chat amiably with police instead of running scared from them, and young Moroccan EYM fans could subvert the larger societal view of them and their music as little more than *bouzebal* ("shit" or "garbage" in Darija), enjoying their festival with relatively the same indulgence as the wealthier Moroccans and foreigners who attended the better-funded and advertised festivals in Rabat (Mawazin), Essaouira (Gnaoua World Music Festival), or Fes (World Festival of Sacred Music). They could even have some edgy political advocacy—Amazigh language rights, homelessness, AIDS, women's rights, globalization—thrown in through activist booths ringing the field and site and public lectures and screenings. But any hope that this marked a substantive shift in the balance of power in Morocco would ultimately prove to have been unduly optimistic. Indeed, intended or not, the Boulevard became, to a certain degree, an example—however edgy—of the official vision of Morocco as a moderate, Western-leaning country, as the other major festivals dotting each spring and summer did (and, in fact, it was that); it was part of what Moroccan anthropologist Aomar Boum, building on the earlier work of Taieb Belghazi, describes as the "festivalizing of dissent" in the Kingdom— although not willingly and only up to a very pointy edge. But at the same time as the King invested in the Boulevard, he and the Makhzen also invested in and otherwise supported specific artists who were quickly climbing to the top of the Moroccan musical universe.

All these political machinations were, however, beside the point in 2008. As Aissam El Hassani, founder of three of the most important Moroccan metal groups of the last decade and a half, put it, the 2008 edition of the Boulevard marked the beginning of the "golden years" of the festival and of the metal and hip hop scenes more broadly. Specifically, the period between 2008 and 2012 (when the Boulevard, for the first time, was not held) was one during which creativity, the possibility for live shows, the viability of independent scenes, and the potential for political openness were all at their peak across the board. Indeed, it's hard to overstate how important having a well-funded and equipped music space was for Moroccan metalheads in the 2000s, who only a decade earlier were stuck in do-it-yourself rehearsal spaces (known as "systeme-D" or "debber rasek"), before the Boulevard offered the chance for young bands to meet, be mentored by more-established musicians, and compete for a chance to perform at the main festival. This was accomplished through organizing the annual Tremplin (French for "springboard" or "trampoline") competition in the lead-up to the Boulevard—in grand metal style, at Casablanca's infamous "anciens abattoirs," a complex of old slaughterhouses in the Hay Mohammedi, one of the city's poorer neighborhoods and historic home to Nass El Ghiwane.

Unfortunately, while the Tremplin had from the start been the "heart of the Boulevard ethos," without suitable rehearsal and recording venues few young artists could realize their potential. And so the organizers of the Boulevard, who'd already accepted sponsorship from the state-owned Royal Air Maroc as far back as the first edition in 1999, accepted a major donation from the King himself in 2009 (most, if not all, Moroccan bands, including the world-renowned and highly principled Hoba Hoba Spirit, have received extra payments from the King when they perform at Mawazine). For the famously DIY and independent Boulevard to accept the King's money might seem somewhat hypocritical or at least mercenary. But beyond the previous history of state funding, the logic for doing so was compelling: the donation from the King not only eased the pressure on the overworked organizers of the Boulevard; it enabled the establishment of a year-round music center—rehearsal and recording studios as well as a radio-training facility and offices—known as Boultek, located in the futuristic-sounding Technopark complex a tram ride away from downtown. Boultek quickly became a "premier center of current music [*musiques actuelles*] of Morocco . . . [and] at the same time a place of work, exchange, and advice for the groups and artists of the urban scene," as the Moroccan magazine *Les Eco* described it in 2013.

As Hicham explained to me over coffee not far from the then still new offices of the Boultek, he and Momo knew from years of experience with both the Boulevard and, as important, the Tremplin that the music scene—and especially the rock and metal scene—could not develop much further without the kind of resources and space such a center would provide, never mind the training in the kinds of DIY activities that first enabled the scene's emergence and growth. And given the reality that even without taking money the Boulevard couldn't cross any of the main political red lines and survive, taking the money and ensuring that a new generation had the tools and resources to develop themselves and their scenes would lay the groundwork for political art in the future.

What's also clear, when looking back on it, is that the victory of the youth in the metal scene in 2003 was not so much a defeat for the government as part of the "authoritarian learning curve" (as scholars like Steve Hyedemann and Raymond Hinnebusch have described it) that most governments in the region were experiencing in the first decade of the new century. The Makhzen had in fact undergone such retooling and adaptations to new circumstances numerous times over the centuries, reformatting and rebooting its modus operandi to ensure greater access to various segments of the population under its control or, theoretically, jurisdiction—in this case the surveillance of fin de siècle youth-cultural scenes even as it enabled their expansion. In the wake of the Satanic Metal affair and the nearly simultaneous terrorist attacks in 2003, this strategy was quite useful, given the far more pressing challenges and crises faced by the government.

Although, as it turned out, even the injection of the King's money couldn't stop the cancelation of the Boulevard in 2012 and 2016, the programming for the tenth anniversary of Tremplin and the Boulevard in 2009 indicates how expansive the programming had become as the golden years headed for their sudden denouement. Confident in its role as a center of "création urbaine" (urban art) and in relations with the large and growing Moroccan diaspora, the organizers brought in Moroccan-origin rappers like Salaheddin from the Netherlands, Cilvarings from the US and the Netherlands (and a protegé of RZA), and the metal bassist Saïd El Yousfi, aka Saïd Guemha, who came with the LA-based band Krashkarma. This was on top of well over a dozen young artists chosen from far more entrants to compete in the finals for the chance to perform at the Boulevard, including fifteen guest groups from Morocco, France, Spain, Burkina Faso, and Algeria.

The year 2009 also saw the creation of a new fan group called the Moroccan Metal Community, which brought together Moroccans of all ages, wages, and interests to support and strengthen both the music and the metal fan community in Morocco. As its Facebook page puts it: "We don't necessarily share the same opinions but we speak the same metal language. We meet each other at shows, we headbang together and we trade MP3s. And then? We scatter into nature. We exist and we know that we are a lot."

CHANGING THE GENDER IMBALANCE IN EYM

The ongoing gender imbalance in the metal, hip hop, EDM, and other scenes in Morocco was still quite strong at the close of the aughts and well into the last decade. The Tremplin is a good barometer of who are the best emerging alternative and indie artists in Morocco; in scanning them for the last two decades it's clear that women remained largely excluded from the rock and metal scenes as artists. As Lazywall singer and bassist Nao put it when we discussed the issue in 2015, it seems that Mystik Moods, the teenage all-female hardcore thrash band whose standout performance at the 2005 Boulevard I discussed in *Heavy Metal Islam,* set a bar that hadn't been reached again in rock-related scenes till the singer-turned-actress Khansa Batma, whom I discuss below, came onto the scene. On the other hand, the number of female MCs has steadily increased, first at the amateur level and now at the highest levels of hip hop as well as pop, which now include at least half a dozen major female stars.

Not surprisingly, the ongoing impediments to women's participation in popular music genres, and EYM in particular, are grounded in good measure in religious and cultural norms. As Nao explained, "I was on the jury of the Tremplin, I think it was 2010, and there was this wonderful young group with a female singer who wore a hijab. Sadly at the last minute she refused to go on because she was too scared of the potential for abuse by the audience and attacks on her and her family for doing metal." The situation has begun to improve in the decade since, but not in a way that would remove most social constraints on girls' and women's participation in EYM scenes, especially metal.

In contrast, however, DJ Amina, one of the rising stars of Morocco's EDM scene, explained to me that "the scene has a politics toward women that is in many ways more progressive than rock, metal, or hip hop." Female rappers have an even longer history, going back to artists like Wydad, Thug Gang, and the group Tigress Flow, formed in 2008. Their frank and socially conscious lyrics were a big inspiration to the scene, and laid the groundwork for

FIGURE 7. Khtek, still from video for her song "KickOff," directed by Alaa Eddine Rais, 2020.

lead rapper Soultana (Youssra Oukaf) to achieve local and even international success (the "voice of women's rap in Morocco" was how Public Radio International described her), particularly with her song "Sawt Annissa" ("Voice of Women").

Soultana straddled the line of political commentary and dangerous criticism by following the well-trodden path of criticizing the situation in the country while professing "to love the King" and be against "revolution" while "imploring him" to improve the lives of young people. Of course, representing what Soultana calls (in her song "Maghrebiyya") "the girls' voice that is lost in this country" and calling out male misbehavior and disrespect may not be "revolutionary," but it does have a direct impact on young women's lives, far more in fact than pushing for major political or economic changes that are quite likely impossible to achieve.

On the other end of the spectrum is rapper Houda Abouz (stage name is Khtek, "your sister" in Darija), who openly talks about her inspiration from the February 20 protests, her strong feminist grounding, her support for LGBTQ+ rights, and her liberal use of Arabic, French, and English profanities in her voluminous freestyle output. Indeed, she has a tattoo of Biggie Smalls on her arm and a fashion sense that calls out old-school female rappers. While Soultana actually appeared in one video wearing a hijab, Khtek is more explicitly secular, describing rap as "my passion and my defense mechanism in a patriarchal society" and putting out hard-charging music that saw her named one of the BBC's "100 Women 2020" globally. Yet even Khtek won't go too far "into *Siba*," as she refuses to acknowledge any political agenda, and has worked with the country's biggest proregime rapper, Don Bigg.

Whatever the ambivalence, it's clear that something of an empowerment subgenre can be said to have emerged in Moroccan hip hop as female MCs, from the stars like Manal and Khtek to more indie hip hop artists like Ily and Krtas Nssa, have developed personas that combine Queen Latifa, Lauryn Hill, Missy Elliott, and Cardi B. Their music can move between social and political themes, between objectified and empowering narratives and videos, all the while reaching anywhere between half a million and tens of millions of views on YouTube per song. Not surprisingly, nothing in the metal scene comes close to this level of popularity.

And yet, while boasting fewer women as musicians and singers, the Moroccan metal scene isn't devoid of female talent. In fact, the last ten years of the scene can be explored through a trio of bands whose core musicians have remained intact from 2011 through today and featured, for a time, one of the best brutal singers, female or male, anywhere: Carnival Slaughter (which lasted from 2011 to 2012), Infected Noise (from 2012 to 2014), and Vile Utopia (on and off from 2014 to the time of writing in early 2020).

The musical motivation behind Carnival Slaughter was owed clearly to bands like Cannibal Corpse and similar, highly evocative extreme metal bands. "We were basically translating horror film themes into music," Aissam explains (not too dissimilar from Black Sabbath when it started out half a century before). And so even their Facebook page was over the top, in a tongue-in-cheek B-horror-movie sort of way "We talk about abominations, Source of Malice, Abnormality, Pathological Disturbances, Maniacal murder, Necrophilia, and the obscured morality of the rapist . . . etc. Yeah we're that fucked up." It was meant to be a joke, but not everyone got it. Nonetheless, musically there was already something special with the band, as becomes apparent when listening to "I Am Nature's Curse" on a compilation released in 2016 produced by the Moroccan Metal Community (and originally uploaded to YouTube in 2012). It's a beast of a hardcore-metal track that starts off with a fifty-second interlude sampled from an unnamed teenage horror flick that features a woman running, screaming, and being attacked in a high school gym, before the blast beats kick in.

Carnival Slaughter seemed destined for the upper echelons of the Moroccan metal scene, but by 2012 it had fallen apart and Aissam and Zakaria formed a new group, Infected Noise, which featured one of the few female brutal singers in not only Morocco but the Arab world—and, indeed, the world for that matter—Nada ElHouari (aka Kucsulain). Infected Noise's Slamdown sound (aka Slamming Beatdown, a hybrid hardcore punk and metal) made a splash across the Mediterranean when it was signed by the Aix-en-Provence-based hardcore label Misos X Anthropos in 2014, for whom it was supposed to release an EP titled "Surrounded by Pigs." A promising collection of high-end hardcore, the music clearly displayed the brutal singing prowess of Nada—whose talent Aissam perfectly captured when he explained that "if [Morocco's biggest female rock singer] Khansa Batma were possessed by a demon she'd be Nada." Indeed the band showed every possibility of heralding a new force on the extreme music scene on both sides of the Mediterranean. But by 2014 Nada as well as bassist Lotfi decided to quit, the album was never released, and Aissam and Zakaria were left to create yet another project, this one titled Vile Utopia. "With this band, the story unfolds around when humanity finally wakes up and realizes nature is revolting, and all the old gods are returning to punish them."

After several years rehearsing and building a repertoire, in 2016 drummer Badr Abouessououd moved to the Ukraine for two years to study to be a pharmacist, an act of migration that has defined far too much music in the Arab world today. As Aissam related it to me, "Each person is from a different city; we met and started playing and our drummer had to go to Ukraine to study, so we already were forced to have a two-year hiatus. Since then we've kept practicing and tried to build despite all the obstacles. Finally, Badr came back home and we are able to record again, and are working on an EP."

As I described at the end of the introduction, that process continued once the pandemic forced the Moroccan music scene, like everywhere else, to move into a largely virtual realm. Indeed, Aissam's description of pandemic-era musical life in Morocco, backed by other musicians in the scene, suggests that the period between the mid-2010s, when Vile Utopia was formed, and the onset of the pandemic marked the end of the "golden years" of Moroccan metal. Piecing together the various factors that in his mind produced an ultimately radical change in the dynamics of the scene, he offered that

> between 2010 and 2015 there was in fact a lot of growth in the metal scene, there were always bands playing, and so on. But then it kind of began to die. There started to be people coming to shows who didn't belong. Not just people there who really loved the music. Shows were always ending up with fights, so organizers didn't want to take risks anymore because it wasn't worth it. The fan base got infected by a new generation—I know I sound cynical but it's true. When we were seventeen or eighteen or twenty we came, had fun,

mosh pit and so on and then just went home. But now people pay the ticket and just chill, they don't even see the band. You could work your ass off for months to organize a show and then it will be canceled because of a fight or something stupid at another show right before it.

In a sense then, far from fading from view, from Aissam's perspective a major problem with the scene was that it was a victim of its own success. It was expanding beyond its natural base and didn't have the facilities or the discipline to grow in a way that could be controlled. This is not a problem unique to Morocco or other Arab/Muslim metal scenes; it's what every underground scene on Earth dreads even as most every band in the scene secretly wishes for it. But in the case of Morocco any growing pains that the scene experiences are inevitably used by conservative forces to push for crackdowns and other forms of harassment.

Interestingly, by some measures the end of the last decade saw somewhat of a renaissance for metal at least, with new groups and new releases, and while there are still too few live shows to nurture a vibrant scene of its own, the combination of sharing music and videos on the Internet and creating local metal communities has created a basis for the future. As Aissam confirmed in early 2020, "We recently had a month of metal shows at l'Uzine with a bunch of new bands. Wassim from Thrillogy was behind the idea, and along with increased presence on the radio, more collectives, and YouTube channels like lMa3adine, Si Kritik, Artwood, and Majmar radio, there is definitely the possibility for growth in content." The "reset" forced on everyone by the pandemic hiatus seems to have strengthened this trend, however unevenly. The long-term consequences of the pandemic's contradictory impacts—making it far more difficult for bands even to practice together, never mind perform live (in a genre that more than most is defined by live performance), while opening new horizons for productive collaboration online—will be played out in battles of the bands like the Tremplin and festivals like l'Boulevard, as well as for years to come.

FEBRUARY 20 CHANGED EVERYTHING. SORT OF . . .

Morocco was the thirteenth out of twenty-two Arab countries to erupt in protests that began with Muhammad Bouazizi's self-immolation in late 2010. However, the deeper roots of the February 20 movement go back to the 1990s, when what Moroccan scholar Mounia Bennani-Chraïbi calls the "cultural arts and crafts" movement emerged and saw increasingly frequent contacts and even relationships among young people who previously would rarely, if ever, have interacted (leftist and Islamist youth, for example). The protests in 2005 against higher prices for food and other staples also led to greater grassroots coordination with groups that were part of the Boulevard as well, especially ATTAC-Maroc. More direct cyber-activism began around 2007 as the lack of a strong government monitoring presence allowed for alternative information, organizing, and debates to occur there that could not occur in the still highly surveilled and policed offline world.

When I first encountered some of Morocco's seminal hip hop artists, such as Don Bigg, H-Kayne, and Fnaire in 2005, they were among the most politically salient voices in Morocco. That sense of social responsibility hadn't changed by 2008, and in 2009 twenty rappers put out a compilation titled *Mamnou3 f'Radio (Forbidden on the Radio)* with the goal of bringing together political and otherwise provocative songs that had been censored on the radio.

But as the situation became more directly political, and, more to the point, directly challenged the system and even the King, something fundamental changed, as battle lines were being drawn that hadn't previously appeared, between the first generation of Moroccan rappers and an emerging cadre of artists. For their part, the metal and rock bands stayed mostly on the sidelines as the initial group of four or five dozen activists came largely from existing political parties, the Sufi-inspired movement Adl wa-Ihsan, and a variety of liberal/Left groups, including ATTAC-Maroc.

Operating on the principal of no concessions—*Mamfakinch!* in Darija— the activists' explicitly political demands (for the dissolution of the current government, increased social spending and a minimum wage, the separation of judicial, executive, and legislative power for constitutionally guaranteed rights for women and for freedom of opinion and dissent, the recognition of the Amazigh language as an official language) were, at the time, too much for most artists to endorse explicitly. A few rappers, like l7a9d and Mr. Crazy, would become more blunt in the years following February 2011, but even the more inherently political hip hop scene was disciplined by their prison sentences. In the new decade, most rappers who wanted to remain political have chosen to do so more obliquely or focus on social, cultural, and family politics rather than direct critiques of and attacks on the Makhzen.

Just as it had learned to wait and infiltrate the music scenes, the Makhzen did not respond with intense repression or mass violence at the start. Instead, it tolerated the protests officially, offering jobs and development programs and even quickly pushing through a new constitution, while behind the scenes smearing its leaders on Facebook, sending thugs to rallies, and otherwise attempting to disrupt the movement. And ultimately, while it's undeniable that the February 20 movement added a new layer to activism in Morocco's vibrant youth culture, it caused divisions between those activists willing to risk the state's ire to press more forcefully and directly for systemic changes and those who were too dependent on the system to join such direct challenges. On the other hand, the movement inspired a new generation of politically charged artists, especially rappers like l7a9d, to directly engage politics through the music. As l7a9d explained to me in his home in exile in Brussels, "Without a doubt the eruption of the February 20 movement encouraged me to become more political with my own music and focus more on the problems in my community." This sense is confirmed by French sociologist Dominique Caubet, undoubtedly the most important scholar of contemporary Moroccan music, in volume 2 of her landmark *Keep It Simple, Make It Fast,* where she explains that "the #Feb.20 movement emerged as a kind of DIY in politics, making the best use of the new media (mostly Facebook and YouTube), although novices in the domain. At that time, artists were trying to live from their art and to become professional, but, due to the setback that followed the Arab spring, a number of recently created festivals disappeared, and with them, the only chance to earn enough money to live throughout the year."

Even before the "successful" constitutional referendum in June (successfully approved, that is, but not successfully implemented by the standards of the rhetoric surrounding it), the regime began to use more violence while also mobilizing the full power of the Makhzen against protesters—meaning that it was not just the ruling elite but the majority of Moroccan society, who over the course of centuries had had the Makhzen "tattooed" onto their minds (as the rapper Muslim put it in his song "Hub lwatan" ["Love of the Homeland"]), that was mobilized against protesters. What is interesting in this regard is not that the Makhzen system, epitomized by the King, remains hegemonic in Moroccan society, but rather that a major split opened up inside the Moroccan youth scene between "Makhzenists" (regime supporters) and the "Fevrierists" (supporters of the February 20 movement) and, equally, that metalheads largely stayed clear of a fight that increasingly became a classic—and for once politically consequential—hip hop beef, between Don Bigg, who'd styled himself as a latter-day Nass El Ghiwane but by 2011 had become part of the very system he'd previously advised people to fear, and a new generation of more directly political oppositional rappers, as we'll see below. Before, however, we need to understand how the King and the Makhzen's strategies played out in the fate of two of Morocco's biggest music festivals in the last decade: the Boulevard and the more mainstream and far better-funded Mawazine.

TWO FESTIVALS, TWO MOROCCOS

Festivals have long been at the heart of Morocco's self-presentation to the outside world (and to the Moroccan people) as a modern Muslim society. The "youth king of youth," Muhammed VI, understood not only that festivals would buttress Morocco's image as a relatively open and tolerant society on the way to some form of democracy, but also that pushing these festivals would help divert attention and energy away from the more repressive activities of the government. Yet the "festivalization of dissent" didn't work for everyone. After all, the Boulevard was not a state-sponsored or -aligned project to begin with (despite the subvention from Royal Air Maroc), but rather was a true space of individual freedom and the transgression of broader social, cultural, and through them political norms. Even accepting money directly from the King was part of a calculation that it was better to have a somewhat more politically constrained Boultek and Boulevard than having them fall apart for lack of finances.

We can understand this pull between politicized and nonpolitical music if we compare the histories of the Mawazine and Boulevard festivals. The split involved two groups of rappers, and could be symbolized roughly by the difference between the Mawazine Festival and the Boulevard, and between two rappers in particular—the Don of Moroccan rap, Don Bigg, and the enraged upstart, l7a9d. Although Mawazine was created in 2001, three years after the Boulevard, no one I know ever mentioned it during the period I was regularly in Morocco researching *Heavy Metal Islam* (2002–08). One reason for this is no doubt that, during its first half-dozen years, Mawazine was poorly managed, focused on a hodgepodge of world music artists, and was regularly in financial trouble. But in 2008, perhaps the peak year for the Boulevard artistically and socially, Mawazine hired a new director, Mounir Majidi, who was the personal secretary of the King. He immediately used the coffers and contacts of the Makhzen to bring in some of the world's biggest pop stars to headline, including Alicia Keyes, Robert Plant, Stevie Wonder, Lenny Kravitz, and Elton John. John's openly gay identity caused quite a stir as the opposition of religious groups to his presence served to highlight even more strongly the ostensibly open and tolerant official culture.

But it wasn't just conservatives who opposed Mawazine. Progressive forces, including many artists and artist-activists, understood full well the propaganda purposes the festival was now serving, and moreover felt that the lavish spending on a festival, aimed largely at the country's wealthy elite and foreign tourists, was unwarranted and even unseemly because of the harsh economic conditions faced by so many Moroccans. Despite—or perhaps in response to—such criticism, Mawazine moved beyond bringing in A-list international artists; taking a page from the Tremplin/Boulevard format, it began offering spots to relatively and even completely unknown rappers, with the difference being that their participation depended at least as much on writing "patriotic" song as on talent. This focus on patriotism became all the more important after February 20, 2011, when prodemocracy forces were labeled as unpatriotic not just by the Makhzen but by leading rappers like Don Bigg, which also had the effect of mobilizing the more working-class Casablanca against the seemingly more cosmopolitan capital of Rabat.

By 2011 Mawazine had become a symbol of two sides in what was becoming a cultural-political war. On one side Bigg, Fnaire, and—surprisingly to me—the previously socially conscious H-Kayne all echoed the Makhzen's narrative, with Bigg's hit "Mabghitch" ("I Don't Want") from 2012 directly attacking the protesters as atheists, Islamists, and unpatriotic, while the collaboration between H-Kayne and Ridfabuleux, "à la Marocaine," called for national unity against the alleged divisiveness of the protests. The Makhzenist rappers were forcing the question, as Bigg evocatively asked in "Mabghitch," of who would "represent the people" as the country moved toward the future. This was a smart and no doubt calculated move, since as long as that remained the defining question there was no way most Moroccans would give any answer but the King, ensuring that the ruling system remained relatively unscathed from the entire episode. For their efforts the Makhzenist rappers received medals from the King.

Yet the other side of what was ultimately a political beef was not without power, just as the *Bled es-siba* for centuries had maintained an undulating level of independence from the forces of official power. On the one hand, Hoba Hoba Spirit, always among the most politically conscious groups in Morocco, put out a song, "Sawt cha3b" ("Voice of the People"), which captured the motivating spirit of the protests and rallied the public toward the cause of the *févriests*. But with a punk aesthetic, rhythm, and sound, it was never going to be a song to march and chant along with. What could be termed the *siba* rappers included artists like Chekhsar, Muslim, Mobydick, l7a9d, and, depending on whom you ask, Si Simo. Out of all of them, l7a9d was the most daring and strident, with "Dogs of the State" leading to the first of his three stints in prison.

It is instructive to compare l7a9d to the "rapper of the Tunisian Revolution," El Général, whose music and career trajectory defined, along with Egyptian revolutionary singer Ramy Essam's, the politicized youth culture of the Arab Spring. In "Rayes Lebled," the rap song that helped launch the Tunisian Revolution, El Général pleads and implores President Zine Abedin Ben Ali that "your people are dying . . . eating from garbage. . . . We are living like dogs," while imploring him to "look at the police with batons. Thwack-thwack-thwack! They don't care!" (*"sha'bak mata, barcha 'abed mezzebla klet, ihna 'a'ishin kaklab. Shuf el hakem bel matrak takatak ma 'albalhach"*). L7a9d's attitude was much more confrontational from the start: rather than describing the people as living like dogs, he describes the police as the dogs, which is among the more highly charged insults one can make in Arabic. Like Essam's lyrics, l7a9d's lyrics take on the most taboo subjects in Moroccan politics—corruption, police brutality, poverty, and the inherently oppressive nature of the monarchy. Specifically, in "Kleb adDawla," l7a9d's signature song, the police—as in every Arab country, the most direct and concrete manifestation of state powers—are labeled "dogs of the state" (the translation of the title). There is no pleading for recognition. There is only derision, anger, and a direct challenge to the core instrument of state power.

In theory, even as central a coercive element of the power structure as the police could have been criticized obliquely. But l7a9d not only insults them; he ties their violence directly to the King. And he was not the only one to do so. Younès Benkhdim, known as the "Poet of the People" because he penned many of the revolutionary poems of the February 20 movement (for which he spent almost two years in prison between 2012 and 2014, and was again arrested in January 2020), explained it in a poem recited at one of the demonstrations and subsequently uploaded to YouTube:

> We are all subjects of the king.
> Left or right . . . we are the property of the king . . .
> His legitimate right is appropriation.

Your slaves have spread in the land.
With your orders, do they have the right to violate?

Similarly, l7a9d's last words before he was arrested for the third time not only continued to directly attack the Makhzen and the King, but also spoke directly as a representative of the February 20 movement:

> May all those who have died for this free land rest in peace!
> The February 20 movement allowed us to raise many questions:
> Why do we pay the police, or rather the slaves of the Makhzen, while this one represses us?
> Why does the government work only for the interests of its own children, and do nothing for the children of the people?

Not just l7a9d but rappers like Si Simo, Mobydick, and Dizzy Dros all in one way or another have directly taken on or at least blamed the state, Makhzen, or King for the rampant inequality, corruption, and violence visited upon the majority of Moroccans in the last decade (during the time when Don Bigg and other mainstream rappers either moved away from politics or became part of the Makhzen). While Makhzen rappers use patriotism to win support from on high, l7a9d's regular run-ins with the government as well as prison time increased his street credibility, especially among Morocco's poor and disenfranchised young people, from whose midst he'd risen in the slum of El Oulfa in the outskirts of Casablanca.

Indeed, as he rose to fame, l7a9d's depictions of the worst characteristics of young Moroccans' lives earned him the sobriquet of the "Gavroche of the Moroccan Revolution." Gavroche was a minor but important character in Victor Hugo's *Les Misérables,* a "street urchin" who joins the revolution and risks his life and in fact dies while collecting ammunition cartridges from dead government soldiers near the barricades during the popular rebellion in Paris in 1832. As I and a group of other musicians and activists worked daily through the organization Freemuse to get l7a9d out of prison and then out of Morocco, his courage in refusing to back down became increasingly evident, as were the risks, including to his life, that were involved in his dissidence.

Epitomizing his single-minded dedication to both his art and his political vision, l7a9d even went directly from prison to the recording studio in the summer of 2014 ("Before I even went home to see my mom!" he joked after recording his verse) to participate in a remake of Fela Kuti's "Zombie" that I was producing with revolutionary artists including Egypt's Ramy Essam, Iranian rapper Salome MC, and Syrian-Palestinian refugee rappers Refugees of Rap. He put it in one of his last big hits before leaving Morocco, "Walou": "Nothing satisfies us.... We are so sick. No culture, no art, no creation.... No, no way.... Put this in your head: Never give up your rights.... This country is ours, not his [the King's]."

THE RISE OF THE MICROFESTIVAL

The Boulevard and Mawazine each continued along their natural and very disparate trajectories, representing two experiences of and visions for Morocco, as narrated by opposing camps of rappers. For its part, however, the metal scene continued in a kind of cruise control. The scene didn't grow much, but thanks in part to the resources and exposure provided by the Boultek, Tremplin, and Boulevard, and newer spaces in Rabat and Casablanca, individual groups developed their sound and became more professional. The Boultek and Tremplin paved the way for other mid-sized venues like l'Uzine in Casablanca and Renaissance in Rabat, and new festivals also emerged in the last decade that built on the energy and eclecticism of the Boulevard, such as the Visa for Music Expo, focusing on mid-level world music artists (largely from Africa), and, as we'll discuss below, the far more grassroots and extreme festival Hardzazat.

After skipping the 2016 edition, in 2017 Boulevard organizers increased the prize money for first and second place at the Tremplin and offered winners a better spot at the Boulevard for their set. (Back in the mid-2000s, when I first attended the festival, Tremplin winners often opened the day's events, performing somewhere around noon when hardly any fans had arrived yet.) The Boulevard program was as impressive as ever, with an international array of artists including American hip hop group M.O.P. and hardcore group Kominas, French metal outfit Dagoba, and Nigerian singer Keziah Jones. These artists were joined by local acts like Masta Flow (one of the great older rappers, who started off as a member of Casa Crew), all-star punk/metal collaboration Betweenatna (featuring some of the original members of the metal scene like Amine Hamma from Reborn and Abdessamad Bourhim from Hoba Hoba Spirit coming together for the first time in almost two decades), and even the soulful alternative voice of Oum. Betweenatna in particular offered a highly sophisticated yet tongue-in-cheek synergy of punk, metal, and popular music that took Hoba Hoba Spirit's already-beloved sound and made it both harder and funn(k)ier.

As in the past, there were numerous booths, panels, films, and artist residencies. Speaking to Morocco World News shortly before the 2017 edition, Momo explained why the Boulevard remained so important for artists young and older alike: "Artists are strong technically [but] lack creativity," because they lost their originality and urgency. "We have big names . . . but their music is just like fast food. . . . Fnair [one of the first big hip hop groups], for instance, they are no longer doing hip-hop; they are variety artists. Things have changed. You can't compare [pop star] Ahmed Chawki with Hoba Hoba Spirit, not the same energy. It is not exclusive to Morocco, it's a global phenomenon. It appears that misery is the source of great creativity."

What Momo was arguing, as Boulevard cofounder Hisham explained to me when we both participated in the 2019 edition of the ACCES Africa music festival in Accra, was that the easier conditions for pop and hip hop artists to become commercially successful, and to a lesser extent for indie and metal artists thanks to Boultek and similar endeavors, took away the struggles and independence that have always been the most favorable conditions for producing aesthetically innovative and culturally and politically powerful music.

It's not surprising, then, that well over half a decade after the last direct F20 protests oppositional movements in Morocco once again were showing how deeply they remained embedded in society. But the Rifian aka Hirak protests that began in late 2016 were not yet connected to or animating music elsewhere in the country, as festivals like the Festival de Gnaoua in Essaouira, Mawazine in Rabat, and the World Festival of Sacred Music in Fes saw no mention of the suffering in the northern steppes. For their part, as recorded by the web-show *L'Ma3adine,* festival-going metal fans at the Boulevard were celebrating the "revolutionary" nature of the increased support by the government for the rock and especially metal scene, which many felt enabled newer bands to achieve higher quality.

However politically off the mark, such assessments of the Boulevard in the final years of the 2010s did to a certain extent make sense in terms of the aesthetics of quotidian, or daily, life. Thinking about the ongoing success of the Boulevard, Hicham explained to me that the main reason so many people were still attending the Boulevard after so many years was not because of the major metal acts they'd brought to Morocco, but rather because of the local bands and, equally important, the everydayness, or at least everyyearness, of the festival—its sheer normalcy at this point after so many years of struggle just to survive and be accepted. And so when conservatives once again attacked the metal scene in the lead-up to the 2017 edition, artists, fans, and organizers were confident enough to shrug them off and even turn them into a joke, as exemplified by a video uploaded on August 19, 2017, by l'Maӡadine, titled 'aibadat ash-shaytan fi-l-bulfar (Lma'adine React to the "Devil Worship at the Boulevard"), in which the hosts searched for Satan worshipers at the festival but found only hilarious metal fans (although the upside-down crosses mascara'd onto one seemingly intoxicated fan's cheeks might have swayed the susceptible to think a few Devil worshipers were hiding in plain sight).

DECOLONIAL HARDCORE

Despite the potentially revolutionary movement in Morocco beginning in February 2011, the metal scene, which earlier in the decade was at the forefront of struggles for cultural and personal freedom against a still-sclerotic (or at least stiff) Makhzen, remained largely absent from the active political engagement of the Arab Spring era. Hip hop as a genre was more implicated in the February 20 movement, although in fact only a few rappers were willing to take on the Makhzen, never mind the King, directly. As for EDM, its presence expanded rapidly in the last decade in terms of the number of festivals but the liberation it promises is more cultural and personal than political.

On the other hand, as scholars like Jim Donaghey, Kevin Dunn, Raymond A. Patton, Paula Guerra, and Pedro Quintela have amply documented, wherever it's landed, punk and hardcore in their various incarnations have almost always had a more directly political edge. This has remained as true in Morocco today as it was in the UK or US two generations ago with bands like the Sex Pistols, Dead Kennedys, Black Flag, and, somewhat more mainstream, the Clash and UB40. The latest example of punk's political edge comes from one of the most interesting microfestivals not just in Morocco, but anywhere today. In the spring of 2015 a group of film school students from the town of Ouarzazate (one of Africa's great medieval mud cities and a UNESCO World Heritage Site made even more famous after its use as a location for Game of Thrones) created a DIY music festival called Hardzazat, its name a neologism of "hard" from "hardcore" and the name of their city. Held in the wilderness outside the town, the festival, whose success in the first year has made it an annual gathering, features hardcore, metal, and hip

FIGURE 8. Moroccan and European fans dancing at Hardzazat festival, 2016.

hop from a variety of artists from inside and—until the pandemic—outside Morocco.

As its own website described its initial focus, from the start Hardzazat has been "guided by a proud punk aesthetic and fierce anti-colonial, anti-fascist rhetoric." Far beyond providing a venue for the still strong DIY aesthetic to express itself musically, the organizers from the start sought to "emancipate all the attendees, . . . gathering the Moroccan libertarian minorities." With a focus on autonomous and self-managed organization and a strong relationship with local inhabitants, the festival took inspiration from the Boulevard in its early days "to create a safe space from the dominant culture, therefore there's no tolerance for violence, sexism, homophobia, or any form of discrimination and . . . all the participants get to be treated equally."

From a political perspective Hardzazat is the realization of the activist dream from the early Boulevards, when film screenings sponsored by ATTAC-Maroc, booths dedicated to Amazigh language and homelessness, and a general willingness to shove metal in the face of a ruling system that had tried to crush it first inspired me to write *Heavy Metal Islam*. Indeed, if the most iconic Boulevard posters, from 2008, saw a bunch of musicians in a beat-up old Mercedes taxi flying toward a glistening modernist urban future, the Hardzazat poster depicts a bunch of musicians on the back of a beat-up pickup truck, traveling down a back-country road on the way to an oasis at the foothills of the mountains.

The similarities and differences between the two images are illuminating. So is the language deployed by the organizers, which is taken straight out of the anticorporate globalization movement. As its webpage explains, "In a time ruled by a globalized economy supported by the political regimes of the states, the festival tries as a result of strong opposition against the current regimes to create a free-living space where people can exchange various experiences about autonomy, aiming to free people from the dominance of the state, the market global economy, and all the traditional power games."

In this context, perhaps the most important aspect of Hardzazat from both a political and an epistemological standpoint was the adoption by organizers of a specifically "decolonial" perspective: "It's a festival by and for non-white people under systemic racism, . . . an occasion to regroup people from southern countries, talk about racism issues, organize local helps, and frequent events. The decolonial issues are part of a more general political engagement of the fest, treating problems like racism, sexism, homophobia, in order to build an autonomous movement of revolted and revolutionaries." As explained briefly in the introduction, and will be discussed in more detail in the epilogue, decolonial theory differs from preindependence anticolonial movements, and the postcolonial theories that attempt to understand the colonial and immediately postcolonial eras. Specifically, it argues that despite decades of formal independence, the countries of the Global South remain mired in relations of dependency and subjugation that are fundamentally the same—that is, colonial—as when they were under foreign rule (and so, the "post-" in postcolonial is seen to confuse more than clarify the situation). What's more, postcolonial states—that is, the states currently in power in countries like Morocco and the rest of the Arab world—are structured and behave like the colonial forms of governance out of which they emerged.

Decolonial theory is one of the most powerful theoretical and methodological interventions in the humanities and social sciences of the last several decades, and even more important for activists looking to more strongly anchor their struggles historically. For a music festival to explicitly embrace it and base its programming and guiding philosophy on it is more or less unprecedented.

But the organizers of Hardzazat took matters one step further, reaching into traditional Moroccan religious culture to adopt the idea of the Moussem, or the annual regional religious festival and market held around harvest times or the birthdays of saints or even natural phenomena. Similar—as we'll see in chapter 6—to how festival organizers in Pakistan have turned traditional *melas* (or religiously oriented festivals) into far more "secular" meetups involving music, food, and corporate sponsors, Hardzazat "intend[ed] to create the first Moussem Hardcore dedicated to the new culture, by and for young Moroccans, and bring an audience from all over the country." And the main focus of the Moussem would be decolonial antifascism.

The 2015 edition of Hardzazat (the second of the festival) featured local bands Chemical Bliss, T-NIN, Tachamarod, Riot Stones, and perhaps the most celebrated of the new era of Moroccan metal bands, Thrillogy, in a loose setup that allowed for late-night performances and a lot of interaction with fans. According to Aissam (from Vile Utopia), who attended the last four editions, the festival represented well the early DIY spirit of Moroccan metal and hardcore: "Every year in fact the festival could have been canceled right up to the last minute. In fact, the first year it was banned, but they did it anyway. . . . But each year there were more techno and hip hop and no French bands, and I think that it lost its spirit a bit."

By the third edition organizers had declared Hardzazat an "antifascist Moussem" and "a resistance event against all the extremists waves, sexists and fascists." But it was the fifth edition, held in May 2019, that was truly explosive. Not because of the music, but rather because of the decision by organizers, in the spirit of its "decolonial" and "antifascist" principles, to prohibit French artists from performing. The pushing-out of French bands came as a shock to many supporters, not least because in previous years the organizers had organized solidarity and fundraising concerts in France to raise funds for the festival and French hardcore bands had been among its most stalwart supporters.

Organizers explained their decision on the Hardzazat Facebook page by arguing that in the context of an unfinished French imperialism in Morocco, "We oppose the excessive importance of Europeans and the way in which they occupy spaces for cultural creation and dissemination." Denying French artists at Hardzazat would thus "allow for a unique creative space made by and for Moroccans. . . . The good thing for white people to do," the organizers concluded, "is to stand back when initiatives are taken and act only when they are asked to."

In the midst of the ensuing trans-Mediterranean debate, I particularly appreciated the comments by Nabil Belkabir, a member of the Union of Students for Change in Education in Rabat and a rising public intellectual voice in and outside of Morocco. He argued simply that there are "infinite festivals where whites can practice their art, but for Africans there are less and less [sic]." Indeed, he added, most French events have no African artists, with no consequences. "For once, an African festival tries to have a program without French artists and it's shocking." If we lay aside the contentious claim that there are "less and less" festivals for African artists (my own experience is that the number had in fact been growing until the pandemic), Belkabir raises the obvious question of whether all that support by European and especially French punks and hardcore fans wasn't more about having a cool Moroccan gig to play at once a year rather than supporting their Moroccan comrades.

Yet if one could find it hard to fault Belkabir's argument as far as it goes, it's also true that for all its talk of decolonial and antifascist attitudes, the festival has stayed clear of directly critiquing the Makhzen or the King, the living embodiments of the ongoing colonial foundations and essence of the Moroccan state and governing system, even when the 2019 edition was officially banned, forcing a smaller version to be held in the desert beyond the original location. It seems that, like so many activists who have been drawn to the idea of decolonial activism and critique, the organizers of Hardzazat assumed that the intended decolonization referred to the former colonial power (in this case France) when in fact at the heart of decolonial critique is the realization that all states are inherently colonial, none more so than post-colonial states whose very existence was germinated and nurtured by the former colonial power—for which the Makhzen is a quintessential example. And so as a small but boisterous crowd of punks, hardcore fans, hip hop heads, and other alternative and extreme music fans gathered, participated in graffiti and other arts workshops, and partied, played, and free-styled late into the night on the makeshift stages, a direct critique of the Makhzen, never mind the King, remained beyond possibility, for obvious and quite understandable reasons.

FROM REVOLUTIONARY BEEFS TO THE AESTHETIC POLITICS OF TRAP

In the mid-2010s, at a moment when the immediate impact of the F20 movement had waned and the Boulevard struggled to organize the yearly festival, a few rappers, most notably l7a9d and Mr. Crazy, refused to back down and more directly challenged the power and prestige of the Makhzen and even the King with each new song. L7a9d's was the most direct challenge possible to "Makhzen power" (as political scientist Mohamed Daadaoui terms it), landing him in jail three times and ultimately exile. At this same time as l7a9d was pushing the limits of expression past the point where he could no longer remain in the country, trap was emerging and rapidly solidifying its position in Morocco as in the rest of the Arab world—and indeed, the world at large—as contemporary rap's dominant aesthetic and form. If hip hop leaped over metal to become the most salient youth music in Morocco in the period around the Arab Spring, in the last half decade there's no doubt that trap has become today the most important and innovative form of youth music—much to the chagrin of older and more verbally dexterous rappers and also those hoping to carry on the more politically critical traditions of the parent genre.

Echoing Momo's complaint that Moroccan pop had become more a variety show than serious music, rapper Lmoutchou (who won the Tremplin back in 2006) explained that "the current trend is not to pass a message through rap, nobody cares about that anymore. What the audience wants is 'trap,' comedy, punch line. . . . If you're an activist, you can help out associations through your art but you cannot be serious like before." But this shouldn't mean that either the artists or their music were devoid of political intentionality. As longtime scene watcher, journalist, and scholar Samia Errazzouki explained to me, songs like Issam's "Trap Beldi," Shobee, Laylow, and Madd's "Money Call," 7liwa's "Nafi," and Issam's "Caviar" all have extremely powerful political messages embedded in imagery and themes that are clearly steeped in working-class urban and rural culture. But unlike l7a9d, they keep these messages below the surface so they don't raise immediate alarm bells with officials, "since if they go full Haqed they know what will happen to them."

It's much better to keep the criticism within acknowledged limits and get an occasional invitation to the Palace to perform at a private party, and perhaps even some funding for your next album, as some of the otherwise political artists like 7liwa have received. Or to be so creative with your lyrics that the censors will accept that when you sing, "You were dear to my heart, but you rotted like caviar. . . . I live in my country as a stranger. . . . I have grown on a path of suffering, there is no hope left. On the road of my dream a policeman has arrested me," as Issam does on "Caviar," you're really just talking about your ex-girlfriend.

One way this is accomplished might well be the combination of the droning, "syrupy" quality inherent in most trap grooves no matter which culture and language they're produced in, and the often-hypnotic vibe of the music videos that inevitably accompany them. In the mid-2000s indie Pakistani artists were in the avant-garde of producing the kind of inexpensive DIY yet highly original music videos that would soon become the norm globally, but the mantle today has surely been shared with their counterparts on the other side of the Muslim world, in Morocco. If you watch videos by artists like Dollypran, Madd, Issam, and other "trappers," what one non-Arab-speaking fan of Issam's captivating "Nike" described as the deeply "wavy" quality of the whole package (the sound, texture, timbre, and rhythms of the rapping, and the aesthetics of the videos) will lull all but the most assiduous censors and Makhzen video police into forgetting about the messages, which are nevertheless easily decoded by the artists' intended audience, largely the urban working class. Indeed, it often seems that the innovative nature of the videos is in inverse relationship to the monotony of the grooves. Perhaps the most shocking example of this comes from the video for the song "Nike" (about the sneaker, not the goddess) by Issam, who in June 2019 signed a record deal with Universal France, the biggest ever for an Arab rapper. The synth heavy track, replete with some retro sounds and incredibly "wavy" autotuned vocal tracks that both celebrate and critique the obsession with flashy brands like Nike and Versace, features a video that is steeped in symbols traditionally associated with magic in Morocco, a level of overt occult referencing that, had these symbols ever been deployed by metalheads in years past, would have driven religious conservatives, and no doubt prosecutors as well, into a frenzy.

But a lot has changed in the last decade, much of it thanks to YouTube and WhatsApp sharing and similar forms of social media, which have brought so many new and different symbols and sounds into peoples' homes that the tolerance for occult imagery (which actually suffuses popular culture not only in Morocco but across the Maghreb and even Egypt), as well as so-called "Western" genres like trap, hip hop, and even metal, is simply at a much higher level than it was previously. At the same time, the level of word play and visual and lyrical sophistication as well as humor in artists like Issam or the up-and-coming Dollypran, as well as in their videos, almost guarantees that most anything they put up will garner at least a million views. And a bit further from the hip hop spotlight, in a one-of-a-kind artist like Cheb (born Nabil Elamraoui), a young pro-Hirak multi-instrumentalist singer-song-writer and video artist who was forced into exile because of his Woody Guthrie (or Ahmed Fouad Negm) level of lyrical dexterity and power, a truly inspiring level of political as well as musical and visual innovativeness is clear, until you realize that, like l7a9d (who is, in his own words, a "very big fan" of

FIGURE 9. Don Bigg, cover art for single "170 KG," released December 2018, from official video. Art by Hamza Zemmama.

Cheb), the power of his music has doomed him to live in exile for the foreseeable future.

Sometimes, however, politics and art smash into each other in ways that shine a klieg light on both. One of these moments occurred on Christmas Eve 2018, while the rest of the world was focused on the brutal murder of two Scandinavian hikers in the Atlas Mountains by self-styled Islamic State supporters. It was at this moment that Don Bigg dropped a new "diss" or "beef" track titled "170 KG" (apparently his weight), which by most accounts is the most vicious beef rap ever produced on the Moroccan scene. To say it "broke the (Moroccan) Internet" would not be an exaggeration in the least in this case.

With a cartoon video depicting him sitting on a throne with several of the main young rappers like Mr. Crazy, 7liwa, Ily, Dizzy Dros, Komy, Toto, and Lbenj around him, the image representing the song announces the tone immediately. Indeed, not only is Don Bigg sitting on a throne, he's holding rapper 7liwa on a leash attached to his little finger and crushing Dizzy Dros's head with his foot. On the floor, we also recognize Komy handcuffed and lying on his stomach and Mr. Crazy dying in the middle of a bloodbath.

Within a week "170 KG" had accumulated over ten million YouTube views, with over fifty thousand comments. It's hard to imagine a better vehicle than "170 KG" to distract people from the most brutal tourist attack in years, never mind the worsening economy, and, indeed, that's what happened. Dizzy Dros, Mr. Crazy, Komy, and 7liwa all responded in kind, setting off what quickly became known as the *guerre de rappeurs* (war of the rappers). Most of the responses also earned at least ten million YouTube views, meaning that the whole episode produced about fifty million views on the participants' YouTube sites, likely confirming Bigg's comment when the responses started being uploaded that he had done them all a favor with his track.

Most if not all of the rappers targeted by Bigg are trap artists, a genre Bigg, like many older rappers, clearly doesn't much approve of. One of the youngest members of the scene, 7liwa, was the first to respond directly, with his track "57 kg," where he clearly taunts Bigg not only for his weight but also for being miserly and cheap, alluding to a Big Mac several times in the song. Dizzy Dros took the situation much further by composing a verbal barrage of a diss track, "Moutanabi," with the video mimicking the style of Bigg's original imagery, but this time with Dros bursting into DBF (Bigg's studio) and dragging Bigg by the neck, while another image of Bigg depicts him half naked, on all fours, with a bondage ball strapped around his mouth. Mr. Crazy's response, "Biggshot," is an even more direct attack, featuring an image of Bigg with a bull's-eye in the middle while he raps about Bigg's lack of bona fides and betrayal.

The beef between Bigg and his once-upon-a-time acolytes puts into context the far tamer feud between Bigg and l7a9d, epitomized by the Enraged One's reply to the Don's attempt to dismiss him and other political rappers as not representing authentic Moroccans in the song "Dahia l7sabbe" ("Victim to the Account"). While calling out Bigg in all but name for his Makhzenist politics, "Dahiya l7sabbe" pales in comparison with the vituperative and directly personal attacks on other rappers by Bigg in "170 KG," a lyrical war that is all the more surprising when you find a YouTube video from 2013 where Don Bigg, Shayfeen, and Dizzy Dros were free-styling together on one of Morocco's most popular radio shows, hosted by Momo Bousfiha.

The focus on YouTube views, never mind beef raps, and on hip hop more broadly could not but have been welcome by the Makhzen, because of the troubles in the heart of the *siba* associated with the Rifian protests of 2017–19. These protests succeeded in once again breaking the "wall of fear," as a leading human rights campaigner, Moroccan Association for Human Rights founder Khadija Riyadi, put it, "electroshocking" the Moroccan body politic. While few musicians were willing to "go full Haqed" in support of the protests, three young rappers—Weld lGriya, Lz3er, and Gnawi—showed great courage by recording and uploading the song "3Ach Cha3b" ("Long

Live the People") in 2019. Showing just the potential of political music, the song quickly garnered well over twenty-five million views on YouTube alone, with hundreds of thousands of comments, most of them in support of the musicians (that pop stars like Douzi, Zouhair Bahaoui, or Saad Lamjarred can achieve one hundred million, five hundred million, and one billion views, respectively, with a single song does, of course, put even this number in perspective). If we read some of the most incendiary lyrics, we can imagine how the government reacted:

> They stifled our dreams
> these sons of dogs
> so that we remain their slaves.
> We despaired of everything
> and we can't take it anymore.
> We have a commander of believers with his Islam burnous [cloak]
> [and] advisers who drain their fortunes abroad.
> Half of the people beg and you enjoy your parties. . . .
> Whoever speaks on behalf of the people
> and says it's the fault of who rules
> Is accused of being radical and terrorist.

Sure enough, the rapper Gnawi was tried and convicted (similar to l7a9d) of insulting the police and sentenced to one year of prison. As he told the court at his sentence, "I am an artist. My job is to defend my rights and the rights of the people. It was not the first time that I had been humiliated by the police. . . . Since I was born, I have been humiliated." Other lesser-known artists, some from the Rif, also recorded songs at the start of the protests.

While written at least partly in response to the Rif conflict, "3Ach Cha3b" was not necessarily on everyone's lips throughout the Rif. Perhaps most telling here is a song by a Rifian rapper named Kalashnikov, "Pik ya wlidi," which was uploaded in June 2017. The title is taken from a phrase first used by a Hiraki activist reacting to a judge's charges against him in court, as a Rifian dialect version of the ubiquitous interjection "pchakh," used in response to hearing something unbelievable or crazy. With a video consisting of a single image of a protest with a giant banner reading "kuluna mu'ataqal" ("we are all [political] prisoners"), the song begins with almost two minutes of audio of a speech and chants led by jailed Hiraki activist Nasser Zefzafi before the music kicks in. The Tamazigh lyrics continue the political refrain, creating a powerful retort to the ongoing abuses of the Makhzen on the Rifian peoples.

Deeper into the Jbala region, in the village of Joujouka (also spelled Zahjouka and Jajouka), a much older musical tradition was continuing, one that in my view has many lessons to teach political artists and activists, not just in Morocco, but everywhere about how to maintain solidarity, originality, and power in the long-term struggles against authoritarian and corrupt political power. According to local lore, the village has existed at least half a millennium, when the founder of a Sufi clan, known to history as Sidi Hmed Shikh, arrived from parts unknown and of uncertain heritage. Dubbed the "4,000 year old rock n roll band" by *Rolling Stone* and Timothy Leary, the Master Musicians of Joujouka (a second group from the village, who spell their name Jajouka, also performs under the broad historical rubric) were first brought to Western ears beginning in the 1950s through the likes of Paul Bowles, Brian Gysin, Hunter S. Thompson, and Rolling Stones guitarist Brian Jones, who recorded the group in 1968 in perhaps one of the first ever attempts at an "EDM" album, released two years after his death in 1969 under the title *Brian Jones Presents the Pipes of Pan at Joujouka.*

Historically part of the *Bled es-siba,* the region of the Rif Mountains including Joujouka has played a central role in the Moroccan economy for centuries, particularly through the widespread cultivation of cannabis, which has made Morocco the primary source for hashish in Europe. A European-requested eradication and substitution program negatively impacted the local economy, leading many young people to leave for jobs in Tangier and other cities.

The Master Musicians exist in a precarious space between poverty and underdevelopment, the preservation of traditions upon which their music and livelihoods depend, and the desire for their children to be afforded the kinds of opportunities that only exist in cities such as Rabat or Tangier, where more and more head as soon as they reach adulthood. I first attended their microfestival in 2012, held yearly in their village for a few dozen lucky aficionados. With the F20 protests still ongoing (though starting to peter out), one of the leaders of the group was asked what the Arab Spring has meant for them. He laughed and shook his head. "We don't want change. We want to preserve what we have," even as he showed us videos on his smart phone purchased during the previous year's tour, when they performed at Glastonbury. With a much more tenuous relationship to central authority than urban-based activists and artists, the musicians of Joujouka exhibit little desire to confront the Makhzen; they want running water and more government services and political patronage for their village while preserving local autonomy and heritage, and spreading their music as widely as possible.

And yet, despite their unique orientation, the music of Joujouka can be heard as a microcosm of Moroccan society; its seeming repetitiveness and predictability (which makes it great trance music) is belied by constant melodic (microtonal) and (poly)rhythmic motion and change that is difficult for the uninitiated to hear when the sound is flattened out on a CD and two speakers or even from the audience at a concert. But if you're lucky enough to experience the Master Musicians live, unmediated, from five feet away (the way they were always meant to be heard) the seemingly effortless blending of melodic dissonance and rhythmic diversity into overall harmony becomes even more impressive. A subtle tone change or slightly harder single beat on the drum can lead the rest of the troupe to an instantaneous change of melody, rhythm, or even song, catching the untrained audience by surprise. Musicians also use their own slang, which is incomprehensible to anyone outside the group, to communicate during performances.

Musicians including Ornette Coleman, Robert Palmer, Billy Corgan, Randy Weston, and Jarvis Cocker have come from all over the world to study with the Master Musicians so they can learn how to interact and adapt to their own musicians more rapidly, to take an audience on such long journeys without anyone seemingly leading the way. What all clearly sensed upon first hearing the group on sonically two-dimensional recordings was that the music clearly had four, and likely more, dimensions. What you realize when you are actually present at a live performance, especially in the village, is not merely that the musicians are breathing music instead of air, but that by the time they're done with you, *you* are breathing music instead of air—that is, you are literally inside their aura.

In the context of an ongoing debate among "Arab Spring" activists as well as progressive activists and movements globally about how "leaderless revolutions" could ever hope to win power from deeply rooted authoritarian and exploitative systems, the Master Musicians offer some of the best examples of the strategies and skills that activists across the region need in these ongoing struggles. If we consider how long the tradition has been developing, how rooted in place it remains, yet how global its impact has become, the group offers many lessons not merely for artists but for activists and scholars as well as to how auratic artistic creation can have profound intellectual and political implications. At the same time, the reality—as expressed by members to me over the years—that their tradition is being lost as their children move away and they've even begun to forget the deepest grooves of the previous generation points to how fragile that aura or art (and similarly, transformative politics) remains. The ongoing struggles between Makhzen and *siba,* between tradition and innovation, authenticity and commercialization, courage and compromise—not just in Joujouka but across the Moroccan musical and political landscapes—encapsulate the myriad musical and political possibilities as well as challenges faced by artists across the MENA and larger Muslim world.

TWO

Yalla, "Let's Play!"

EGYPT FROM THE PHARAOH TO THE GENERAL

With Anonymous 1 & 2

Oh SCAF, you bastards. How much money is a martyr's blood!?
 You sold our blood cheap: to protect the regime which you
are a part of.
 Unleash more of your dogs [police] and spread chaos everywhere.
 I will never trust you nor let you control me one more day.

—"OH COUNCIL OF BASTARDS" *(Ya maglis ya ibn haram),*
chanted by thousands of Ultras Ahlawy fans in front
of the Egyptian Parliament, April 2012

AS WE ALL NOW KNOW, the rising hopefulness of the years before the Arab uprisings exploded in late 2010 masked a roiling below the surface, as millions of people's lives felt just like the region's burgeoning metal scenes sounded. In Egypt we can see this from a debate in spring 2010 on the program *al-Haqiqa* on Egypt's Dream 2 TV channel, which pitted several young metalheads (the young woman among them wearing a hijab) against a conservative former assistant to Egypt's grand mufti named Tuhami Muntasir, who began his career two decades earlier condemning "crass" cassette tapes and "vulgar" pop songs before turning his attention to a far easier victim: Egypt's "shabab al-metal," its "metal youth." The program's host, Wael El Ebrashy, introduced the debate by declaring to the metal youth that while there were "unfortunately many misconceptions in society" about metal (*"lil-asf 'adid min al-mufahim al-mugtama'"*—lit. "understandings," but in context it clearly means "misunderstanding"), nonetheless, "Let's be frank, people call you

---

Anonymous 1 & 2 are a longtime Egyptian male MC and female music writer who, because of the ongoing political repression against artists and journalists who in any way criticize the system, have chosen to remain anonymous.

Satan worshipers" ("'abad ash-shaytan"). "Some of your parties," he continued, "have developed into national security issues [al-'aadiya 'amni]."

The idea of metal as a national security issue might seem ridiculous today (and should have then), but the metaliens (the Egyptian word for "metalheads") nodded in agreement as he spoke; how could they not, since if the government and religious establishment declared someone or something a national security issue, then it was, until declared otherwise, a national security issue. Perhaps a more accurate word choice would have been "state security issue" rather than "national security issue," since there was little evidence that the small but plucky metal scene threatened the actual security of Egypt, but a perspicacious security or intelligence official might have been justified in wondering whether these kids might someday threaten the security of an increasingly out-of-touch, sclerotic authoritarian state.

Of course, for the regime, the state and the country were the same thing. Indeed, unbeknown to the government and probably even to themselves, the young fans of the metal and other underground scenes had developed the skills, ideas, and courage that would soon threaten the survival of the military regime or system (nitham) that had run the country for decades.

As for the former religious censor, Muntasir played his role well, accusing the kids, who grew increasingly exasperated as one lie bled into another, of being part of a "sponsored organized Zionist activity" (nashat sahyuni) that gets "money [amwal] from many sources. Maybe Cyprus, maybe Israel." Even the host El Ebrashy couldn't let that accusation go unanswered. When he asked the kids if they received outside money, one of them retorted, "If we did, would we be in such a poor state?"

Muntasir claimed that this information was "from confessions from people who were caught" before being interrupted and then finishing by stating that "the phenomenon we are witnessing right now is a clear manifestation of a well-funded Zionist campaign, which is based on a Constitution [dustur]—The Protocols of the Elders of Zion," at which point one of the most vocal metalheads on the panel leaned back so far in his chair in disgust that it seemed he might tip over backward. Muntasir would not even let the kids respond. "Please, excuse me, excuse me. I'm not done yet . . . " (Min fadlak, law samaht, law samaht. khalasna), he decried, in a staccato cadence, while he put his thumbs to his fingers in the ubiquitous Mediterranean gesture signaling "wait!" until he got to the money line: "What does Zionism want? You know this as an intellectual: To rule the world [yusaitr al-'alam]." He then declared that Zionism has the "means" and "priorities" to accomplish this by "establish[ing] clubs that will draw people who have certain characteristics and who are willing to collaborate *[isti'idad lil-a'amala]* . . . and will bring them to the top of the pyramid of power *[qimat al-haram as-sulta]*."

The look and body language of the metalheads as he said this were utterly memeable. Before he was finally shut up, Muntasir declared that "the third priority of the Elders of Zion [the current elders, one supposes, not those of the book] is drug trafficking and facilitating the spread of abomination so that societies become enslaved to their desire and urges. . . . Let's turn [them into] to heavy metal fans. That way the countries will collapse with no need to resort to weapons."

We can easily dismiss Muntasir's diatribe as theater. But in fact his accusations played on tropes that had been inculcated into Egyptians by state-controlled media and religious authorities incessantly for half a century and more, and against which there really isn't any defense because their validity isn't measured by their fidelity to reality, but rather their fidelity to the patriarchal authoritarian narrative that has always defined the dominant Egyptian (and, to some extent, Arab) culture. All the metaliens could do in response was declare loudly that they "renounced every Satan, from the smallest to the Minister of all Satans" *(wazir kul ash-shaytan).*

What is most interesting for our purposes is that, coming three-quarters of a year before the Arab uprisings hit Egypt, the arguments put forth by Muntasir mirrored those deployed by the Egyptian military in the wake of the youth-led #Jan25 Uprising to delegitimize young activists and young Egyptians more broadly as untrustworthy and a threat to the security and stability of Egypt moving forward, even as they were being celebrated by the entire country for the incredible feat of toppling Mubarak. The kids were a potential cancer and a fifth column, Manchurian candidates simply waiting to be "activated" by the sound of heavy metal, an accusation that would legitimize the worst sorts of state violence against them in the coming years: mass imprisonment, torture, mass shootings to blind and otherwise disable, and even outright murder.

Although attacked relentlessly by Muntasir and barely allowed opportunity to respond by the host, the fearless *shabab al-metal* fought back as best they could. Indeed, they were not only unafraid to speak back to someone representing governmental authority; their exasperation and anger were on full display. Few moments better reflected the contest of power, worldviews, and vision that would explode approximately ten months later than this, and the back-and-forth and ultimate silencing of the youth by the cartoonish representative of the Old Guard mirror what actually happened in Egypt over the next three years.

The conflict between the metaliens and the establishment depicted in this episode of *al-Haqiqa* reflected the changing calculus—if not balance—of power between the "new generation" *(ig-gil ig-gadid)* and the system at the end of the 2000s. Readers who remember the end of the Egypt chapter in *Heavy Metal Islam* will recall the words of Marz, lead guitarist of the band Hate Suffocation, which had just changed its name to Scarab as the book went to press to highlight Egypt's glorious ancient past. "WRITE MY NAME!" he wrote to Mark in an email, declaring that he wanted to "let the fucking world know what we're doing." It was not an easy decision to make, but in hindsight he realized it was the right one.

Simply put, like his comrades on TV, Marz knew that something was changing in Egyptian society, even if he, like most other people, couldn't quite put his finger on what the change was. But as was becoming clear across the MENA region, nowhere more so than in the music, the time for staying quiet or remaining cowed by authoritarian regimes was ending. Indeed, by the end of the twenty-first century's first decade, it was increasingly clear to most Egyptians involved in some way in activism that the country was on the brink of major change. The system had become so corrupt, the chance for improvement and development so stunted, and the pressure from the burgeoning millennial population so high that something was going to give in the near future. In chapter 1, we saw that Morocco had been poised for greater cultural and political liberalization on the eve of the Arab uprisings era. In this chapter, we will see that Egypt's metal scene equally epitomized the political potential of underground music in the MENA region at the turn of the twenty-first century's second decade.

In December 2008 Mark organized the first metal show in central Cairo in almost a decade, at the Sawi Culture Wheel Zemalek, the island between downtown Cairo and the Dokki neighborhood, as part of the filming for the documentary that would become *Before the Spring, after the Fall*. The venue was filled nearly to capacity. Upward of eight hundred kids, some with their parents in tow, were there to support the bands who performed that night, including Egypt's first all-female metal band, Massive Scar Era (Mascara), its first "Oriental" death metal group, Beyond East, and the emo-metal group Your Prince Harming, fronted by Shady Nour, son of then imprisoned former presidential candidate Ayman Nour. The lead-up to the show was as eventful as the show itself. After taking the courageous step of agreeing to host a metal show, Mohammed Sawi, the proprietor, got cold feet and informed the groups that he wouldn't allow brutal singing. Backstage, Shady mentioned the Satanist accusation to Troll, lead singer of the evening's headliner, Beyond East, who agreed that "We are Muslims, not Satanic." He explained, "During soundcheck I will go up and just say 'Check, check' and that's it." The real singing, in all its brutal glory, would be saved for the show.

As hundreds of kids hurried down the narrow alleyway between the Zamalek Mosque and the entrance to Sawi, one young fan declared to Mark, "You can't imagine how important this is to us as metalheads in Egypt." The evening itself started off in proper metal fashion, with a fight, or at least a scuffle (it was hard to tell from the side of the stage). Shady's older brother Noor went into the crowd to break it up while Shady pleaded for people to calm down from the stage, telling the crowd it was really important to respect the rules. As if on cue, a guy in the crowd immediately yelled back, "We don't give a fuck about rules, man!" Noor fought his way to the front of the crowd and motioned Shady to bend down, whispering to him, "Mom says be careful. There are undercover police everywhere." "I know, it's crazy," Shady replied. With that, with everything to lose, Shady cued the band to hit it.

Let us recall here that on this warm December evening, with Shady and Noor's father Ayman still in prison as an enemy of the state nothing would have made Mubarak happier than a front-page story about his Satan-worshiping sons leading a crowd of hijab-wearing girls into an orgiastic frenzy. Luckily, whoever was there either liked the show or couldn't be bothered to write a report, so in fact the concert helped (re)normalize metal shows at Sawi and, soon enough, other venues across Cairo. In the opening song (he no longer remembers its name), Shady began singing, "Confide in no one with your secrets, or begin to lose your mind. The promise is they make you drink this poison, and say it's your medication." As so many Egyptian metaliens have said over the years, if the lies of the "system" (the *nizam* the revolutionaries in Tahrir chanted that they wanted pulled down two years later) are the disease, then metal is the best medicine, at least for them.

Your Prince Harming got the largely teenage audience, at least half of them girls and young women, moving with their catchy and bouncy riffs, and Shady's seemingly improbable combination of boyband looks and expertly brutal singing. The evening got even more exciting when Massive Scar Era took the stage, performing what for them had become a standard powerhouse set, with the song "Nothing." There were hundreds of hijab-wearing fans headbanging.

Yet the large number of young women with headscarves (see figure 1 in the author's note) who were enjoying the show dancing right next to young men in a public setting in a manner that was ostensibly at odds with existing gender norms did point to something different about Egypt, compared with other countries in the region, when it came to how young women and men performed their gender roles in the context of metal shows. In Dubai, for example, Sara al-Baba, the young woman on the cover of *Heavy Metal Islam,* was fairly unique as most women were unscarved; in Morocco headbanging *muhajabat* were present but sparsely so; in Cairo the majority of female concert-goers were *muhagabat,* as women who wear the hijab are known in Egyptian dialect (where "j" is pronounced as a hard "g"). The culmination of the evening was Beyond East's performance; as Troll sang, guitarist Shung shredded, and Slacker—one of the seminal figures in the Egyptian metal scene whom we met in *Heavy Metal Islam*—filled in the choruses with his tenor voice, the crowd reached a frenzy, especially when they performed their eponymously titled "Beyond the East" (whose lyrics, like the music, call for a hybrid of "East" and "West," an Arab version of Israel's "Oriental metal" pioneers Orphaned Land with a sound even more powerful and from the gut).

Troll was in rare form when Mark and the filmmakers met him the next morning at a brutally poor corner of the Nazlet El Semmaan neighborhood, home to the camel and horse drivers who took tourists for rides around the pyramids (and who, two years later, would infamously attack protesters in Tahrir in the infamous "Battle of the Camel"). They'd agreed to meet there so Troll could take them to the spot where, years earlier, he'd first sung brutally after escaping from the police, who were chasing him because of his (then) long hair and metal T-shirt. Troll was in a rage, for reasons that were difficult to understand given how well the show had gone. But as horses were hired and loaded up with cameras and supplies, and everyone rode out into the desert sun (about the worst lighting imaginable in which to film) to find the spot where he had had his musical epiphany, it became clear that Troll's story was even more interesting than the music he played.

About two kilometers into the desert, with the pyramids fading into the ever-brighter sun, Troll told everyone to stop and, after setting up the shoot, began what seemed like an hour-long uninterrupted rant as the sun moved ever higher in the sky. Finally, director Jed Rothstein and cinematographer Tom Hurwitz decided the shoot was a bust and called the wrap. If Troll realized their disappointment at not getting any usable footage, he didn't show any remorse, and indeed he kept on ranting, about his family, his friends, his bandmates, the music scenes, and life in Egypt, all of which had conspired to destroy his life.

But then, as Hurwitz was about to put the camera away, Troll suddenly unleashed what remains one of the most powerful, poignant, and prescient soliloquies I've ever heard about life for the emerging generation of Egyptians, and Arabs and Muslims more broadly, in the waning years of the first decade of the twenty-first century:

"In the United States they say that we are camels, we're riding horses, we have galabia [the long tunics traditionally worn by Arab men] and we have pyramids," Troll began, his head nodding backward to the pyramids in the distance. "That's it. And we are pharaohs." He stopped to inhale. "Fuck off! FUCK OFF! Step away," he screamed, brutally, his fingers punctuating each syllable. He continued in a slightly softer voice, "We love you, we love you guys, we know, we knew the whole culture of the United States, we love the United States, we love any world, we love any country. But, do not say . . . like . . . " he shrugged as he said this, not finding the words to continue. A few seconds later, he asked, "You got me?" and after we all replied "yes" in unison, Troll said, "Thanks," took a final sip of his beer, and lit a cigarette.

There was no need to ask Troll to finish his last sentence or elaborate on his remarks. It was the essence of everything Mark had been hearing for the last half-decade—the same schizophrenia that Fanon had, decades earlier, diagnosed in *The Wretched of the Earth* (written while he served as a psychiatrist in Algeria during the war of independence against France), and that defined the attitude not only of Arabs and Muslims but of most of the world's colonized peoples toward Europe and later America.

Thankfully, Tom had filmed musicians many times in the past, and so he'd kept the camera rolling after they had ostensibly wrapped while chatting nonchalantly with Troll, just in case—as had happened so many times before—he suddenly became focused once he thought the camera was off (good audio engineers do the same thing when they're recording difficult artists, knowing the best vocals or guitar solos often come when they don't think the tape is rolling). Troll's main point was that, whether it was metalheads or geeks, the relationship with the West had been so needlessly one-sided for so long that it couldn't continue. For decades in fact it had been the region's leaders who were most interested in keeping that imbalance of power and dialog; but after two decades of structural adjustment and the forced neoliberalization of their economies and cultures that came with it, and more positively with the arrival and rapid spread of the Internet across the Middle East and within the emerging generation of Middle Eastern and North African youth, particularly its cultural creatives, the balance of power was suddenly shifting rapidly away from seemingly worn-out elites and the systems that preserved their rule and toward an increasingly educated and energized generation, which only made their marginalization that much more actively felt.

Heavy Metal Islam described the well-formed subcultures seeking spaces of autonomy and freedom from oppressive regimes and conservative societies. The years immediately following its publication in 2008 saw the transformation of those subcultures into countercultures whose members advocated a very different vision for their societies and a belief in the possibility of achieving that change. Finally, by the beginning of 2010 it had become clear that the counterculture could and would become a revolutionary culture, moving from merely articulating a different vision of the future to trying to enact it on the ground, through mass protests led in good measure by the artists who were articulating that different vision of the future.

As Egypt society started to boil toward the revolutionary uprising that would begin in early 2011, metal was not the only genre of music that was indicating just how close the country's young people were to bursting at the seams. As occurred in Morocco and so many countries of the Arab/Muslim world, hip hop was quickly becoming even more central to youth expression, with upward of a dozen groups emerging by the mid-2000s. A host of rappers with social and political messages emerged in this period, including Asfalt, MTM, Y-Crew, F Killa, Arabian Knightz, Wighit Nazar (Point of View), Kordy, Ramy Donjewan, and MC Amin. Strongly influenced by American gangsta rap and Maghrebi, Lebanese, and Palestinian hip hop as well, Egyptian hip hop progressed rapidly in the years leading up to and following the publication of the book, with such regular lyrical themes as unemployment, poverty (most powerfully recounted in the collaboration "Slums," featuring F Killa and Kordy, among others), sexual harassment, and the lack of Arab unity.

More broadly, in the years before the Revolution rappers were imagining a different Egypt, one where "everything's fine" (as the rapper Haty titled a song in 2007), because the Mubarak regime was gone. The early success of songs like "Fokkak" and "Yalla" by Arabian Knightz and the growing popularity of hip hop, as a medium for the rising generation of actors like Ahmed Fishawy and Ahmed Mekky to extend their street cred and broader fame, helped launch hip hop in the second half of the 2000s into the mainstream.

While most crews were located in Cairo, some of the most innovative were in Alexandria (which a *New York Times* profile in 2012 described as "the pacemaker" for political and social developments in Egypt, as well as provincial cities like the Nile Delta town of Mansoura). As metalheads who came of age in the 2000s were well trained for the DIY political activism of the moment, Egyptian rappers, like their counterparts in Tunisia, Morocco, Palestine, and other Arab countries, were well trained and placed to produce songs that would articulate the direct criticism of the system in a language and style more accessible to the public.

Epitomizing the steady growth of hip hop was Arabian Knightz, who had the most expansive vision of a region-wide Arab(ic) hip hop collective. Formed in 2005, the band reached one hundred thousand MySpace views within a couple of years (back when that number still meant something). Many other groups also pushed the edges of social commentary, receiving warnings from the government and even seeing their music censored because of the lyrics (in contrast to the metal scene, where the lyrics remained largely incomprehensible to unaccustomed ears and the censorship and persecution were for the alleged meaning of the music as a whole). But such attempts at silencing or at least quieting the music simply couldn't slow down the genre's steady growth.

The various concerns and elements of the burgeoning hip hop scene were on full display around the time of the eruption of what became known as the January 25, or #Jan25, Uprising. As the one-evening protest quickly morphed into a sleep-in and then an attempt at a long-term sit-in or occupation, Arabian Knightz were in the process of recording their song "Rebel." Quickly understanding their auspicious timing, the group released a rough mix of the song early on in the protests, and when the Internet was turned back on at the beginning of February, fan-made videos of the song went viral. What was Egypt rebelling against in the view of Arabian Knightz? "Against the birds of darkness. The people want the overthrow of the regime. They killed us, slaughtered us, put us behind bars, tortured us, robbed us, scared us, terrorized us, and ignored us."

For young Alexandrians who lived through the brutal police murder in June 2010 of Khaled Said (whose killing prompted the creation of the Facebook page "Kuluna Khaled Said" ["We Are All Khaled Said"], which became a primary organizing node for the #Jan25 protest), there was even more reason to support the protests half a year later. So it's not surprising that two of the most important and provocative songs in the lead-up to the #Jan25 protest, "Revolution Time" and "Change Is Forbidden," were written by the Alexandria-based group Revolution, in part to help motivate people onto the streets.

Rapper Ramy Donjewan summed up the anger in those last preuprising moments in the song "Against the Government":

> Against the government. Against the thuggery and the injustice.
> Against the government. Against the ruler and the authority . . .
> Your blood, they're spilling it. Your death, they're sanctioning it.
> Your voice, they're silencing it. Your rightful due, they're devouring it.

As we'll discuss below, before hip hop could settle itself in as the dominant youth musical force in Egypt, two new and far more controversial genres, *mahraganat* and trap, swept in and changed the musical and political landscape. Once the coup occurred in 2013 few artists were willing to take the risk to continue making directly antiregime songs. Karim Rush well summed up the attitude of most artists who remained in Egypt and out of jail because they stopped being politically engaged directly. As he explained to Mark in late 2018: "We are more helpful as free artists than we are as incarcerated artists and I'm not going to do the Ramy situation and flee the country. . . . I can't never come back."

THE EXPLOSION

It would be ridiculous to argue that Egypt's metaliens (or any genre of artists for that matter) were singularly or even primarily responsible for the revolutionary outburst on January 25, 2011. Yet it would be equally inaccurate to ignore the fact that so many of the young activists who were at the core of the protests and uprising came out of (and a good number were still part of) the scene. The cultural marginalization of the metaliens from society enabled the possibility of being on the political avant-garde. And it's from that position that we must understand the meaning of Shady's seemingly innocuous explanation that "I'm using my voice. I don't have weapons. I'm just singing and I think I should have the right to do that." Similarly, the skills developed participating in and even building an underground, DIY movement were, to say the least, transferable to the act of political organizing against the same system that oppressed them culturally.

Certainly not every metalien became a political activist—indeed, most didn't. Marz, Troll, and countless others certainly supported the revolutionary wave, but for various reasons were not in the middle of Tahrir, on their phones, leading the resistance. But others—Noor and Shady Nour, Hossam el-Hamalawy, Cherine and other members of Massive Scar Era, and particularly Alaa Abd el-Fattah, all of whom were deep into the scene earlier in the decade—were front and center, whether as part of the hundreds of thousands of protesters or in leadership roles. And then there was a young metalhead named Ramy Essam, who showed up on the fifth day of the protests with nothing more than a sleeping bag and an acoustic guitar and within forty-eight hours had written one of the most important and consequential protest songs since the Russian Revolution. But we're getting ahead of ourselves.

The year leading up to the eruption of the Revolution was an eventful one for the artists from *Heavy Metal Islam*. Massive Scar Era were getting their first taste of recognition; the band was part of the award-winning documentary *Microphone*, which chronicled the underground music scene in Alexandria (which was also home to bands like Massar Egbari and Eskenderella, and rappers like Y-Crew and Revolution, all of whom would also offer important musical support to protesters during the Revolution). They even played in the US for the first time and released their first EP, *Unfamiliar Territories*. Hate Suffocation changed their name to Scarab, both to better reflect their focus on ancient Egyptian iconography and to move away from the anger that, as their original name suggested, had defined them up to that point. Shady and Noor joined various bands and developed as musicians, but everything took on a more hopeful hue with the sudden release of their father from jail, and then the decision by their mother to run for Parliament. On the other hand, like many other "maturing" metalheads, Slacker slowly moved away from the scene as he realized, with youth sliding into the rearview mirror, that he had to put his hacking skills to more remunerative use—doing cyber security for big banks in the Gulf.

Hossam el-Hamalawy stayed true to his metal soul. As he became better known as a journalist, he also became more active in the Revolutionary Socialist Party, perhaps the most progressive social and political group in Egypt, which was then still banned. While outlawed, the Revolutionary Socialists became increasingly popular with young people after the outbreak of the al-Aqsa Intifada, as the activists aligned with its views were meeting regularly via the Center for Socialist Studies in Cairo, where other well-known Revolutionary Socialist activists and thinkers would visit to discuss both classic works (especially of Trotsky but also of Lenin and other major figures) and contemporary strategy. One of the most important British Revolutionary Socialist figures, Chris Harman (who wrote a book about how Revolutionary Socialist activists should not demonize Islamists titled *The Prophet and the Proletariat*), actually died after speaking at the Center in late 2009. For their part, Alaa and his (then) partner Manal moved to South Africa during this period for work, although their fathers—human rights pioneers Ahmed Seif and Bahey Eddin Hassan—continued to push the increasingly powerful human rights agendas right into the Revolution.

Because of their years spent studying the organizing and theories of revolution, when the uprising did erupt the Revolutionary Socialists were able to play a key role in the organization not only of Tahrir but also of protests across the country. Hossam, already one of the most driven people imaginable, was in overdrive—how could he not be—as he was both helping organize and reporting/blogging about the rapidly escalating protests. For their part, Manal and Alaa quickly returned to Egypt from South Africa once the seriousness of the protests became clear. From the moment they landed they were in Tahrir, on the front lines, and participating in the Revolutionary Youth coalition, which would negotiate a truce with the military and security forces that would shut down the uprising and initiate the transition period after Mubarak's removal from power on February 11, 2011.

In retrospect, it's hard to understand why the #Jan25 Uprising was a shock. By late 2009 most everyone who was in any way politically or culturally active, or even merely aware, was expecting an explosion sooner or later. Hossam explained then, "You take a cab and start to talk about the traffic and in one minute the talk will shift to Mubarak, how he's a dictator, you feel it in the air, you just talk to anyone in the street there's so much militancy, so much courage to speak out, that me, as someone who got into politics in the second half of the 1990s, we could not sense it back then." About a year later, after perhaps the most corrupt election in modern Egyptian history, Hossam strengthened his remarks: "In Egypt we have a saying, 'You can't make a sweet drink out of rotten fish' *[Yemel min elfesikh sharbat];* and the Mubarak family is a rotten fish, it doesn't matter if it's Mubarak Jr. or Sr. . . . This state has to be dissolved. We need a new state with new institutions, and I'm afraid that this would only happen via . . . a revolution."

In the lead-up to the November 2010 elections, regime thugs stuffed ballot boxes in plain view of the candidate, well-known broadcast journalist Gamilla Ismail (who was married to imprisoned former presidential candidate Ayman Nour) at her home polling station, and then, while the camera crew of *Before the Spring* continued filming, ran down the street with the box, trailed by her sons and other supporters screaming at them. Egyptian colleagues were increasingly sure that an explosion was immanent. Yet Noor for one wasn't completely pessimistic. "I still have hope," he explained as he was filmed for *Before the Spring* in the aftermath of the vote-stealing against his mother, "because we can't stay like this forever. We can't stay on a tight leash forever. There is a threshold and, once it is broken, that's it."

Six weeks later, what quickly became known as the Egyptian Revolution began.

The same DIY skills that enabled a small subcultural scene to survive and grow in a still hostile political and cultural landscape helped some of its members lead a countercultural and then revolutionary movement against the same forces that were oppressing them to begin with. Specifically, the ability for socially and politically marginalized young people to create, circulate, and consume powerful cultural products below the official radar that were inherently subversive to the values and politics of the existing order, to command new technologies with greater facility than those in power, and to harness the anger of their generation all characterized the metal community, and the rapidly expanding hip hop scene as well. It's thus not surprising that metaliens became activists, especially those with university educations, a good command of English, and an already progressive political bent.

Metaliens didn't just play an outsized role in the ranks of young people on the front lines and as organizers of the increasingly coordinated protests compared with their rather small number. Any time the young protesters were together, especially organizers of the Tahrir occupation, when they would meet in one of several "safe houses" (apartments, really) or similar locations, they would play the most aggressive metal and hip hop they could, like soldiers preparing for or resting after a battle. For the young Egyptians who helped ignite and fan the flames of the revolutionary uprising, Sabbath, Maiden, Slayer, Rage Against the Machine, Public Enemy, 2Pac, NWA, and similarly amped-up and highly politicized (or at least politically sympathetic) artists helped set, and keep, the mood. If Spotify had been popular in Egypt in early 2011 the local revolutionary playlist would have included a lot of metal, a bit of 'Umm Kulthoum, with a liberal dose of Sheikh Imam and Ahmed Fouad Negm (Egypt's most famous political musical duo), Sayed Darwish, Black Theama, Baraka Band, and Mohamed Mounir's rocking "Ezay" ("How?")—ostensibly a song of unrequited love but clearly about the Egyptian state, which from the moment it was released on February 6, 2011, was played incessantly in Tahrir, and some traditional anticolonial songs thrown in for good measure. Such a playlist might give the impression that these were simply "Westernized" young people who were somehow out of step with the rest of their society—certainly that's how they were depicted by the government during the protests, and later on by the armed forces leadership and the Sisi regime. As Sphinx, one of the two main rappers of Arabian Knightz (who spent much of his adolescence in Los Angeles), explained to the *San Francisco Chronicle* in 2012, "Since the revolution, you will hear a lot of our music and think we wrote it about what is happening. But we had actually written that four years prior, calling for what happened to happen."

The story behind Arabian Knightz's "Rebel" was particularly portentous. As lead MC Karim Rush explained it to Mark,

> The music we, Donjewan, and MC Amin did was like a manual, what we thought was the way Egypt should go with the revolution we knew would come. On January 28 we had "Rebel" out; on February 4 we had "Prisoner" out. In fact, we actually recorded it first back in 2007, one of the first singles we released on MySpace, and then remixed with the great Palestinian rapper Shadia Mansour as the Revolution unfolded. While I was in Tahrir I was calling my sister asking her to take all the footage and edit a video for "Prisoner," and then she took my password and uploaded it to YouTube for me.

Karim continued,

> I listened to Lauryn Hill's "Rebel" on YouTube months before the Revolution and I felt that she was talking about us, about Egypt: Are you satisfied? If not, rebel! I think I had the beat from 2009 or 2010. It took years to sit on the beat but ten seconds to record it! And I recorded 'ash-sha'b yurid isqat an-nizzam', which became the iconic chant in Tahrir, the last second. Mc and sphinx sat there and said there's gonna be a march, what happens if it actually works? If it does what no one expects and [bears] fruit? We gotta be talking about this. We are reality rappers and this is reality. We were moved by all the vids being made to motivate people to go out on Jan 25 so this was our contribution.

More than in Tunisia or any other country, the winds of revolt could be detected through the music of Egypt's bursting youth cultures. Mohammed Deeb, another of the pioneering rappers who cut his teeth with crews like Asfalt and Wighit Nazar, also had a preuprising history of producing critical commentary through his rhymes, such as focusing on the corruption that led to the drowning of over one thousand people on a *hajj* ferry returning from Saudi Arabia to Egypt, and using Tahrir as a backdrop for broader criticisms of the Mubarak regime—he fortuitously had filmed a video near Tahrir for his song "Masrah Deeb" ("Deeb's Stage") only weeks before January 25, and released it at the end of the uprising's first week. He also performed in Tahrir during the protests.

FORESHADOWING RESISTANCE

The music many of the young protesters were listening to during the eighteen days was not necessarily the same music they were listening to in the period leading up to the protests. In fact, when searching the past for moments of musical foreshadowing of the #Jan25 Uprising, the clues can be found more so in music productions that were in some way rooted in Egyptian pop culture, rather than European and American metal, hip hop, or rock music. Bands like Black Theama, Baraka Band, and even Wust El-Balad were important vehicles through which poets such as Mido Zoheir, Diaa El-Rahman, and Rami Yehia broadcast increasingly powerful messages to Egyptian society. While the sound of Egypt before the revolution and after has taken on many timbers, the lyrics penned by these poets offered a good mirror for Cairo's disenfranchised urban youth, with themes ranging from migration to dystopian narratives, voices from the margins, fear, and, at times, subversive sociopolitical commentary.

Since their formation in 2010, the Egyptian band Black Theama has written upward of fifty songs heavily laced with social and political themes, particularly during their early years. Founded by Ahmed Bahr and Amir Salah El Deen, and later joined by Mohamed Abdo, the band pulls heavily from its Nubian heritage both sonically and thematically, as it has simultaneously reflected the daily lives of Egyptians, in addition to expressing the experience of Egyptians from the south.

In an interview in the *Egypt Independent* published in 2010, Bahr explained that "our project is not to croon about starry-eyed love and teenage heartbreak. We assumed that there was a wide array of emotions and issues not yet tackled in contemporary singing, and we think that there is an insistent demand for that genre." As writer and musician Fayrouz Kawala describes in an article about the band from 2010, "Black Theama's rebellious lyrics are written in colloquial Egyptian Arabic and reflect the sociopolitical scene in Egypt. The poets writing for the band (among them Ramy Yehia, Mido Zoheir, and Diaa el-Rahman) drew from the group's focus on black musical traditions—jazz, R & B, soul, rap, blues—to help shape songs that voice the sentiments of today's marginalized and underrepresented youth in Egypt."

The lyrics to Black Theama's song "Zahma," by Mido Zoheir (who tragically died of a heart attack at forty-six in 2020), reflect the prerevolutionary "misery" of the mass of urban Egyptian youth waiting for "miracles and prophets" *(al-muegazat wa-l-anbia)* in the midst of too many illusions *(wahumah)*. Meanwhile, Wust El-Balad was also working with Mido Zoheir, who penned love songs like "Aneqini" ("Huge Me") and the more rocking "Damiruna Mashawy" ("Our Conscience Is Grilled"), both of which have clear political undertones.

Another important voice was singer, composer, and songwriter Maryam Saleh and her group Baraka Band, formed in 2008. Baraka Band launched Maryam into the consciousness of many Egyptian youth, largely because of her throwback voice and keen appropriations of pop-cultural relics like Sheik Imam and Ahmed Fouad Negm, reworked with contemporary arrangements and aesthetics deeply steeped in underground electronica. When Maryam released her solo debut, *Mesh Baghany,* in 2012, she once again used the poetry of Zoheir for her lyrics, and her duet with Lebanese electronica pioneer Zeid Hamdan, "Watan el 3ak," resonated with a wide spectrum of Egyptian youth, more than most metal or even hip hop songs of the period. No doubt, this was owed in good measure to the deep roots of the music in Egyptian pop culture, such as rearranging classic movie songs with contemporary instruments while foregrounding the sarcasm that increasingly defined the attitude of Cairo's youth. Indeed, from the point of view of impacting the youth who would be at the forefront of the revolutionary wave, artists like Maryam Saleh, Black Theama, and Dina El Wedidi staked the avant-garde for the Tahrir Generation *(ag-gil at-tahrir).*

Ramy Essam, known internationally (more than locally, in fact) as the "singer of the Revolution" in the wake of the #Jan25 Uprising and one of the stars of the film from 2013 about the Egyptian uprising, *The Square,* had a very different background and route to fame. On January 25, 2011, Ramy was a more or less unknown twenty-three-year-old singer from Mansoura, a provincial city one hundred kilometers (over sixty miles) north of Cairo, which is the birthplace of both Adel Imam, an actor whose comical depiction of a *zar* exorcism ceremony in his film *al-Halfut* first suggested a relationship between the headbanging of metalheads and of Sufis, as well as the birthplace, more importantly, of none other than Umm Kulthum.

Before becoming a revolutionary icon, Ramy was a dyed-in-the-wool metal fan: Slipknot, Korn, Maiden, Metallica, and Rage Against the Machine, among others, all shaped his musical consciousness. But knowing the difficulty of making a living in Egypt as a metal singer, he tried his hand at singing pop, without success. Like so many others of his generation, watching the increasingly intense daily battles between protesters and security forces in Tahrir compelled him to head for Cairo, with nothing but a sleeping bag and his acoustic guitar. Despite suffering a head injury while battling police almost as soon as he arrived, on February 1, he took out his guitar while sitting among the tents of the Mansoura contingent of protesters, pitched opposite the enormous mugamma' building on the east side of Tahrir, and started strumming the few chords he knew—all variations on the first position bar chord every beginner guitarist learns, with a simple two-bar chord and rhythm pattern (I-♭II-♭III-♭II), while singing the chants he'd been hearing one after another with an even simpler melody, changing up the order until they fit together just right. Within a few hours Ramy had "composed" the song "Irhal!" ("Leave!"). Picking up on the French chant of "Dégage!" (which also means "Leave!" in English), which was ubiquitous in the Tunisian Revolution only weeks before, "Irhal!" became the refrain for other powerful chants like *"ash-sha'b yurid isqat an-nizam"* ("the people want the downfall of the system/regime"), another historic chant also heard in Tunis before Tahrir, and other lyrics that united the crowd in a single thought and purpose: force Mubarak from power and, if possible, fundamentally change the political system.

"Irhal!" was a massive viral hit. When Mark first saw the grainy video of an early performance late at night on Facebook (it showed only the crowd and didn't even mention Essam's name), it had three hundred views. When Mark met him in Tahrir a couple of days later after tracking him down through his producer (who uploaded the video through his YouTube account), the same video had thirty thousand views. By the time Mubarak was removed, it had three hundred thousand views. In the meantime, in the space of eleven days Ramy had gone from metal-hearted pop wannabe to, at least for a moment, one of the most celebrated singers on Earth, even if in Egypt his position remained much more ambivalent. A decade later, debate remains among Egyptian activists and musicians about whether "Irhal!" even counts as a proper song (since the lyrics were simply repetitions of chants heard in Tahrir), as well as about how impactful it was outside of Tahrir. But there's little doubt that inside the Midan and during that period, as well as in the subsequent two years of periodic occupations, it was among the most powerful sonic symbols of the spirit of Tahrir and the uprising at large.

A month after Mubarak was ousted, Ramy was recognized by the *mukhabarat* (the Egyptian intelligence/security forces) at a protest in Tahrir,

FIGURE 10. Revolutionary Artists Union corner, Midan Tahrir, during the #Jan25 Uprising. Photo by Hossam el-Hamalawy.

kidnapped, brought into the National Museum at the far west end of the Midan, and brutally tortured for several hours. He assumed he would die; when he didn't, he thanked the military for what it had done to him. "I have no more fear. There's nothing else they can do to me," he told Mark while he was still recovering a month later.

One reason "Irhal!" was so popular and effective was that it was a rap song, or at least 80 percent one. The words were sung-spoken by Ramy in a kind of Dylanesque rasp and the groove of his acoustic guitar was so bouncy that the first thing Mark did after watching the grainy video was send the link to his producer, and they together recorded a hip hop drum pattern under it, with the goal of playing it for Ramy as soon as he met him (which he did several days later). But Ramy was far from the only person chant-rapping. Tahrir was filled with people doing the same thing day and night, from five to eighty-five years old. People were dropping rhymes of incredible creativity and complexity at every spot in the Midan, most of them flanked by other people playing real or makeshift percussion instruments, while multiple stages blared out recorded songs or live bands. The use of chanting, in both a syncopated or a melodic style, along with makeshift percussions, hand drums, and rhythmic hand-clapping is not surprising when thinking of Egypt's folkloric cultures, particularly that of Nubian, Bedouin, or Upper Egypt traditional music. The

Revolutionary Artists Corner was on the west side of Tahrir, right in front of KFC (which somehow remained open during the whole eighteen days), where actual rappers would drop by and spit rhymes; but these paled in comparison to the power of the children who often led and even created the chants that were viewed and heard all around Cairo, Egypt, and the world.

In the next two years when not gigging and performing almost daily—and indeed, camping—whenever Tahrir was reoccupied, Ramy became a regular guest on the numerous news programs that sprung up after Mubarak's ouster as well as traveling regularly to Europe and the United States. He also became the unofficial bard of the Ultras movement—the fervent soccer fans who'd spent years chanting antiregime slogans and battling police and in football matches. Between February 11, 2001, and the military coup on July 3, 2013, they were perhaps the most powerful force on the Egyptian street, suffering immensely for their temerity when seventy-four Ultras were killed in a riot likely provoked by the security services in Alexandria on February 1, 2012, and in their increasing oppression by the government in subsequent years. It is next to impossible to explain the energy and power generated by 10,000 Ultras scream-chanting the epigraph at the start of this chapter, at the top of their lungs while jumping up and down in unison in front of the Parliament in April 2012, perhaps the last moment when revolutionaries still owned Tahrir, and with it, could shape the national narrative. The em*u*rgent, transversal, and viscerallectric power of the music gave it an aura that made the revolution still feel irresistible, even if it was no longer inevitable. Quite simply, it felt like a concert by a transcendently powerful live band: Zeppelin or Maiden, Public Enemy, or Rage Against the Machine—*only the people were the band, and they knew it.*

In addition to giving new voice to their anthems, Ramy's songs, which often included collaborations with both established poets like Ahmed Fouad Negm and younger poets (several of whom have received long prison terms because of their association with him), rarely lost their political or musical edge. This is, no doubt, why, once the coup occurred, his days in Egypt were numbered. Faced with a literal choice between exile and death, like so many of Egypt's most important young activists, intellectuals, and artists of the post-2011 era, he accepted an offer to come to Sweden to live and study music. As of late 2021 he still can't go home.

Ramy Essam was far from the only revolutionary artist in Egypt, nor were rock, metal, and hip hop the only genres for revolutionary musical expression. Traditional and resistance music from previous revolutionary eras and from labor struggles was also repurposed for the latest revolutionary moment by more established groups, most notably the Nile Delta folklore group El Tanbura.

Equally, if not more, politically innovative artists included singer, artist, and actor Maryam Saleh (mentioned above), who was already writing powerful music before the uprising; singer Dina El Wedidi; singer and accordionist Youssra el Hawary; singer Mohammad Mohsen and his lyricist, the revolutionary poet Mostafa Ibrahim; and finally singer and guitarist/'oudist Yasser El-Manawahly, whose "Ya Sundu'" ("Oh Fund"), a sarcastic ode "thanking" the International Monetary Fund for destroying Egypt, is unquestionably one of the most powerful (and catchy) critiques of finance imperialism of the neoliberal era.

Together, these artists and their music equally represent the richness and sophistication of the revolutionary music of the #Jan25 era, even if they didn't achieve the same level of immediately local and international acclaim as Ramy. And beyond music, art, poetry, photography, and theater were all equally crucial, before, during, and after the #Jan25 Uprising. Together, they became the arsenal deployed by those on the front lines in the war for the hearts and minds of their fellow Egyptians. Collectively, the power of the revolutionary music and art more broadly of the Tahrir period was like the AK-47 favored by guerrilla armies the world over; the fusillade of artistic bullets—songs, photos, poems, graffiti, memes, placards—was overwhelming in its firepower, at least for a while, before regimes decided to counter the cultural weapons with sniper rifles, grenades, and torture chambers.

MUSIC AFTER THE REVOLUTION

The revolution was the easy part. Removing the corrupt mentality that is inside all of us is the hard part.

—NOOR AYMAN NOUR, APRIL 2012

In the immediate aftermath of the #Jan25 Uprising in Egypt and the Arab uprisings more broadly, the situation for hip hop improved even more than for metal, largely because of the opening of commercial as well as performance opportunities for local artists. Arabian Knightz created their own label, Arab League Records. Other rappers began doing commercials or receiving sponsorships from phone companies, and also were able to collaborate more easily and frequently with other Arab and international artists (as opposed to previously, when they would mostly do unofficial "remixes" of well-known tracks with their own verses added over the original ones).

Despite ongoing violence against civilians, particularly young people, by the military and security forces after Mubarak's ouster, there was an unprecedented level of freedom of expression in the two years between then and the coup that ended the tenure of Mohamed Morsi, Egypt's first and so far only democratically elected president. This allowed not only the metal scene to become more popular, but also hip hop to become a defining sound of young people, in both its commercial and its more politically aware variants. Groups like Arabian Knightz, Zap Tharwat, MC Amin, and others routinely released new music that criticized at first the ongoing power of the military and then the Muslim Brotherhood–created Freedom and Justice Party and Mohamed Morsi even more vehemently after they came to power. For example, Arabian Knightz and Revolution took on the military with songs like "Kazeboon" ("Liars"), a term popularized by the Mosireen (Insistent Ones) collective formed after Mubarak's departure to educate the public about the cascade of lies military leaders told the Egyptian public. Another important track released in the post-Mubarak period was by the rapper F Killa, who in 2012 released "A Message to Every Harasser" (as the title suggests, about sexual harassment), which addressed what to this day remains one of the most pressing problems in Egypt.

After the incomparable joy felt in Tahrir in the hours after Mubarak's ouster, the next morning a massive impromptu cleanup began throughout downtown Cairo, with people scrubbing the streets clean in an act of collective catharsis that for many Cairenes was a "spring cleaning" of a political system that had made their lives a political winter of thirty years. They hoped that this was its end. Unfortunately, no sooner had they thrown the dirt from three decades of Mubarak into the dustbin than a host of social and political forces that had remained on the sidelines during the previous eighteen days suddenly pushed their way onto the stage.

In Tahrir it was Salafis, in particular Salafi women, who stormed onto a newly erected stage for a celebratory concert February 12, interrupting Ramy Essam as he was walking to the front of the stage to perform. In the crowd a group of aggressive Salafi men barreled into the area right in front of the stage and pushed everyone back about five meters, opening a space for Salafi women to congregate without fear of coming into direct contact with anyone outside their group. It wasn't to have a better view of Ramy's show, however. Rather, it was to cheer on the three Salafi women who grabbed the microphone and started haranguing the crowd, yelling that their actions were against God and they were going to suffer God's punishment, while Ramy stood at the back of the stage sheepishly strumming his guitar. They were eventually forced off the stage, but their point was made—religious forces might have remained more or less publicly quiet during the eighteen days, but they were going to exert outsized influence over whatever was to come next.

The other group that began (re)asserting itself directly on day one of the new era was the military, which had brilliantly positioned itself as the honest broker between the people and the regime during the eighteen-day standoff in Tahrir, even as behind the scenes the leadership expertly managed the government's response to the uprising. While the military leadership was willing to throw the increasingly troublesome Mubarak family under the revolutionary bus, they were not willing to cede any real power. So at a meeting of revolutionary youth and more senior human rights activists that Mark attended after leaving Ramy's aborted Tahrir concert on February 12, the subject of discussion was whether it was possible for the forces behind the uprising to press their demand that Egypt follow Tunisia's path and have a civilian-led transition government, or whether the country was too close to the edge to endure weeks more protest (the consensus was that too many Egyptians were too close to running out of money to support another round of protests then).

Whatever its faults and failures, the thirty months between Mubarak's ouster and the coup that brought an end to Egypt's first and so far only era of (at least formally) democratic rule offered an unprecedented level of cultural freedom and freedom of expression more broadly, which would have a major effect on the country's various arts scenes, including music. Specifically, the political opening inside Egypt was more than matched by a cultural opening that not only provided more free and uncensored and unsupervised art, but European and North American governments, NGOs, and corporate actors (such as Red Bull and Boiler Room) were suddenly taking a heightened interest in an Egyptian youth culture that had seemingly brought down one of the world's most stable authoritarian systems.

Indeed, the cultural opening that occurred in the period between the #Jan25 Uprising and the coup on July 3, 2013, constituted one of the most culturally effervescent periods in modern Egyptian history, on par with the post-1922 era when Egypt first became nominally independent and, however imperfectly and corruptly, was governed as a constitutional parliamentary monarchy. While Morsi and the Muslim Brotherhood held cultural views that were far more conservative than most Egyptian artists, they were neither able to impose nor seemingly interested in imposing any kind of significant restrictions on artists of any kind, including music. One could describe not only a cultural flowering, but an explosion of cultural production that involved theater, the visual arts, poetry, cinema (particularly locally produced documentaries), and music.

This situation should have constituted the perfect opportunity for a significant expansion, if not explosion, of the metal scene, after so much hard work had been put in to build the scene while it was underground and even then barely tolerated in the late Mubarak era. But as it happened, the metal scene broadly stagnated during this era, even as the challenges to performing from government and social opposition clearly lessened. Cherine Amr of Massive Scar Era has a theory about why this happened. Echoing Reda Zine's comments in the previous chapter about Moroccan metal, as Cherine explained to Mark in early 2020 during a chance meeting in Cairo, the answer is simply that metal "didn't speak the language" of the people since the bands mostly wrote in English (not to mention sing in a "brutal" style that's impossible for nonfans to understand or even enjoy). Also, she explained, drugs and girls, two themes that are common in American hip hop (and also hair metal, if not its more extreme subgenres), became more common in Egyptian hip hop in ways that Egyptian metal artists generally haven't wanted to touch upon.

To understand this, it is important to look into the aesthetics of metal versus *mahraganat,* the content of the music, and the larger socioeconomic cultures in which they are rooted in Egypt. With some exceptions (such as Shung from Beyond East and Ahl al-Sina), the metal scene was and remains a middle- and upper-middle-class phenomenon in Egypt, with kids who had some education in or knowledge of English, a familiarity with and even affinity for European or American culture more broadly, and access to friends and peers who did, even if they didn't travel themselves. Even a relatively open and welcoming venue, such as the Sawi Culture Wheel, was actually a "harsh space" (in Shady Nour's words) for metal artists to perform because of the patina of conservative sensibilities governing how bands were chosen to perform and treated by Sawi and his staff (for example, generic metal might be okay but brutal metal less so, and so on). Moreover, not just the sound but the lyrical content of metal—to the extent that it's possible—was monitored by the Sawi management, as well as security personnel and even the *mossanafat al-fania* (the foot soldiers of the music syndicate who attend events to make sure artists have a valid license to perform from the syndicate and, if not, heavily fine and even jail event organizers).

More than most new genres of art about which it is said, *mahraganat* as a whole is truly far greater than the "sum of its (musical) parts." While it's not often discussed as such, the scene was inherently, if not directly, political, just as metal and hip hop were at their dawns. But the fact that the roots of *mahraganat* go back at least half a decade before the eruption of the uprising in 2011 shouldn't surprise us; the same uncontrolled energy that produced one no doubt helped spark the other. Moreover, that one of the first certified hits, DJ Figo's "Ana Baba, Yalla," was released during the eighteen days certainly isn't coincidental; it's just one of the many songs that could also be heard blasting from the myriad PA systems rigged around Tahrir during the uprising. Similar to Morocco's Boulevard Festival, it straddles the edge between acceptable liminality and opening new space for political dissent, however couched in the language of weed, women, and partying.

Moreover, unlike metal's largely if not exclusively middle- and upper-class base in Egypt, *mahragan* and hip hop (before it became respectable or at least accepted as a mainstream genre) originated in the *'ashwiyat* (or informal poor and working-class neighborhoods) in weddings and street festivals, where the government has rarely interfered, let alone the music syndicate. In this way it is similar to Algerian raï, which has long been a staple at weddings because its transgressive lyrics and aesthetics corresponded to the liminal nature of a social ritual based on procreation, where highly libidinal and even ecstatic energy is not just accepted but expected to be released.

While the legend has it that one pair of artists—the DJ known as DJ 7a7a (Haha) and DJ Figo—was the first to create the sound, the reality is more likely that it coalesced out of the sounds being produced by many DJs in the period, not only in Cairo but in Alexandria as well. Yet for all the focus on its roots as working-class party or "festival" music (the English meaning of *mahragan*), *mahraganat* was from the start inherently and intimately political. As one of the seminal *mahraganat* singers, Oka, put it in another documentary in 2013 about the music, *Underground/on the Surface,* "Do you know why our music is called sha'bi? It's not because of the rhythms. The rhythms exist in all genres. It's called sha'bi because it comes from the people. It represents the people. It's the music of the poor."

Oka's good friend Sadat similarly explains in *Electro-Chaabi:* "We can tell the story of the street. That's also politics. If I talk about something that happens, that's politics. . . . Politics doesn't have to involve the government or the regime." Of course, what starts in the streets can quickly move up to the penthouse. Oka's song "Ana Aslan Gamid" ("I'm Originally Awesome"), one of his early songs as part of the duo Oka and Ortega, has over thirty-four million YouTube views and counting. And the video of his collaboration with Ortega, "El3ab yalla!" ("Dude, Let's Play!") has over 190 million views—this despite the lyrically playful teasing of the protagonist throughout the song by Satan to stop praying and start partying.

Lyrically, this positioning afforded more freedom to *mahraganat* to speak honestly about the lives of the community. At the same time, as in hip hop, lyrics are rooted in stories from the margins—that is, the popular classes that make up the majority of the country. Sonically, *mahraganat* is also rooted in familiar sha'bi musical timbers and rhythmic structures that themselves carry strong echoes of the rich history of Arab music, with particular devices arguably derived from the hypnotic effects and use of repetition found in Sufi and *tarab* music.

The working-class sonic grounding of *mahraganat* is in obvious contrast to metal, which from the start attracted more middle- and upper-class Egyptians because they had access to the music before the Internet made it more widely available, and because they could better negotiate the social marginalization of the scene by the conservative majority. Perhaps most important, because most any form of dissent or counternarrative against the Egyptian state rhetoric has always been banished to the margins and even criminalized, *mahraganat* and other music that comes from the margins is much harder to crack down on.

Mahraganat's roots in working-class or "street" culture have been used to explain the alleged prevalence of lyrics seemingly glorifying drugs and misogyny. But this argument is problematic on several fronts. First, drugs and misogyny are prevalent in many forms of popular music lyrics locally and globally, including in genres like hip hop and heavy metal and in pop songs written by artists with an entirely different set of life experiences and positionality. *Mahraganat,* hip hop, and occasionally sha'bi music more broadly also discuss drugs because it is a plague across all socioeconomic classes (not just the poor). Thus in the song "Kharban" by Sadat and Wegz, for example, the lyrics make repeated reference to being *kharban* (literally "out of order," but used colloquially to mean "destroyed" or "wasted" from alcohol or drugs), making the song simultaneously a pro- and antidrug anthem in the manner of Mike Mosner's "I Took a Pill in Ibiza." Of course, then there's Sadat and

Alaa 50's collaboration with Cypress Hill on the group's hit from 2018, "Band of Gypsies"—whose video featured the Egyptian stars and their American counterparts smoking blunts in a Cairo studio and shisha spot (a café where customers smoke water pipes while drinking tea or coffee, or, in a few places, beer) while Sadat ululates to his dealer for a nice soft piece of hash, all over a mélange of what the Egyptian music portal *Scene Noise* described as "Egyptian *maw'wal* with authentic West Coast hip hop." It is hard to understand the song as anything other than a paean to the favorite pastime of millions of young Egyptians and Californians, and everyone else for that matter.

Sexism is also much more ambivalent in *mahraganat* that it seems at first listen. While songs like Oka and Ortega's "Al-Wisada al-khalya" might feature far-from-enlightened views on women (but certainly no less than pop star Tamer Hosny's laughably sexist duet with Snoop Dog, "Si Said"), other songs have explicitly criticized sexual harassment, such as Sadat's clear anti-harassment song "Aakis ah, at-tharrash la" ("Flirting Yes, Harassment No"). In the broader public consciousness, however, fighting against sexual harassment is rendered more difficult when many female pop artists, such as Jannat Mahid and Donia Samira Ghanem, endorse the dominant patriarchal view of women as subservient to men's uncontrolled desire on songs such as "Estahmelny" ("Be Patient with Me") and "Wahda tania khalas" ("A Completely Different Person").

Indeed, the commitment of *mahraganat* artists to what could be termed "social realism," or at least an honest narrative of "life in the 'hood," is made clear by the fact that, by highlighting painful truths, they are harming their chances to get air time or sponsorships, even as it enhances the street credibility of the artists. In this regard, *mahraganat* is following a well-worn script in the history of hip hop the world over. It's clear, then, that *mahraganat* displays a much higher level of linguistic multivalence and sophistication (including parody, irony, and sarcasm) than most commentators give it credit for, allowing lyrics to be read in multiple dimensions that appeal to different people in various ways. At the same time, the fact that the key figures in building the genre have created alternative revenue streams (the deals with foreign labels, YouTube, and concerts outside Egypt) not so easily controlled by the government and its economic allies allows the artists to maintain more independence and ambivalence as well. (This became even more important when the government effectively banned all live performances by *mahraganat* artists in 2020.)

On March 5, 2020, the Musicians' Syndicate announced its intention to issue one-year public singing permits to *mahraganat* singers, provided that they pass a test before a union jury. Recipients of these permits would also have to comply with union rules and rules regarding censorship. According to Donia, the objective of these conditional permits is to "monitor the lyrics of the *mahraganat*."

A final contributing factor to the relative decline in popularity of metal compared with the rapid rise of *mahraganat* and hip hop more broadly concerned the realities of live performances. The kinds of live performances at the heart of most metal scenes require far more sophisticated, high-quality, and expensive equipment than that required for hip hop or *mahraganat* shows (never mind punk/hardcore, which isn't a major presence in Egypt). Because of this, they need to perform in more "legitimate" spaces in order to expand their base and to get the proper sound, as well as needing to have a significant budget or to perform in venues that own high-quality backline and PAs. Such a budget is simply beyond the reach of most underground groups, for which sponsorships approved by the government or musicians' syndicate would have to be obtained, which are neither possible nor desirable for most metal bands.

This dynamic creates a kind of self-fulfilling prophecy, since without the higher-quality equipment it's hard to raise the level of performance, whereas popular groups like Cairokee and Wust El-Balad (whom we discuss below, and who also generally come from well-to-do families and thus can afford expensive equipment to begin with) get access to major corporate sponsorships like Pepsi and Coke and appear on major TV programs (like revolutionary comedian Bassem Youssef's *El Barnameg* while it was still on air). This exposure in turn yields exponentially higher YouTube or Spotify numbers, and thus much larger fan bases. Unlike the "indie" or "independent" label, metal will never function, as musician Rami Abadir argued in a *Mada Masr* article in 2015, as "just a transition or interim choice that qualifies artists to enter the mainstream and produce popular music."

Violinist and original Massive Scar Era member Nancy Mounir had a similar argument when she and Mark met unexpectedly at a conference on the architecture of sound in Egypt at the American Research Center in Egypt in late 2018. Speaking about the rise of both the experimental/avant-garde and the *mahraganat* scenes, she explained that "the expense (for security and other reasons) of doing really big shows for artists like Amr Diab after the 2011 uprising opened spaces for other artists and scenes that were closer to the street. Newer artists were willing to perform in free public concerts as part of the 'placebo effect' of the revolution, which also saw the opening of many new spaces for young and nonwealthy people."

FIGURE 11. Cherine Amr and Nancy Mounir in studio during rehearsals in 2019 for Massive Scar Era performance, Cairo. Courtesy of Cherine Amr.

To this we can add several other elements. As Shady Nour explained,

> The problem is certainly venues, as Sawi still remains one of the few places to play and it has so many rules and fees and remains really locked up and even harsh to play. But the very familiarity of metal now—yes, people don't like it, but they're know what it is and are more or less used to it—has paradoxically made it less appealing to potential fans or musicians. It used to be something forbidden. Black and death metal were strange; bands had an aura of mystery before social media; they were played by guys who looked like they just walked out of some Scandinavian forest. But with social media now we know everything about them. It's kind of like when Kiss took off their makeup; it's just not as interesting anymore.

It's important to note that it wasn't only harder or extreme forms of youth music like metal and hip hop that were part of the aesthetic soniscape and, to varying degrees, helped to inspire and shape the #Jan25 Uprising. Pop rock and even traditional/folklore artists also played an important role in the uprising. Of the many groups that stand out in this regard, we can discuss six who achieved particular recognition or fame, or at least participated, in the revolutionary outburst of 2010–12. These included Massar Egbari and Eskenderella from Alexandria; Wust El-Balad, Cairokee, and Maryam Saleh from Cairo; the Nubian-influenced trio Black Theama; and the folklore band El Tanbura, whose members hail from the Nile Delta center of Port Said but are based in Cairo. With a slightly smaller fan base but equally important in terms of their impact on the local youth music scenes are indie-folk singer-songwriters like Dina El Wedidi and Youssra El Hawary, who along with Maryam Saleh created music that blends with and crosses over to the Lebanese indie scene centered in Beirut (which itself blends back into the Cairo independent electronica scene, which is among the most avant-garde today). Perhaps most notable in this regard are Saleh's collaboration in 2015 with one of Beirut's leading producers, Zaid Hamdan, on her album *Halawella* and El Wedidi's work with 'oud virtuoso, composer, and singer Kamilya Jubran. Indeed, both Saleh and El Wedidi garnered significant fan bases with their interpretations of songs by Sayed Darwish and Sheikh Imam even before the #Jan25 Uprising. Their music, which is clearly revolutionary in spirit and content, forces a different assessment of the musically simpler and less subtly subversive music of better-known revolutionary artists like Ramy Essam, reflecting a different view of what lyrically, and sonically, resonates with Egyptian youth culture.

Meanwhile, more in the "rock" vein, Massar Egbari's blues- and funk-tinged grooves, Wust El-Balad's folk-tinged rock, and Cairokee's more sophisticated and highly produced hits have each, in their own way, pushed the boundaries of Arab pop rock forward over the last two decades. To these can be joined El Tanbura's re-creation of the virtuosic music of the Nile Delta. What unites these groups is the music they created and performed before, during, and after the #Jan25 Uprising, whether it was coming to Tahrir to perform classic resistance songs and poetry (Tanbura and Eskenderella) or composing some of the most memorable revolutionary songs of the period (Cairokee, Wust El-Balad, and Massar Egbari). In the wake of the Uprising all received increasing international recognition, while the three pop groups and Eskenderella went on to major commercial success inside Egypt, garnering millions of social media views and performing to ever-larger crowds as well as appearing on important television programs (such as, again, *El Barnameg*), and even squaring off against one another in friendly battles of the bands.

As Massar Egbari founder Ayman Massoud explains, "After the revolution we saw an increase in people who were willing to listen to independent, different music. That for sure couldn't have happened without the revolution. The revolution was a revolution on everything, including music." In so doing, then, even though none of these bands was in the musical/aesthetic avant-garde in Egypt, they helped blaze the trail for a new generation of artists who were not part of the existing, previously state-controlled cadre of popular artists to take the stage and achieve success outside of either government or other mechanisms of elite control.

As we've seen, while from the start *mahraganat* lyrics have dealt with drugs, women, and betraying friends, with the eruption of the uprising in 2011 the first *mahraganat* artists did take on politics directly in some songs. Perhaps the seminal example of this is the collaboration between Figo, Alaa 50, and Sadat along with Abdel-Aziz in the song "ash-Shaab wa-l-hukuma" ("The People and the Government"), whose lyrics declare: "The people and the government, the machine guns and clubs / Egypt rose up, and even those who didn't steal dove into it / I'll talk about those standing, the survivors and the dead / I'll talk about the church, the mosque, and the Brotherhood." From conversations with artists and other participants in the scene, what seems clear is that the lack of a more prominent place for politicized songs in *mahraganat* owes less to the risks involved in putting out critical music than the fact that most marginalized young Egyptians don't see the point of hitting the streets in another revolutionary outburst if they don't see it leading to actual change at the heart of the system and broader society. As Sadat put it, "The revolution removed a president, which was not the big deal. . . . The big deal is justice and that things become better."

In that regard, when security forces shot and killed the rising *mahraganat* star DJ Ahmed "Zo'la" Mohsen on the fourth anniversary of the #Jan25 Uprising, his bandmate Alaa 50 directly accused the police of his murder, refuting their claim that Brotherhood supporters at the protest that they were walking past were responsible. "Police are ignoring the vivid terrorism in Sinai and instead killing our youth," a Facebook post read that would likely have landed anyone other than one of the most popular *mahraganat* stars in Egypt in Sisi's torture chamber jails.

In a situation where metal remains too culturally "foreign" to reach most Egyptians, and where rappers know the full limits of the regime's toleration, does the nonpolitical politics of *mahraganat* in fact constitute the most powerful—never mind practical—form of protest politics in Egypt? Can it at least keep the reality of people's difficult lives at the surface, rather than merely serving as a fantasy escape as so much pop—Arab pop no less than any other—does? Is it a weapon in the "war of position" in which Egypt will remain entrenched for the foreseeable future? It's hard to answer in the negative once you've seen a *mahraganat* show in person. Meanwhile, according to Sadat in the video interview for the documentary *Guardians of Joy*, *mahraganat* is helping to overturn the elite- and government-perpetuated stereotypes, where certain neighborhoods that were once associated with drugs and poverty like Madinet el Salam are instead becoming synonymous with music.

FIGURE 12. Islam Chipsy performing with EEK at Nuits Sonores, Lyon, France, 2016. Photo by Robert Brice.

As one of the scene's seminal artists, virtuoso keyboardist Islam Chipsy, put it in the documentary, "People learned to say no, even with music."

Of course, it wasn't just musicians who learned to say "no"; visual artists like the calligrapher and graphic designer Bahia Shehab stenciled "La" (no in Arabic) 1001 different ways across Cairo and later the world during and after the uprising. And as documented in books such as Sherif Boraie's *Wall Talk,* street artists during and after the #Jan25 Uprising covered Tahrir and the surrounding area in graffiti, elaborate murals, portraits of martyrs, and even installation art using the hulks of abandoned and destroyed security vehicles to establish their presence and continue to reject the clearly undemocratic rule of the Supreme Council of the Armed Forces (SCAF), which governed Egypt from Mubarak's removal till the start of Morsi's presidency.

The sheer volume of artistic production in so many media makes clear that, while extreme metal remains one of the most powerfully negative artistic forces imaginable, in terms of reaching a broader public and helping direct that anger (toward what end is a different question) hip hop was far better suited to the task, as is the case in most every latitude south of Scandinavia.

However new and innovative, listening to *mahraganat* and talking with both its practitioners and with the generation of rappers who immediately preceded them make clear how deep are its roots in hip hop. The major artists have specifically talked about the influence not only of 2Pac but of Bob

Marley as well, a fact notable and melodically relevant. Moreover, Karim from Arabian Knightz argues that rappers were not just part of the scene from the start; they were the ones who started to add hip hop elements to sha'bi music. Many *mahraganat* singers started off as rappers before turning to the simpler rhyming style and meter of *mahraganat*.

This narrative is at least partially confirmed by Sadat, one of the first and best-known *mahraganat* artists, particularly for his work with his longtime friend and partner Alaa 50 Cent. As he explained in an interview in 2013, "Before the revolution we rapped about what is going on in the streets and our social relations, for example friends who turn out to be dishonest, etc., this kind of stuff. Not directly about politics ... it's politics, but not that direct. ... After the revolution we had more freedom to say what we want, so rapped directly about in politics."

Such dynamism could also be seen on the dance floor at *mahraganat* events (until they were officially banned), whether weddings, concerts, or festivals. As much as the music, dancing in *mahraganat* reflects a kind of fragmented, nonlinear journey that breaks through many narrative and physical conventions. When on the dance floor, *mahraganat* dancers combine an amalgamation of dance styles, from heavy metal's headbanging, to punk's frenetic moshing, hip hop's breakbeat footwork, and techno shuffling, along with the swirling hips and shaking shoulders found in belly dancing, in addition to traces of Egyptian folkloric rooted movements. Indeed, the aesthetic is at least partially metal, just as punk and even hip hop have always had some metal in their genes, which isn't surprising given their common origins in the early period of deindustrialization and "structural adjustment" in Europe and the United States. So it should be equally unsurprising that some of the most devoted metaliens in the Egyptian scene, such as guitarist Shung, come from the same kinds of sha'bi neighborhoods (in this case, al-Munib across the Nile from downtown Cairo) from where *mahraganat* sprung forth. While the majority of metal artists and fans were at least middle class or above, Shung's family was effectively working poor. When he spoke about how the anger of the music reflected the difficult circumstances of his life, it made as much sense as the anger and harsh energy underlying *mahraganat*. As Mahmoud Refat explained in a *Vice* interview in 2017 describing the sound of the Sadat and Alaa 50 Cent's classic "Hooga," "The dirtier, the crazier, ... more dangerous ... you get, the better. As if you're threatening someone almost. ... You have to scream." It's hard to get more metal than these instructions.

Indeed, this energy is the same whether it's metal, punk/hardcore, hip hop, or *mahraganat,* even if each has its own particular aesthetic brew and mechanisms of gathering the tribes: metal requires more formal shows with vaguely proper PA systems; hip hop in Egypt as in the rest of the world increasingly relies on much-hyped and über-intense rap battles, most now filmed for YouTube and receiving hundreds of thousands and occasionally millions of views (when they're not canceled or raided by police); *mahraganat* merely needs a wedding or other public celebration, a cheap DJ and sound system, and, if possible, a drum set to keep the intensity and party going well into the night.

In the meantime, particularly after the coup in 2013, rappers like Arabian Knightz moved from engaging Egyptian politics toward the politics of hip hop in Egypt, criticizing the rapping/rhyming skills not just of *mahraganat* artists, but even more so of the new generation of rappers, and for more than half a decade they have been using the mechanism of diss or beef raps to go after what they feel to be their lazy and less talented younger generation. Recalling the lyrical feuds launched by veteran Don Bigg against his former protégés in Morocco, the viciousness of their takedown is apparent from the beef rap of the AK/MC Amin iteration known as the Arab League All-Stars, "Respect," in which they dissed all the newer rappers who were recording diss tracks against not just them but their families as well. In the video the rappers even beat up the fictional rapper who attacked them. This was an early indication of the rise of "battle rap," which has become a global phenomenon and features rappers squaring off in front of an audience for freestyle diss contests that can achieve hundreds of thousands of views on YouTube and other platforms.

As Karim describes it, battle raps are like metal fifteen years ago, forced to take place out in the desert and often raided by cops (ironically, Shady Nour says the same thing about electronic and dance music for the same reason). But this too is changing as there are actually leagues, such as Rap or Die *(Ya tarab ya tamut),* that are gaining sponsorships and credibility as their YouTube views and Instagram views pile up. Not surprisingly, the one genre of rap that doesn't find much of a place in this hypercompetitive and virtuosic lyrical and flowing environment is the quickly accelerating "mumble rap" scene, which is sure to set up some big beefs in the near future. Most established rappers have nothing but praise for the fans' devotion to the genre, and little but disdain for how rappers have scoffed at it. As Karim explained, half exasperated and half excited by the conflict:

FIGURE 13. Egyptian rapper Karim Rush performing with Arabian Knightz and MC Amin in Mansoura, Egypt, 2015. Courtesy of Karim Rush.

Mahraganat artists are the best people. They make sure they support their shit for real and when they get exposed to good music they like it . . . 50 and Sadat recorded songs with MC Amin and every time they do other rappers start dissing Amin about it: "Why are you going to that fan base and low IQ and uneducated people," etc. But I'm like, "How you gonna talk about rebel this and rebel that and revolution when you're actually classist?!" Now you're gonna tell us what we're supposed to rap to. That we're not supposed to rap to poor people? Are you fucking crazy? Even worse, other rappers claimed that Arabian Knightz and Amin were "dirtying hip hop" by working with these guys but then the same rappers, like Y Crew, went and did collaborations with Sadat.

As with metal and hip hop, technology was crucial to the rise of *mahraganat:* Here it was not just the cheap yet professional recording technologies, which had already enabled the rise of "bedroom music" across the MENA and wider world, or the increasing ubiquity of the Internet, where music could be freely circulated and consumed. Also important was the new digital DJ equipment, which allowed the highly improvised *mahraganat* to be performed live, often with trap drums and, in the famous case of Islam Chipsy, keyboards as well. Indeed, a seminal example of the sound and energy of this fusion can be found on "Islam Chipsy Boiler Room Cairo Live," on YouTube, which features Chipsy on his famed Yamaha PSR OR-700 Arabic keyboard, backed up by two of Egypt's funkiest drummers—a perfect storm of technology, aesthetics, and space. When you listen to the music, the clear affinities (though different sonic signatures) between Chipsy's music and more avant-garde electronica by Egyptian artists like Onsy, Alternative Matter, and 100Copies artists like Andro El-Hawy and El-Sweasy are inescapable.

IS EGYPTIAN METAL DOOMED?

Since *Heavy Metal Islam* was published in 2008, hip hop has divided between battle rap and trap while *mahraganat* emerged and went mainstream. But what of Egyptian metal, which found such powerful and unique expression in *um ad-dunia,* the "Mother of the World," as Egypt has long been called? One basic problem with the Egyptian metal scene, even more than other scenes in this book, is that many of its most devoted musicians and fans don't venture far from their musical home turf, limiting their ability to stretch out and expand their audience or minds. On the other hand, *mahraganat* has been a happily and promiscuously hybrid, bastardized music from the start, its seminal artists constantly collaborating with rappers, DJs, EDM (even Shady Nour's favorite, "Berlin techno"), avant-garde and experimental musicians, and the complete spectrum of Egypt's youth music. And when judged by Alexandria-based DJ El Dakhlwya's track "Dakhlwya wa Simsimiya" ("Dakhlwya and Simsimiyya"), released in summer 2020, bringing together *mahraganat* with the traditional instruments of the Nile Delta, the sonic possibilities of *mahraganat* are pretty endless.

If metal and *mahraganat* finally meet, the offspring will be ferocious indeed. In fact, a metal-*mahraganat* mash-up would most certainly help the metal scene gain new relevance for young Egyptians, especially as the very circumstances in which *mahraganat*'s natural fan base lives are so amenable to metal. The problem, according to Reda Zine, is that while the lives of "mahraganians" (to borrow the syntax that produces "metalians" even though the actual colloquial name for a mahragan fan is *sarsagi*) "are metal," it's take a lot more time and money to learn to play drums, guitar, or bass at a high level, find a band, rehearse for months or even years, and then organize shows when half the population think you've become, if not a Satan worshiper, then at least weird. Indeed, if a metal band ever wrote a song with lyrics similar to Oka and Ortega's smash hit "Elʒab yalla," whose lyrics repeatedly if playfully refer to Shaytan enticing people to play, drink, and party all night (the *elʒab yalla* of the title, plus *eshrab yalla* and *wala yalla*), it wouldn't be surprising if the grand mufti dusted off that fatwa from 1997 condemning metalheads to death for apostasy in what was Egypt's first metal moral panic.

Even if the lyrics could be kept halal (or at least brutal enough to be indecipherable to the untrained censor's ear), the timeline and financial burden of becoming a rapper or *mahraganat* artist are much shorter and lower than becoming a metal or other serious musician. So there's not much chance that a critical mass of *mahraganat*'s core fanbase and practitioners will make the jump to metal on their own; if a metal-*mahraganat* mash-up is going to happen, the initiative will have to come from the now far more established and financially and culturally (if not politically) secure *mahraganat* side, although the radically different tempos, instrumentation, singing, and production styles would make a successful meeting a true accomplishment.

So we are left with a nagging question: Can the metal scene survive, never mind recapture some of the energy it had a decade ago? And is its demise a canary in the coalmine for Egypt's political, never mind musical, future? Or have hip hop and even more so *mahraganat* simply taken over metal's affective, social, and even political functions and terrain in the post-Tahrir generation? Certainly, many metaliens have a particularly negative view of *mahraganat*. One musician who grew up in the same neighborhoods out of which *mahraganat* emerged told Mark that it was "much more dangerous than radicals and extreme religious culture," an attitude that well reflects the anger coupled with jealousy that an allegedly musically "low" and lyrically "vulgar" form of music could become so popular and accepted while metal is still attacked as un-Islamic. Frank Sinatra, we might remember here, had much the same opinion of rock 'n' roll.

Variations on these questions have been asked by most of the metaliens Mark has come to know. Almost no one who's been in the scene at some point thinks of metal as a musical waste of time; quite the opposite, in fact. Nancy Mounir well summarizes one aspect of the problem: "The thing is, with metal, we've all been in that phase, and then other things happen. So it was important for everyone, . . . what made it easier to jump through different projects." Mahmoud Refat, founder of 100Copies, perhaps the primary label and management company both for *mahraganat* and for Cairo's avant-garde electronica scene, had words almost identical to Nancy Mounir's in several conversations about the metal scene, which is not surprising, given that he started off as a metal drummer before moving to the production and promotion side of the business.

Another reason that metal is sidelined despite the political-cultural environment being otherwise ripe for the energy it brings is the importance of humor as a major coping mechanism under the Sisi regime; it shouldn't be hard to imagine why extreme metal will not likely make the turn toward humor, or even parody. Shady Nour explained to Mark: "As people are being more and more desensitized because of the massive human rights abuse, humor has become the number one way to criticize the regime or its supporters. And so while I've stopped doing metal, I now spend much of my time creating memes, which have become super popular in the last few years."

Together, these issues help account for why the total number of metal bands in Egypt remains comparatively small (Alexandria in particular lost a significant share of the total, dropping from one-half to less than a third of Egypt's metal scene). And yet, there are some major positive developments for the scene. Most important among them, the further development of digital recording technologies and the devotion of most artists to their craft, along with the growing recognition of the best Egyptian bands, and other bands from the MENA, in Europe—which led to record deals and opportunities for tours and performances at the ubiquitous summer metal festivals across the Continent (until, of course, the pandemic of 2020–22)—have meant that, even as the live metal scene became less robust, those bands that have persevered have matured as musicians and writers, producing increasingly sophisticated and high-quality music that has earned Egypt an international reputation for producing some of the best metal anywhere.

In short, a decade ago a band like Beyond East showed the potential for an indigenous Middle Eastern/Arab metal that pushed the idiom in new directions as well as to one of its ancestral homes. Today the mature sounds of bands like Scarab, Odious, Tafaqum, and Beyond East guitarist Shung's more recent project, Ahl Sina (The People of Sinai), demonstrate that what was first popularized by Israel's Orphaned Land as "Oriental Metal" has grown far beyond its early incarnations and can now take its place as a fully fledged subgenre alongside all the other iterations of metal.

FIGURE 14. Scarab, *Martyrs of the Storm*, album cover, 2020.

More broadly, while on the daily level there is a big differentiation between various scenes, particularly between the seemingly insular metal scene, on the one hand, and the hip hop, *mahraganat,* and other subgenres within electronic and dance music scenes, on the other, in reality they share roots in the metal scene. Specifically, several of the most important artists and producers in the *mahraganat* and electronic and hip hop scenes, people like Mahmoud Refat and Abyusif, began their musical life in the metal scene in the late 1990s and early 2000s, and served as inspirations (sometimes directly) for artists such as Scarab and Massive Scar Era. Marz explained the dynamic to Mark as they stood on the balcony of his Zamalek apartment when Mark mentioned the sold-out Chipsy-Abyusif concert the evening before at the American University in Cairo's old downtown campus: "You have to understand, he used to be a metal drummer. When I was starting out and everyone was dissuading me from playing guitar he invited me into the studio to jam. He was an amazing drummer and was one of the only people who supported me as a metal guitarist at the start." Similarly, Massive Scar Era's Nancy Mounir recalled fondly his time filling in on drums for the band when they lost their female drummer. The pieces are in place; if the right people just need to start moving them, who knows what mayhem the metal-*mahraganat* fusion would produce?

THE PRICE OF POLITICS, THE COSTS OF SEXISM, AND THE HEALING POWER OF MUSIC

After coming out of nowhere to become the most visible and provocative politically engaged artist in Egypt during the revolutionary era, Ramy Essam left the country in 2014 after being warned directly by security personnel that his life would be in danger if he remained in the country. Fortunately for him, an international initiative cosponsored by the Scandinavian music freedom organizations Freemuse and Safemuse provided a scholarship opportunity to study music in Sweden. But before he left, he sent one more missile at the postcoup Sisi regime in the form of a song, "Mahnash min Dol" ("We're Not from Them"), whose video he uploaded while blockaded in his apartment, blocks from Tahrir, on the third anniversary of the #Jan25 Uprising. While friends called every few minutes to warn him that people were instructed to attack him on sight, he uploaded the just-completed video of the song, whose heavily distorted riff and chords and screaming voice marked the closest to pure metal he'd come in his career.

The video was as powerful as the song, featuring a shirtless Ramy, his body painted red and black (the anarchist colors), screaming in a decrepit apartment that the Revolution "isn't a match where whoever scores a goal wins our revolution and takes it home," and calling for the "remnants of the regime to be the next to be overthrown," before exhorting the people to remember that "we don't belong to them, or them, or them." The video ends with Ramy throwing a Molotov at a brick wall, which, when it explodes, showers fire across a set of images, including Nasser, Sadat, Mubarak, Morsi, and other leaders. While Sisi's followers cheered for their coup leader turned soon-to-be president with Trumpian abandon five hundred meters away in Tahrir, Ramy, his video editor, Mark, and a couple of friends sat and watched the YouTube views go from several dozen to several hundred to thousands in the first few hours after it was uploaded. Within a few days "Mahnash min

Dol" would reach hundreds of thousands of views. Within a month, Ramy would be gone from Egypt, unable to return.

Ramy could afford to take the risk of producing a song and video like "Mahnash min Dol" because of his global recognition and the international protection that came with it, including a Scandinavian safe haven and steady income waiting for him as soon as he was ready to leave Egypt. Most others weren't so lucky. In 2018, after the release of his track "Balaha" (which translates to "Date," and is considered a derogatory reference to President El Sisi), several artists and activists associated with him were imprisoned even though they had no part in that or other recent songs. For example, while Rami Sidky worked with Ramy in the past, and is featured on the track "Mahnash min Dol," he had no part in the production, performance, or dissemination of "Balaha," the track he was arrested for.

Many artists and activists who have remained have lingering anger at Essam for "planning his escape and leaving others to suffer," as one former collaborator put it, while most everyone still inside more or less feels he's no longer relevant to the local musical or political scene, whatever good he might be doing keeping the revolutionary flame alive among foreign supporters or diaspora Egyptians during his frequent concerts in Europe and occasional ones in the US.

Most other artists, with little opportunity for a similar safe haven or desire to leave Egypt for the foreseeable future, have kept a lower profile politically while hoping to stay relevant enough to maintain credibility among Egyptian fans regardless of the country's political future. But politics is not the only thing that's driven some of the best artists out of Egypt. For example, Massive Scar Era's Cherine Amr, who moved to Vancouver in 2015 and later Montreal, left the scene, and the country, she'd worked so hard to build up "because of sexism, plain and simple." As a female metal musician in a country that remained deeply patriarchal, where sexual harassment and violence against women continue at epidemic levels, the more successful she became, the more of a burden and block sexism became. Indeed, even at the height of the #Jan25 Uprising, during one conversation filmed for the *Before the Spring* documentary, Cherine and then Massive Scar Era bassist Perry Moataz sat across the Nile from Tahrir wishing they could just "get the fuck out of here" and go "somewhere like Canada to play music and walk the streets freely." Cherine could overcome the inherent patriarchy in Egyptian society broadly; she could even take the casual but usually not toxic sexism of the metal scene. But what she couldn't take was the sexism and harassment of and by her own fans.

I had worked hard to create a second band, a rock band, Cheen, and we were doing very well. Mahmoud Refat even signed us to 100Copies, saying that while it wasn't his normal music he thought there was a niche and saw I had a connection with the younger and especially female audience, who related to my lyrics. Then I was doing shows and there was so much harassment of the female fans by guys in the crowd. Finally, I had to stop in the middle of a show and yell at the guys who kept pushing the women out of the front and to the back. I mean, I'm singing for the girls!

Not surprisingly, when the chance finally came, Cherine in fact did move. With Nancy Mounir remaining in Cairo, Massive Scar Era became a long-distance project, with occasional shows with Cherine and Nancy together during yearly tours or her return visits to Egypt and Nancy's visits to Vancouver for periodic recordings.

It's worth noting here that a similar trajectory was followed by one of the few other Egyptian metal bands fronted by a woman, Enraged. As lead singer Rasha Magdy explained in a 2016 interview with the German magazine *Deine Korrespondenti*, "Growing up as a girl or a woman in Egypt sucks. It's terrible. A fate that I do not wish for anyone. When I was pregnant, I wished they were boys [they are]. I just didn't want to raise a girl in Egypt because it would have been hell—for her and for me." It took becoming financially independent (as a high school economics teacher) and a "thick enough skin" to deal with regular abuse by male metal musicians and fans. Even then, ultimately, she and her bandmate and husband Wael Alsoukkary relocated to New Zealand, where a reconfigured version of the band continues under the name Medjai.

Massive Scar Era has managed to continue producing high-quality music despite the distance. One such recording that marks a highpoint in Massive Scar Era's discography is "Unfollow," part of the band's *Color Blind* EP, released in 2019. The first demo for the song was recorded by Cherine and the band on her computer, and then sent to Nancy to inspire her own parts and arranging. Ultimately, Nancy flew to Vancouver and the band spent a week or so jamming and finalizing the structure and then rehearsing the song, after which they recorded it at Rain City Recorders in Vancouver. Like all the best metal from the MENA region, "Unfollow" manages to faithfully capture the spirit of death metal with rhythmic and melodic orchestration that places it unmistakably ahead of the aesthetic and cultural curve. To this day, the combination of Cherine's beautiful-to-brutal vocals and Nancy's aggressive but filigreed violin melodies is one of the most recognizable combinations in the metal world for those who know it. Here their sound is overlaid with a powerful paean to resistance, "the many forms of resistance, the consequences, and the aftermath," as Cherine explains it.

Indeed, as she and Mark discussed the track, halfway around the world rockets were passing each other in the night between Gaza and Jerusalem as Palestinian resistance to Israel's takeover of the Sheikh Jarrah neighborhood of East Jerusalem reached the boiling point. "I found the romanticization of war very disturbing in the West; aggressive and physical resistance gets a spotlight yet they are ignoring the soft war that is happening in its political textures, like ongoing colonialism, destroying the land and the mistreatment of indigenous people, especially women." The video is even more shocking, with a postapocalyptic tone and a cast that includes African, Muslim, lesbian, transgender, and other characters fighting over the scraps of what remains after the world has ended.

The kind of sophisticated and global sound and visual styles of Massive Scar Era today are far from the norm across the MENA region. Like their male counterparts, most female underground or alternative artists in Egypt don't have the ability to pick up and move, nor do all or even most of them want to. While still somewhat marginalized in Egypt, a small group of female rappers has, like their counterparts in the metal scene, helped break down gender boundaries and genre borders at the same time. One of the most talented to emerge since the Revolution is Yukka Shahin, who like many of the best male MCs in the scene started rapping in Alexandria at the start of the 2010s. While some male rappers have attempted to highlight the ongoing problems of sexual harassment and gender violence, Yukka's personal experiences with these issues naturally inspired some very powerful lyrics and a sense of activism as the center of hip hop. Another rapper, Mayam Mahmoud, originally gained fame as a "veiled rapper" (in contrast to Shahin, who removed hers not long after starting to get some recognition), making several appearances on the widely watched program *Arabs Got Talent,* which became widely discussed, not just because of her undeniable talent but also because she refuted so many preconceptions about the relationship between gender, art, and religion among ostensibly conservative Egyptians.

The cadre of innovative and powerful female artists extends deep into the DJ and experimental scenes in Egypt as well. Artists like Bosaina (who has worked with several projects like Wetrobots and Bikya on Mahmoud Refat's 100Copies label), as well as noise and electronic artists like Jacqueline George and Yara Mekawei, join the singers, rappers, and musicians as well in creating some of the most groundbreaking as well as culturally and politically salient music anywhere.

Yet perhaps because of their creative power, existing in the alternative, never mind underground, music scenes as a woman remains a herculean task, especially if on top of this one wants to challenge a political system that is, now more than ever, held firm by rape and other forms of extreme violence against anyone who challenges it. Shady Nour powerfully captured the feeling of so many artist-activists in Egypt during a Q & A at a screening of *Before the Spring, after the Fall,* which centered on the story of his and his brother Noor's musical and political evolution in the years before, during, and after the #Jan25 Uprising. It's worth quoting in full:

> All the revolutionaries I know have not only been desensitized but we've all reached a horrible state of apathy because of all the crazy and horrible stuff that's happened. All the people who've died, been jailed. You'd think it would have mattered, but it all went to waste and you think it would have an impact on society but it didn't. All the hope . . . what could happen, and then didn't. I saw the *Before the Spring* documentary in 2013 at a screening at the Williamsburg Film Festival when it came out as I happened to be in Brooklyn at the time, and I just started crying because things had already gone so bad. . . . Today the people who took part in revolution are all depressed and letting out negative energy in so many ways. One of my friends, a filmmaker, was called into secret security because of a *Facebook* post, another [Shady Abu Zeid] was arrested and spent two years in prison before being released in October 2020. And we're all very aware of each other being apathetic and depressed. I see [another artist featured in *Heavy Metal Islam*] and we chill and have drinks and we look each other in the eye and we know. We are unable to give a shit. We cannot give a shit. Because if we do give a shit we get imprisoned. So we have to be quiet and act like nothing happened, leave, or get locked away.

Other activists remain engaged, often at great peril, although few if any musicians still in the country remain overtly political. Shady began DJing, moving from metal to EDM not long after the uprisings began, followed a couple of years later by taking up creating and circulating memes as a way of dealing with the stress of a life seemingly on hold permanently. His brother Noor helped create the group No to Military Trials with Alaa Abd el-Fattah's sister Mona Seif, and then moved into environmental activism, running an NGO working to preserve the region around Lake Nasser before moving to Cambridge to complete an MA in environmental activism. Reflecting his growing environmental commitments, Noor moved from metal to creating street music with found instruments in the years after the uprising, even as he remains a metalien at heart.

Noor's old friend and Mona's brother Alaa, who was one of the first people Mark met on his journey into Egyptian metal over a decade and a half ago, had a characteristically unique insight into *mahraganat,* whose origins he'd in fact investigated when not imprisoned by the Morsi and then Sisi governments. As he and Mark shared a strong early morning coffee at a friend's house (to which Alaa often decamped after leaving the nearby prison where he was forced to spend every night from 6 PM to 6 AM), he challenged the ubiquitous assumption of hip hop and Egyptian sha'bi origins. "You think *mahraganat* is so related to hip hop, but do you know what the most direct influence on it was?" he asked, as he typed in Arabic into the YouTube home page. "Here, listen to this."

What he pulled up was the song "Sahranat tul al-layl" ("Party All Night") by Libyan singer Hala Shaaban. The song was produced by the well-known Libyan singer, composer, and producer Hamid El Shaeri, who has spent much of his career in Egypt working with some of the biggest names in Egyptian pop. The song is forgettable today, but it was banging out of tuk-tuks (three-wheeled minitaxis), the uncontested "influencers" of popular musical taste, when it was released in the summer 2010. What made it immediately relevant to Alaa and Mark's discussion, however, were the sonic elements it was based on: a mid-tempo sha'bi-sounding drum part, a cheesy retro-sounding synth line, and an autotuned voice—that is, all the elements of a proper *mahraganat* song, several years before the genre stormed into public consciousness seemingly fully formed. "You gotta understand," Alaa explained as Mark listened to the track, a bit confused at the sound, "this sound didn't just emerge out of nowhere in the 'ashwiyat by a few DJs and MCs in Cairo; its origins are much broader and more complex and need to be taken into account to understand its origins and popularity. It was particularly because of this kind of sound, which El Shaeri is known for and which comes out of a similar working-class environment." Sadly, Mark and Alaa never got to finish their conversation. Not long after, Alaa was again illegally imprisoned as he was leaving his nightly jail term, and remains in maximum security as of winter 2022.

The *mahraganat* scene, its roots and routes better understood, is still immensely popular despite the government crackdown, the hip hop scene somewhat less so; the experimental electronic and dance scene is achieving more and more international recognition and producing highly innovative music, but remains a small scene circumscribed by class and education levels and a high level of transcultural experience. With politics all but impossible inside Egypt, an entrepreneurial attitude and agenda naturally emerged in the wake of 2013, focusing on corporate-sponsored "hackathons," highly polished festivals, and conferences like the "Rise Up Summit" that bring together leading representatives of the business, tech, and art worlds to figure out a way forward, at least economically and culturally, within the tightly constrained political environment of the Sisi regime.

In this broader situation the metal scene might remain small, but the music is still developing and improving. Massive Scar Era keeps pushing Egyptian metal forward from afar, Shung's most recent band, Ahl Sina, keeps Alexandria in the game, and both OG and newer metal bands, like the Alexandria-based Odious and Cairo's Tafaqum, have added powerful symphonic elements, complex rhythmic changes, Arabic vocals, and high-level production to Middle Eastern inflections as they push metal to new levels of sophistication and power. The Odious album *Skin Age,* released in 2015, is sure to be remembered as one of the defining albums of the genre, with the band hoping to go even "more Oriental" on their next album. Occasional stories about the scene in cultural portals like *Scene Noise, Rock Era Magazine,* and *Mada Masr* enable fans to keep tabs on its progress, and who's coming out with a new album.

For its part, Scarab has been carrying the banner of Egyptian extreme metal as far as humanly possible, with several albums released in the 2010s that expanded the boundaries of production and writing quality in the scene to new frontiers, as demonstrated by their release in 2018, as part of the album *Martyrs of the Storm* (officially released in 2020), of the track "Circles of Verminejya." Dedicated "to the Voodoo Culture of great Africa," with a video featuring vintage footage of ritual African dancing and the most brutal delivery vocalist Sammy Sayed has ever mustered, the song is an absolute "fuck you!" to all the forces of darkness that have again descended upon Egypt—the government, religious forces, hypocrites, and poseurs alike. But even with such a high-quality product, cofounder and lead guitarist Marz continues to struggle to work, maintain his family, and produce metal in an environment where it remains very difficult to give metal the time, energy, and respect it demands.

As he put it one afternoon as he and Mark chatted on Facebook, "I think the scene did very well throughout this decade, honestly. . . . No time for bullshit. Attitude is crucial to rise up in the current chaotic world we live in. So the scene is slowly taking a fast pace to evolve in the sense of inviting more international bands for our scene here . . . and also because of the hunger for all kinds of bizarre genres. Metal will always stay underground, especially genres like black and death. But honestly, it's better that way. It's what binds and unites us."

In one of the most original and far-sighted analyses of the #Jan25 Uprising and how it was coopted and repressed, Oxford University anthropologist Walter Armbrust uses the anthropological figure of the "trickster" to explain how what should have been a transversal revolutionary moment in Egypt was ultimately merely a liminal one, as 'Abd al-Fattah al-Sisi played the part of trickster to coopt the majority of the movement and convince people that he was the fulfillment of the revolution while, of course, harshly repressing any attempt to challenge his and the military's power. Armbrust's explanation is as disheartening as it is illuminating, revealing just how easily so many supporters of the Egyptian Revolution were played by the very people who oppressed them. But it also intimates why creating art beyond the edge of that liminal space that Sisi was able to invade and capture remains singularly important in ensuring the chances of success for a revolutionary moment: Artists have themselves long been among the most talented and adept tricksters, using the magic of creative culture to reach people and deliver messages those in power are desperate to silence. There are few tools more powerful for achieving this end than music; however Egypt's politics unfolds in the coming years, there is little doubt that its metal, hip hop, *mahraganat,* and electronica scenes will retain their subversive and transformative potential to push the country over the edge again.

THREE

Palestine/Israel

UPRISINGS IN MUSIC

Composed and arranged by Mark LeVine and Sameh
"SAZ" Zakout, engineered and mixed by Mark and Abed Hathout

THE DECADE SINCE *Heavy Metal Islam* was published has not been kind to the majority of the people and territory of historic Palestine (including Israel, the West Bank, the Gaza Strip, and East Jerusalem), particularly for the Palestinian inhabitants of the Occupied Territories and the hundreds of thousands of migrants from across Africa, Eastern Europe, and Southeast Asia who live and work in Israel with no protections or rights. Thousands of Palestinians have been killed by Israeli occupation forces, tens of thousands permanently maimed, much of the infrastructure of governance and daily life destroyed, the dream of independence buried for good. For Israeli supporters of a "just" peace, the dream of creating an Israeli state and society based on democratic rather than colonial values, of liberating Prophetic from Settler Judaism, has been permanently discredited. But as so often happens when politics become irredeemable, art—particularly music—fills at least part of the gap. At least until the next round of colonial violence erupts, as is happening as we write these lines, in May 2021.

How to sum up the last ten years of music in Occupied Palestine/Israel? It's hard to pick one episode, but a good candidate would be the scene of DAM coming onstage to a raucous welcome in Ramallah, at the 2019 edition of the Palestine Music Expo (PMX), not long after Gaza's most famous garage band finished a medley of songs including Rage Against the Machine, the Scorpions, and a popular (sha'bi) groove, only to see a coordinated protest break out among fans angry at lead rapper Tamer Nafar's just-dropped video calling on Palestinians citizens of Israel to vote in the upcoming elections.

The eight years following the eruption of the al-Aqsa Intifada in September 2000 witnessed the most violence and oppression in the Occupied Territories since their conquest in 1967 (at least until the Occupation went into a

FIGURE 15. '48 Palestinian hip hop pioneers DAM performing at the 2019 Palestine Music Expo, Ramallah. Photo by Wael Abu Jabal.

previously unknown gear of overdrive in the last few years of the 2010s). There were, in these eight years, upward of five thousand killed, tens of thousands injured, thousands of homes destroyed, hundreds of thousands of trees uprooted, and several hundred thousand more settlers implanted in the West Bank and East Jerusalem. If someone would have asked Mark in November 2008 if it could get much worse in the decade to come, he would have responded, "No, it couldn't, because it was already that bad." Saz and Abed knew better.

But in December 2008, Israel launched its largest military attack on Palestinians since 1967. The assault, dubbed Operation Cast Lead (the name is even more menacing in Hebrew), was launched in response to an increase in rocket attacks from Gaza, which were themselves launched in response to increased Israeli violations of a recently declared ceasefire. The fighting killed twelve hundred Palestinians (compared with thirteen Israelis); untold thousands more were injured. The attack elicited unprecedented outrage internationally and led to a UN fact-finding report, the Goldstone Report, which blamed Israel for the wildly excessive death toll among Palestinians. It had no impact on the ground, however. Israel moved further to the Right with each election, while Palestinians remained politically and economically frozen. The violence only picked up in the ensuing years, with major Israeli assaults in 2012 (Pillar of Defense) and in 2014 (Operation Protective Edge), the latter far deadlier, killing well over two thousand Palestinians, at least three-quarters of them civilians (versus six Israeli civilians) and destroying even more of Gaza, while land seizures, settlements, and home demolitions (among other routine violations of international law) continued apace in the West Bank and migrants and refugees were squeezed even harder by the Israeli government.

A MUSICAL EXPLOSION

If the political situation in Palestine/Israel has regressed in the last decade, musically it's evolved in many noteworthy ways. A number of sonically and aesthetically innovative scenes either expanded or developed anew in each community, from the explosion of EDM in Ramallah to the rise of Ethiopian hip hop across Israel. On the Israeli side, Orphaned Land became even more overt—and playful—with its use of religious imagery. Indeed, a well-known photo shot as a promo for the album *Or (Light) Warrior,* released in 2010, featured lead singer Kobi Farhi dressed as Jesus, complete with a crown of thorns, while other members were dressed as Bedouin reading Jewish prayer books and Hassidim kneeling on Muslim prayer rugs. At the same time, the band extended its international stature with regular tours across the length and breadth of Europe and the US, including tours with Khalas and—in an international first, to be sure—a double bill across Europe with the Tunisian metal pioneers Myrath. Orphaned Land also opened for Metallica and Ozzy Osbourne when each performed in Israel, in 2010 and 2018, respectively. But with founding guitarist Yossi Sassi-Sa'aron leaving the group in 2014, the "Oriental" component was perhaps a bit less organic, even as the iconography of the band became more outrightly syncretistic.

One of the few other Israeli "Oriental" metal bands, Arallu, continued to record its blend of Mizrahi folk and death metal sounds, mixing in 'oud, saz, and sitar into brutal death metal with, at least at times, a much more Zionist edge than Orphaned Land. Recent years have also seen the beginnings of a Yiddish scene, with bands such as Parve and the Chabad-affiliated band Chasidica, which blends klezmer sounds into the mix, if not always so originally.

As British metal scholar Keith Kahn-Harris explains, "There are loads of bands, but—as in every scene—most are fairly generic." The broader Israeli scene did not feature much sonic development, with bands like the Mortuus

FIGURE 16. Cover of Orphaned Land's album *The Never Ending Way of ORwarriOR*. Art by Zen Two and Native. Band photo by Ofir Abe and Adam Nishma.

Umbra, Dim Aura, and Lehavoth (extreme/black), Shredhead (thrash), and Sonne Adam and Dukatalon (death metal) joining more established groups like Betzefer and Khalas on the scene without changing its fundamental sonic palette. Politically, hardly any Jewish Israeli artists, particularly in the metal scene, came out with any overt political messages, while in the hip hop scene rappers like Subliminal and his acolytes either became more openly nationalist and racist or, with the rise of a new generation of Ethiopian and other subaltern voices, limited criticism to intra-Jewish racism within Israeli society, as we discuss more below.

But Orphaned Land remained at the apotheosis of the Israeli metal scene once Khalas, after producing the innovative *Arab Rock Orchestra* album with superstar Israeli producer Yossi Fine in 2013, went on semipermanent hiatus. As Kobi explained to Mark at the end of his marathon US tour in 2018, during the last decade "Orphaned Land has turned into an idea more than just a band for the fans. . . . Everyone comes to our shows and that's something great because for an hour or two you have this utopia where everything is okay and coexistence does exist and the fans do feel that. In that way I think that OL is some sort of torch of hope that unites people. It's a huge responsibility, but OL . . . is an idea that proves that music is a great weapon, that BDS is not the right way even though we don't like the government's deeds."

The "Boycott, Divestment, and Sanctions" (hereafter, BDS) movement, which, inspired by the anti-Apartheid movement of a generation before, has seen the large majority of Palestinian civil society organizations ask international artists not to perform in Israel, hadn't been brought up by Mark before this. But it's something that is regularly on his mind because the movement demands of Israeli as well as international artists not merely to be positive and provide a space for hope, but to engage in concrete political warfare against one of the world's most powerful states and efficient propaganda machines—that is, to take sides against not merely their own government but their own society, something that is the opposite of the utopic space Orphaned Land has always tried to create.

The clash between utopia and reality surfaced when Kobi sought the opinions on Facebook of his large Arab fan base about whether it would be a good idea, or even possible, to perform in Egypt. In so doing, he began one of the most telling discussions about the relationship between art and politics of the Arab Spring era. As violence has flared across the region, Orphaned Land has continued to represent for many of its Arab fans both a critique (however safely unfocused) of the present and a positive vision of the future, which have always been at the heart of the international—and, within it, Arab/Muslim—metal scenes. These fans remained devoted to and protective of the band, but Orphaned Land's refusal to engage explicitly with the Occupation also caused a split in the Arab fan base when the issue of the band actually performing in an Arab country like Egypt became a possibility.

"My dream is to meet our fans in the Middle East, Egypt, Syria, Lebanon or any other place. I have played in Australia, China, Japan, USA, South America, Europe, but I never played next door, and these are the fans I want to meet the most," Kobi said in the Facebook discussion. The feeling was surely shared by Arab fans, but a large number nevertheless didn't support the idea of OL performing in Arab countries, with some "haters" (in Kobi's words) offering a harsh judgment of just his consideration of the idea as long as the Occupation continues. Not surprisingly, Kobi took issue with attacks ostensibly blaming Orphaned Land for the ills of the Occupation and asked how that's any different than blaming all Palestinians for the actions of terrorists, or all Egyptians for the actions of the Brotherhood or government.

It seems, in fact, that the issue is personal: "I grew up and still live in Jaffa in an amazing co-existence of Arabs & Jews who are nothing but beloved cousins. My Jewish Grandma and her Muslim friend Yusra were calling each other on every Jewish/Muslim holiday to greet each other. I know stories of a Jewish/Muslim mother who gave milk from her body to a Muslim/Jewish baby since his own mother couldn't." As someone who spent the better part of a decade researching the history and contemporary realities of Jaffa and its daughter-turned-conqueror Tel Aviv (as explored in the book *Overthrowing Geography,* released in 2005), it was hard for Mark not to notice that Kobi's narrative avoids the huge imbalance of power between the Israeli state and its

Jewish citizens, on the one hand, and the small and largely poor Palestinian community of Jaffa, on the other.

As he continued, "We wrote songs/albums about the conflict for the past 27 years ... We were the first ... who took a Palestinian band [Khalas] on a one hell of a tour with us + when we got the glorious *Metal Hammer* award we shared it with a Palestinian band. I have recorded a song with a Palestinian singer and I'm doing my small efforts for a better future." For Kobi, the personal is political in a very deep way (going as deep as his tattoos deliberately inked by Arab artists). One can say that it substitutes for the actively political; or rather, his personal relationships with Arab and Palestinian artists and fans are his political statement.

It's thus no surprise that Kobi faulted the "haters" for heaping scorn on Israel when the death and brutality of Assad or numerous other regimes far exceed Israel's. "Please tell me my dear haters—what have you all done except drinking an eternal poison and swallowing all the hate you've been brainwashed to eat? ... Yes, it's true; I'm not standing with only one side here, because both sides are mistaken, I do not support the Israeli government nor the Palestinian one, I think they are both pieces of pure shit."

And it's these two sides that in his mind must be maintained for the positioning of Orphaned Land as heralds of something beyond itself to work. Israel, even as a colonial occupier, can't be uniquely and irredeemably responsible for the Occupation and wronging Palestinians, and attempts to create such a narrative, like the BDS movement, are a clear threat to Orphaned Land's sense of itself (even if members agree with the broader critique of Israel and the Occupation) as much as to Israel. Thus he continued, "Someone mentioned Roger Waters: well, though I think he is one hell of an antisemite jerk. ... The thing about Waters is that he did play a show in Israel, grabbed his millions of $, and only then started to preach about boycotts, he never wrote a song about it, never did a concert about it, never thought to do a concept album about it and as much as I know he never gave 1$ from his own pocket to try and solve problems and help. ... It appears that we, with our little metal band[,] succeeded to do more than the hate and separation he is spreading. ... Art is the best way to protest," he concluded, "boycott is the wrong way."

In fact, Waters has written songs and donated money on behalf of justice for Palestinians, and has never been accused of animosity toward Jews by anyone who actually knows him. More interesting is Kobi's belief in the possibility of a depoliticized "protest" art—that is, art that criticizes the situation (*hamatzav* in Hebrew), broadly apportions blame, and offers a vision of a different future, without directly choosing sides and joining the fight. Kobi's feelings raise important questions about the role and responsibility of artists in societies dominated by prejudice and oppression, as is Israel (and the US for that matter). How far must artists go in their music and public positions to oppose their governments (and even societies) directly in such situations? And if their message is positive and at least not supportive of such actions, is that enough?

Arab fans were surprisingly split on the idea, with a majority supporting Kobi's position and at least wishing he could play Egypt. One Arab fan even compared Orphaned Land to the moment in Medina when the early Muslim community lived harmoniously with their Christian and Jewish neighbors; another lamented that "in our society, as Arabs, we are taught to hate you since our early childhood." Not surprisingly, Shung—the guitarist of Beyond East and Ahl al-Sina whom we met in chapter 2—was initially quite supportive. During this initial debate, he joined another fan in the sentiment: "Do most of hate commentators love orphaned land? Yes."

Yet another Arab fan offered his support: "Kobi, never mind the haters, they are a product of a system that demonizes Israel and blame it for any problem that arises in the country, so that they would create a scarecrow that they can unite people against, and justify their military rule over [us]." A fourth exclaimed: "Music is supposed to have no limits or bonds[. The] same people who are against Orphaned Land listen to bands that have anti-Islamic and or anti-Semitic lyrics and be like 'oh I just listen to their music for music's sake.'"

But many Arab/Middle Eastern fans extended notes of caution, both because of the dangerous situation in the Sinai and with an even more emphatic situation: "Kobi, you performing here—which is not possible anyway—will open the gates of hell once again and will kill the metal scene in Egypt For Good my friend. Sorry to burst your 'dream' but that will never ever happen. Ever. Over so many people's dead body."

A Palestinian fan was, not surprisingly, the most critical: "Not acceptable [for OL to play] for the simple fact that u took our land. . . . tell me if I took ur home would keep saying that? U want to live in peace then you must know that the land ur stepping on isn't urs." Even Shung had changed his tune when Mark spoke with him later: "Maybe it was a good idea when Orphaned Land was a much truer underground metal band, [but] not now, because this will be more for political propaganda than an underground musical event if it happened."

With the exception of a few bands like Khalas that include or are fronted by Palestinian citizens of Israel, the metal scene in Palestine/Israel continues to be dominated by Israeli Jewish bands and fans. With the ubiquity of metal scenes across the MENA region and particularly in neighboring Arab countries, it's always been a mystery why there was never much of a metal scene or even small cadres of musical devotees in either "'48" or "'67" Palestinian societies. Haifa University anthropologist Nadeem Karkabi offered one explanation as he and Mark geared up for the first night of the PMX in 2019. He felt that, unlike in other Arab countries from the 1970s through 1990s, when hard rock and metal penetrated into the youth culture, in Palestine traditional music like Dabke and even *mijwiz* (Levantine reed flute)—so-called "village"—music took on overwhelming symbolic importance as national symbols of resistance for Palestinians. Because of this, it was very hard for other styles of music to find a space to grow and wind up being performed.

Not everyone from the small community of metal players pointed to the same problem. Haifa-based synthesist and bass player Raymond (Rimon) Haddad—today mostly a jazz player, but thirty years ago a member of the seminal local rock band Shatea (Shore)—disagreed with his good friend and fellow *haifawi* (Haifa native) Nadeem. A day after his amazing modular synth set at PMX (no keyboard, just a lot of improvisational sequencing, knob turning, and patch cabling on about a dozen "Eurorack" modules), he reminisced about the old days of the scene and the passion his generation had for the music, but lamented that there just wasn't a critical mass of artists to sustain it.

For ex–Orphaned Land guitarist Yossi Sassi-Sa'aron, other issues come to mind. Catching up together for the first time in over a decade, he explained to Mark that

I've actually thought about why there isn't any real Palestinian metal scene, and also talked with Abed from Khalas about this. There was, of course, plenty of music produced by different camps in Palestine, but it was all underground because there were never any real vehicles to get an audience or pay for it. In fact, back in the day [Israeli rock legend] David Broza told me that he met a lot of Palestinian musicians and they'd play for him in their basements or in hidden places because the music wasn't accepted. Today of course there's hip hop and artists like DAM. But still, living as a minority is very challenging and you know the big picture. If you're an electronic musician all you need is computer and keyboard, you can share your music, etc. But metal musicians need places to rehearse that will not be bombed tomorrow. You need big initial costs, the down payments before . . . a band collectively [is viable are] considerably more than with any other genre. Even to play hip hop in a challenging place, in third world country, it's doable, because the basic prerequisites are not that big; but in metal it's all about money, instrumentation, places to rehearse, rehearsals, all just to sound professional.

Yossi's old friend Abed Hathout had a more historically rooted but similarly nuanced take: "I think the *mijwiz* and Dabke [were] prominent then because the leaders of the PLO in this era mostly came from the Palestinian villages where that was the dominant music, rather than the towns, where there was always more modern and even Western music. But my uncle had a band in the '80s; he loved Sabbath and would occasionally play them live but it was mostly a wedding band, so the most metal he could do in that situation was Europe's 'The Final Countdown' or Survivor's 'Eye of the Tiger.'"

Mark and Abed both laughed at his mentioning these songs because thirty years later at PMX Gaza's newest phenomenon, the band "Tybo" (the Arabic pronunciation of the English word "typo," in Arabic also known as Hata' Matba'i) started off the evening with a medley of their own sha'bi grooves interspersed with Rage Against the Machine's "Wake Up!," the Scorpions' "Hurricane," and, of course, "The Final Countdown." As for Abed, he'd been exposed to bands like Metallica and other Western bands early through the particular cohort of teenagers he'd hung out with, but Khalas became perhaps the first Arabic-singing metal band in the world because he'd never heard anyone do it before.

That was actually the main reason we decided to help create the genre of Arabic metal. Back then we were unique. There was a band, Chaos, from Nazareth, that was around a couple of years, and of course Melechesh from Jerusalem, but that was it. We knew about the metal scene in Israel of course, but all the other scenes back in the day were too small for us then, even Egypt. In fact, it wasn't until MySpace in the mid-2000s that we really began to learn about other bands. I actually first found out about Orphaned Land through MySpace! Same with Melechesh, and I'm from Haifa so I had access to everything.

On top of all these particular reasons, of course, was the sheer scale of other scenes, particularly Egypt's scene, compared with Palestine's. "In Egypt even if only 1% liked your music, you could create a metal scene. But here that would mean a few dozen people, just you and your friends. It just wasn't enough for a full-fledged scene to catch on, and then when the digital era began with MySpace young people quickly gravitated to the far easier hip hop scene."

Indeed, even in Israel Orphaned Land, for all its growing international presence, cannot compete with more mainstream Israeli pop artists, particularly the Mizrahi/Sephardi music scenes or the hip hop scene, which are all far larger in terms of sales and media presence. As Yossi Sassi-Sa'aron explained to Mark,

> The progressive metal scene in Israel is doing well, with lots of young bands still performing, still creating. But there's a sort of soberness now; ten years ago we had big bold dreams, everything felt possible, but not now, it's more sober and realistic. And perhaps because of this, there's less experimentations and innovations. Bands are sounding alike, the new bands aren't taking chances. Rather than investing in high-quality recording, they have to invest in videos or running ads on Facebook and social media. Once you invest a lot of resources in how to get the music to people and less on the music itself, it affects everything.

Similarly, Arabic pop and traditional Palestinian nationalist songs remain at the center of Palestinian popular culture. The most prominent popular singer today is no doubt Gazan crooner Mohammed Assaf, who took the Arab and broader Muslim world by storm with his historic victory on *Arab Idol* in 2013. But other comparatively less commercial artists, like Trio Joubran, 47 Soul, and Dub-Kcy, have also become part of the global music ecumene. As PMX demonstrated with its doubling in size in the first three years, while the territory of Palestine was ever more quickly disappearing into Israeli control, Palestinian culture, particularly music, was conquering new territory with each passing year.

HIP HOP OCCUPIES HEARTS AND MINDS

I consider Arabic hip-hop as an uprising in music.
—PALESTINIAN RAPPER SHADIA MANSOUR

In *Heavy Metal Islam* we discussed how hip hop became such an important and meaningful metaphor for the larger conflict between Palestinians and Israelis, particularly around the competition between DAM's Tamer Nafar and his one-time mentor, Subliminal. As with most other regions of the world, hip hop has continued to develop and expand in both Israeli and Palestinian societies. Much of the most innovative music came from the Palestinian side, but there were some important sonic innovations on the Israeli side as well, as we document below.

More broadly, most of the sonic and social innovation has remained on the Palestinian side, with a couple of contrary examples. If we start inside the Green Line in the Jewish Israeli rap scene, nationalist artists like Subliminal and his acolyte, Yoav Eliasi, aka Hatzel (The Shadow), continued to dominate the scene, with their collaboration "Tikva" ("Hope"), released in 2010, displaying a more nationalist streak. In a Facebook post in 2013 in response to a Palestinian killing an Israeli soldier, Subliminal declared, "Damn all those savages, we should burn the jails with all of them inside! And a second later we should destroy Jenin whose inhabitants gloat that they are the stronghold of terror against Israel. . . . And all the lefties who hate what I wrote here—kill yourselves already!" The Shadow organized violent counterdemonstrations at anti–Gaza War rallies in 2014. The next year, after an off-duty soldier sent him the ID of a left-wing demonstrator that he had illegally obtained at a rally, the Shadow doxxed the protester on his page, leading to fifty thousand views and numerous death threats against the protester, whose identity and address were shared with his followers.

As a *Haaretz* profile of the Shadow in 2016 explained, after burning through his money in true rock star style by 2011 and going bankrupt, he reinvented himself as a social media force largely through a constant stream of incendiary posts on Facebook that attacked left-wing Israelis and Palestinians in equal measure. In short, the Shadow became the avatar of the emerging ultrarightist generation of Israeli youth, who by the end of the decade would become the dominant trend in Israeli society (in the national elections in 2019, young Israeli Jews favored Prime Minister Netanyahu by upward of 60 percent). Not surprisingly, the Shadow joined the Likud Party in 2016.

The interpenetration of anti-Palestinian/Arab nationalism and hip hop was epitomized by Subliminal's performance at a rally to support an IDF soldier, Elor Azaria, who was on trial for shooting a bound Palestinian in the head, where supporters were carrying signs including "Kill them [Arabs] all!" The Shadow was one of the main boosters of the rally, but at the last minute was disinvited from performing because organizers felt that his "extreme" views would distract from its—in their minds, at least—nonpolitical message.

If politically the Zionist rap scene became more nationalist, musically there was not much aesthetic development, although Subliminal's stature allowed him to experiment with different genres. Thus on the track "Srotim" ("Scarred," released in 2017, thirteen million views and counting as of mid-2019), he raps, while dancing with children and a big band plays, about reconciliation between Israelis despite their differences:

> This is not a crazy world
> Everyone here is scratched
> And I'm scratched for life
> Scheming intrigues and biting
> Everyone here is scratched
> In the end, everything is transparent to God.
> Israelis are one tribe
> And despite the differences the faith in my heart is forever.

One year later he dropped the song "Ten lamusika ldaber" ("Let the Music Speak"), a reggaeton/Naija pop-inspired song with various African percussion and voices. It is in fact a brilliant piece of propaganda, if not a very original-sounding song (although it is original in an Israeli context, which hadn't seen the ubiquitous dancehall sound dominate the scene yet). Not only does the song contain many antiracist messages, including "There will be equality, there will be justice, there will be good here, regardless of background or color," but the video was filmed in Cape Town, South Africa. As Subliminal raps in the video, "I came to one of the most deprived and difficult places in the world, and I experienced a warm experience, love and modesty with music streaming through them." While he was singing about brotherly love, the people he was referring to were not Israel's Arab or Palestinian neighbors, or even the world as a whole, but rather yeshiva students, soldiers, and reservists. It was intra-Jewish Israeli racism that he was combatting. The prejudice against Palestinians remains untouched, a bait-and-switch discourse he's been deploying at least since his collaboration with Miri Ben-Ari in 2007, "Adon 'Olam, 'ad matai?" ("Oh Lord of the World, When Will It End?").

Artists like Subliminal and the Shadow might dominate the politics of Israeli Jewish hip hop, but there remains plenty of room for other rappers to continue and break through, albeit without much in the way of political content. This lack of politics isn't surprising, as protest music has been a rarity in Israel, and those artists over the years who have expressed deep criticisms

of the Zionist project have been, like the protest singer and accordion virtuoso Sara Alexander, unceremoniously forced into exile, or they, like Aviv
Geffen, have ultimately switched their politics from anti-Zionist to virulently
Zionist. One of the few voices since then to take a more assertive stance has
in fact been a female Orthodox rapper, Rinat Gutman, who after years spent
moving away from her religious roots with her music came back after a long
hiatus to release the song "Shirat Ha'asavim Hashotim" ("Son of the Weeds"),
an early Israeli #MeToo song that took on the sex abuse scandal among rabbis
in her community, which had just been exposed.

Hadag Nahash, a hip hop funk group well into its third decade, continues
to make danceable music with vaguely left-wing messages, while Sagol 59
remains one of the few mainstream Jewish Israeli rappers with a social justice
(if not overtly political) message. Relative newcomers like Tuna and Peled
have become rising stars in the last decade, with millions of views and listens
per song directly related to their musical talent, their humor, and the quality
of their videos. (If we think that there are roughly seven million Jewish
Israelis, versus tens of millions of Moroccans, Egyptians, etc., the number of
views is remarkable.) But perhaps the most interesting of the new breed of
mainstream rappers is Lukach, a phenom who was accidentally discovered by
Subliminal at a gig of his in 1999, when the then fifteen-year-old, fairly obese
young aficionado asked from the front row to join his idol onstage and pro-
ceeded to drop a rhyme (while managing to knock Subliminal off the stage)
that launched a career that has since expanded into TV and other media,
including a successful food show on Israeli TV. His piercing parodies of other
rappers, including Subliminal, earned him not just a huge following but the
attention of the next generation of rappers, including Nechi Nech, an
Ashkenazi rapper who started a group with two Ethiopian immigrant friends
(his stage name is Amharic for "white boy") and, after sending Lukach their
first demo, was quickly catapulted to fame.

ETHIOPIA RISING

While Nechi Nech saw his fame rise in the ensuing years, and even some
American Black Israelite rappers such as Blackwell garnered success, perhaps
the most important new scene to arise since 2008 was Ethiopian hip hop
(otherwise known as "Ethio-Israel" music). Groups like Axum released irre-
sistibly catchy songs like "Ma 'im ha-kesef?" ("What about the Money?") in

2008, "Cafe Shahor Hazak" ("Strong Black Coffee"), "KGC," "Shasha ve Shrulik," "Bilusa," "Surafel," and "Jeremy Cool Habash." Among the most talented of the rising Ethiopian generation are indie singer Ester Rada, female duo M-Ya, and rapper and model Eden Derrso, whose flows and grooves are easily the equal of any male MC in the country. Far more commercially successful is pop sensation Moti Taka, whose Afro-Mizrahi-inflected Hebrew pop songs—what *Haaretz* calls "Amharic soul" (epitomized by the track "Balbale," released in 2017)—rack up as many as twelve million views and counting.

These young Israelis, who in the words of sociologist David Ratner have been "marked as black" their entire lives and who have faced several generations of entrenched discrimination within society and against skin color, have quite naturally looked to American hip hop for inspiration for a situation that in many ways seemed very close to that of black Americans. Indeed, KGC in particular has cultivated a bad boy image that developed when they first started rehearsing in one of the country's ubiquitous bomb shelters as teenagers. But their social justice message is focused on self-help aimed at "black youth" rather than accusations against the broader, Ashkenazi-dominated society.

Equally important, they unabashedly employ symbols, colors, and even flags from Ethiopia as part of their visual markers. As Ethiopia develops further and these young artists become a bridge between the two countries, there is little doubt that they will become a unique bridge not just to Ethiopian society, where many have already returned, often with official Israeli delegations, to perform and learn about their heritage, but also to what they conceive of as an Afro-diasporic culture in which, perhaps more than anywhere else (including Israel), they feel at home (something Mark has seen visiting Addis Ababa). But what they won't be mediating at all is the Israeli-Palestinian or even Israeli-African migrant relationships. As was the case with Mizrahi and Sephardi Jews before them, rather than leading them to seek alliances with or even show vague sympathy for Palestinians, the racism against Ethiopians has led the vast majority of them to become that much more Zionist/nationalist. As Ratner explained to Mark after he returned from the 2019 PMX, "Finding solidarity with Palestinians is extremely rare; the vast majority [of Ethiopians] sympathizes with the right-wing ultranationalist worldview that portrays Palestinians as the ultimate 'other.' I guess Ethiopian rappers are no different; at least their lyrics or acts give no reason to think otherwise."

Even as they critique the systemic discrimination against them, the new generation of Ethiopian rappers "rarely connect the dots" to the system that affects them and Palestinians alike. A large share of Ethiopians have proved their Israeli Jewishness through their active and enthusiastic participation in the defining policy of that identity, the Occupation, a well-honed, time-tested strategy that has been adopted by "ethnic" European immigrants in the United States for centuries, and similarly by Mizrahi and Sephardic Jewish immigrants (that is, "Arab" and other "Middle Eastern" Jews) who have come to Israel since the 1950s. But to be fair, as Ratner points out, "What other local acts nowadays, whether Ethiopian or non- exhibit any form of such solidarity?" Indeed, to find such solidarity, you need to look outside of Israel, to scenes such as hip hop, EDM, and even metal, which are more open to supporting them. Even when protests reemerged in the spring of 2020 among Ethiopians around the international Black Lives Matter protests, they remained largely focused on international Jewish dynamics rather than the structural racism of the Occupation.

'48 HIP HOP AT THE EDGE

For the Palestinian Israeli, or "'48 Palestinian," hip hop artists we met in *Heavy Metal Islam,* the last ten years have been especially eventful. For their part DAM remained one of the most acclaimed crews on the international scene while also having an impact inside Israel and the Occupied Territories, which we describe below. Saz continued to focus on encouraging equality and coexistence through his music, similar to Jewish Israeli rapper Sagol 59 and the much newer Israeli and Palestinian duo Zoolod, although, not surprisingly, with far more emphasis on justice and equality versus merely coexistence.

At the same time, one of the most interesting and innovative groups ever to appear on the scene was formed not long before *Heavy Metal Islam* was published. System Ali comprised Palestinian, Jewish, and Uzbek Israelis, rapping not just in Arabic and Hebrew but in Russian as well. The group came together in a bomb shelter-turned-community center (and, during the J14 protests in 2011 [discussed below], a protest encampment) and saw its first performances as part of resistance to the announcement of home demolitions in the Palestinian neighborhood of Ajami. The band was also, from the start, un-afraid (although perhaps not always of one mind) both to claim a Palestinian identity and to encourage fans to imagine alternative perceptions of territory and identity by incorporating Palestinian flags into their iconography and rapping Arabic as well as Hebrew. A song from their album *Building the House Anew!* starts with the words: "Ihna 'arab 'arab an-nizam harab / Ihna 'arab 'arab kul ishi indarab / Ihna at-tabib at-tabib / Jorh falastin ma bteeb" ("We are Arabs, Arabs, the regime ran away / We are Arabs, Arabs, everything is fucked / We are the doctor, doctor / Palestine wound will never heal").

The contrast between System Ali's and Kobi Farhi's imaginations and experiences of Jaffa is hard to miss. As Israeli ethnomusicologist Nili Belkind describes it in her book *Music in Conflict: Palestine, Israel and the Politics of Aesthetic Production* (2020), "Unlike sanctioned multiculturalist musical narratives, System Ali's presentations do not aim for static 'harmonious' images of coexistence (there are no 'peace songs' in their repertoire), nor for sublimation of individualist voices, but rather, for grit, friction, energy and motion. The main theme that emerges out of their songs is an imaginary of 'home' that is eclectic, diverse and full of contradictions." The band itself is a kind of "borderland" performance, moving back and forth across identities and both territorial and discursive locales. But unlike in, for example, Mizrahi music, which uses the affect of Arabness to articulate a specifically Jewish and almost always explicitly Zionist identity, the affective power of System Ali is that it problematizes most every possible identity out there.

DAM has remained, however, among the most important voices in the Israeli and Palestinian hip hop scenes. Because of its ongoing relevance, the song "Born Here" was adopted for a public campaign for better services in Palestinian towns and neighborhoods. Drawing support from leading Jewish artists like Moni Moshonov and Aviv Geffen, it forced the Israeli government to build a bridge over the very train tracks depicted in the video for the song, thus ending the spate of killings of people forced to cross them. Unfortunately, the female lead singer on "Born Here," Abeer Zinati (who is the cousin of the DAM rappers Tamer and Suhel Nafar), had to drop out of the project and stop singing after she and Tamer received death threats from her family because of her singing.

This incident ultimately led DAM to tackle women's oppression in their community, most notably with the collaboration with Haifa-based singer Amal Murkus titled "Law arju' bil-zaman" ("If I Could Go Back in Time"), one of their most powerful songs. Two prominent diaspora Palestinian professors, Lila Abu Lughod and Maya Makdisi, took issue with the song and video, accusing the band of being "seduced" by the Western stereotypical discourse on honor killings and the oppression of women more broadly in Muslim societies. The band, however, was quick to respond, declaring in a text published on the Jadaliyya.com website (the same location as the original article) that "For the last two years, we have witnessed political revolution and upheaval in the Arab world. It is for many of us perhaps the greatest historical moment we have ever experienced. This is the moment when we should dispense with concerns over how we may be read (particularly by the West). . . . We see 'If I Could Go Back in Time,' as one effort of many in these momentous times." Most important, DAM's members continued, "We are part of a new artistic movement in Palestine that is secure enough to take on occupation and domestic violence, racism and sexism. We will not shy away from engaging our society's taboos."

It wasn't just Palestinian Israeli artists who saw increased success at that time. That same year, the documentary *Slingshot Hip Hop* was released by filmmaker Jackie Salloum. A Sundance selection and international hit, the film put Palestinian hip hop on the world music map, featuring not just DAM and Abeer, but also several Akka-based groups and, perhaps most powerfully, Gaza-based artists like Palestinian Rapperz and Ibrahim. What in retrospect is most telling about the film was strong cultural and musical connections between Palestinian artists on both sides of the Green Line and the common desire to fight the Occupation, highlighting the Israeli attempts to separate them, which have occurred for a long time and still continue.

MUSIC AND SOCIAL (IN)JUSTICE

The opportunity for a fundamental change in Israeli cultural politics arrived with the outbreak of the "social justice" protests on July 14, 2011, four months after the successful toppling of Mubarak in Egypt and as the Arab uprisings were spreading across the region. The "J14" protests were clearly and admittedly inspired by the uprisings, which led organizers to erect a tent city on Rothschild Boulevard in Tel Aviv in emulation of the tent city of Tahrir. Almost from the start, however, it was clear that the largely Jewish Israeli organizers of the protest movement, backed by liberal Zionist groups in Israel and internationally, had no intention of addressing the underlying political issues tied to the unending Occupation that were clearly at the root of the crisis. Not surprisingly, the apolitical focus on housing prices and diminished public services was easily parried by the government, which offered enough promises and funding addressing the complaints of the protesters, who were largely young students, to diffuse the protests before the year was out. When organizers tried to reestablish the tent city a year later, they were quickly arrested and the movement fizzled. Few artists participated in any significant way, likely because the self-generated energy of the movement was never as strong as initial celebratory accounts indicated.

A more serious challenge to the status quo was growing in this period within Palestinian youth culture on the "occupied" side of the Green Line. Already in early 2010 in Gaza, one of the ur-texts of the Arab Spring era was released by a new group calling itself Gaza Youth Breaks Out, or GYBO. Utterly frustrated by the unending Israeli siege, Hamas's rampant violence, oppression, and corruption, and the complicity of the international community at so many levels, their manifesto begins with a scream: "Fuck Hamas. Fuck Israel. Fuck Fatah. Fuck UN. Fuck UNWRA. Fuck USA!" (the verb was written originally in English because the Arabic equivalent does not have anything close to the power and anger of the English word). It ends by declaring. "We do not want to hate, we do not want to feel all of these feelings, we do not want to be victims anymore."

The GYBO manifesto was, in Mark's view, the first salvo in a generational war for independence that pushed its way into world consciousness not long after its appearance with the uprisings in Tunisia and Egypt. It is an act of extreme will by young people who had nothing left to lose, and its poetic meter and naked eloquence are a work of art as powerful as any produced during revolutionary times in the last half-century or more. Even visiting Gaza months later after spending time in Egypt, Bahrain, Tunisia, and other locations of the Arab uprisings, it was clear that this text, as well as the anger it reflected, was a seminal moment in the coming of age of the new generation of Arab activists.

Unfortunately, the energy generated by GYBO's manifesto was dissipated by the kidnapping and brutal murder of Italian activist Vittorio Arrigoni by a breakaway radical religious cell. Vik, as he was known to everyone, had spent the previous three years in Gaza chronicling the suffering of the people of the Strip, creating the Guerrilla Radio website and publishing one of the most powerful eyewitness accounts of the Israeli invasion of 2008–09, titled *Restiamo Umani* (*Gaza: Stay Human* in English). During this time he become a dear friend and inspiration to young Gazan rappers, many of whom were also involved in GYBO; so it was not surprising that his senseless murder produced some of the most powerful music of the Strip in the last decade.

In particular, the DARG Team crew recorded the song "Onadekom" ("Calling You"), in which members apologized to him for his murder and declared that they wouldn't veer from the path he showed them.

The West Bank's most powerful institution of cultural resistance against the Occupation, the Jenin Freedom Theater, suffered a similarly terrible blow when its founder, Juliano Mer-Khamis, was gunned down outside the theater a week and a half before Arrigoni was killed. A well-known half-Jewish, half-Palestinian actor and director of DAM's "Born Here," Juliano (as he was known to everyone) was the kind of liminal and provocative figure whose undying devotion to freedom for young Palestinians put him, like Vik, at odds not merely with Israel but equally with powerful forces inside Palestinian society.

Even as Israel imposed a permanent closure on the checkpoints out of Gaza, the two years between Mubarak's ouster and the coup of 2013 saw the Egyptian military allow far more regular and open movement through its border at Rafah. Many of GYBO's leaders and even more musical artists left Gaza for Egypt and elsewhere in the Arab world and Europe. Of those, a large share was able to leave through invitations to various meetings, tours, and conferences across the region and in Europe, where they were asked to discuss the implications and future of the "Arab Spring," and to participate in various musical workshops and collaborations with other Arab and European artists. Rapper Muhammad Antar made his way to Cairo in 2014, where he remained, living precariously without papers until obtaining a humanitarian visa for Turkey in 2019.

Antar was clearly one of the most talented rappers in the Strip when he and Mark first met in Gaza in June 2011. Sitting along the sea at one of the few open restaurants that day with a group of GYBO activists, he and fellow rapper Ahmed Rezeq explained that hip hop and activism could not but go together at a moment when young Gazans were taking the lead in calling bullshit on all the institutions involved in their oppression. "I can't go to the university, I have nothing except my words," Ahmed said, to which Antar elaborated, "Art is crucial because it leads people to the truth. It shows them how we suffer and how much we struggle, that we are human." Even if a few lucky artists and activists could get out of Gaza, most of their peers remained trapped, "despite doing everything we could to try and create our lives."

Gaza is a place of incredible improvisation—electricity, cars, building materials, music, and, yes, rockets, are all created out of seemingly nothing. So it's not surprising that well past midnight on a warm summer night, the Strip's best rappers might decide to head to the beach, where, in the cover of darkness, with smaller crowds and less heat, they can spend a few hours talking, laughing, and rapping on the sand while smoking shishas and eating kebab. To say that you haven't really heard Arab hip hop till you've heard it at 3 AM on a Gazan beach might sound like a pseudo-cliché, but in fact it's the truth—albeit, sadly, a very partial one. With the sounds of the waves breaking on the shore providing the tempo, the rhymes feel even more rooted in the sands of this place, like the vegetation that improbably explodes from the sands. But the laughter of the children playing in the middle of the night, whose only sense of freedom comes in the dark when the Israeli navy boats and the immiseration of their lives are out of sight, makes sure the pain of Gaza is never out of mind.

Antar is not just an artist, but a gay artist who was just coming out to himself and his closest friends when he and Mark first met in mid-2011, an extremely dangerous act because of the obvious aversion Hamas and even ordinary Gazans would have for a secular gay rapper working with a new youth organization that had just told it to go fuck itself. And indeed, not long after he and Mark first met Antar was arrested by Hamas for the first of many times. "I was treated like one of the most dangerous criminals in the city, and they investigated me as if I were a spy!!!" he explained. Recalling his experience to Mark several years later in Cairo, he explained,

Hamas [asked] why I am dressing this way and who my friends are and how we got girls in the group and if I have sex with them. They asked about my family's history of working with Fatah, and said that there was an investigation about my sexuality, showing me a list of guys and asking which one of them I had sex with. After a short break the monitoring started again, now focused on the music, my lyrics and my network. This was part of a broader attack on the whole hip hop scene in 2010.

After I traveled abroad the first time they arrested me and tried to force me to tell them what I'd done and whom I'd met, etc. I was being regularly beaten in this period. I remember one time, after an Italian film crew came to interview me on my roof in 2013, they arrested me again as a spy, claiming the crew were in fact Israeli spies using the interview as an excuse to take up close images of the area. . . . They even took my passport and put me on a blacklist for traveling; but ultimately I got a new passport thanks to connections and entered Egypt.

Unfortunately, Antar's life in Egypt was little better than in Gaza, especially as it coincided with the military coup and the constant smearing of Palestinians by the new regime.

The situation was even harder in Egypt by myself, with almost no ability to break into the local hip hop scene despite trying for several years, and having a very hard time even to find occasional work. . . . When you have artists like [actor-turned-rapper] Mekki doing kids' songs during Ramadan boasting of all the money he has, you know we're in a bad place. . . . So I held my pen and paper again and realized that art and music are the only things I know how to do, and started writing again. I realized that Palestine, Gaza and the revolution are a part of me, and my lyrics changed from just Palestinian-related topics to also for people everywhere looking for peace in this crazy world, especially who had to leave their own country and find themselves out somewhere, and find peace and safety first.

PERFORMANCE AS ACTIVISM

One of the key issues in this book has been the relationship between music and activism across the region for the young artists and fans who perform and enjoy the music, and nowhere has the relationship between music and activism been more direct in the region than in Palestine/Israel. Music is by no means the only artistic medium that has played an important role in the two societies, but this is particularly so in Palestinian culture and politics. Art, poetry, dance, and film have all long taken on foundational political themes in each community—what the Jenin Freedom Theater, one of the most important front-line Palestinian cultural organizations, has described as "creative resistance" and "resistance through art."

Collaboration with international supporters, particularly in the arts, has been a very important component of solidarity and the possibilities of resistance and *summud,* or remaining steadfast on the land despite all the attempts to uproot them. While the artistic initiative and aesthetics have always been unmistakably Palestinian, the financial, political, and diplomatic support and solidarity offered by foreign activists, organizations, and in a few cases governments helped enable a local cultural sector to not just survive but thrive, even under the most adverse conditions. Among the most recent examples of this collaboration has been the Walled Off Hotel in Bethlehem, created by a group of Palestinian and international artists and activists including Brian Eno and the artist Bansky. The hotel's location across the street from one of the largest and highest concrete sections of the Apartheid Wall is the reason for the name, an obvious pun on the Waldorf-Astoria Hotel, which has long been known as the epitome of luxury in New York.

But whereas the Waldorf had million-dollar views of Park Avenue, the Walled Off Hotel is billed as the hotel "with the worst view in the world," a perfect stage for revealing not just the horror and insanity and absurdities of the Occupation but beautiful possibilities for a very different future. Through the artwork provided by Bansky and local Palestinian artists, and the recording of international musical collaborations there, the hotel has become a wonderful example of how creative resistance can, at least in certain spaces and for certain periods, hold the line against even the most powerful forms of colonial power.

The collaboration that brought the Walled Off Hotel to fruition was also involved in the creation of PMX. Conceived, or so the preferred origin story at each introductory dinner tells it, after a night of Ramallah drinking involving Rami Younis, Martin Goldschmidt, DAM's Mahmoud Jrere, and Khalas's Abed Hathout, the idea of PMX has from the start been twofold: bring leading European and American music industry professionals to Ramallah to be introduced to the best Palestinian musical talent in the Occupied Territories and among Palestinian citizens of Israel, with the goal of both making connections that could lead to great exposure, provide professional education through panels and listening sessions, and distribute their music and invitations to perform abroad, while, at the same time, help educate the industry about the realities of the Occupation and in so doing increase understanding of and, it's hoped, sympathy not just for Palestinians broadly but for nonviolent strategies of solidarity and resistance, including BDS.

The first thing you notice when you meet the organizers is that almost to a person the Palestinian ones are in fact Israeli citizens, almost all from Haifa and Akka. This makes sense on two fronts. First, Palestinian citizens of Israel have a lot more mobility than residents of the Occupied Territories (outside of the dwindling number with Jerusalem IDs), which is crucial in order to successfully organize and pull off such a big festival. Equally important, however, the presence of Israeli, or '48, Palestinians in Ramallah and their close coordination and collaboration with their compatriots from the Occupied Territories reinforce the claim—already alluded to above—that Palestinians on both sides of the Green Line constitute one indivisible community. Indeed, "We are artists [all] under occupation," DAM's Mahmoud Jrere put it in a promo for PMX; his identification with his compatriots across the Green Line couldn't have been clearer.

Over three years PMX more than doubled the number of international delegates attending, averaging over fifteen hundred people per night in year three, despite the violence of the Gaza conflict and obvious surveillance by Israeli intelligence, which included pulling delegates off planes to question them before arrival, which led to a purposefully low-key public campaign for the festival. If the musical highlight of the first edition was Khalas's killer reunion show, the second edition had more star appeal as well as political poignancy. The star in question was celebrated British musical artist and producer Brian Eno, who along with Roger Waters has long been among the most powerful and public supporters of Palestinians in the United Kingdom and larger European music scenes.

It was quite a surprise to see Eno at PMX because only months earlier he did the Walled Off Hotel collaboration remotely from London, as it was felt that Israel, which controls all the entrances into the West Bank, wouldn't let him into the country if he tried to come because of his well-known advocacy of BDS. As it turned out, Eno came in on his own, with no fanfare and not even a single question at Ben Gurion airport, a pleasant surprise, if not shock, to PMX organizers.

But there he was, and with his presence the importance of PMX as both a gateway to the elite of the music industry and a vehicle to share the Palestinian experience of Occupation couldn't have been clearer. His presence was nearly eclipsed, however, by Lebanese alternative rock and soul diva Yasmine Hamdan. It's hard to overstate what a thrill it was for Palestinians in the West Bank to see Hamdan in their midst. As a Lebanese artist, it's more or less impossible for her to travel to the Occupied Territories, but thanks to her French passport she was—like Eno—allowed in by Israel.

Without a doubt, Hamdan's entrance was the grandest of any artist at the Expo, involving five cameras surrounding her and her mother as she regally walked through the hotel lobby to the restaurant where most of the delegates and artists were sitting after the first night's dinner, in an outfit and makeup that were made for a red carpet, and a diva's aura that was in complete contrast to the more laid-back attitude of the Expo as a whole. But from a media perspective, Hamdan's presence, along with Eno's, was a publicity coup of the highest order.

Aside from Eno's collaboration with Trio Joubran (the three brothers who all are virtuosi 'oud players), the reunion of the seminal Palestinian electro-sha'bi group Ministry of Dubkey, one of the pioneers of Arab-flavored EDM (their name is a direct shout-out to the seminal EDM group Ministry of Sound), also marked a historic moment in Palestinian popular music whose importance was best summed up by Eno during an afternoon panel on the second day:

> This is going to be a question we will deal with many times as popular pressure builds up to support Palestinians: The Walled Off Hotel was created in the context of Trump and [Theresa] May and we are constantly being told the most important thing is to divide [and separate] people. But this project celebrates exactly the opposite. What happens if we bring people together and see what happens when they meet. Make the best of differences, because they are the root of creativity. It's when they crash together that new ideas are born. The sterility of walls is what this project is against.

Eno well summarized perhaps the most important element of the practice of "solidarity" that artists and activists around the world have shown with Palestinians. It's not about dividing; it's about bringing people together. If the participants in the Walled Off Hotel music project, hardly any of whom had ever met before their collaborations, were "eating off the same plates" after twenty-four hours of working together for what became the Block 9 Creative Retreat Palestine project, that camaraderie carried over to PMX, giving the second edition an aura and buzz that made it clear to attendees that they were not merely at a festival but participating in a moment of cultural—and, through it, political—transformation.

PMX 2018 was a "happening" not only because of the dozens of foreign delegates and musical dignitaries in attendance, but even more so because so many of the most important contemporary Palestinian musical artists were there. Boikutt from Ramallah Underground, one of the seminal global "sound catching" hip hop artists, did an incredible improvisational DJ set, which highlighted the presence of other amazing DJs, especially women like Sama' Abdulhadi (aka Skywalker) and multi-instrumentalist Rasha Nahas, who's at the helm of an up-and-coming generation of experimental trip hop artists like Moody (who along with Rasha relocated to Berlin in 2019). What is striking about all these artists is not just their talent but their originality; none could easily be placed into an obvious genre or clique, the way one could fairly easily place most artists you might be exposed to in Cairo or Beirut. It was as if, given the small size of the Palestinian scene on both sides of the Green Line, each of these artists constituted an entire subgenre on their own.

Even more powerful than the presence of so many great acts was the absence, at least in person, of two of Gaza's most important groups, MC Gaza

I got sick and tired

FIGURE 17. MC Gaza, still from video for "We Didn't Fear the Snipers," 2018.

and Watar Band. Both bands, who've achieved a measure of international renown in the last decade, were prohibited by Israel from leaving the Strip to come to Ramallah for PMX, no doubt in good measure because of the intense protests (and Israeli violence) associated with the Great March of Return then occurring in Gaza. Instead, both groups sent videos to be played for the crowd. MC Gaza's was particularly powerful. Titled "Koshok" (Arabic for the tires that were ubiquitously burned during the protests, as shown in the video), the song is a powerful attack on the violence of Israel's response to the protests; it features a relatively slow groove punctuated by sharp and stabbing synth riffs that sound like sirens and the sounds of the protests. Over this purposeful cacophony, MC Gaza delivers a shockingly mellow rap: "Who started first? He occupied me and confronted me. He thinks the blood will go in vain," he begins, rapping from the front lines of the protests and fighting, the video interspersed with images and footage of bloodied protesters and young men hurling sling shots into the clouds of tear gas toward the unseen enemy far in the distance across the separation barrier. Indeed, filmed with a drone in the midst of the protests and fighting while MC Gaza rapped for his life next to the field of battle, the images were more important than the words. After DAM's "Min Irhabi" ("Who's the

Terrorist?") and "Born Here," "Koshok" is surely among the most powerful audiovisual testaments to the violence and struggles associated with the Occupation imaginable. And it's not just about the fire and brimstone of direct conflict.

For its part, Watar Band's video was a far mellower, featuring them playing acoustic instruments on a rooftop that could be taken for any seaside location on the Mediterranean. With a sound reminiscent of Egypt's Eskenderella or Cairokee, Watar Band projects the future possibility of a Gaza Strip that has escaped the hell of interminable conflict and siege and become a place of beauty and normalcy. Unfortunately, as they are the first to admit, that vision is a very long way off.

The 2019 edition of PMX didn't have quite the star wattage without Brian Eno, Yasmine Hamdan, and the Trio Joubran, but it did have Sepultura drummer Igor Cavalera, who was clearly impressed by the quality and dedication as well as courage of the dozens of artists he saw perform. Most of the Palestinian artists who performed were repeat performers from the first or second edition of the Expo. There was palpable tension in the lead-up to the first day as Israel had once again been attacking Gazan protesters and, more troublingly in the immediate sense, had in the week before PMX kidnapped a group of student activists from Birzeit University, shot dead a Palestinian at the Qalandiya crossing outside Ramallah, and staged several raids inside the city. With the history of closing down Palestinian cultural events, there was every reason to suspect a similar fate would await PMX in 2020, especially after many foreign delegates were questioned at length on the way to Tel Aviv. (No one could figure out how delegates, whose names weren't publicly announced, were discovered, but it was clear that somehow the Israelis had hacked or otherwise penetrated their computers.)

There were numerous standouts at the 2019 edition of PMX. Young experimental electronic musicians like Rasha and Moody showed increasing maturity and stage presence during their sets. Veterans like DAM showcased new members and materials, which in their case meant singer Maysa Daw, who'd replaced Suhel Nafar (who'd left DAM to head up Spotify's Middle East division), stealing the show with her powerful voice and command of the stage (no doubt by design, given DAM members Tamer Nafar and Mahmoud Jrere's well-known proclivity to promote women artists and issues).

But for most delegates there were two standouts among the several dozen artists. The first was Bashar Murad, one of the first, if not the only, (relatively) openly gay musical artists in the Arab/Muslim world, whose highly polished

Arab pop sound and out and open queer identity (and fashion sense) blew everyone away. For purely musical edge, however, no one came close to Haifa-based bass player, OG metalhead, and composer Raymond Haddad, who did a half-hour-long improvisational EDM set with nothing but a dozen or so modular synths linked together with dozens of patch cables. Standing amid the delegates to the side of the stage, one could see their forty-, fifty-, and sixty-something faces light up at the old school artistry displayed by one of Palestine/Israel's most talented musicians, and so it wasn't surprising when Raymond was mobbed by business cards and offers to support him while he walked off the stage.

Saz's set was also among the most musically explosive sets of the 2019 PMX, while opening act rapper Dave Kirreh also demonstrated the power of contemporary Palestinian hip hop. After a decade spent honing has craft through numerous ups and downs, from relationships to managers to stardom on his own TV show, Saz had reached a level of professionalism that was reflected in his stage show, which featured a full band and enough sweat to make James Brown proud. Hanging out in the days before his show, he and Mark talked about his evolution since they first met almost fifteen years earlier. As he put it, "Mark, I've been through so much and made and lost so much, I had to learn and grow up, even as the politics got worse. . . . In fact, I also learned how not to put too much politics into the music, so it can speak for itself." Kirreh also shone through with a far more pop-oriented style mixing singing and rapping, with a tight and powerful band on his hit songs like "Aysheen" ("Living").

But for audacity and hope the most inspiring and politically important artists were the Gazan trio of bands, Tybo, Sol Band, and Watar Band. None of the bands was complete; the Israelis seemed to choose who wasn't allowed out in order to prevent one full band from getting to Ramallah, but with the members who made it and two days of intense rehearsals, all three bands managed to pull off three exciting shows. Night two featured two of the groups, Tybo and Sol Band, and they were both a treat to watch and listen to, made all the more poignant by the ongoing protests and violence eighty-two kilometers to the southwest in Gaza.

Tybo got things going with a powerhouse medley of metal covers mixed with sha'bi grooves, which began with Rage Against the Machine's "Wake Up!," "Rock Me Like a Hurricane," and even "The Final Countdown," with the crowd switching effortlessly within the performance between headbanging with delight to the metal and dabke'ing to the local grooves. If there were an award for "Palestine's greatest garage band," surely Tybo, the youngest of

FIGURE 18. Palestinian-Israeli rapper Saz, publicity photo from 2019. Photo by Moshiko Tishler.

the three bands, would win it hands down. Indeed, what made for likely the most heartwarming experience of any PMX was listening to their music, and feeling their evident joy (clear from their smiles as they lived the dream of finally playing outside Gaza without either Hamas or Israel to fuck every-thing up), first, in not performing in front of Hamas security agents ("It's our first time ever not performing in front of Hamas!" one member exclaimed during their last rehearsal) and, second, in trying to bridge iconic rock songs of a bygone era with Arabic grooves.

Sol Band was created amid the Israeli offensive on Gaza in 2012 with the goal of using music to lift the spirit of beleaguered Gazans. In contrast to Hamas's image of Gaza as a conservative space that rejects Western culture, the band specifically brings together Western and Arab styles. No doubt this is one reason that the band has long had problems getting permits to perform in Gaza, and that they were so excited to play outside Hamas's clutches for the first time. Indeed, the situation became untenable enough that the band relocated to Istanbul after the 2019 edition, and have been making a living doing weddings and other shows ever since.

The standout player of Tybo and Sol Band was eighteen-year-old multi-instrumentalist Mohammed Shoman (who even played with Watar Band on the final night as well). One of the few members of any of the bands to have spent significant time outside Gaza, Mohammed knew Ramallah well as he'd spent several years studying at the Edward Said Conservatory, where he developed the skills of a young John Paul Jones. (Although his main instrument is keyboards, for these shows he played guitar and bass and is studying composition.) Mohammed is a big fan of metal and all styles of music. But as he explained to Mark at the hotel after the first show, it's still very hard to play any kind of nontraditional music in Gaza. In fact, Tybo is presently the only rock band in all of Gaza, and because of Hamas's tight grip on the Strip, it's almost impossible to obtain permission to perform in the few venues that regularly allow music. Mohammed was only guesting for Tybo on guitar because the Israelis had refused permission for their regular guitar player to travel. He felt far more at home playing bass (as most keyboard players do) with Sol Band's more sophisticated songs.

Despite the ad hoc nature of the bands, all the performances on the first night were solid and even inspiring, as it should be, given that the Expo was able to choose the top twenty out of almost two hundred submissions. Indeed, it was clear that PMX had quickly succeeded in becoming *the* showcase of the best of Palestinian contemporary music. The morning of the third day, a delegation of attendees at the Expo made the half-hour trip from Ramallah to Nabi Saleh to visit the family of Ahed Tamimi, the young activist who was jailed by Israel for physically attacking soldiers who'd invaded her house. Even the delegates like UK music industry icon Martin Goldschmidt, one of the founders of PMX, were shocked at what they experienced in Nabi Saleh, as family members, including Ahed and her cousin Janna Jihad (considered one of the world's youngest journalists), showed videos of the violence visited on their village and their family by Israeli Occupation forces. Despite having years of experience in Palestine, Martin was particularly "stunned" (as he put it) by what he saw. Afterward he explained that the visit affirmed his belief that "music is the Palestinians' secret weapon" because it could be used to bring people to places like Nabi Saleh, where they experience the Occupation in a way that bulldozes even the most deeply held beliefs about Israel.

It took Ahed's father Bassem (who the previous year had met with Brian Eno at PMX while Ahed and her mother were still in prison) nearly five minutes to list all the shootings, maiming, kidnapping, and killing his immediate family has endured, made all the more real by the presence of his son, Mohammed, who was sporting a cast on his right arm, broken during a recent Israeli invasion of their house when the tear gas fired into it became so suffocating that he had to break and jump out of the upstairs window to survive. But Bassem and Ahed agreed with Martin on the role of music in their struggle: "It's a weapon," he explained as he talked about the festival that he hopes to organize in the summer to highlight the ongoing attacks now that the weekly protests have been stopped. "Music and culture are the most powerful way to resist."

The final night of PMX 2019 was more subdued than that of the second year, in good measure because of ongoing Israeli "operations" around Ramallah, which Mark and several other participants ran into not far from the festival hotel the night before. But the performances were still in top form, none more so than Watar Band, the most professional of the three bands, having performed outside Gaza, at a TEDx at Jerusalem's al-Quds University, in Ramallah, and on a European tour (with Palestinian Rapperz's Ayman Mghames). Their appearance was especially poignant for anyone who was present for their forced remote appearance the previous year. When viewed against bands like Egypt's Eskenderella, Massar Egbari, and Cairokee and Mashrou' Leila from Lebanon, it's clear that Watar Band, along with similar indie-rock fusion bands in the West Bank and Occupied Golan Heights like TootArd and ElContainer, has more than enough talent to become staples of the world pop circuit if given half a chance. Indeed, their four-song original set was one of the most powerful of the entire Expo, but half a year later, speaking with Mohammed Shomran in Gaza, he explained that since then there were almost no opportunities to perform at home. His main group, Sol Band, was trying to get authorized to travel again to the West Bank through UNESCO, from where they hope to make it to Istanbul for as long as they could get a visa to meet other artists, do some shows, and perhaps record.

But the political highlight of the day was clearly DAM's performance closing the show and the Expo. The crowd was surely primed for the performance, and as Tamer, Mahmoud, and Maysa took the stage, everything seemed set for a great show, as the crowd in front was chanting Tamer's name. Or so it sounded at first listen. Then it became clear that in fact they weren't chanting for Tamer; they were chanting *at* him. A group of young "'48" fans had come, equipped with signs, to protest his recording of a video earlier that week in which he had urged Palestinian citizens of Israel to vote in the elections scheduled for the next week. This was a controversial move that resulted in international coverage, including in the *New York Times* and the *Guardian,* and there was a lot of opposition among his natural consistency inside Israel, who felt that the system was so stacked against Palestinians that they no longer saw a point to electoral politics (for most West Bank and Gaza Palestinians, the debate was meaningless). For Tamer, however, the alternative to not voting could well be mass expulsion if the worst elements of the Jewish Right took power in Israel. As he put it in the song, voting would at least enable him to "sing to the boycotters, rather than talk to them in the transfer trucks."

As if to prove the point—it's not clear whose point, but it was pertinent to both sides—just as DAM took the stage news alerts started appearing on people's smart phones that Netanyahu had announced he would annex the West Bank if reelected. As DAM broke into a new track featuring Maysa on a powerful vocal, a dozen or so '48 Palestinian fans held up their signs and chanted "Yuskut Tatbi'a!" ("Down with normalization!"), a play on the ubiquitous phrase "yuskut hukm al-'askar" ("Down with military rule!") during the Arab uprisings. After their set, Maysa, who's also an Israeli citizen, engaged them in a heated discussion by the side of the stage about whether PMX was the place for such a protest, but what was clear was that, even at the most Palestinian-focused cultural event possible, Israeli politics still intruded; such is the overwhelming imbalance in power between the two sides.

DANCING THE NIGHT ELECTRIC

Out of the many stories that have arisen through PMX, the maturation of the Palestinian industry and its openness to the world are surely one of the most important. But equally important to anyone who's observed the Occupation from the front lines is the total absence of even a single Jewish Israeli artist supporting their Palestinian counterparts. This is in stark contrast to

American and South African freedom struggles, where white artists played important roles in supporting and magnifying the black voices for justice and equality. With or without them, however, each successful event like the Palestine Music Expo or Palfest, the equally entertaining literary festival that occurred in 2019 on the heels of PMX, brings the Palestinian struggle for freedom and justice one step closer to full recognition and acceptance in the global public sphere. Here it's worth noting that while in a country like Morocco—as discussed in chapter 1—the government has been engaged in a decade-long process of "festivalizing dissent," in the more straightforward colonial conditions of Palestine art remains largely impossible to coopt or defang by the occupying power, which is why there has been so much violence and repression against Palestinian artists of all kinds over the decades.

Thinking about the lack of metal in Palestinian society, Nadeem Karkabi ruminated for a minute before exclaiming, "How can you punk your own culture if you haven't had your traditional music recognized?" In that sense, rather than rock or even hip hop, for a culture so steeped and so politically invested in dance and rhythm, music becomes a natural expression and development of that tradition, one that brings the kind of joy that everyone from Bassem Tamimi to Brian Eno reminds us is absolutely essential to surviving the nightmare of unending occupation and colonization without losing one's humanity and even soul.

But it's not the Dabke, perhaps *the* cultural symbol of Palestinian identity, that defines the night for young Palestinians; rather it's techno, EDM, and electro-sha'bi. For EDM artists and DJ Sama', who was one of the highlights of the first two years of PMX, EDM's existence is nothing short of miraculous. As one of the first DJs of the genre in the West Bank (and the first but no longer only female one), her set in 2018 for the famed Boiler Room series is one of the most viewed ever, with just shy of three million views and counting. She has picked up the mantle from artists, like Ramallah Underground and Tashweesh, who have struggled to prevent the "erasure of Palestinian history" (as Ramallah Underground and Tashweesh founder Muqata'a put it), by the Occupation and Israel's appropriation of every possible element of Palestinian identity and culture.

While it will likely remain among the most marginalized styles in a marginalized scene, metal might yet have a future in Palestine. One of the highlights for me of PMX 2019 was the performance by Beit Sahour guitarist and bassist Usama Allati, one of the premier talents in the Palestinian music scene, with singer and rapper David Kirreh. With his Gibson Flying V and goatee, never mind distorted guitar sound, immediately differentiating him from most other musicians at PMX, Usama is the embodiment of Palestinian metal, such as it is. As we sat in the lobby of the Park Grand hotel after the second evening of the Expo, sweat still dripping from his closely cut head, he gave me his take on the history and future of metal in Palestinian music, which continued over the next twenty-four hours via WhatsApp and phone conversations. Starting off with a broad panorama of popular music, he explained that "in Palestine metal hasn't always been a popular genre; the most popular genres have been Western and Arabic pop, Latin and flamenco, folk and disco stuff. After the nineties rock, blues, jazz, and reggae started developing and having their way into the Palestinian community." But metal was never totally absent. "Step by step and through rock and blues the upcoming generations of musicians started approaching metal, knowing that Arab communities don't generally appreciate or stand loud and aggressive music. It was in the [new] millennium that old school rock, hard rock, and some metal genres started appearing in the community through fashion and musicians who began to play it publicly." He explained:

> Metal bands arose but the majority of them faded away because metal didn't have enough of an audience like the other genres. But after 2005 the metal scene got a bit stronger due to technology and the Internet. So people started being open more and more to the loud and aggressive-sounding genres like rock and metal. Nowadays, the presence of metal is very strong among Palestinian youth but only through listening and fashion. Sadly, bands have come and gone because metal still doesn't have the needed audience or the venues. Musicians who play metal try to practice it through solo projects and collaborations rather than through bands, since the musical techniques and nature of solos that most bands [pursue don't] need the aggression and speed that characterizes metal.

From his performance with David Kirreh, it was clear that he was speaking from experience. But this is clearly not a hardship for him to stretch beyond his metal roots. A beautiful collaboration in 2017 with Lina Sleibi featuring him on a six-string bass covering Nancy Ajram's "3am Bet3alla2 Feek" (literally, "I'm Getting Attached to You," also known as "Derniere Dance" / "Last Dance") has over 1.5 million views on YouTube alone.

Usama sees a future for metal, as long as Palestinian listeners can learn to appreciate more aggressive music and, as important, as long as venues and engineers can learn to mix the sound and not ruin it with too many effects or incompetent mixes. For him metal doesn't have to be political at all, but no matter how you conceive of it, it's clear that ultimately metal will become indigenized in the soil of Palestine simply because more than most any place on Earth, their lives remain, for lack of a better word, "metal" to the core.

ANOTHER YEAR, ANOTHER INVASION, ANOTHER SINGER

As this book was being edited, in early May 2021, a new round of violence erupted between Israel and Hamas after Israeli Occupation forces brutally cracked down on protesters against ongoing Israeli evictions in the East Jerusalem neighborhood of Sheikh Jarrah. As the resistance escalated Israel occupied the Haram al-Sharif/Temple Mount, which led Hamas to threaten retaliation if soldiers weren't removed, at which point rockets began to be fired into Israel and Israel responded with its usual large-scale bombing of Gaza. What made this episode unique was that Palestinian citizens of Israel staged strong protests in support of their compatriots across the Green Line, and even attacked Jews and Jewish property, which led to violent Jewish mobs rampaging through mixed and Palestinian neighborhoods in towns like Jaffa, Lydda, Ramla, and Akka, all of which overshadowed the air war between Hamas and the IDF: Hamas launched thousands of rockets from Gaza that killed half a dozen Israelis, and Israel launched massive strikes that killed several hundreds Palestinians and made thousands more homeless.

We began this chapter with Orphaned Land's Kobi Farhi ruminating about performing in the Arab world and how his relationship to Jaffa and its Arab heritage and inhabitants shaped his beliefs as well as music. So it wasn't surprising that many fans, especially Palestinian and Arab fans, anticipated that he or other members of the band would put out a statement when fighting erupted, especially since his home neighborhood of Jaffa had suffered some of the worst intercommunal violence inside Israel. That statement came in a public Facebook post on May 13, in which Kobi explained to OL fans that, while many fans were asking how he and the band were doing and wishing them well, other comments "do not ask if we are safe at all. People just contacting to show their disappointment from us, as if we are our government/army/police/airplanes and bombs, they are just bashing us for not being one sided as they are, for not seeing the world and situation as they see it. . . . To them there is a very clear truth that everyone shall embrace and we shall see everything as they see it."

To their critics, Kobi declared that "We wrote just above 60 songs about our Orphaned Middle Eastern Lands for the past 30 years. We are not a customer service to keep you pleased at times of stupid and useless wars. . . . But in our songs, dreams or shows—there is a different reality that exists for only 90 minutes. We adore the people who join us, living this dream. However, most people are not interested in leaving the cave."

Kobi's musings about playing the Arab world are, for the moment, firmly in the realm of dreams. Few Palestinian or Arab/Muslim fans more broadly bothered to comment on the post, with the vast majority of the 150 or so replies from European or Jewish fans offering their support. One Arab fan, however, well summed up the predicament: "I like your music and your message, but there is sometimes a need to tell the truth and to move away from impartiality and this is what I very much want to see from you." This has always been the fine line that the band, like most successful artists, has to walk: create an imagined world beyond politics and actual history, where a common future can be imagined without having to address the realities of the present, or enter the fray directly and, most likely, lose a large share of your fan base (especially in as militantly nationalist a society as Israel today).

I couldn't help thinking of Iron Maiden, who released the song "Writing on the Wall" not long after the latest round of violence in Palestine/Israel. The song is not an attack on any particular politician or party in particular (although the cartoon fat cat at the beginning of the video seems like a clear cross between Donald Trump and Boris Johnson), but its lyrics are a clear warning of how the "writing on the wall" is already warning us of impending civilizational disaster if humanity doesn't change drastically, and soon. It's an indictment of humanity but not of particular people, leaders, or corporations, much like Orphaned Land's music. It's arguable whether naming names would have made the song stronger as a song or a message; in fact, the power of the song lies in the breadth of the indictment—and the killer riffs. Bruce Dickenson doesn't live in Jaffa, and the UK, whatever its myriad injustices and inequalities, isn't presently in the midst of an ever-deepening settler-colonial occupation. If it were, what would we expect him or other artists to say if the violence reached their doorstep?

A month to the day after the latest conflict erupted, Orphaned Land celebrated its thirtieth anniversary as a band with a big concert in Tel Aviv. Meanwhile, System Ali, which has long been far more active in the local community, recorded a video titled "I Can't Breathe," featuring each member beating their chests in mourning while describing the pain of the intercommunal violence for their community. Saz and Israeli Jewish rapper and educator Uriya Rosenman collaborated on a musical video confrontation-*cum*-song, "Let's Talk Straight" ("Bo, Ndaber Dogri" in Hebrew, "Ta'al, Nihki dughri" in Arabic), which saw each rapper begin by engaging in stereotypical tirades about the other community before working through the pain and trauma of the last century to reach the beginning of an understanding of how to move forward. The video quickly garnered millions of views and even Roger Cohen of the *New York Times* did a long article about the project, hailing it as a model for how the two sides could move forward-at least within Israel.

Meanwhile, in Gaza, twelve-year-old rap prodigy MC Abdul (Abdalrahman Alshantti) recorded a song and then a video in the rubble of the latest assault titled "Shouting at the Wall." In flawless English he described trying to "protect my brother under the bed while my dad risked his life to go out for bread." Within days the video had gotten tens of thousands of views and his Instagram post over three hundred thousand likes. That dichotomy, between a group able to "live the dream"—however frustrating the reality—and a young boy forced to walk through a constant nightmare, is impossible to miss.

FOUR

Lebanon

REMIXED BUT NEVER REMASTERED

Composed by Mark LeVine and Jackson Allers,
arranged and mixed by Mark

In Lebanon, there's this mixture of cultures and religions, so obviously it's hard for us to be . . . minimalis[t]. . . . Silence is not really our environment. Normally our impulse is toward energy and to fill the space with sound.

—SHARIF SEHNAOUI,
musician, Beirut, 2013 interview with Music Works

It's too easy being a metalhead in Lebanon since all the ingredients are there.

—PATRICK SAAD,
Lebmetal, 2017

NEARLY EVERY LEBANESE MUSICIAN who was alive and conscious in the 1980s has the same story: they listened to music, often the loudest and heaviest music they could get their hands—and ears—on in order to drown out the bombs and gunfire that defined daily life during the Civil War and Israeli Occupation, which lasted from 1982 through 1989 (the war) and 2000 (the Occupation). In *Heavy Metal Islam* Moe Hamzeh first brought this phenomenon to Mark's attention. Since then, it's become almost a truism. Once you've actually lived through days of bombings and machine-gun fire, Metallica, Maiden, Zeppelin, NWA, and Wu-Tang take on a whole different meaning.

Two decades after the end of the Israeli Occupation in 2000, but only half a decade since the last major Israeli bombardment, "Beirut is definitely not the ideal place for any metal musician. . . . But it's still as metal as it gets." So explained Anthony Kaoteon, lead guitarist of the black and death metal band Kaoteon—whose sound follows the logic by Sharif Sehnaoui in the epigraph to this chapter to a T—in an interview with *Revolver Magazine* in February 2018. Kaoteon is one of the more adventurous metal projects in Lebanon of the last decade, but the description of his hometown is not entirely accurate; at the height of its popularity in the middle of the last decade, metal shows by top Lebanese bands could draw well over one thousand people, a number most groups in New York or London in whatever decade could only dream of experiencing. Even in the relative doldrums of the last decade, metal bands in Lebanon could still attract hundreds of fans to their shows.

Indeed, with a total population of roughly a third of Cairo, Lebanon manages to have one of the more robust live scenes not only in the MENA region, but anywhere. From hip hop to indie and alternative rock to EDM and metal—never mind Arab pop, jazz, world music, and various forms of "traditional" Arab music—Beirut compares favorably with most any world city in terms of the possibilities for high-quality live and recorded music. Music is, as Kaoteon continued, "a way of life." If only the country's politics were as vibrant as its music.

Most Lebanese have a variation of the same story to explain how their country has managed both to avoid dictatorial rule and, until the combined disasters of Covid and the massive explosion on August 4, 2020, at the city's port, to function continuously at a level just above ungovernability and widespread poverty in the thirty years since the end of the Civil War. "We can say anything we want here because nothing we say matters" is how one professor put it to Mark at a lecture at the American University of Beirut, way back in 1998. A similar view is expressed by the well-known claim that while most Arab countries only have one dictator, "We have seven or eight"—or however many of the eighteen-odd religious and sectarian communities one decides to count. Similarly, more than one commentator has pointed out that while most authoritarian countries have seen major protests against family dynasties (for example, against the Ben Ali/Trabulsi clan in Tunisia, against the Ghaddafi and Mubarak families in Libya and Egypt, and against the Assads in Syria), Lebanon remains one of the few nonmonarchies in the Arab/Muslim world where family politics still defines the political system without much protest.

It is true that there are few cities besides Beirut where people have partied in the center of the city to the sounds and sights of bombs exploding a few kilometers to the south, as happened during various Israeli bombardments of the southern, Shi'a neighborhoods of the city in the mid-2000s. More recently, of course, we could ask what other governments, no matter how incompetent, could allow 2,750 tons of ammonium nitrate to be stored in the open for years on end at the country's main port despite repeated warnings that it was a potential nuclear-sized explosion hazard. Indeed, given the level of dysfunctionality, one might ask why Lebanon did not have its own "Arab Spring" moment in 2011.

But spring in fact came early to Lebanon, in 2005–06, when the eruption of protests after the assassination of former prime minister Rafiq Hariri both pushed Syria out of the country after a nearly thirty-year occupation and offered a seemingly unprecedented chance for one of the region's few nonauthoritarian governments to achieve a decent measure of democratic accountability. Indeed, the assassinated journalist Samir Kassir predicted as much in his book *Dimuqratiya suriya wa-istiqlal lubnan* (*Syria's Democracy Lebanon's Independence*, 2004), where he wrote that "when the Arab Spring begins in Beirut, it will herald the blooming of roses in Damascus." Sadly, the roses turned out to represent the wrong red.

It's hard to overstate how powerfully generative an aesthetic force violence can be even on its victims. Two generations ago and a continent away, the great Nigerian Afrobeat pioneer Fela Kuti watched as his mother, the independence and women's rights pioneer Funmilayo Anikulapo Kuti, was thrown out of the second-story window of his compound, causing injuries from which she would die. True to his—and his mother's—evolutionary spirit, Fela marched his mother's coffin to the presidential compound with his supporters, and soon thereafter created a song and album (and album cover), *Coffin for Head of State,* that shook the Nigerian regime to its foundations.

Fela didn't have much over the young Lebanese artists who came of age in the midst of a brutal civil war, a nightmarish Israeli occupation and even longer Syrian one, and a seemingly permanent state of violence and corruption. Readers of *Heavy Metal Islam* will recall how artists like Moe Hamzeh of The Kordz and a host of Iranian musicians discussed how they listened to the loudest possible music as loudly as possible to drown out the sounds of guns, artillery, and bombs (not completely coincidentally, Fela's first manager, Faysal Helwani, was Lebanese). This idea didn't disappear when the war ended in 1989 or the Israelis withdrew in 2000. And so, when in 2006 Israel launched another war against Hezbollah in response to a tit-for-tat series of border attacks between the two sides, Lebanese rock musician Mazen Kerbaj recorded several hours of the nightly bombardments and used the recording as the core "track" over which he recorded almost an hour of electronic improvisation. It is truly a frightening, if ultimately uplifting, composition, the rhythm of the bombs being turned into the pulse of a powerful meditation on war, creativity, and the power of music to turn even barbarity into a tool for transcendence, if only momentarily. As Kerbaj explained (with more than a hint of irony) in an interview in 2013 with the magazine *Music Works*, "Sometimes I want to find the pilot who dropped the bombs, and say, 'Thank you. And sorry that I never gave you any royalties.'"

Lebanese music continued to play the role of regional "disruptor," helping to spread new styles and, as important, encouraging "pan-Arab" collaborations between artists, especially in hip hop, that laid the groundwork for the far more political collaborations of the Arab uprisings era. A new music scene, created by musicians born during the war, emerged. It stood in stark contrast to the highly commercialized pop industry and, as in so many other places, from New York to Peshawar, a record shop was at its heart. As many of the musicians who came of age in the 1990s and 2000s tell it, in the mid-1990s local music fanatic and entrepreneur Tony Sfeir started a specialized music store called La CD-Thèque, in the Mount Lebanon area. It then moved to Kaslik by the coast and then opened branches in Achrafiyeh and Hamra. La CD-Thèque became the most important CD store that sold jazz, classical, and alternative music, and as the store's success grew Sfeir started to produce many of the talented young Beiruti artists. His goal was, and remains to this day, to challenge the pop market with music that is well ahead of the popular curve.

Even with the pandemic and explosion of 2020, it's hard to surpass the intensity of the year in which research for *Heavy Metal Islam* began in Beirut. The assassination of Rafiq Hariri unleashed a tidal wave of events: the creation of opposing pro-Syrian "March 8" and anti-Syrian "March 14" coalitions, the pushing out of the Syrian army after a thirty-year presence (for those opposed to it, "occupation") of the country, the election of a new parliament led by the March 14 coalition, the explosion of several more car bombs, the charging of four pro-Syrian Lebanese generals in Hariri's assassination—all of this just in 2005. More car bombs and the Israel-Hezbollah war in 2006, a failed tribunal to investigate Hariri's murder and the declaration of a state of emergency by outgoing president Lahoud in 2007, gunfights and a near civil war in 2008 followed by a power-sharing pact in Doha and the reestablishment of diplomatic relations with Syria for the first time since the 1940s.

One of the best exemplars of this trend was the release in 2007 by Lebanese turntablist extraordinaire DJ Lethal Skillz of his first album, *New World Disorder,* which, though aimed at a Western or even global (rather than just Arab) audience, contained a smorgasbord of local and regional talent, each distilling their rejection of the rampant corruption and social neglect inherent in their societies in witty metaphorical turns of phrase and in very grave tones. Collaborators included Lebanese rappers MC Moe and Malikah of 961 Underground, Rayess Bek of Aks'ser, RGB and Siska of Kita3 Beyrouthe, Chyno and El Edd of Fareeq al Atrash, Omarz of Dezert Dragons, Grandsunn, and Matthew Noujaim aka MC Zoog, as well as Ramallah Underground's Boikutt, aka Muqata'a, Asifeh aka Stormtrap, and Aswaat (Muqata'a's brother and member of their multimedia sound collaboration Tashweesh alongside Ruanne Abou-Rahme); most of the songs presaged the messages that were echoed by the demonstrators that took down the Tunisian and Egyptian regimes and that now threaten the regimes in Bahrain, Syria, Yemen, and Libya.

It only got crazier in the decade after. A failed attempt by the International Criminal Court to try Hariri's suspected killers was followed by the freeing of the four detained generals by a Lebanese court and the inauguration of a Hariri-led March 14 coalition government with none other than Hezbollah in 2009. And then, as the Arab Spring was just erupting (two days before Tunisian president Ben Ali fled the country), Hezbollah broke the coalition, and the UN-backed Special Tribunal for Lebanon handed down indictments in the assassination, but they were kept secret to prevent violence and so were to be forgotten until arrest warrants were handed out for more junior figures in the early summer, which inevitably led to a brief exchange of rocket fire between Hezbollah and Israel but still relative calm.

In the meantime, Lebanon did have a brief *intifada al-karama* (Intifada of Dignity) in 2009, but that had dimmed before the year was over, and was replaced by sectarian violence as the dominant public narrative by the next summer. By the time the Arab Spring began in late 2010 the country was already half a decade on from its cedar-scented eruption; as the uprisings began to degenerate into renewed authoritarianism, bloody repression, and civil war in 2012, the *New York Times* declared that "Resurgent Beirut Offers a Haven amid Turmoil of Arab Spring." Even more exuberantly, writing for Red Bull Music Academy, Jackson described Beirut's allure the same year as "its diversity, ethnic and religious, [which] is unmatched in the Arab world, and since the 1950s, its capital city Beirut has become the fulcrum between oriental and occidental, creating the 'perfect storm' of influences that has made it the mecca for progressive musical trends in the Middle East and North Africa (MENA)."

The same sectarian dynamics that could have motivated people toward pushing for revolutionary change in a corrupt and barely functioning political system instead acted as a "demotivating" factor that prevented the kind of cross-sectarian solidarity and collaboration that could achieve it, particularly when in the background lurked a history of disastrous civil war, which, with Syria in flames next door and most of the major Lebanese factions already lined up behind one or another side, was only a spark away from reigniting. And yet, at the same time a new cadre of independent artists emerged, including Zeid Hamdan, Yasmine Hamdan, Scrambled Eggs, the Wanton Bishops, Who Killed Bruce Lee, Munma, LUMI, Malikah, Postcards, Fareeq al Atrash, Chyno, Edd, El Rass, A Trio, Hello Psychallepo, Lazzy Lung, Tanjaret Daghet, Lilian Chlela, Kinematik, and, perhaps the biggest rock band in Lebanese history, Mashrou' Leila (whom we'll discuss at length below).

Indeed, by the summer of 2012 the expanding Syrian Civil War reached Lebanon, as Sunni-Alawi clashes erupted with deadly results in Beirut and Tripoli, followed by more bombings. These events were accompanied by the influx of 160,000 Syrian refugees. The war next door continued to make its presence felt in Lebanon in 2013 and 2014, with occasional clashes, both between various Lebanese factions and between Hezbollah and ISIS, as well as bombings of targets including the Iranian Embassy. But the violence was largely overshadowed by the almost unfathomable refugee influx, which reached upward of one million people by 2015—far surpassing the total number of Palestinians forced into exile in 1948. In the space of three years the population of Lebanon swelled by more than 20 percent—as if sixty million people had entered the United States during the same period, or fifteen million into Germany, instead of the one million refugees that did come.

By 2018 the total number of refugees in Lebanon, including the 450,000 Palestinians who've been languishing in camps since 1948, approached two million, approximately one-third of Lebanon's population. Not surprisingly, as their numbers swelled, the Lebanese government engaged in a de facto process of "criminalization" of the refugee population, using claims that the influx included significant numbers of ISIS members or other foreign fighters to generate fear among the normally generous Lebanese population in the hope of preventing the newcomers from becoming too implanted and acclimated in Lebanese society.

Exacerbating the difficulties of acculturation of the refugee, protests on behalf of, never mind by, refugees were ultimately banned. And so to the present day the integration of refugees, whether Palestinians in 1948 or Syrians today, into Lebanon's political and cultural economies remains haphazard, below the surface, and filled with exploitation and violence. The Syrian influx should have permanently changed Lebanon's politics, economy, and culture. But the country's already fractured, sectarian, and dysfunctional system managed somehow to continue on, although under an increased level of strain.

On the other hand, however, musically the arrival of so many talented Syrian musicians, singers, and rappers naturally led to many collaborations between them and their Lebanese counterparts. As French-Lebanese journalist Emmanuel Haddad described it in a report in 2017, *Contemporary Performing Arts in Lebanon:* "Beirut became the echo chamber of Syrian creativity in the face of the nearby slaughters and destruction." Its size—not too big like Cairo, but not too provincial like Amman—made it the perfect incubator for artists to relocate to and have a critical mass of other artists and musicians with whom one could collaborate without getting lost in a sea of competing agendas.

ART DON'T STINK!

While Lebanese politicians feared a "terrorist onslaught" via infiltration in the midst of so many refugees, the country miraculously managed to avoid a descent into mass violence, whether internally or transnationally motivated, during the refugee wave. But by 2015 another seemingly irresolvable problem began to plague the country, this one caused by a complete breakdown in garbage services in Beirut in the summer of 2015 after the city's main dump was closed and garbage collection suspended. The corruption and failure to provide basic services, along with high levels of corruption in the public sector and the high and even duplicate prices for them (Lebanese as a matter of course wind up paying twice for electricity or water, once to official state-owned companies that often fail to deliver them, and a second time for price-gauging private companies) prompted mass protests led by a new, grassroots movement called You Stink! (tol3et re7etkom!), which brought to Lebanon the kinds of artistic satire against the government and corrupt politicians and businessmen that had long characterized the Arab Spring protests, along with chants of some of the uprisings' most famous slogans, such as "the people want the downfall of the system."

Ironically—or perhaps fittingly—the garbage crisis achieved what even civil war couldn't, as new cross-sectarian alliances were formed by citizens utterly fed up with the putrid politics as well as realities on the ground. A temporary solution for the trash crisis was agreed to in late March 2016, when the Lebanese government reopened the main landfill and set up two new ones, with the goal of holding off the problem for half a decade or so until a permanent solution could be found.

The garbage crisis revealed the intensity of discontent on the Lebanese street over the direct and maleficent impact of the country's politics on every aspect of life—housing, utilities, garbage, pollution, healthcare, and innumerable other local problems. For its part, You Stink! rearranged the status quo of Lebanese politics in an almost unprecedented manner through the cross-sectarian alliances forged in response (although most didn't last more than the next electoral cycle).

A new political movement was born out of the protests in Beirut, Beirut My City (Beirut Madinati), which in focusing on the epidemic of trash that overtook the entire city, showing how citizens were in fact united in common suffering at the hands of their political system, looked poised to achieve municipal control over the city before Saad Hariri's coalition claimed victory in the elections the next year. Beirut has been the subject of numerous songs in the last half-century, from Fairuz's "L'Beirut" and "Ya Mina El Habayeb" and her son Marcel Khalife's "Toot Toot 3a Beirut" ("On to Beirut"), to fighter-turned-singer Kahled al-Haber's "Beirut Bokra" ("Beirut Tomorrow"), Yasmine Hamdan's "Beirut," and Eben Foulen and Rayess Bek's "Madinet Beirut" ("City of Beirut"). Yet while many of the city's leading young(er) musicians like Zeid Hamdan, Anthony Khoury (of the pop band Adonis), Michelle and Noel Keserwany, Karim Khneisser, DJ Ali Ajami, and others were part of the movement and performed at rallies and benefits, no anthem-like song emerged during the movement that captured its frenetic energy or encouraged wider popularity and mobilization.

Perhaps one reason is that the garbage crisis was only one of multiple crises facing Beirut and Lebanon more broadly. During this period Beirut was rocked by two massive ISIS suicide bombings that killed over fifty people and wounded almost three hundred. The political outcome of all of these developments was the election of the Christian, Hezbollah-backed Michel Aoun as president, who then chose none other than Saad Hariri to be prime minister.

Just when it seemed that Lebanese politics couldn't get any stranger or more dysfunctional, however, in late 2017 Saad Hariri suddenly flew to Saudi Arabia and announced in a strange televised speech that he was resigning because of assassination fears and Hezbollah and Iranian "meddling" in his country. The timing as well as the strange appearance and diction of Hariri's speech led to widespread speculation that the Saudi Crown Prince, Mohammed bin Salman, had kidnapped him or threatened to expropriate billions of dollars tied to the Hariri family companies operating in the Kingdom (with bin Salman's later ordering of the brutal murder of journalist Jamal Khashoggi and his contemporaneous kidnapping and extortion of much of the royal elite, this claim doesn't seem so far-fetched). An uproar ensued in Lebanon, with campaigns launched on social media demanding his return, and ultimately he rescinded his resignation and returned home, still prime minister, although he's refused to discuss what actually happened in Saudi Arabia. In May 2018 Hariri won yet another term as prime minister with wide parliamentary support, only to resign in October 2019 in response to the massive protests that again swept across the country in response to the lack of any movement toward functioning governance in the previous years. Those protests were intense enough to lead celebrated novelist Elias Khoury to declare in a column for the *al-Quds al-'Arabi* newspaper that the movement was moving "from intifada to revolution" *("min al-initifada ila-th-thawra")* because of the strong role of culture in emphasizing social justice. Sadly, however, whatever momentum it might have had was squashed with the onset of the coronavirus pandemic a few months later, and the devastating explosion that rocked the capital on August 4, 2020.

More broadly, however, the problem for Lebanese protesters was that there was no system or regime, similar to the Moroccan Makhzen, Algerian Pouvoir, or Egyptian and various other deep states, to try to topple or replace. The durability of the post–Civil War political system was owed to its amorphousness and spread-out nature and what could be termed "effective ineffectualness" (that is, it was effective enough in distributing power and patronage to prevent a new civil war, but utterly ineffectual as a form of governance). Epitomizing the fleeting nature of the "victory," by 2019 the Youstink.org domain name was pointing to a web aggregator for German furniture.

Red Bull through its now defunct subsidiary Red Bull Music Academy had done wonders for music in the Middle East, Africa, and beyond, providing funding for artists to travel, connect, and collaborate who otherwise wouldn't have the chance to. But Mark couldn't help thinking, as he watched a Red Bull documentary from 2012 on that year's Bass Camp—boot camp, really—in Beirut, that the city was in fact the last place in the Arab world that needed Red Bull Music Academy to develop and professionalize its local music scene. If anything, the opposite was and remains the case: Beirut and Lebanon more broadly have been at the forefront of regional and global changes in the music industry for decades, and will remain so for the foreseeable future.

As leading local musician Zeid Hamdan points out, since the end of the Civil War in 1989 Lebanese have used music as a key tool to understand "What is Lebanon today?," doing so through an alternative music scene that can accurately be considered the first of any consequence across the Middle East and North Africa, and one—at least at the start—equally steeped in the Arabic musical traditions and those of Western rock. Similar, rapper El Rass explains that "this phenomenon [of change] is happening on all levels in the Arab world, including on the musical level and artistic level. There's a dialog going on without any rules besides the artistic rule—which is to do great things that touch people, enlighten people, and give people more awareness toward how they experience what they're living and their surroundings."

This dialog didn't just involve straight-up hip hop à l'américaine. It also involved experimental music, live improvisational DJ'ing (that is, where the DJ is playing the turntables like an instrument, using effects, processors, and other tools that radically change the sound of the music she or he is spinning), and other, more experimental forms of EDM in a manner very similar to what was developing at the same time in Cairo. But even more than in Cairo, there was a very clearly traceable historical trajectory going back decades to the music and politics of artists like Ziad Rahbani and Marcel Khalife, Computer Zaki Nassif, and others, who during the Civil War laid the groundwork for what can be called contemporary "resistance music" in Lebanon. These artists inspired the postwar generation of artists like El Rass and Jawad Nawfal (aka Munma) and Mazen Kerbaj to create music that was both sonically innovative and still political at its core. They in turn provided lyrical images and sonic affectations that perfectly captured the hypocrisies, corruption, and horrors of life in Lebanon and that provided both a dissonant soundtrack for a new generation of activists and a space for connection and solidarity between them. They also happened to be part of a larger arts industry that was flourishing in Beirut thanks to generous foreign funding, largely from European consulates and NGOs.

As part of the entrepreneurship that has defined not just Lebanese music but the larger Lebanese personality for well over a century, there have been several sustainable labels formed in this period, including Zeid Hamdan's Lebanese Underground and the regional music agency Eka3, Forward Music, Fantôme de Nuit (FDN), and Ziad Nawfal's Ruptured label and of course CD Techque. When the label Incognito folded, Ghazi Abdel Baki's Forward Music kept the discography alive, a sign that whatever one throws at Beirut's alternative music scene—civil war, political assassination, socioeconomic depravity—it keeps on going.

And then there was the country's proper indie scene, which more than any other captured the imagination of both the international media and the middle- and upper-class college set. Groups like Soap Kills and Scrambled Eggs saw their profiles rise abroad and at home, epitomized by the invitation given to Scrambled Eggs to play at the 2008 edition of SXSW. Blend was signed to EMI and bands like Meen and LUMI achieved notoriety as well. However, for most of these bands the difficulties of translating talent and potential in the local rock scene into successful careers in and outside of Lebanon took their toll (as we saw it did on The Kordz).

Hip hop has from the start followed different paths when it has come to the experience of Lebanese artists outside the country, as we'll discuss more below. To be sure, in the last decade, as places to perform rock and metal have disappeared in Beirut (and Lebanon more broadly), new venues have opened to cater to the seemingly ever-expanding hip hop scenes, epitomized by clubs like Metro al-Madina, an old cabaret located on Beirut's famous Hamra Street, where some of the best shows involving Lebanese, Syrian, and international hip hop artists have taken place.

THE SYRIAN "INVASION"

For its part, the increasing lack of regular places to perform hasn't hurt the quality of the metal scene. Indeed, Lebanon continues to be a site where the music just naturally "fits in with" young fans, as Patrick Saad, the founder of the Lebmetal web portal, put it to Mark. And so it naturally encourages musical innovation; even if stylistically it hasn't developed that much, the quality of the bands definitely improved, or at least was distributed deeper into the scene as even amateur bands improved the quality of their playing. According to Bassem Deaibess,

How has metal changed in last decade? After 2010 or 2011 the scene shrank considerably. Why? Well you have to first ask, "Why did it expand after 2005?" Because before 2005 there was a big metal scene; 800–1000 people would show up for a concert. From 2005–2009 we'd have as many as 2,000–3,000 people at a local gig! And the number of active bands reached as high as fifty—actual bands, not simply "projects." That was what I would call the "liberation metal" period. The scene expanded because it was no longer under scrutiny, because local clubs and gathering places increased steadily in the previous decade.

"This was, of course, before social media took off," Bassem continued, moving toward why the scene stagnated.

So people needed a location to meet and share information. And many members of the band went on to develop their own . . . bands in the scene. Now it's totally different. There's no point signing with a big label because it won't do anything for you. Despite cheaper production technologies it's still expensive to do a professional video, especially if you're paying for it, and to distribute your music outside of it becoming viral. There's still a hundred-day rule. If you play somewhere and it's successful you need to get back within one hundred days, but that's very difficult today in Europe because of tightening visa rules, especially as our drummer is Saudi. It's even hard to go to Syria now because of the problems between the Saudi and Syrian governments.

In this regard, the various Lebanese music scenes have benefited from the arrival of many of Syria's best metal musicians and singers to Lebanon with the onset of the civil war. In fact, according to Bassem, who echoes the opinion of several other rock, metal, and hip hop artists with whom Mark has spoken about the issue,

My personal opinion is that the Lebanese scene owes the Syrian scene its continuity because at a certain point, around 2012–14, it was the Syrian metalheads who showed up to concerts here. Sometimes half the audience would be Syrian at shows, at least 20 percent other times. And the musicians are amazing as well. There weren't many but that's the period where, up till 2017, you'd have one hundred or two hundred at most at concert. It was really small compared to the two thousand people that used to come to shows. And half these one hundred people were Syrian.

Indeed, several dozen Syrian rock and metal bands moved to Lebanon, with Maysaloon and Tanjeret Daghet the best known of them. While many groups disbanded in Lebanon or moved on to Europe if they could, many musicians joined Lebanese bands. And so, Bassem argues, "The Syrians are contributing to the scene as bands, musicians, fans, and technicians as well." Certainly, they brought an even more intense form of energy to the scene. As Sepultura founder Max Cavelera said to Jake Shuker of Maysaloon during a World Metal Congress webcast from December 2020, while metal bands like Sepultura were writing and singing about fictional wars, "You were living the real the real war." Shuker nodded, explaining, "It's like we were living the song, the dream, and passion. But we were frightened because at some point you realize this is [actual] death you're talking about." His way of dealing with experiencing the horrors of the war was to go as deep as possible into the music, not just metal but the music of his furthest ancestors. Similar to how the members of Egypt's Hate Suffocation and Late Scarab used Ancient Egyptian iconography to root their extremely modern—even postmodern—music in a country that didn't much want it, Maysaloon (whose name is taken from the village where Syrian rebels defeated the French Occupation forces) incorporated the oldest music of their country, including from the Ugaritic period ("the oldest note in the country"), in order to stay connected to their history and "mix up and channel" all the energy into "a really, really dark epic full of violence, full of anger."

Not surprisingly, a similar situation arose with Syrian hip hop artists (DJs, MCs, producers, etc.), as rapper Osloob explained: "The Syrian rappers changed everything. Such a burst of energy. The rappers who came to Lebanon were both smart and good and had amazing lyrics." Normally, however, these bursts of creative energy only lasted a relatively short time. "It happens and then it was over. . . . The scene here is just too small; you see the same people every day so, the music wears out and people want something new."

But there is agreement as of late 2020 that the burst of Syrian energy has yet to fade. Their arrival in fact had a more profound effect than just energizing scenes that had gotten flat creatively. Besides just adding bodies to the scene, the Syrian bands helped the Lebanese sound evolve. According to Bassem Deaibess, "This is the schizophrenia of Lebanese identity. We want to be Europe. When I wanted to fuse Oriental music with metal, I had opposition within band members. The drummer and bassist at the time resisted, thinking it was too cliché. But when I listen to bands that left Syria, like Ascendance (who are now in Dubai), they started putting more and more

Oriental touches with vocals in the music." Even here, though, it's not just Syrians, as the push to add local elements—sometimes ornamentations, but often structurally at the core of melodies, rhythms, and instrumentation— was also observed by Lebanese metal artists through interacting with local metal artists in Egypt, Morocco, and other Arab countries.

Indeed, whatever the complaints of some scene veterans who, like musicians the world over, are having difficulty maintaining a place in changing musical ecosystems, the present generation of Lebanese metal musicians have broken through to the highest echelons of the global metal scene, facilitated no doubt by the fact that there have been so few restrictions on metal over the years, while rehearsal spaces with decent equipment are ubiquitous and, at least until recent years, gigs were relatively plentiful. It's thus not surprising that one of the premier metal magazines, *Metal Hammer,* did a special issue on Lebanon in 2017—although here again we see the misrepresentation of countries of the regions and the scenes that inhabit them right on the cover, which declares that Lebanese bands are "fighting for their lives" in "war torn streets" that lead to the creation of "war ensembles" in the country.

It's hard to generalize across disparate genres like rap and metal. But there can also be significant divergence within the rock scene broadly understood. Perhaps the best evidence of this dynamic involves two bands, The Kordz and Mashrou' Leila. The Kordz were among the most powerful rock/metal outfits in the entire MENA region and even larger Muslim world. Moe Hamzeh's soaring and melismatic vocals matched the band's "Arab"-tinged grooves, creating a true hybrid, "Oriental" groove metal in the style of Junoon more than the more death metal style of Orphaned Land and the many bands it inspired. After almost a decade of performing across Lebanon and occasionally Europe, the band finally had the resources to record a full-fledged album, which they did in 2008–10 with metal producer Ulrik Wild. The story of the album is a powerful example of how great art circulates—or doesn't—across cultures and continents in the Internet age.

As he and Mark reminisced over the last decade of work, Moe recalled:

We went to Canada to record because it was cheaper to record and get Ulrik. Then we came back to Lebanon to record all the Arabic instrumentation, and then sent all the tracks to Ulrik, who finished producing and mixing the album in Los Angeles. I released it on my own label, a small pressing to launch it here in Lebanon and then another pressing with a small distribution service in Germany. I did this smaller pressing because the limited PR release enabled us to get some gigs and the tour with Deep Purple, and to be signed with Ear Music, Purple's label as well as Skunk Anansie's, and then a licensing deal that enabled us to release the album as a deluxe set with a DVD. After that we charted in Italy, which was very encouraging.

With the high quality, beauty, and sophistication of the music and production, Mark was sure that *Beauty and the East* was going to put The Kordz on the international rock 'n' roll map, with major festival gigs and tours to follow. In the end, however, it didn't happen, and for the usual rock 'n' roll reasons: too much pressure, not enough money to invest in marketing the band, difficulties in finding international distribution, too much investment of time and energy without a big payoff, and band members needing to get on with and even move to a new phase in their life, whether that meant moving to a different continent or having kids. Between 2012 and 2016 the band was on hiatus more or less as guitarist Nadim Sioufi moved to Canada. When he returned in 2016, a reunion gig was organized with the original lineup in the coastal town of Batroun, a little more than halfway from Beirut north to Tripoli. "We had around thirty-five hundred people at the show. It was a great way to come back. But afterwards Nadim returned to Canada and it just wasn't possible to find the right replacement. I couldn't keep putting all the energy into this when everyone couldn't be on the same wavelength, and with our manager in Germany as opposed to being here it was hard to keep us motivated. Simply put, you can't write new music if you don't have or take the time to sit together."

Aside from the ongoing difficulty of international audiences taking rock bands from the Arab/Muslim world seriously on their own terms as opposed to as a novelty, the very originality of The Kordz's music, the fact that the band doesn't fit easily into a "metal" or contemporary "rock" category, made it hard to break through. "In Europe we were labeled as a metal band, but we should have been positioned—not labeled, positioned—more toward hard classic rock. We don't do what's metal today, and we're not 'Wacken' material. Making it even harder is that the rock scene here in Lebanon is almost entirely indie."

With Moe's position in the Lebanese and broader Middle Eastern music industries, it's hard to dispute his (self-)analysis. Most interesting is that today so many more bands are mixing together the "Arab" or other local sounds, melodies, rhythms, and instruments into their songs, a testament to The Kordz's pioneering vision and sound even as the more indie sound of a band like Mashrou' Leila ensured greater international success. Indeed, being ahead of one's time rarely pays the rent, as the saying goes. It's also true that much of the "hybridity" between various styles and genres one hears in Lebanon, or anywhere for that matter, is not that well thought out or executed. "I don't think it's as simple as just adding Arab or Oriental elements. It's a tricky mixture and can feel forced very easily. It took a long time for us to get that seamless, organic mixture of the two you hear on *Beauty and the East.*"

Whatever the path that history ultimately laid out for the band, *Beauty and the East* remains one of the most beautifully produced and original-sounding rock albums of the last decade, a landmark in the evolution of what many now call "Oriental" rock or metal. The album enabled them to do concerts and even tours with legends like Deep Purple, Robert Plant, and Placebo, to be sure. But despite pouring their souls into the album, and Moe much of his savings, it didn't open the band to the broad international audience it had hoped to reach.

Mashrou' Leila had a far different experience than The Kordz. Formed in 2008 as part of a music workshop at the American University of Beirut, the band's sound was far mellower and more commercial than that of their compatriots in the rock and metal scenes. With tinges of Armenian folk music mixed with indie, Arab melodic tinges and rhythms, samples, and hip hop beats (or at least synthesized drums), the band moved from a largely college fan base to concert halls around the Arab world and the world at large. In a sense Mashrou' Leila benefited from not being a straight-up rock or metal band in their ability to self-promote their music, which allowed them to break through internationally without constant live touring, even as their sound is closer to Egypt's Cairokee than The Kordz's *Beauty and the East.*

Mashrou' Leila was also lucky to start gigging with major shows like the Byblos Festival and could be selective about gigs. The band's notoriety jumped even more when lead singer Hamed Sinno came out as gay and began advocating for LGBTQ+ rights, which became an important part of Marshou' Leila's public identity. This led to the banning of the group's concerts for two years in a row in Jordan and an even more infamous massive crackdown on LGBTQ+ activism and gay people in Egypt after a fan at a concert outside Cairo held up the international pride flag. How this played out within Lebanon will be discussed at the conclusion of this chapter. But internationally, it was the perfect publicity storm.

Mashrou' Leila caught lightning in a bottle with their sound, look, politics, and indie sensibility. They were the perfect band for the liberal youth of the post-2011 Arab uprisings. Edgy and independent, advocating radical changes in social morality, but all within a market-friendly framework that is very progressive socially (especially around LGBTQ+ issues), but that doesn't directly challenge the ruling systems in place around the region. Musically, their sound was far less avant-garde, particularly considering how innovative Lebanon's indie scene and sound had been for decades before.

HIP HOP AT THE AVANT-GARDE

The greater level of innovation today comes from the hip hop scene, and few artists in the last decade have shone through as much as Osloob, whose skills as a rapper have always extended to collaborations with musicians. Particularly powerful was his collaboration with Syrian French flautist Naissam Jalal in a project called al-Akhareen (The Others), which has been described as "a hip hop/jazz reflection on alterity." Having met in Beirut when Naissam was invited to sit in with Osloob's then band, Katibeh 5, the two met regularly during her visits to Beirut until Osloob moved to Paris, where he's now based, in 2014. Over the course of the next year or so, Osloob and Naissam expanded to a trio with the addition of DJ Junkaz Lou on turntables, and then a sextet after adding sax player Mehdi Chaïb, bassist Viryane Say, and drummer Sébastien Le Bon.

Al-Akhareen is one of the best jazz-inspired, or "acid jazz," hip hop collectives working anywhere today. A lot of rappers have a knack for rhyming over jazzier grooves, but what makes Osloob's style so strong is his collaboration with Naissam, whose flute lines, through the use of Arab maqamat, or modes, as the basis for many of her melodies, immediately lift the music out of the ersatz acid jazz imitating A Tribe Called Quest, De La Soul, or, on the funkier side, the Brand New Heavies, which so often can date attempts to recapture that sound. While the combination of rhyming and flute works well enough live with just the two of them and a DJ, it really kicks into high gear when they have had the chance to perform with their full, six-piece lineup.

Al-Akhareen is also one of the most quintessentially Lebanese bands today: that is, it is very much a Lebanese project but with roots and most of its time spent in the diaspora—specifically France—just as the majority of Lebanese in fact live in the diaspora today. Indeed, the band isn't in reality a "Lebanese" group per se: Osloob was born in the Bourj al Barajneh Palestinian refugee camp and carries a Palestinian refugee passport rather than a Lebanese passport (which remains exceedingly difficult for Palestinians to obtain even if they were born and have spent their whole lives in Lebanon); Naissam is the daughter of Syrian immigrants in France who grew up partly in Lebanon. As Osloob explains it, "My being a refugee was important. Between the Palestinian and Lebanese communities in Lebanon there are a lot of borders; you're always a stranger. I'm still Palestinian, even if I was born in Lebanon." The band reflects this experience of rejection, as explained by its Facebook narrative: "What we embody is linked to a violent history, to wars in which we did not participate but whose consequences we suffer. We have had to face the rejection of societies which, in different ways, refuse our presence and our existence within them. Despite ourselves, each of us embodies the other, the foreigner, the enemy." It's not surprising then that the music of al-Akhareen is conceived of as a "bridge between two worlds," in Naissam's words, while creating a "veritable ode to alterity," as the band's Facebook page points out.

It's worth noting here that the aural innovations of al-Akhareen wouldn't have been possible without the near-complete takeover by hip hop of the aural culture of the Palestinian camps, and Lebanon more broadly. It's clear visiting them today that hip hop is more dominant than ever. As Osloob reminded Mark,

> To wear baggy [clothes] or tell people that you were a rapper used to be strange, but now it's really normal. Everyone knows about hip hop, everyone has his own special rapper, etc. And it was always political. But now, with al-Akhareen, I can be political as an Arab in France, or as a Palestinian or Syrian in Lebanon. At the same time, to stay rooted I try to keep the instruments as real as possible. That I couldn't really do in Lebanon the way I can in France. In fact, not only can I live on my music for the first time ever—I don't have to do shitty jobs to survive and pay for my art, but you can find any musician you want in Paris: a beautiful clarinetist, amazing guitar player, or whatever. And you get exposed to so much more music live, so many concerts, whereas in Beirut all the concerts take place on two streets. Even Berlin doesn't have this feel, it's a lot more electro/techno. Paris is still the place to be for hip hop.

We can see the lyrical power of this collaboration in the words to "Fight Back," a track equally vulgar and profound:

> Fuck government, authority and the occupation.
> Fuck kissasses, dicksuckers, and traitors,

Those who lost the way, and those who lost sponsors.
One left you chaos and the other a pickaxe.
Go tell the refugees we don't need all the land back. I mean convince refugees
  that we're fine where we at.
While the occupation is busy taking lands, and betting on us forgetting their
  whole plan.

In their eponymously titled song "al-Akhareen" ("The Others"), the band
similarly declares:

We are the others who live on the other side but close to you
We feel pain and tolerate it like you do, we inhale polluted air before you
Among us there are haters, motherfuckers, and fake suckers.
Among us are scientists, dreamers, and mystics, the intelligent and those who
  are waiting for real shit, and those who go wherever the wind takes them,
  Struggling not to cry, not to fall.
Sometimes the others are shapes, sometimes numbers, and sometimes houses,
  Sometimes they are outlined by a picture of a terrorist. A refugee camp or
  the suburbs in Europe.
The others are the others no matter where they are exiled.

RIGHTS OF SPRING

More than most countries across the MENA, Lebanon experienced the Arab
uprisings from a position of ambivalence because of its long history of instability, political disappointment, and violence. The constant level of political
instability "has always h[ung] over your head in Beirut," DJ Lethal Skillz has
said, and with the Arab uprisings that instability has become generalized
region-wide. Music has become not merely a weapon against oppressive systems, but, as Salman Ahmad of Junoon put it about his home country of
Pakistan, a medicine to help cure the many ills they cause. And so in Lebanon
too, whether individually or through pan-Arab and international collaborations, music has remained one of the most powerful ways to combat oppressive systems, to bring a musical order to the political chaos.

What has become clear over the decade since the Arab uprisings began
and the Syrian Civil War sent a million people across the border is that whatever one throws at Beirut's alternative music scene—civil war, political assassination, socioeconomic depravity—it continues and even develops further,
a kind of *summud,* or "steadfastness," as Palestinians describe it, that pro-

duces continual innovation, from backwater garages in the Shuf Mountains to the high-rises of Beirut. Ernesto Chahoud, along with Rami Obeid, a founder of the Beirut Groove Collective, explained to his partner Jackson back in 2012: "For me, the alternative scene in Beirut is like a bunch of outcasts accepted by hardly anyone. The political powers or political players in and outside the government don't acknowledge them. So, when you have these outcast musicians—or DJs, or artists—that are expressing themselves and nothing but themselves, without care for anything, this is Beirut's alternative scene. And it is what makes Beirut an underground trendsetter in the region."

Similarly, poet/MC El Rass recalls Ramy Essam's notion of the role of the musician to reflect and intensify the sentiments of society when he explains that "I want to synthesize and absorb the cumulative experience of the culture I belong to on a musical and artistic level and be a continuation of this culture. This is what is happening in the Arab world. Now it's prime time and it's at some sort of peak. I know I'm not alone when I say this, but I always see myself as trying to create something that's going to be perceived as traditional music a century from now."

Ultimately, the "outcasts" (as Osloob describes them) inhabiting or moving into and out of Lebanon's alt-music scenes have succeeded in keeping the intensity and innovation at a level disproportionately high to the small population. But as in most other countries they lack the power to push the broader society further than it would otherwise go. Despite the pansectarian, pan-Arab, and international environment they've fostered, the "seed of the revolution," as El Rass rhymes in the song "Borkan Beirut" ("The Volcano of Beirut"), "sprouted when our spirits were foiled from immobility"; they were and remain incapable of enabling the kind of collective political mobilization that could overcome the "suppression" of the deeply entrenched sectarian political economy of the country.

STEPPING ON THE THIRD RAIL

Like the literary *Nahda,* or "renaissance," that jump-started modern culture in the Arab world, the last ten years have seen an explosion of new music developing out of the music that had taken root in the generation before. Certainly Lebanon and its youth were influenced by the rise of DJ culture globally, and in keeping with Lebanon's neoliberal free-market system, its entrepreneurial base also saw a perfect opportunity to take part in the huge amounts of money being made at raves and techno events in the world's major capitals. These elite stakeholders had no overt sectarian loyalties. In fact, religious institutions, political parties (at every level of society), and these elite businessmen understood Lebanon's number one religion: money.

Crucial to this process was the need to create or rehabilitate spaces where the burgeoning youth population could hear music. But by and large this didn't happen for the rock scene, because that required a great investment of funds for better PA systems, backlines, and other expensive items. Hip hop was and remains much easier to market and produce events around.

On the other hand, and similar to the Egyptian experience of Mahmoud Refat's 100Copies label and roster of artists, there has been a rise in Lebanon of smaller, all-in-one labels, which also serve as publishing, video production, and music distribution outlets. This returns all the way to the 1990s when the small independent CD Techque label was founded out of the back of a record store of the same name. To this day, such smaller boutique labels not only offer unique alternative and electronic music; they also are at the forefront of the vinyl revolution—or return—across the MENA region.

Around 2008 another important change in the Lebanese scene occurred, which was the reemergence of vinyl-only formats, and the music this format was attached to: collaborations like the Beirut Groove Collective, Diamond Setter and Jade, Ziad Nawfal's Ruptured label and his large roster of Lebanese artists, and then DJ Lethal Skillz, Ernesto Chahoud, and composer, film scorer, and DJ Jad Taleb. The Arab uprisings produced a slew of compilation albums across the region and internationally. Some were put together by European or American producers and artists who wanted to support and publicize their comrades from a region in the midst of seemingly epochal change. Others were produced by local artists themselves, as a way to curate and perhaps catalyze the music that had played such an important role in the uprisings.

Perhaps the most important example of this trend was the album *Khat Thaleth*, a hip hop compilation involving twenty-three tracks, a dozen MCs, five producers, and two turntablists, along with some of the best musicians around.

Khat Thaleth wasn't created in the immediate aftermath of the revolutionary outbursts, when they were still largely optimistic. Rather, it was released in 2013, after the violence in Syria, Libya, and increasingly Yemen had begun to take its toll while Egypt's democratic experiment was hijacked by the Sisi coup. So the album has little of either the pent-up frustrations waiting to explode of compilations like DJ Lethal Skillz's *New World Disorder,* Mark's *Flowers in the Desert,* Skillz's *Karmageddon,* or the Nomadic Wax disc *Thawra* (Revolution), which were released in the immediate aftermath of the Tunisian and Egyptian uprisings.

Khat Thaleth is direct and even incendiary in its lyrical diatribes and stories related to the uprisings, much of it pushing the boundaries of contemporary Arabic syntax and lexicology. In particular, according to Ahmed Khouja aka dub Snakkr, the DJ/producer behind the project, "My initial reaction to the revolutions was that we have to grab as much of the space that was carved out by others as we can . . . the artistic space that was sacrificed for! And that is particularly important for those who feel silenced now or feel threatened— a renewed threat. It's simple—if we lose that artistic space then it will really feel as if what has happened in the Arab world (these past three years) was in vain." For Khouja the path to that space is the third way between the two increasingly polarized sides in the various societies under stress where there's still room for creative expression, for a kind of *zajal,* or "battle poetry," that can create what has come to be known as *shiq*—a combination of *sha'r* (poetry) and *iqa'a* (beats) that is both totally ancient and utterly fresh. Snakkr's narrative has been borne out with the exploding popularity of the kinds of rap battles and diss raps, many with elaborate music to match the lyric fireworks, now dominating most every Arab hip hop scene, as the Morocco and Egypt chapters have already shown.

If *Khat Thaleth* captured the increasingly schizophrenic (and paranoid) zeitgeist of the later Arab uprisings era, DJ Skillz's second album, *Karmageddon,* captured the potential of Arab(ic) hip hop even more fully, featuring many of the greatest MCs of the generation, from Omar Zeneiddine to Fareeq al Atrash and Ramcess l'Hamorabi. It's part of a trend that involves Lebanese artists like El Rass, Osloob, and others collaborating as far and wide in the Arab world as possible. The larger album features twenty-three tracks with twenty-nine artists from twenty countries, but the unity of vision under one core or executive producer and impresario enabled the album to, in Skillz's words, "spread a wake-up call and bridge cultures through soulful, funky, raw beats, a microphone, and two turntables." Indeed, *Karmageddon* was one of the first Middle East–produced hip hop albums, featuring only Middle Eastern artists, to be available at a major music store (Virgin Megastores, Lebanon), meaning that an album intended to give young Arab artists unprecedented opportunities to express themselves could reach the greatest possible audience. Of course, major label backing didn't translate into sales success as sales of physical formats were already in rapid decline.

A THOUSAND TIMES MUSIC

All these DJs and MCs, many of whom are also excellent musicians and composers, have affirmed Lebanon's pride of place as one of the most intensely innovative experimental electronic and EDM scenes on Earth, and with it Beirut's position as a premier destination globally for the EDM avant-garde. Aesthetically and artistically, the trend is epitomized by the group Alif, an all-star collaboration from the mid-2010s that brought together some of the most innovative artists from Cairo and Beirut, including the Beirut-based Iraqi 'oud virtuoso Khyam Allami, Egyptian singers and multi-instrumentalists (and electro-scene trend-setters) Maurice Louca and Tamer Abu Ghazaleh, and Lebanese drummer Khaled Yassine and bassist Bashar Farran.

Alif takes the artistry of the electronic and DJ scenes but foregrounds live instrumentation, creating a sound that channels Led Zeppelin's acoustic yet superheavy third album, mixing intense acoustic jams with Arab(esque) melodies and vocals that, if they were one or two octaves higher, could be mistaken for Robert Plant channeling 'Umm Kulthoum. When listening to the band, it's hard not to think that one of the tragedies of contemporary Lebanese music is that Alif and The Kordz never collaborated, because the latter's heavy riffs and drums coupled with the former's folk meets indie-Arab rock sounds would have surely produced some of the most powerful rock music anywhere this millennium.

The scene described here is not just on the musical and political avant-garde; it's also among the most business-savvy scenes in Lebanon, enabling promoters and event producers to engage directly with local youth and the larger cultural sector, and partnering with local and international record labels and foreign cultural agencies anchored in Beirut. A good example of this trend was Beirut Jam Sessions, founded in 2012 by arts promoter and musician Anthony Semaan with the idea of reestablishing the importance of live music to counter a youth base obsessed with electronic dance music. These popular Jam Sessions on YouTube showcase live unplugged video performances resembling filmmaker Vincent Moon's "Take Away Shows" for the French video podcast *La Blogotheque,* thus helping to create a digital footprint that has resonated with local and international audiences well past the actual musical event itself. New festivals also emerged to accommodate growing demand for live music, such as the indie festivals like Wickerpark in Batroun (the biggest indie-music festival in Lebanon) and the more jazz-oriented Beirut and Beyond Music Festival (a collaboration with the Norwegian Oslo World Music Festival Foundation), alongside older and better-known festivals like Baalbeck and the Byblos Festivals.

Between 2009 and 2021, the all-vinyl socially conscious party collective—the Beirut Groove Collective—emerged as one of the planet's funkiest weekend dance events, gathering fans from different class and sectarian divides in what became a rare and safe place to showcase local indie-music talent. Unfortunately, like many social functions in Beirut, because of the continuing demise of the state between the start of the October 2019 revolution, the 2020 Beirut port explosion, and the ongoing economic and political collapse, it became untenable for the core members of the BGC to maintain their Beirut-based operations.

Already in 2009, writing in the leading journal of Middle Eastern cultural criticism, *Norient* editor Thomas Burkhalter argued that Lebanon's avant-garde musicians were "creat[ing] alternatives to the over-represented mainstream pop culture. . . . They can afford to take the risk to choose alternative lifestyles, and to live biographies that are based on possibilities rather than on security." It is true that their impact on the Lebanese society broadly might remain limited, but it's undeniable that these artists have long shaped and continue to shape the sonic as well as economic contours and possibilities of the Lebanese music scene and, through it, that of the region as a whole. Similarly, in a more recent survey of the Lebanese scene, composer and curator Nick Storring explained that, while it might still be relatively isolated from other global music scenes, Beirut in particular has undoubtedly become "a dynamic hub for a dense concentration of fiercely independent musical voices, hot-wir[ing] dub, Egyptian sha'bi, experimental rock, improv, and electronica to produce a hybrid rife with odd timbres and melodies of explicitly Middle Eastern orientation."

REACTIVE METAL

As should be clear, the hip hop and metal/hard rock scenes certainly diverged in their fortunes in many ways in the last decade. But sometimes roads traveling in different directions curve their way back to the same place, or at least nearby. In a way this is what happened with the metal scene. On the one hand, stylistically speaking there was less development in the Lebanese metal scene (which was already quite developed musically) than in the hip hop or electronic scenes, where there was a greater premium on constantly putting out new sounds and styles.

We've already discussed the problems faced by The Kordz. Their difficulties got Mark thinking of whether, with the changes in the industry, such a band could be successfully "broken" today. Moe was not so sure about the prospect. "For a band like The Kordz it would be as tricky today as it was in the past." Sitting in the same apartment where he and Mark first recorded together, in 2005, he explained that "it's still about performing live and targeting [an] audience that would listen in an environment in which the mainstream media is not very supportive, it's hard to play live, and streaming demands curation that might not exist. But mostly, the band would have to be playing regularly. Otherwise you can't build an audience, especially if you don't fit neatly into one of the many niches where marketing can take place more easily. And finally, there's no radio support for whatever identity you do choose for the band." One of the leaders of the long-standing metal group Kimaera—who are considered one of the great doom metal groups in Lebanon and who, aside from regularly touring Europe (they were in fact the first Lebanese band to do so), were featured on *Metal Hammer*'s *Global Metal Volume 3* compilation—similarly explained to Lebmetal.com in an interview in 2020 about their new album, "I honestly miss the old days. There was no social media but still we managed to gather almost every couple of weeks for a metal night or a concert. Things were different, more 'intimate' and 'genuine.' . . . Now the online community took over and it will stay like that, and we can't deny that it is the best way to give bands exposure and the chance to be heard and getting your music everywhere in the world."

While older and more established metal artists lament the loss of live performance opportunities and the difficulties of maintaining a strong following without them, the number of standout bands in the metal scene actually increased in the last decade. Indeed, bands both old and new came to fill prominent places in the country's rock and metal scenes. At least half a dozen unique and highly creative groups have emerged in the last decade who together are keeping Lebanon at the forefront of the MENA metal scenes. It's hard to name or do justice to them all, from the one-man ambient post black metal project Black Folly, to Weeping Willow, Deathlam, Voice of the Soul, and Sound of Degeneration (many of whom were featured in the 2018 Beirut Metal Fest), to bands like Kimaera, the more groove-oriented melodic

FIGURE 19. Slave to Sirens, performing at l'Boulevard Festival, Casablanca, 2019. End of show photo with audience. Courtesy of the band.

black metal outfit Langrima, and the more symphonic and bluesy metal of Ostura, the thrash sound of Phenomy, and, finally, the most recently established major Lebanese group, Turbulence, whose album *Disequilibrium,* released in 2016, comes closer to capturing the classic Kordz sound than perhaps any other band in the country.

Among all these bands however, Slave to Sirens stands out as one of the more original, and not only because it's one of the few all-female metal bands in the Middle East. (Another Beirut band, Zix, had a female lead singer, Maya Khairallah, equally adept at wailing soprano melodies and brutal choruses. But Maya wound up leaving Zix to join Slave to Sirens.) But with their infectious combination of thrash and death metal, the five-piece band, formed in 2015, hews most closely to the path blazed by Egypt's Massive Scar Era, mixing highly melodic and brutal singing with English lyrics geared toward reaching a non-Arabic-speaking audience.

The band's first EP, *Terminal Leeches,* was released on March 11, 2018. The band played in various local metal events, and also got invited by Earache Records to perform at the Glastonbury Festival 2019, where metal was only introduced two years before. The first Lebanese metal band to perform at Glastonbury, they performed three sets, sharing stages with bands like Venom Prison and Gojira, and went to even higher (metal) heights soon after when they played Wacken as well. And completing a historically unprecedented trifecta, they also played the Boulevard in Casablanca the same summer. Literally, no one had done that before.

Not surprisingly, as soon as word of the band got out, most every article about or interview with the band described them as "growl[ing] a message of empowerment" for women *(The National)* or "breaking norms" and making a "feminist stand" in a region unused to nonnormative female singers *(The New Arab)*. Less remarked upon is the band's inherently anticapitalist critique, as the name refers specifically to the fact that "everyone is a slave to something," as Maya put it. "We are slaves to money, slaves to power." But for women, as the band expresses, the burdens are even harder, never mind when one is trying to front an all-female band: "Just the idea of rehearsing at night, so simple and normal, for women is a problem because if the neighbors see you out at night they hint you are using drugs, crazy or are Devil Worshippers," she explained in an interview in September 2018.

Despite, or more likely because of, these unique challenges for female metal musicians, Slave to Sirens's lyrics and music have a strongly political air without even trying. In the words of bassist Alma Doumani, the band sees itself as directly challenging the hypersexualized, feminine, and objectified vision of women in both metal and Arab pop music: "Other girls can also feel like maybe they [want] to do something but they are ashamed or they don't have the guts," while listening to the band will hopefully help them "have the guts to do it." With such attitudes, it's obvious why Slave to Sirens is adding a refreshing twist to a metal scene that, since the fading of the uprisings era, has seen metal become increasingly divorced from the political context and become more of an escape, without a direct political agenda behind it.

We can experience the tension driving the band's lyrics in songs like "Terminal Leeches," where Maya sings:

> Possess not a human
> Obsess not over his flesh
> For you shall be slave of time
> Greed and hate is all that we know
> They fill your head with lies
> Ignorance, your ultimate demise

Similarly, in "Humanesticide," she declares:

> Aggression dominion
> And hate are your ways.
> Prepare for the final scene
> Where we end your game

While its female lineup and powerful lyrics made Slave to Sirens particularly noteworthy, other bands were even more adventurous and boundary-pushing musically. Damage Rite, founded in 2013, is definitely one of the most rhythmically sophisticated hardcore speed and thrash metal groups in the MENA region, while Tripoli-based "depressive black metal" bands Death Is Painless and Hatecrowned have even heavier yet groove-oriented sounds with lyrics that address the usual extreme metal themes of "hatred, misanthropy, darkness, and death," and, in Hatecrowned's case, "Anti-Cosmic Luciferianism."

If we recall how small Lebanon is and how many competing scenes there are for musicians to devote their time to, and the lack of places to perform or ways to promote one's music, the resilience of the local metal scene is remarkable—the number of high-quality bands equals that of Iran or Egypt or Pakistan, for example, countries that dwarf the country in terms of population. Two bands that are at the pinnacle of the scene in terms of originality and sophistication are Kaoteon and Blaakyum, two groups whose roots go back to the dawn of the millennium.

Ironically, both of these bands, which go back to the 1990s OG era of Middle Eastern metal, are among the few in the country to face actual harassment and even arrest for playing metal (as usual, the charges involved convoluted accusations of Satan worship). Indeed, Kaoteon was forced to change the original spelling of their name, Chaoteon (a symbiosis of "chaos" and "eaon," or historical "age"), because it was misread as being "Satan" in Arabic. Members of Blaakyum were arrested multiple times on accusations of Satan worship and similarly sordid claims.

Kaoteon might be the only band in the region to be arrested, as they tell it, *while performing.* Of course, if one is trying to create a B-movie version of Beirut and Lebanon, it's not surprising that this would be the response. The group's Bandcamp site describes them as an "extreme metal band with origins in the devastated Middle East, with a sound blending a brutally dark atmosphere with riffs that range from anthemic post-rock to oriental/Middle Eastern folklore and incendiary lyrics driven by the band's background in turbulent Beirut, Lebanon." Of course, this description is no closer to the truth of Lebanon than devil worship is to the truth of the band.

For their efforts the band was most recently awarded the "Global Metal" award at the 2018 *Metal Hammer* Golden Gods Awards. As lead singer Anthony Kaoteon explained to Mark, however, if Kaoteon might be considered a global metal band, it's because of their location, not their sound: "Geography doesn't have as much to do with our sound in Kaeteon as just learning and maturing. The metal scene in the region is doing a lot, but the majority of the bands are going in the wrong direction, copying the sounds of Lamb of God or Gojira, so they sound like cheap copycats, underproduced, made in a garage."

Interestingly, given Beirut's history of having great bars for live music, the relative stagnation, if not decline, of the metal scene is due, in Anthony's view, to the lack of venues to perform today. "In particular, there're no meeting points for metalheads. There used to be more. We would argue about which metal bar we would go to. These were our problems in the late 1990s and early 2000s." What's more, even as metal is becoming more accessible, it's losing its meaning "because metal in the beginning was about revolt, but [today] very few bands are taking on the idea of speaking political things. Metal has become just like fashion and branding as it's become more accessible. Metal is driven by a certain ideology. . . . Without the politics, it just becomes fantasy, power metal, images of bling and money."

Formed half a dozen years before Kaoteon, in the early years of the post–Civil War recovery, Blaakyum started off doing rock and metal covers as well as church songs (the band members were all Maronite) before moving through grunge and punk and toward thrash and ultimately to a heavier groove-oriented sound with strong elements of Arab/Middle Eastern rhythms (brought in with the incorporation of the darbuka, or Arabic percussion). Its original lineup was talented, but the pressures of a still-stunted economy and the need to earn money led to the demise of the original group in 2001, the year Kaoteon was formed.

The main members of the group reformed in 2007, with a new generation of musicians under the direction of lead singer Bassem Deaibess. After winning the Lebanese leg of the Global Battle of the Bands, it was able to represent Lebanon in London, ultimately being named seventh place out of the three thousand bands who auditioned. It also made its "pilgrimage to the holy land of metal" (in Bassem's words), the Wacken festival in Germany, where it won another competition at Wacken's Metal Battle in 2015 in what's been described as "a legendary landmark in the history of the Lebanese Metal scene" (as the website Lebmetal.com put it). Blaakyum was not only the first Lebanese band to perform there; they were profiled by the German television network Deutsche Welle TV.

The trajectories of the Kaoteon and Blaakyum are quite similar: larger bands ultimately paired down to a more manageable size; the need to have other sources of income outside the band to survive. The struggles against religious

FIGURE 20. Social media banner for World Metal Congress video podcast, episode 5, November 2020. Courtesy of Lina Khatib.

authorities, as well as the ascendance of hip hop and EDM, forced even the most talented Lebanese metal bands to reach a different level in order to stand out, never mind prosper. The epitome of the local absurdities—or so one would have thought—occurred in 2018, when the seminal band Sepultura was banned from performing in Lebanon a day or so before their show for officially indeterminate reasons, which were clearly tied to the band's assumed irreligiosity. Fittingly, then, Blaakyum led an all-star concert in their honor to protest their ban from Lebanon, doing a set of covers while the band watched on Skype video from Istanbul, from where they were supposed to leave for Beirut.

The black, death, and experimental metal band Khavar, founded in 2018, is another standout new band in the scene. With a lineage that goes back to one of Lebanon's first metal bands, Opposite (founded in 1996), and then the Weeping Willow. The band also features extreme metal drumming icon Derek Roddy, although he and other members float in and out of the lineup depending on their other touring responsibilities. After their first performance at Metro El Madina in June 2019 (alongside Kimaera, atmospheric death metal band Nocturna, and a young rock group, SOD), Roddy declared Beirut to be "one of my favorite places on Earth," a view shared by most musicians who spend any amount of time in the city. In the wake of the explosion, he explained to Lina Khatib in an episode of the World Metal Congress podcast on the Lebanese scene in November 2020 that the fact that "the Lebanese people were able to pull themselves up out of the ashes, [after] everything the country has been going through," made him reevaluate his own positionality as an American. Indeed, more than most cities, Beirut has earned the title *Umm al-musiqa* (mother of music), although, ironically, it has rarely if ever been called that among its innumerable sobriquets over the centuries (including "Berytus Nutrix Legum," roughly translatable as "Beirut, Mother of Breastfeeding and Laws," in the late Roman era).

FROM DEVIL WORSHIP TO LGBTQ+ IDENTITY: THE FIGHT FOR EQUALITY NO ONE REALLY EXPECTED

With the history of threats, arrests, and attacks for being a devil worshipper, it's not surprising that Blaakyum founder Bassem Deaibess would be supportive of other Lebanese artists who are threatened with censorship or worse, even if the band is Mashrou' Leila, whose peppy, indie sound is in many ways the antithesis of the metal aesthetic in Lebanon, or anywhere else for that matter. Yet when in late July 2019 the band was attacked by local Catholic authorities, who demanded their concert be canceled at the Byblos International festival, Bassem was in fact among the first artists to jump to Mashrou' Leila's defense.

LGBTQ+ activism has a longer history in Lebanon than just about anywhere else in the Middle East, save Israel. Although various courts in Lebanon have ruled that articles of the penal code barring sexual relations "that contradict the laws of nature" should not apply to LGBTQ+ people, the law continues to be used to harass and even arrest suspected gay people. Nonetheless, since the early 2000s LGBTQ+ activism has been a major issue in Lebanon, spearheaded by the founding of the group Hurriyyat Khassa (Private Privileges) that year. Several Beirut Pride events have been organized beginning in 2017 but each time threats and arrests have forced the cancelation. Nevertheless, there is less stigma and attacks against gay people in Beirut than most other cities in the MENA region, and to the present day there are bars and clubs that openly cater to a gay clientele, usually (but not always) without fear of closure. Lebanon remains "the exception" to the Middle Eastern rule when it comes to tolerance for openly gay people, the *New York Times* has declared, quoting activists in an article from December 2017, "Coming Out in Lebanon," who said that, despite the difficulties, their activism has made it possible "not to be scared," at least in Beirut.

Indeed, dozens of politicians have run for office in Lebanon publicly endorsing proposed laws to decriminalize homosexuality and well-known artists have joined public media campaigns calling for greater tolerance. At the same time, public events in support of gay rights have been banned in the last year by the security services, ostensibly because of threats by "radical Islamic groups" against organizers and marchers. So it was something of a shock when, deep into the summer festival season, leaders from the Maronite Catholic Eparchy of Byblos, where Mashrou' Leila famously played its first major gig, in 2010, and another in 2016 (more recently, Elton John, Lana Del Rey, and Jethro Tull performed at the city's famous annual music festival as well), suddenly came out demanding their show be canceled because the band's songs were "offensive to religious and humanitarian values and Christian beliefs." Not long after, a complaint was filed with the public prosecutor calling on the state to prosecute the band for insulting a religion, for inciting sectarianism, and for "spreading and promoting homosexuality," which, it was falsely claimed, is illegal under the penal code. Perhaps the band's biggest hit, "Djinn," which means both spirits and the alcohol gin, came in for particular attack because its lyrics seem to encourage "immoral" behavior.

Amnesty International swiftly entered the fray, declaring that "the authorities, mainly the Ministry of Interior, have a responsibility to take the necessary measures to ensure the band is protected from this spiteful campaign, and to ensure that the concert not be cancelled for security considerations. It is unconscionable that there continue to be such calls emanating from institutions that are meant to serve as role models to their constituencies, and can and should be upholding the right to freedom of expression and protection of vulnerable groups, instead of enabling hate speech, including homophobia."

That it was the local Catholic authorities and not Muslims who were at the center of this controversy was lost on no one. Indeed, Hezbollah has long been supportive of the arts scene, including festivals held in the Shi'i south of the country (which both bring in crucial foreign currency and help protect it from Israeli attacks). For Blaakyum's Bassem Deaibess, the situation cut directly to his own personal history as a metal artist. As he explained to Mark: "When I was arrested in 1998 [for being a metalhead/devil worshiper,] I was a Christian believer. I was studying to become a priest. I had a rosary with me in fact. I told the investigator, 'Look, I'm a Christian, you can find my rosary.' . . . But the name devil worshiper was catchy."

In fact, the episode brought back some issues he had had with Mark's description of Lebanon and the MENA metal scenes more broadly when he read *Heavy Metal Islam*. As he explained to Mark,

When I was reading the chapter on Lebanon I felt that Hezbollah was the problem, but in fact the main problem was not Hezbollah, it was the Christian—that is, Catholic and Maronite—Church! We recorded the first single we did in Haret Hreik! [the Hezbollah-controlled Shi'i quarter of southern Beirut where most of the destruction had occurred during the war in 2006]. The studio was named Ramadan Studio and it was also used to record Hezbollah *nasheeds* [a cappella religious songs venerating the Prophet]. We started recording in 1997; the owner, Kareem Ramadan, was a big glam metal fan. And there were huge posters of Poison and Cinderella on the wall, but suddenly in 1998 he put up wood paneling and pictures of al-Aqsa Mosque because Hezbollah started recording there. But he had a secret refrigerator with all the beers that he'd hide when Hezbollah would come.

For Bassem, there was no doubt that he had to stand up for Mashrou' Leila, even if they were on the opposite end of the musical spectrum. On behalf of the entire band, he posted:

We take a break from our long slumber and form the work we are doing on the new album and its promotional material to take a moment and stand in solidarity with fellow artists from Mashrou' Leila. Regardless of our opinion [of] them musically, Mashrou' Leila is a Lebanese band, that was able to rise up the complex Lebanese and Arabic pop culture ladder in an area where anything other than cheap Arabic pop barely ever makes it anywhere. Their open support for LGBT especially that their frontman is openly gay is another reason to admire them. Now there are attempts by some backwards Christian extremists to censor them and ban them from performing in Byblos.

NO ONE has the right to censor arts.

We stand with you Mashrou' full support.

Within a few hours upward of one hundred people liked/loved/angry-faced the post and other artists and bloggers also voiced support for the band.

Mashrou' Leila were as shocked as everyone else about the attempts to cancel their show, having just returned from a long sojourn, which included teaching a course at NYU and an extensive tour of the US and Europe, and they'd already played some of their most important shows at the very festival that now was considering banning them. While apologizing for any pain their music or videos might have caused, they remained steadfast in their argument that they'd done nothing wrong and complained about their music being "distort[ed] and understood in a wrong way."

Most of the mainstream media came out in support of Mashrou' Leila, with *an-Nahar* declaring that the conflict was now about the "meaning of

Lebanon" going forward into the future. But such support only emboldened the attacks against them, ultimately leading to the show's cancelation for "security reasons." Many artists and supporters of the band called for a boycott of the festival and the Dutch metal band Within Temptation in fact pulled out, while Yo-Yo Ma closed his show with a performance of their song "Taif."

CAN THE BC RICH REPLACE THE AK-47?

A dozen years ago, the rejection of the sectarian status quo was the creation of the party Hezb El Rock (or the Party of Rock), a spoof on the Hezbollah (or Party of God), complete with its own flag, which, in a clear play on Hezbollah's iconic flag, featured in green calligraphy the words "Rock Resistance in Lebanon" *("al-muqawwama al-rokkiya fi lubnan")*—again, a play on the Hezbollah flag's "Islamic Resistance in Lebanon" over a yellow field with a first rising—much like Bob Marley's famed *Uprising* album cover, but instead of holding an AK-47 (as in the Hezbollah flag), this hand is clenching a BC Rich guitar, the very symbol of heavy metal shredding. It was very confusing whether in fact the Party of Rock was a real political party. Facebook seemed to think so and actually banned the group's Facebook page, claiming it was sectarian, but then apologized when the members of the group protested that they were not in fact an actual political party but just a Facebook group of Lebanese metalheads who loved the music and were against all the sectarianism and corruption that defined Lebanese politics. As one of the original members, Maroun Habibi, explained to Mark, "While Hezb el Rock used to be a huge thing for us, I am sorry to burst the bubble but it was just a Facebook group between 2004 and 2010; it was the biggest Facebook group back then for rockers in Lebanon, it was also against all political heads back then. We were never a real Hezb. But we gained so much reputation!"

One of the early acolytes of the Party of Rock was Anthony Kaoteon. Almost a decade later, he's carrying on the spirit. In June 2019, not long before the Mashrou' Leila controversy, he took to Facebook to vent his frustration at fans who think metal and politics shouldn't mix. "So many metalheads show hate when all our songs are about stopping wars, poverty, prosecution. I think metal is not getting the attention it deserves as somehow we are sending the wrong message as depressed, angry, all hating people while metalheads are the funniest, friendliest, most open and inclusive people [I've] met." Kaoteon was particularly angry that people assume that metalheads are just aimlessly angry. "That's Emo," he explained. "We say fuck you to oppressors, suppressors, haters, and commanders but we should just spread a positive message and not one of hate, crime, death, and torture."

One can disagree with his understanding of Emo and even gangsta rap, which he also believes is too nihilistically negative. But he perfectly sums up the views of most metalheads I've met anywhere in the region when he declares that metal "should be a revolution AGAINST all that is wrong in the world. It is a call to stop ignorance and spread light and education." But Kaoteon is based in Europe, where despite all the problems there is a lot more light to be shared. In Lebanon and the region more broadly, what's always defined metal was how powerfully it's pointed out the darker recesses of the region and the hypocrisies of the hegemonic cultures. As we've seen, metal has had a harder time offering a positive vision through the music. As with Kaoteon and so many other members of the Hezb El Rock in Lebanon, it's largely the musicians and the communities they've created that transform the negative power of the music into the positive power of community and solidarity. And nowhere is that solidarity more needed today than in our next stop, Iran.

CONCLUSION: AN APOCALYPSE CHANGES ~~EVERYTHING~~ SOME THINGS

If a picture is worth a thousand words, how many songs is a two-minute video of one of the largest nonnuclear explosions ever produced by humans worth? For anyone who knows Beirut, the scene of the explosion at Beirut Port on August 2, 2020, was as shocking as it was tragic. The Port was the lodestar of the city, a place you drive or run past regularly when moving through the city and a place that was before the explosion equally known as a central site for the criminality, cronyism, and corruption that have long defined the city's, and Lebanon's, political economy.

Lebanon had already been hit hard by the coronavirus pandemic, even if, like most of the Middle East, the majority of Lebanese had little choice but to continue living their lives more or less as (ab)normal. But the explosion, which despite its miraculously low death toll damaged upward of half the city's buildings and displaced a quarter of a million inhabitants, made that impossible.

With its power—the equivalent of at least five hundred tons of TNT, more than many tactical nuclear warheads—it was "an apocalypse," as Moe Hamzeh explained to Mark when they spoke the day after the explosion. Much as the smell of 9/11 lingered in New York for weeks after the 9/11 attacks, the smell of the explosion and the ash still hung freshly in the air for days, followed by the smell of death and destruction for weeks and months afterward. Moe continued,

> I lived and witnessed all the wars we've had. I lived all of them, unfortunately. But this blast I never could imagine. It was an earthquake. And then the blast. I thought a missile had hit my street. Families were panicking everywhere and then the main one came and it was so huge. Everyone's windows and all curtains gone, people couldn't reach their families who were outside. Half the city is destroyed. . . . Really it's an apocalypse.

After half a year in which the Covid-19 pandemic all but destroyed Beirut's live music scene, which more than most places on Earth was so crucial to the identity of the city, the Port blast destroyed the better part of the city itself. Bassem Deaibess took Moe's analysis another step further less than a week later, explaining in a Facebook post on August 7: "I am under occupation. I believe we are all under occupation. The enemy is the whole political class who are occupying us, is it possible to refuse to abide by their rules, by the rule of their laws, refuse to pay anything to them, refuse to execute their demands? Isn't it time for armed resistance against this enemy, an enemy as equally inhuman as the Zionists and the Terrorists?" His fear that even this level of destruction would change nothing in Lebanese politics was borne out when, after much posturing about rooting out the corruption and malfeasance that made the blast possible, the Parliament chose none other than Saad Hariri to assume the post of prime minister, reaffirming the impossibility of changing the Lebanese system ever after a cataclysm.

Despite the almost Armageddon-like physical destruction, artists quickly began organizing online and, where possible, physical benefit concerts. One group of local and international musicians and Beirut-lovers, Beirut Calling, held four virtual concerts in a month that raised over $10,000 for relief. Iron Maiden donated $1,000 worth of merchandise and memorabilia to the initiative. While some artists have finally given up and have left the scene and even the country (including, as of the time of writing, Blaakyum), others released some of their best work in the wake of the explosion. No band more exemplifies this than Kimaera, which put out several singles in late 2020. While the album as a whole features a theme about Ancient Rome and its fratricidal politics, the star track of the new album is undoubtedly the band's cover of the Majida El Roumi classic "Ya Beirut," which they remade as a symphonic metal anthem with local chanteuse Cheryl Khayrallah.

As lead singer JP Haddad explained in the World Metal Congress podcast on Lebanese metal,

> When the [pandemic] happened, like everywhere else we thought, "It's about time we start working on the new album, let's take advantage, we're not doing anything." . . . We had planned to do "Ya Beirut" for a long time and we were supposed to meet with Cheryl at 7 PM on the day of the explosion, [but] it happened the hour before. But we decided to go on anyway, there was so much mixed emotion, such a feeling of anger and disappointment. The city we grew up and lived in was destroyed in a minute. . . . It would be a good chance to do something that would actually mean something to people that they would relate to and this song was perfect.

Both the song and the video are, deliberately, over the top—a fittingly kitschy yet utterly engrossing riposte to the devastation of the explosion. It truly was a breath of fresh air and musical joy in the midst of so much suffering and dislocation in a city that, despite everything, is loved by most all who have had the fortune of calling it home. And indeed, according Haddad, "Sixty percent of those who loved [our] song have nothing to do with metal and we just introduced them to metal, that you can take an Arabic song and do something new with it. . . . Most of the feedback we got were extremely positive."

The lyrics, which in El Roumi's voice seem to be a lament for a lost lover, become politically supercharged for the present moment:

Oh Beirut, Lady of the World	(Ya Beirut ... Sitt ad-dunya ya Beirut),
We confess in front of the One God	(na'atarif 'amam allahu al-wahad) ...
[We] gifted you a knife instead of a flower.	(wa'ahdaynak makan alwardat skynaan) ...
Rise from under the rubble	(Qumi min taht ar-rahm) ...
Like an almond's rose in spring	(kazahrat lawz fi nisan) ...
Revolution is born from the womb of sorrow.	('iina althawrat tulad man rahim alahzan)

Sadly, in a development that wouldn't surprise anyone, Majida El Roumi—who uploaded a new video mash-up of her song with patriotic images the day after the explosion—sued Kimaera, arguing not only that they engaged in an unauthorized broadcast of "her" song (in fact, she has no standing to sue, since she's not one of the songwriters) but, worse, that they created "a hybrid work that spreads violence and blackness and includes strange sounds and melodies that aroused astonishment." Rumors of Satanic means naturally followed, like the shockwave after an explosion. As Haddad pointed out, "You can't change people overnight." And so, despite garnering tens of thousands of views in its few days on YouTube, Kimaera pulled the song rather than go to war against El Roumi and the Lebanese musical and cultural establishments.

Beirut and Lebanon, it seems, are still waiting for their song, and their revolution.

Postscript: On February 25, 2022, tragedy struck the Lebanese music scene and the metal world at large when Kimaera founder JP Haddad died in Cairo, where he'd moved to work at the Cairo Jazz Club after the economic situation in Covid-era, post-explosion Beirut made it impossible to continue working there. His death, from a gas leak in his apartment only weeks before the release of the band's new album, was yet another senseless loss that reflected the costs of a disastrous political and economic situation across the MENA that has forced so many extremely talented young people to leave their homelands for uncertain and sometimes perilous and even deadly futures abroad.

FIVE

Iran

LIVING IN THE UPSIDE DOWN AND INSIDE OUT

Composed, arranged, and produced by Mark LeVine and Salome MC

MORE THAN MOST ANY OTHER MUSLIM-MAJORITY country with a viable metal scene, Iran has always embodied, if not epitomized, the Middle Eastern metal experience. And this hasn't changed in the dozen years since *Heavy Metal Islam* was published, although the dynamics and the locations in which metal is produced and experienced have changed in some crucial respects. Perhaps the first hint at how things were changing was the appearance of the band TarantisT, whom Mark introduced in that book, at the 2009 edition of the SXSW festival in Austin, Texas, where he'd been invited to curate a night of Middle Eastern metal and hip hop to celebrate its publication. In fact, the whole band didn't quite make it to Austin; only founder and bassist Arash Rahbary succeeded in making it all the way.

Arash's herculean effort to get to Texas all the way from Tehran—his fellow band members either didn't get visas or weren't allowed out of the country—made him something of a celebrity at the festival as media picked up on the story. Making his trouble worse but the story better, his car broke down and he ran out of money along the way; he arrived literally with nothing but the clothes on his back and his bass. Luckily, Mark had organized a band for him, and after a half-hour rehearsal everyone was good to go. It may not have been the tightest or most musically extraordinary set in metal history, but it was undoubtedly one of the most impassioned and inspired. The media dubbed Arash and his makeshift band the "Metallica of Iran."

Jump ahead almost nine years. Tehran. A concert. Not in the basement where Mark first met Arash and so many other Iranian metalheads and rappers in 2007. True, once upon a time basements were the site for "underground" music in Iran, so much so that the term for underground music, *zirzamin,* is the word for basement, and *musighi-ye zirzamini*—literally, "music of the basement"—means "underground music." Nevertheless, neither rock, metal, nor hip hop was in the underground anymore, at least not usually and not deeply. And this moment was definitely not underground, although it was certainly not mainstream either. The concert in question, which took place in January 2018, could have been in Berlin, Birmingham, Los Angeles, or Tampa; the theater, the lighting, the sound, the bands, and even the audience were all professional enough to be anywhere. Only the Persian banter in between songs, the lack of a mosh pit and general politeness of the crowd (most of whom were seated while enthusiastically headbanging), and the fact that the majority of the women were sort of wearing headscarves suggested this was Tehran.

This particular show was part of a "festival," more accurately a weekly Saturday Night gathering—*Shab shanbehah* means "Saturday night" in Persian (the *-e* that would normally come after *Shab* was left off to make the word sound cool). The gathering occurred with various levels of frequency in the last half of the 2010s, although it had largely stopped by 2019. That night, a German metal drummer, traveler, and vlogger named Andi Rohde was there, as surprised as Mark was the first time he had seen a metal show in the Middle East. The evening featured several bands from the first decade of Iranian metal that, unlike the majority of their peers, had remained in Iran. 5grs is recognized today as one of the more important bands of the 2000s, although so dense was the metal scene then that they weren't on Mark's radar during his first visit. Even older still was the band Avesta, who formed near the dawn of the metal era in Iran, all the way back in 2000, and whose lyrics were drawn directly from Zoroastrian themes (the Avesta is the Zoroastrian holy book). Many musicians inside and outside Iran's metal scene have simultaneously praised the originality of the bands and lamented the lack of professionalization in the scene caused by lack of regular access to live performing. But at least for someone reared in the New York and Los Angeles rock and metal scenes, bands like Avesta and 5grs, never mind all the bands Mark wrote about in *Heavy Metal Islam,* can stand toe to toe with any up-and-coming metal band in the US. If there was anything approaching a live scene in Iran, there's little doubt that it would be world metal central.

And yet, as quickly as the scene reblossomed, it retreated again. As Ali Azhari, guitarist of the seminal death metal group Arthimoth, put it, "Six to seven months ago suddenly the authorities withdrew permission and silenced us and now [late 2019] we are in an era of silence again. And that was that." (In fact, there would be some loud shredding going on in 2020, as we'll see

FIGURE 21. Still from video of heavy metal show in Tehran, January 2018. Video by Andi Rohde.

toward the end of this chapter.) But the official silencing of public performances doesn't mean that there aren't still a lot of young bands emerging, even if they're emerging underground again—however paradoxical that spatial analogy seems, it well captures the reality of trying to break a band in a truly under-the-ground scene. And some musicians and even filmmakers have utilized the combination of ambivalence and oppression to produce fictionalized simulacra of the realities of life as a rock or metal musician in Iran today, epitomized by the award-winning film *No One Knows about Persian Cats* (*Kasi az Gorbehaye Irani Khabar Nadareh,* 2009), by director Bahman Ghobadi, and more recently, *Forbidden to See Us Scream in Tehran,* by Farbod Ardebili. Not surprisingly, both films focus on the heightened challenges faced by women singers and musicians to reflect the struggles of the scene.

Whether cover bands or focused on original music the situation today is, according to Ali (who would know better than almost anyone else), "the same as always. It's not like there's a truly ongoing, uninterrupted scene. Instead, with Ershad [the Ministry of Culture and Islamic Guidance] it's like whenever someone takes charge of permissions who happens to like metal then it goes on, and when he's replaced with someone who doesn't like or at least tolerate metal, then there's a crackdown. It's not even a *basij* [the self-styled religious morality police created as a volunteer paramilitary force by Khomeini in 1979] thing, it's just internal to Ershad, who's working where at any moment."

Ultimately, however, it's not merely chance that determines the official mood toward metal, or other forms of music and expressive culture more broadly. After thinking carefully how to most accurately choose his words, Ali explained, "Look, the long-term policy of the Islamic Government is to put more pressure on people when there's pressure from outside in order to control them. So, for example, one of the direct effects of the pressure from outside is that the pressure on women in terms of the *hijab* or art and music gets worse because they know that dissatisfaction is rising across society and they need to take charge of that before sentiments get out of hand, so they start with the simple things. And the two most simple are music and *hijab*."

HAPPINESS IN A MINOR KEY

Just how complex Iranian music has become is even more apparent if we explore the music of 1980s Iranian pop icon Shahram Shabpareh, who was the drummer of the rock band the Rebels in the 1960s, developed a successful solo career, and then had to flee the newly established Islamic Republic after the Revolution. As avant-garde singer and setar player Mohsen Namjoo explained in a talk in 2014, Shabpareh's music reflects the discursive as well as affective tensions in modern Iranian pop music, which point to the similarly affective dimensions and power of contemporary underground youth music today through a mournfulness that allows the aesthetic and political power of the music to be fully exposed in a way similar to gospel and blues in the United States. In so doing, the very sad and mournful affect leads the listener—at least potentially—to a state of perceived happiness.

This is not a religious or ecstatic type of happiness, of the kind that occurs with an often similarly minor-sounding Sufi chant or the kind of *tarab* performance associated with virtuosic Arab art music (termed *ghena* in Persian music), which conservative religious authorities consider *haram* because it brings listeners as well as performers to a highly emotional state not involving God. Rather, it's a far more ordinary—and, in that sense, more profound— sense of happiness, "like at a celebration or party when you're dancing," Namjoo continued, because it allows one to continue, and cope, with one's day.

This secular experience of mourning is in direct contrast to the manner in which public occasions in Iran are dominated by mournful performances associated with the martyrdom and death of the sons of Ali, Hussein and Hassan (the foundational events of Shi'ism), and is reflected in the large number of songs that are both in minor keys and 6/8 time. As Brooklyn-based Iranian singer Carmel Kooros explained to Mark, the 6/8 time "swings, and it creates melodic rhythms that are easy to copy and make you happy to sing, regardless of whether they're in a minor or major mode. Sorrow is a deep concept. . . . Iconic pop singer Shahram Shabpareh has all three catalysts of sorrow—the lyrics, the way that a singer utters the sounds and words, and the [mostly minor] scales. And yet he's the icon of cheerfulness and happiness in Iran!" Not surprisingly, lyrics, performance, and melody continue to be foundational vehicles for both sorrow and mournfulness, but also anger and resistance as well. Whether in post-Revolution, wartime Islamic Republic Iran or across the battle lines in Iraq, Egypt, Syria, or Palestine, or indeed globally, conservative governments repress popular music (until they realize it's counterproductive and try to coopt it).

"Think about the 1980s in Iran," Namjoo continues, bringing up the moment when most of the first two generations of metalheads and rappers came of age, or at least became in any way socially conscious of the world around them. There is little space for happiness in the midst of war and authoritarian revolutionary governance. This grotesque mournfulness inevitably becomes subverted from all directions—from the joyfulness of Googoosh to the brutality of death metal and the "thug life" of gangsta rap. But there is a specific historical, semiotic, and cultural context in Iran that links the minor and major, the happy and the morning, together in ways that don't occur in the same manner in the music of surrounding cultures.

THE GREEN WAVE AGAINST THE POWER SLAVES

Not long after Mark first visited Iran in 2007, a major crackdown began that was given the name "Project for the Elimination of Underground Music." It was a response to what performance studies scholar Heather Rastovac describes as the "ongoing challenge by underground musicians to the dominant discourse on questions of national identity and the meaning of being Iranian." At the same time, the official intelligentsia also tried to understand from a more scholarly—if still judgmental—perch why the music had such power.

Thus the Mehr News Agency convened a research seminar on underground music in the summer of 2007. What became clear from the panel was that what makes underground music unique, powerful, and popular in Iran was that it contained protest that was prohibited in legitimate music. At the same time, a generational conflict was clearly in evidence, as the older and more established (and largely classically/conservatory-trained) musicians were angry at the international attention being garnered by the young pop and rock artists, while the young musicians had little regard in their complaints against censorship for the fact that the older artists had spent decades working through the same system. Even then, the relative success of slightly more recognized artists generated criticism and even suspicion and accusations of collaboration among their peers. It's not surprising that, for very different reasons, many of the same artists soon made their home outside the country. Not unrelatedly, this aesthetic brain drain occurred just as the government realized that it needed to figure out how best to coopt and control the alternative scenes, capture the energy, and redirect it away from politics.

Iran's musical trajectories have in many ways mirrored—if sometimes inverting—its political trajectory since 2008, which in turn was a harbinger of both the explosion of the Arab uprisings and the difficult and often violent path they've followed. While Lebanon's Cedar Spring in 2006 provided the first indication of the explosive political power of the emerging generation, Iran's Green Wave (referred to in Persian variously as *jonbesh-e sabz*, "Green Movement," or *mowj-e sabz*, "Green Wave"), which emerged in the wake of the highly contentious and disputed presidential election in June 2009, signaled the first popular youth revolt against the established political systems. The last years of President Ahmedinejad's first term were marked not only by a weakening economy and increased international isolation but also by growing anger at his rule in Iran by a large section of Iran's overrepresented young generation. It was thus not surprising that, when he ran for reelection in 2009, he would face a serious challenge from whatever more "liberal" candidate was allowed to run against him. Indeed, fearing this, the Supreme Guardian Council vetoed several candidates for being insufficiently supportive of the goals and ideology of the Revolution.

However, one major reform-oriented candidate, Mir Hossein Mousavi, who was Prime Minister during the eight-year war with Iraq, was allowed to run, and the Green Wave emerged to support him as part of a wider attempt to challenge the near stranglehold on executive power held by religious hard-liners, not just via Ahmedinejad and the presidency but through the Revolutionary Guards and, of course, the highest echelons of the religious establishment. It was after the allegedly (and, indeed, likely) fraudulent victory by Ahmedinejad over his popular challenger that the movement morphed into a more directly political force, demanding the annulment of the official results and a restoration of many of the freedoms lost with the Revolution three decades earlier.

Implausibly, the government announced the election winner—Ahmedinejad—less than two hours after the polls closed. Confused yet hopeful, the youth took over the streets. The initial peaceful protests saw people singing "My School Mate" ("Yar-e Dabestani-e Man"), an anthem of friendship that has long been the go-to revolutionary song in various protests in Iran's history. Unfortunately, they quickly turned violent as the police and then the *basij* started attacking protesters. When it became clear that the people wouldn't back down easily, the movement's symbol, Mousavi, was placed under house arrest—where he remains to this day—and several hundred students were detained. Unprecedented youth-led protests erupted across the country. The movement used well-known dates on the Islamic revolutionary calendar to attack the governor, going so far as to call Khamenei "a murderer" whose rule was "null and void." They transformed Quds (or Jerusalem) day—where "Death to America!" had long been shouted—into a day to condemn Russia for its recognition of the Ahmedinejad "victory."

Then, on the anniversary of the US Embassy takeover, protesters shouted, "Death to No One!" in a newfound attempt to discredit the symbolically violent chants that have been embraced by the public and authorities alike since the first days of the Revolution, as epitomized by the well-worn and by then clichéd chant "Death to America!" As momentum grew behind the Green Wave, the government response was increasingly tough. Fearing that the legitimacy, and potentially the survival, of the Islamic Revolutionary state was threatened, the government cracked down harshly during the course of six weeks.

We know how the story ended—the Green Wave was effectively crushed by the Islamic government, supported by its *basij* militia (although by the standards of Assad, Sisi, and even Erdoğan, its reaction was by no means among the region's most violent or deadly). President Obama was warned that anything he might say in the way of supporting the protesters would only delegitimize the Green Wave, and so he kept silent for several crucial weeks until intensified government repression led him from cautious commentary to describing the crackdown as "violent and unjust." In the meantime, *basij* members were filmed firing into crowds and breaking into houses. Hospital staff protested after people were transported to the hospitals dead or in critical condition with gunshot wounds. The Islamic Revolutionary Guards Corps (IRGC) and the *basij* also attacked universities and students' dorms at night and destroyed property. European embassies were getting the word out to bring injured protesters to them rather than hospitals, where they were being arrested upon arrival.

The death of a young woman, Neda Agha-Soltan, caught on a video that immediately went viral, became a rallying point for the opposition. Indeed, *Neda* in Persian means, among other things, a "voice" or "calling," which is why she was called the "Voice of Iran" after her murder. Neda was by some accounts an underground musician, or at least an aspiring one, who tragically didn't live long enough to see the piano she'd purchased before the protests delivered to her home.

In the fall of 2009, more than one hundred of the Green Wave's most important leaders, activists, and theorists appeared in show trials. The regime also shut down newspapers, magazines, and websites close to the Green Wave. One year after the Green Wave's birth, Mousavi published a proposed new covenant, in which he declared that the regime represented "institutionalized corruption hiding behind a pretense of piety." He placed the Green Wave in the context of Iran's hundred-year-old quest for democracy. He was silent on the *velayat-e faqih* (the Rule of the Jurisconsults, the governing system designated by Khomeini for the new Islamic Republic), but he clearly stated that a government's legitimacy can be founded only on the will and support of the people. Nothing in the constitution is sacrosanct, he declared, and every article of the law should be subject to debate and reconsideration.

Whatever their ultimate failure, the Green Wave protests generated unprecedented support for Iranian young people globally. Well-known Armenian-Iranian pop singer Andy (whose full name is Andy Madadian) teamed up with Jon Bonjovi and Ritchie Sambora to record a special version of "Lean on Me" in support of the protesters. Artists from Joan Baez to Guns N' Roses and Pakistan's premier rock group, Junoon, sent messages of support. Many if not most Iranian artists in the diaspora actively supported the protests; those that remained quiet did so for fear of what might happen when they returned to Iran to perform or visit family. As the protests spread, Mark organized a running blog page with the *Huffington Post* to put up reports from artists taking part in the protests, publicize new songs, and share messages of support. Writing from Egypt, where his father had just been released from prison, Shady Nour wrote: "You guys in Iran have all the worlds' music scenes' respect for dealing with all of this right now. . . . It's a pain, I know. I had to go through the same childish works of Mubarak here in Egypt when my dad ran for president. He was jailed. I let out all my anger and hatred in the form of music. It worked. Good luck and stay strong everyone."

Singer Hamed Nikpay recorded a song, "Maalek-e Een Khak" ("The Owner of This Land"), riffing off Ahmedinejad's insulting dismissal of protesters as "worthless" and "riffraff" (ashghal). While he didn't actively participate in the protests in 2009, Iran's most beloved singer, Mohammad Reza Shajarian, backed the protesters and refused to allow his music to be played by the government, threatening "to file a complaint if they continued to use my music." This stance was all the more powerful because he'd been one of the most important musicians to turn against the Shah, resigning from his position at the State Radio network before the Revolution, and singing the prayer before sunset each night during Ramadan in the years after the Islamic Republic was established. While writing a song, "Zaban-e Atash o Ahan" ("The Language of Fire and Iron"), in support of dialog between the government and protesters, he predicted that the opposition by artists to the government after the elections in 2009 would produce a "confrontation between the artists and this government."

Besides these icons of a previous era, older songs with themes of oppression, corruption, and justice were repurposed with new YouTube videos featuring images of protesters. Social media showed its political muscle for the first time during the protests, though not inside Iran, where only a few dozen activists were using Twitter regularly in comparison with the far more important use of texting and other older alternatives. Where Twitter was important was both in the awareness raised by diaspora Iranians and other supporters of the protesters in the broader media universe and, to some degree, in the confusion of the regime about who was doing all the tweeting (whether the campaign to have people globally make their Twitter locations Tehran, which initially gave the false impression that thousands of Iranians inside the country were tweeting, actually did any good will remain a subject of debate for a long time to come).

As the protests grew more intense and violence began to be unleashed against demonstrators, one metal musician wrote, "Now we've got lots of ideas to transform to rhythm and blues. we will create new music to fuel the protests." As the government's filtering and blocking of Iranian music platforms intensified, local artists used virtual private networks (VPN) to get around the censorship and have their music reach the audience by any means necessary. One of such websites was now defunct Zirzamin, a credible platform for the review and presentation of artists in the alternative music scene. Fereidoon Tafreshi, the website's editor-in-chief, remembers Kiosk as the most vocal band that followed the Green Wave developments closely: "Kiosk's music became a 'news channel' with multiple songs that touched the current affair at that time and this aspect made their songs a bit mortal"— that is, gave them a more limited musical shelf life. Shahin Najafi, on the other hand, who remains one of the most popular diaspora musicians, had greater intellectual depth with his lyrics, Tafreshi recalls, which kept him more relevant as time has passed. But it wasn't just Kiosk. As documented by Shabnam Goli in her comprehensive PhD exploration of Persian "underground rock music," from rock to metal artists like the Ways, Electroqute, and Hooman Ajdari, extreme youth music has cultural and political resistance inscribed in its aesthetic, sonic, and performative DNA.

A percussionist Mark had worked with who was in the middle of the fighting explained that "Tehran is burning in extreme brutalism of Islamic fascists," but he also realized the creative potential of these liminal experiences: "i hope there be a good outcome from all this. Im thinking about a concept album regarding the events."

Salome MC expressed the frustration of Iranian youth at the prodemocracy and reform crackdown through music, seeing it equally as representing an increasingly bitter culture war as well. The music video for the song "Do Not Muddy the Water" (the title references a poem by the renowned Iranian poet Sohrab Sepehri, and Salome later changed the name to "Constant Pain of Mine" for her mixtape *Paranoid Descent*, from 2009) featured cell-phone videos shot by protesters that she edited together. In the song, she raps:

> It was a murderer who killed my friend's hope,
> I had this wish to go live on top of a mountain, staying away from it all
> But I couldn't, because what they're doing is hard to swallow
> This constant pain of mine emanates from being a human
> Because one night, they stole my light of hope
> If I stay silent, if I stay still
> Who is gonna write? Who is gonna sing? Who is gonna move if I am also passive?
> Don't be silent, because if you keep silence, it will be your turn soon.

Despite the threat of arrest, torture, and even death, most young artists believed, as one put it in the blog, "Our parents are afraid to show up, so we young people go there knowing that we might get shot and end up dead, but if we don't go out to make our voice heard, who will?" On the other hand, some artists seemed to relish the chance to fight the hated *basij* on more equal terms, becoming almost delirious in the heat of battle. As one told me after Khameini came out against the protesters in his Friday sermon of June 19, they were quick to post reactions, claiming that he was inciting more violence: "His speech means death for many young people tomorrow in Tehran. He basically OK'd their murder & arrest. Bastard!! He is losing his mind ... it's not politics it's JONOON [crazy/insane]! Haaaaaaa haaaaa haaaaaaaaaaaaaaa."

Ironically, given how pessimistic their lyrics had tended to be, the metalheads who were taking part in the protests tended to be upbeat during the first few weeks. As one wrote Mark,

> I am fine but so worried and restless because the situation is so fragile and dangerous but of course hopeful.... I don't think that the regime could extinguish the fire.... It is so difficult. I enjoyed fighting on the street with different people from different cultures! ... these 2 Nights.... Poor amateur police is so loose and frightened. This seems to be the hugest culture jam one can see.... Some of Hezbollahiz [members of a pro-Government religious vigilante and paramilitary movement] and religious fellas and women also are fighting with guards with us and once i was carrying a Woman in her Chadorr full hijaab!!! The Spectrum of people types seems to be rich (wide).... Variety of people ... all the streets ... different cities. P.S. It seems this fuckin' gas that police uses has no effects on me other than losing sleep!

Despite his wonder at how "all parts of Tehran had united against *basij* violence," he sensed that the momentum could turn against protesters very quickly if they weren't very disciplined: "Mark, please name your article: 'A Flower to the Police'! after our album *Flowers in the Desert*. We have to control our thoughts." More ominously, however, it seemed the metalheads were being targeted by the regime specifically, as "they easily located and arrest[ed] people, especially rockers ... who [thus] prefer to wait and see. But the rappers are out there."

Indeed, artists wrote of being physically attacked and beaten with batons, of how violence was being used as a strategy "to keep the people away from protesting by creating Fear." One metalhead who was on the front lines wrote to Mark,

The point is this, it's like that we have two different buses in Iran, going straight in two opposite ways and they are going to hit each other.... they are going to hit and there will be massive massacre.... in one hand we have guardless people, university students , ordinary people that you may see each day in the streets, and in the other hand, there are National Guards and *basij*, etc. They Have used Us, ... can you feel me!? They have USED us to show the world that we accept Islamic republic and islamic government of Ahmadinejad.... i can easily say that iranian youth feel like this.... they feel like they have been raped!? can you feel the heat in my words.... we really need global attention, cause we don't have no media to express what's going on in iran.... and let me say it in this way ... i need some kind of thoughtful help! don't really know what to do ... these people have no leadership

In the song "Sarbaze Vatan" ("Soldier of the Homeland"), released several years after the aborted elections, the rapper Yas rapped, "We're the children of the underground. We will keep on shouting," which was interpreted by some as a warning against the country's leaders. But in the end, as in most other countries of the region, their voices were silenced, at least publicly, by the overwhelming power and violence of the state. Yet as these words make clear, the youth-led Iranian protest movement was encountering the same problem that stifled the anticorporate globalization and then antiwar movements in the 1990s and 2000s, and that would doom the Occupy movements in the years after: the near impossibility of achieving long-term success against powerful states and vested economic interests without identifiable leaders and organizational structures (which in this case were destroyed by the government). Furthermore, the average Iranian who wanted to earn a living and go on with their lives was growing tired of closed streets and daily violence. "You kids should just go home, enough is enough!" Salome recalls a cab driver saying, as she was commuting to Valiasr Square to join a protest.

Nevertheless, the eruption of the Arab uprisings in late 2010 did lead to attempts to resurrect the Green Wave, or at least bring it to public attention again. And so on January 27, 2011, in support of the protests in Tunisia and those that had just started in Egypt, the Green Wave called a series of protests for prior to the Revolution Day march on February 11. Various groups tried to obtain official permission to protest, but it was denied, and Mousavi and others were placed once again under house arrest after calling for a "Day of Rage" only three days after Mubarak was forced from power. When protests did occur the government arrested as many as fifteen hundred people during three months of protests. The *basij*, including female "stormtroopers," were also heavily involved in the crackdown.

In the wake of the crackdown, two major processes were unleashed. First was the mass exodus of musicians, artists, filmmakers, and activists abroad, one way or another. Even artists who went abroad for work or study often stayed away or didn't return in good measure because of the crackdown. Solidifying the clear intent of the government to use religiously justified condemnations of music to go after any young activists who might be a threat, in 2010 the government not only banned musical instruction in private schools but also saw the Supreme Leader Khameini declare that music was "not compatible with the highest values of the sacred regime of the Islamic Republic."

With these musicians leaving, many of them pioneers in their respective genres, you had a new generation of Internet music taking over by kids who had come of age in Ahmadinejad's Iran, as opposed to the previous generation, which had experienced a relative freedom under Khatami's government and had taken it for granted. Having emerged under such trying circumstances, these younger artists were a lot more equipped to make music inside Iran and survive, including monetizing music in ways the previous generation couldn't have imagined. For the previous generation such resilience and entrepreneurialism are both fascinating and admirable.

On the eve of the elections in 2009 Iranian youth culture was at a crossroads. As Sohrab Mahdavi of the then web music portal and news site Tehran Avenue recalled to Mark, "Ahmadinejad had become president by refiring, reigniting the revolutionary propensity to fight the 'elite,' who in this case were, beyond the actual rich, the middle classes who emerged during the post-Khomeini era. At the same time, the Ahmadinejad administration wanted to create its own understanding of culture, and so redirected government funds to activities it saw as culturally aligned to its project, meaning that the creative middle class had to look elsewhere in and outside Iran for support."

Arash Rahbary from TarantisT, who was out of Iran during the protests and returned in October 2009 as they died down, explained that even if the people were ready to explode in the lead-up to the elections, they had already been shoved down by the time he got back. As for the hip hop scene, Salome MC well remembers the feeling in the air:

FIGURE 22. Ali Sana'ei peforming with Googoosh at the Hollywood Bowl, 2018. Photo by Payam Arzani.

> In the midst of it, I wasn't thinking about [the] future of music personally, and I don't know anyone who did. It was more fundamental than that; we thought of our basic rights, and the travesty of justice that we'd just witnessed; everything was fresh and burning, and for a while there was an air of hope that something will happen. That Ahmadinejad would go away. We had high hopes for Mousavi. Those hopes of course died away slowly, and once we came to terms with the fact that Mahmoud is here to stay, well, it wasn't the end of the world anymore. It was just going to be another three years of the status quo.

So things didn't get worse for musicians; they just stayed exactly the way they were, and whatever trajectory, hopes, or possibilities these scenes thought they'd had before them in May 2009 were gone, but by year's end it seemed that all hope was lost.

With most every form of music or activism repressed, if not completely shut down, it's not surprising that by 2012 most of the Iranian rockers, rappers, and metalheads Mark first met in the mid- to late 2000s had left Iran or were trying to get out. Farzad Golpayegani had moved to Istanbul and ultimately landed in New York and then Los Angeles. Ali Sana'ei traveled to

FIGURE 23. Salome MC performing at the Music Freedom Day Festival, Harstad, Norway, February 2016. Photo by Andreas Leonardsen.

Los Angeles to study English, and his bass playing skills quickly cemented his place at the highest rung of the pecking order, especially in the vibrant Iranian-American music scene, where he's "played with more or less every famous Persian singer there is :-)," as he put it to Mark when asked for a synopsis of his work in the last decade. Arash returned several times to the US before moving permanently in 2011 and spending the next half-decade doing everything possible to get the rest of his family out. Rapper Salome MC went first to Japan and got a master's degree in audiovisual arts, ultimately landing in Seattle, where she is active as a music producer, educator, and multimedia artist. Hichkas now calls London home, while Mahdyar, one of Iran's most renowned hip hop producers, lives in France.

And so it goes. It was simply too difficult and too dangerous to stay for artists who performed music that challenged the political, cultural, or religious status quo. And despite the success of some of the artists over the last decade, life as a migrant could be and usually was very difficult. As Arash Rahbarry explained it, "This migration has its own disasters and hassles. The minute you go to another country you realize that there is no more parental support here and no one gives a flying finger about you and who you were."

At the same time, the opportunities for success outside Iran were, in general, greater than inside, especially for metal musicians (rappers had a slightly easier time of it if they weren't political or too profane with their lyrics). And yet not everyone left in the immediate aftermath of the crushing of the Green Wave. Guitarist Ali Azhari went to Jordan to study film before returning home for several more years. As he explained to Mark, the promise of the Rouhani era was quickly frustrated by the "iron ideological axe of the Islamic state.... Meanwhile with the emergence of a new generation of self-taught musicians and their access to the World Wide Web (thanks to VPNs), the underground scene was taken to a new level of technical standard. If back in 2007 everything from playing skills to mix and mastering stage was based on numerous trials and errors, today it's all based on sophisticated practical methods."

Even more than in the previous decade, social media and the Internet have been key to the evolution of Iranian youth music, especially toward the more extreme/avant-garde edges. Ali Azhari continued: "With the aid of the Internet, the millennial generation learns the roots from the best and infuse their taste into that knowledge. This movement seemed to be growing vividly after the election of President Hassan Rouhani in 2012. The new Islamic government attempted to increase the social freedom 'not entirely' by giving a chance to some of the Western music genres to have a limited publicity under 'certain' circumstances." And indeed, the number of approved concerts did increase significantly.

Despite the conservative judiciary's regular indictments of musicians—widely believed to undermine Rouhani's moderate policies regarding culture and music compared to his predecessor—the real players behind the regime decided to use the powerful tool of music, which they'd been so afraid of, as a tool toward their own favor. Suddenly, there were rappers who made songs in support of nuclear power accompanied with elaborate music videos, clearly with funding from the government. There were even musicians who endorsed political candidates and appeared in photo ops. There are backroom deals, and as long as you stay out of certain topics, you are allowed a relative freedom within the Islamic Republic's framework. It's not that different from how the music industry works in many other parts of the world, but instead of the government, big labels and corporations call the shots. It shows how powerful a tool music can be and the popularity of musicians over politicians that, when pop singer Morteza Pashaie died of pancreatic cancer in 2014, Tehran saw the biggest crowds since the protests in 2009, which led to some police violence against mourners.

The international media, meanwhile, increasingly woke up to Iranian artists, as TarantisT was able to open for several major acts, and Salome MC was featured in *Time* in 2014 as one of the "world's best rappers" people didn't know about. Still whether in or outside the country, the struggles continued, as did the need to persevere. In lyrics that well summarize the attitude of most of the country's metal and hip hop artists, in her song "Riddle" from 2018, Salome MC sings: "All the hardship is alike a sledgehammer to your steel. If there's not enough meat, double the broth and deal" *("Potk-e sakhtiha vase poulad pustet, Gusht ke kam bud dubl kon abgushtet").*

In fact, the Rouhani government understood the power of music, and so the Culture Ministry tried to legitimize the issue by labeling rock and metal concerts as "musical performances" under the supervision of Theatre Administration of the Ministry of Islamic Cultures. But according to Ali, "This literally means that they look at them more of a freak show rather than a musical genre. But at the end of the day this approach led to a good number of gigs in Tehran."

Iranian artists are by now well used to the rhythm of tightening and relaxing restrictions on their art, as the government regularly adjusts its control over the ever more youthful population just enough to prevent a return to full-blown protests. Not surprisingly, as documented by Finnish metal scholars Pasqualina Eckerström and Titus Hjelm, the tension caused by the alternating relaxation and stiffening of control has led to intense debates within the extreme metal community inside Iran as to whether bands can be considered extreme if they in any way compromise with the government in order to be allowed to perform or release music legally inside the country. But even after forty years in power, the Islamic government doesn't always get it right, and in 2017 and 2018, as the Trump Administration moved to leave the nuclear deal and the economy went into a tailspin, protests again broke out that were some of the biggest since 2009, with protesters—including, for the first time, a large number of poor and working-class youth—shouting "Death to the Dictator!" and "Death to Khameini!" instead of the infamous "Death to America."

At the same time, one of the effects of the renewed sanctions was that musical instruments suddenly became far more expensive, out of reach for most young people, which artists fear will slow down, if not stop, the new generation from taking up the challenge. This was not necessarily reflected in the hip hop scene, as production depends mostly on the pirated software readily available to most aspiring rappers. But the ailing economy did take a toll on the direction of the lyrics, which started to get heavy on the burdens of the working class, and the once popular party songs—pioneered by Zedbazi—became rare or nonexistent, at least coming from Iranians living inside Iran. And when the coronavirus pandemic hit like a sledgehammer in early 2020—Iran was among the first and most severely affected countries—it brought even more economic desperation, amplified by Trump's maximum pressure campaign. However, at the same time, for a certain subset of relatively economically secure musicians, being stuck at home with little to do encouraged a greater level of collaboration and even "shredding competitions" (about which more below) that saw many of the younger generation of metal musicians, especially guitarists, trade solos over prerecorded tracks that were filmed and uploaded onto Instagram and YouTube, intensifying a trend that was already becoming common with the crackdown on live performances.

CRACKDOWNS YES, BUT ALSO OPENINGS

Over the last decade, it's actually been quite impressive how the stream of newcomers in the Iranian music scene keeps their spirits up despite all the hindrances, epitomized by the prosecution, imprisonment, and escape into exile of members of two of Iran's seminal metal bands, Confess and Arsames. There has been a surge of great new artists—rappers, singer/songwriters, and rock/metal bands—as the demand for better music in more quantities has increased consistently throughout the past few years among the Iranian youth, as access to international music has increased through the surge of streaming platforms. Artists like the rapper Ali Sorena, the folk-pop singer Faravaz, the female-led metal band Sanam Pasha, and the rock band Shahrivar are a few of these new artists. In the fast-moving alternative music scene in Iran ten years has created three different musical eras and generations of musicians, as if the late-blooming scene is trying to catch up.

In hip hop in particular it can often seem like everything has changed. In the early 2000s rap songs were very much experimental, not only in how the music was made, but in the ways of distributing it and making sure it reached an audience. This process was inherently one of trial and error. Since they didn't have a model, they had to create models of their own. There were at most a few websites that collected hip hop tracks, fewer still that curated, and not many more Orkut and Yahoo! groups. Direct artist-to-audience distribution, through mailing lists and streaming platforms like MySpace (today it would be SoundCloud or Bandcamp), was also a popular way of making one's songs heard.

But as the numbers of artists grew, two things happened. First, the popularity of alternative music alerted the Iranian government, and many of the platforms and early websites used by artists were blocked. Second, the number of emerging artists increased as an inevitable result of the popularity of hip hop and its appeal to the youth. If you were a newcomer, standing out among so many new faces became an issue; you couldn't just pop your song in a MySpace or Facebook page and be assured of at least five hundred downloads. So an opportunity was there and it was seized by some music fans/website developers who devoted themselves to exclusively distributing music in an easy-to-navigate manner.

The tech savvy administrators of these websites changed their names as soon as the government blocked them, usually by adding numbers at the end of their domain name, therefore never losing any visitors. Artists who were already popular would be on the websites, no questions asked—obviously since they brought with them a larger number of clicks—but emerging artists would have to go through a sort of curatorial process, at least in the beginning of this trend. However, in time, as the demand grew, a new opportunity emerged for the website owners: monetizing the music. Many of these sites turned into a fee-based submission system, but this inevitably led to a decrease in the quality of the songs, and since then, many of the more popular artists have turned to the old-school direct distribution, which was easier for them since they already enjoyed a massive following, multiplied by years of support from the popular websites. This is also a general trend in the world, and even major artists turn to Bandcamp or Patreon for direct support by their audience.

Currently, for Iranian artists the most popular platform is Telegram, a Russia-based encrypted messaging application that allows artists to have a page that users can follow, and where the artist can upload files, which in turn can be forwarded and distributed among fans. A popular artist's release can reach millions of listeners with this app alone. Many Iranian artists use international platforms too, like SoundCloud, Bandcamp, and paid streaming services such as Apple Music, Spotify, and Amazon Music. These platforms, not surprisingly, are not popular inside Iran, as buying music from them can be very complicated due to the country's banking system, which remains cut off from most of the world due to ongoing sanctions, made worse by President Trump. But the reach offered by the international streaming platforms makes them still a favorable option to add on top of the Iran-only systems like Telegram, even though most artists living inside Iran will need to forgo their earnings or share them with the middle men who run their accounts from abroad, again, due to economic sanctions, unless the Biden Administration lifts some of the heavy sanctions imposed by Trump.

But that's not to say that there are no monetary gains for Iranian artists inside the country in the international game. Even in the early 2000s a rudimentary domestic fee-based download system existed, although it remained fairly old-fashioned in its technology, a situation that continues up to today. The artist or the distributer website gives a bank account number; the customer transfers the cost of the music and emails the receipt; in return they receive a digital or physical copy of what they purchased. This allowed artists, at least the more popular ones, to have an income that would allow them to continue to produce new music. It also changed the culture of alternative music scenes to an extent, with fans not expecting the music to be free by default. There is also a hunger for physical copies of music, with designed jackets and album art, since it's been missing from the scene for decades. Eventually though, all releases end up available for free and the financial gain from the direct-deposit sales is negligible compared to those available for similarly popular international musicians.

There's a relatively humble earning potential from the sales of merchandise too, which many popular artists have sold. But the lack of reliable revenue has led to an unlikely and unfortunate trend among some artists both inside and outside Iran, including some big names with millions of followers like Erfan Paydar and Sepehr Khalse: the promotion of various fishy gambling websites on their Instagram and Telegram pages, which seemingly earns them a lot of money, at least much more than they can make from selling their music to Iranians. This has become such a huge online phenomenon that extensive investigative pieces have been published on websites like Hipgah and Meidaan, and Sweden-based columnist Behrooz Aghakhanian has written on its broader cultural implications. There have also been reports from within the Iranian media that have traced massive scams and phishing scandals on the websites that steal money directly from people's accounts.

One thing that has remained unchanged, at least for hip hop music, is the lack of live performances. Hip hop artists inside Iran still remain recording artists, but for the most part the only way to have their music heard by their fans is through speakers or headphones. But that's not the case for many other types of alternative music. Especially in the last few years of Rouhani's government, there has been an opening up of genres like rock, pop rock, and folk-fusion in the public sphere. There are many concerts and live shows. In fact there are so many shows that some of them get canceled due to not selling enough tickets, meaning the supply is exceeding the demand in some cases. It's very different from the early 2000s, when any alternative music concert was a big event and would undoubtedly be sold out, because of how hungry people were for live music.

Why did this happen? There has been a shift of strategy in how the Islamic regime's elites want to deal with the ever-growing young populations' demands. They clearly came to understand that censorship, demonization, and negative campaigns have been counterproductive, so they implemented what could be termed a rapprochement policy in recent years: "If you can't beat them, recruit them." By letting musicians perform and release music, but in a controlled manner still acceptable within the framework of Islamic values, they managed to create a less-asphyxiated young population whose energy isn't channeled into dissatisfaction and political rallies. Some musicians in the Iranian diaspora are not necessarily happy with these developments, and think the local musicians are playing into the government's hands. But in the end, a new generation of teenagers is taking for granted that they can buy the music they want and go to concerts. This is something that will be hard to step back from.

FROM THE INSIDE OUT

In the last dozen years, Iran has seen its rock, metal, hip hop, and related artists, musicians, singers, and rappers leave for what they all hoped would be greener—and safer—pastures overseas, more than in any other MENA country. This process was already underway in the mid-2000s, but it not surprisingly picked up quickly after the crushing of the Green Wave in 2009. The reasons for this were, and sadly today remain, fairly simple. First and foremost, Iran's Islamic government restricts the public performance and consumption of music more than most any other government on Earth, even more in some ways than Saudi Arabia, which is increasingly opening up culturally, if not politically. It also enforces a level of public religiosity that puts the official culture at odds with much of the country's youth. Even though a large share and likely majority of the population opposes such harsh conservatism, the Iranian state remains split between more moderate political institutions that are part of the elected government and the institutions and apparatuses, especially the religious institutions, the ruling system, and the religiously grounded security services (the Revolutionary Guards, the *basij*), allied and loyal to them alone. It's clear that in Iran today, the religious-military-security state ultimately controls most of the levers of economic as well as political power—never mind security—but these forces aren't strong or hegemonic enough simply to crush those who oppose their conservative ideology and rules.

And so there's a constant war of position, not merely within Iranian civil society but also between various factions in the ruling system as a whole, and between the conservative institutions of the state and a large share of young people. In this competition the freedom given to youth music and the arts more broadly will wax and wane for a host of reasons, from the shifting balance of power and allegiances of various parts of the state, to the strength of the economy, the broader position of Iran in the world, and how much push-back youth are giving to restrictions on their public behavior. But even under the best of conditions, it is very hard to make a living as a musician or musical artist in Iran, and practically impossible to do so as a metal, rock, or hip hop artist.

Because of this, the majority of the artists Mark came to know in the mid-2000s ultimately left Iran, most but not all for the United States, in the ensuing decade. The solidification of a specifically musical diaspora created unique conditions for the music scenes, in which there was little corporate continuity, as it were, in their evolution. And because so many of the artists who left did so in part for political reasons, their ability to return has remained limited, particularly when the government has a well-known habit of jailing Iranians who return home, regardless of the reason. This raises the question of their relationships to the scenes back home: how the music differs or remains similar between the two scenes, what kind of influence/cross-fertilization there is, and how the two streams of musicians/artists understand the changes to each other.

Some artists who left Iran prefer to identify as artists in exile; others would consider themselves just immigrants in search of a new home. Either way, it's impossible to have the same social relevancy they used to have for the Iranian public when they lived inside Iran, especially now that so many great musicians are emerging within the country. This is a crucial way of defining how being in or outside can radically change one's perspective. If an artist considers themselves in exile and dislocated, they'll continue to make music for inside Iran, and for Iranians living in diaspora. They might maintain a level of impact and popularity among the audience in Iran, but they'll always be in that in-between spot where you belong neither to Iran nor to the place you are currently residing. They will always be defined by exile.

It seems that one's perspective is determined in good measure by the success one has had performing outside. For metal artists like Ali Azhari and TarantisT the scenes haven't really developed much since their departure. For Ali, it's impossible to imagine Iran today accepting what he did as a young metal artist when he released the critical track "Baptized," which attacked the government harshly and brutally for brainwashing an entire generation with religious propaganda. This condition creates the need to live outside the country. Arash Rahbary of TarantisT has an even more negative view of what he imagines the scene is like today, almost a decade after he left. "They don't know any better," he explained, by way of understanding why artists inside are more sanguine than those on the outside about the present situation for metal in Iran. "They are fruits of this fucked up situation. No one showed them anything different so they're a product of the environment. They are controlled up to that point and have no other choice. Some people are just happy to have space to play and won't publish anything."

Looking back on it, he feels that the situation was dissimilar for the previous generation of artists, most of whom are not in the country anymore or have stopped playing. "It was so different for us, not only about playing music. Metal was some sort of fighting, standing against system; it was a weapon, was meaningful, and wasn't just about drawing attention, going after girls, getting media attention. Not all that matters is getting on social media, Instagram likes, etc."

Although according to Arash the new generation of Iran-based bands has been forced by the government to avoid mention of or support for bands like TarantisT that are outside and that are critical, he's done recent albums in Persian to reach the local audience more directly. Music apps like Radio Javan (which is like Spotify for Persian-language artists) allow the band to put its music on the site, but they do nothing to promote it.

One artist who never planned to be in this situation is Hichkas, the seminal rapper with whom Salome MC recorded her first song. Hichkas was among the first to publicly produce rap that was critical of the government and about the growing disparities between the wealthy and the rest of society. Despite constant harassment and even detention by authorities, he seemed to be the last person who would leave the country. In the documentary *No One Knows about Persian Cats,* released in 2009, he was asked why he doesn't leave Iran. His response was telling: "What do they call what we sing? They call it rap-e farsi. Okay? What's farsi for? It's for right here." But when he did his song "Yeh ruz-e Khub Miyad" ("A Good Day Will Come") criticizing regime violence during the Green protests, he crossed one too many lines, and fearing long-term detention, he chose to leave and relocated to London.

If we don't count the innovation of the music as an important measure for success and only go by the numbers, a good example of such "success" would be the rapper Tohi, who first went from being an average party-rapper within Iran to being a well-known pop singer, and after leaving Iran, he sky-rocketed as a mainstream recording artist who sells out venues and collaborates with international musicians for catchy summer hits. His regular collaborator and R & B singer Tatloo is another similar example: he signed with Universal Music Germany in 2020 and has been releasing music regularly to the delight of his large fan base.

As we have seen throughout this book, and particularly in the chapters on Morocco and Egypt, the question remains whether such power can continue when one enters the diaspora. No one has any illusions that the diaspora can maintain the same necessity; they know there's little choice for many artists who've moved to the diaspora but to "take the freedom we have and create what we can while staying in touch back home," as one successful diaspora artist explained to Mark. Depending on the kind of artist and the dislocation or relocation, one can make an impact locally that is greater than the long-distance impact one can achieve back home.

A good example of this dynamic occurred with Salome MC when she started making video art, sound art, and installations in Japan, where she moved in 2010. Even as she began creating various forms of visual art and music there, she continued to produce music in Farsi for her fan base. Having moved to the United States in 2016, she adapted her sound yet again, releasing another self-produced album, *Excerpts from Unhappy Consciousness,* in 2017, which still gets airplay on the local Seattle radio station KEXP. Salome has received multiple scholarships and art grants from American institutions for her projects such as "Seven Climes," an initiative that aims to present the cultural and lingual diversity of the Iranian hip hop scene that was partially funded by Washington State's 4Culture organization.

Like Ali Sana'ei and many other talented musicians in the diaspora, and like previous generations of virtuoso musicians like Shajarian, Salome MC also turned to teaching, working with the Pacific Northwest's only auditory arts organization, the Jack Straw Cultural Center. And similar to Ali Azhari's, her self-directed videos continue to get screened in American festivals, the most recent one at the Local Sightings Film Festival in 2019 in Seattle. She has also become a vocal activist against the US-imposed economic sanctions on Iran, and sits on the advisory board of Code Pink, a DC-based, woman-led grassroots organization that advocates against militarism and economic warfare.

Other Iranian artists are also adapting in whatever ways they can musically to their environment. Ali Sana'ei's work with the diaspora Persian music elite reached its zenith when he joined the legendary singer Googoosh's band in 2016, first as the bass player and ultimately as bandleader. But because Googoosh is persona non grata in Iran, Ali has not returned home since he's performed with her, even though their burgeoning musical output remains explicitly apolitical.

For his part, Farzad Golpayegani moved first to Istanbul in 2009, and then to Los Angeles in 2013. In both places he was consistently doing both his music and his artwork. Unlike Ali Sana'ei, he has spent the last seventeen years working largely on his own, producing eight albums that have demonstrated increasing musical complexity and diversity, beginning particularly with the album *Four,* released in 2010, which didn't use any electric guitars or drums, but featured Farzad on several traditional Iranian instruments. *Five,* released the next year, saw the return of electric guitars, but it was still over a far more symphonic or cinematographic sound than his earlier, purely metal attempts. The albums in which he has pushed further into the progressive "Oriental" metal genre were produced, recorded, and performed almost entirely by him alone, with the exception of a few guest spots by close friends like Ali Sana'ei, whereas most artists doing that are in bands.

Not surprisingly, given the amount of time he's spent recording on his own, Farzad has come to understand deeply how technology can both enable and stifle artists in situations like his: "Yes there are a lot of improvements in terms of production and quality. It applies on arrangement and orchestration as well, but in my opinion, not as much in production, which mostly follow Western bands as references." This sentiment is shared across the board among diaspora Iranian artists Mark has spoken with, except for Salome MC, who places a definitive advantage on those artists who've remained rooted in Iran in terms of capturing and maintaining the allegiance of home fans.

The situation inside Iran remains confusing, even for the artists. Yes, there is still censorship, harassment, and even arrest. But there are also concerts featuring singing metal bands and a lot more really good hip hop. Indeed, not only is hip hop flourishing despite the focus on the music by the authorities;

female hip hop artists are doing some of the most groundbreaking work. Shaya Zandi is a rapper/singer who took a break from making hip hop music during Ahmadinejad's presidency and focused on performance work permitted by the Ministry of Culture, such as choral opera and musicals (as solo female singing is not permitted). She just recently started making new music and sharing it with fans online. Having experience working in highly developed musical genres like opera has made it important to push the sonic boundaries of hip hop as well. In her talks with Salome MC, she explained: "When we started making hip hop, despite the fact that everyone was imitating foreign rappers, there was a realness to the scene. Over the following years, we've witnessed fresh, unique styles emerging, but this trend didn't continue and those original styles kept getting recycled. Today it's in arrangement and mix that we see lots of creativity, but not in vocals; the thing is people like it that way. Our people love repetition. Another new development is the decrease in the median age of the audience, which can be good and bad."

As with the rock and metal scene, it's been hard to get authorization to perform live for rappers. This puts a definite ceiling on how far the scene can evolve aesthetically and politically. (However, it can make some rappers rich quite easily thanks to the monetization of the Internet and performance opportunities abroad.) If we recall the description of rappers meeting in the park to trade beats on their phone and battle with rhymes in *Heavy Metal Islam,* the next step in this development, as witnessed in Morocco, Egypt, Lebanon, and other countries, was the live public events where rappers could hone their skills and verbal dexterity and rapid improvisatory skills. But with the government prohibiting even more rap shows than metal shows, it's hard to continue to do that.

Of course, most of the rock/metal concerts used to happen without official permission as well, in public places such as cafés and galleries. When the government cracked down on these performances, the bands organized jamming sessions open to friends, and so on. Basically they kept going until they met more red tape. But hip hop took a different route as mentioned above, and another reason on top of everything that's been said could be the fact that in Iran, rock/metal bands have several members who bear the brunt of the pressure equally, but a rapper, usually working alone, takes all the responsibility, which means they would prefer to keep the risk at a minimum. Despite this, there were a few hip hop albums that received official permissions and were legally released, largely due to the backroom deals mentioned before, and occasionally live performances do happen.

Ali Nodism, director of the alternative music site Aamizeh.com and a publicist for various Iranian artists, also focuses on the lyrics as the key issue today (as opposed to a decade ago, when the aesthetics of the music and the style of dress were more important). For him, as he explained to Salome MC, "It's too hard for rock and metal concerts to get permission these days. But it's always the lyrics that are the main problem, and that's why the government had problems with rap from day one."

> They will ban anything that they don't understand, and rap is one of those. Unfortunately, there's no light at the end of tunnel either. I think the "unofficial" status of Iranian rap has made it "official," and the most important difference it has from American hip hop is in its texts and lyrics. Structurally and from the literature point of view, Iranian rap has its own identity. Yes it is still possible to do political rap. Lyrics with complex connotations and structures allow for political concepts, usually manifesting in rather philosophical form, so even though somehow indirect, the objections are still expressed. I think the era of speaking directly and straightforward has ended for Iranian rap and artists now try to place their sociopolitical protests inside multiplex metaphors and similes. So the spirit of rebellion and protest is still alive and well in Iranian rap, but it has shape-shifted and has become similar to what Iranian poets used to do back in seventh and eighth centuries of the Iranian calendar [twelfth and thirteenth centuries CE].

Shaya Zandi has her own take on the special nature of Iranian rap lyrics, which became clear during discussions with Salome MC on this issue: "I think rap inside Iran is mostly the glorification of suffering that we have in our country, just like cinema and theater. People are competing to say I got it worst, it's all complaining. But Iranian hip hop abroad is more about success stories and being a winner." At the same time, however, it seems that there's an equal lack of political engagement today among artists—as is the case in Morocco, Egypt, and other countries—because it's the only way to get by and not face severe surveillance and even arrest and prosecution. So for Shaya "rap shouldn't be political, and it can't be. First because most rappers are not political people, and second if they do want to make political songs, it's not about change, it's just whining and complaining."

Perhaps the dichotomy between stylistic innovation and political commitment is a false one. Navid Sadr, for over fifteen years one of the most important underground rappers working with Divar Records (an arm of the biggest underground hip hop organization in Iran), thinks back to the earlier days of hip hop when he and Salome MC were coming up and sees the biggest change since then as surrounding the sound of the music more than the politics of the country. "Persian rap is not the imitation of American rap anymore, like it used to be," he told Salome MC, continuing that today it has its own sound and identity. "We have masterpieces that we are proud of, such as 'Ye Ruze Khub Miad' ('A Good Day Will Come') by Hichkas, 'Sokout' ('Silence') by Bahram, 'Aavaar' ('Ruins') by Soorena, and many others." But even as the scene has developed stylistically—much as metal has as well—the maturity of the scene has been accompanied by silence politically in a genre that was at the forefront of critiquing the Iranian system for over a decade. As Navid explains it, "I don't think the audience has changed much though. . . . If I can be blunt, there's only one difference I can think of. In the light of hip hop being more widespread and more people listening to it, and the information technology and more access and acceptance that exists today compared to then, I am gonna say that the audience is more passive and dumbed down."

Dumb here doesn't mean unsophisticated or stupid, but closer to silent—a willing dumbness of a generation that has come of age since 2009 and doesn't see the point in taking political risks or even focusing on political music. And especially as more opportunities for making money exist, the costs of being political are far higher than the potential profit for being commercially successful, even without live shows. Unfortunately, the lack of live shows also makes the situation even harder to justify taking political risks, at least inside Iran.

Babak Khiavchi, who was an active musician and guitar instructor in Tehran's alternative music scene before the 2000s, and the owner of the Bamahang Productions label, which provided digital distribution for Iranian underground artists until 2010, explains further in his talks with Salome:

A lot of the early Rock concerts managed to find loopholes in the Ershad regulations and get permits by performing instrumental music ranging from Pink Floyd and Camel covers to Thrash Metal concerts, which opened up the possibilities to performing with English lyrics that were difficult to comprehend and therefore were not deemed threatening by the authorities. Rap, on the other hand, cannot be performed instrumental due to its dependency on lyrics, so there were always fewer performance opportunities to begin with, but there has always been a lot of Ershad sensitivity around Farsi lyrics with double entendres and social commentary, however conservative they may have been written.

And here is another issue that would seem to separate the rappers from the metalheads: regime violence. A decade or two ago most of the regime's suspicion and ire were directed at metal and other forms of at least somewhat "extreme" rock because they were the cultural threat to the hegemony of the Islamic regime. More recently it's hip hop that has taken on this possibility, because it appeals to a far larger segment of the youth population and the lyrics have far more often strayed into directly political territory. Yet even if audiences are less political for a variety of reasons, rappers remain, at least potentially, quite political. As Navid explains, "Rap inside Iran is more political than ever. I think there can be political hip hop inside Iran, of course having certain red lines in mind. . . . Is it the artist who couldn't engage the society, or is it the society that's not ready?"

Ali Nodism sees definite maturation in the last ten years.

> One of the most important things that happened in the scene during the last fifteen years is the rising awareness about the societal problems and using the platform as a means for social change. Of course, we can't ignore the progress in lyrics and writing either. When we compare today's pieces with the early days, we can instantly notice the difference, how far we've come in terms of poetry and expression. In terms of music production too, considering the relatively short history of this genre in Iran, there's been immense progress, and we have world-class producers now, for example, Mahdyar has worked with Snoop Dogg—albeit indirectly—and has collaborated with Birdy NAM NAM. Mita Maleki has worked with Tech N9ne, and Farshad could make a song with Hollywood musician Junkie XL. As far as the audience, I think today the audience is not only the younger people like it used to be, and hip hop has found its place among people of all ages and is accepted, of course not by the government but by the citizens.

And found its place it did. In fact in the past few years, the Iranian hip hop scene grew far beyond the confines of big cities and middle-class kids, with youth from various ethnic groups adopting and creating scenes within their own communities using their own languages, dialects, and accents. Turkish and Kurdi rap are predictably pretty popular since these two groups constitute the largest ethnic groups in Iran, but you can also hear Arabic, Lori, and Laki hip hop all over Instagram, and rappers with accented Farsi that differs from the standardized Farsi learned in schools are not shying away in reflecting their heritage in their verses anymore. Recently there's a big push in online communities to replace "Persian Rap" or "Farsi Rap" with "Iranian Rap" to reflect the multicultural and multilingual nature of the scene. One of the early champions of the movement is Salome MC— a Turkish-Iranian herself—who in 2021 produced the album *Seven Climes*

Vol. 1 (Haft Eghlim) featuring seven Iranian rappers who rap in a language other than the standard Farsi. One of the rappers featured, Javid, who raps in the nearly extinct Tati language, told Salome: "I was the first person to rap in the Tati language, and my song in *Seven Climes* is the first rap song in Tati. My hope is other rappers will emerge who would continue this trend and preserve the culture and language long term." Due to increasing economic pressure caused by historically high levels of inflation, which has affected not only large cities but also towns and villages, protests are today occurring with greater frequency. These are being shut down with brutal tactics by the recently installed government of President Ebrahim Raisi. Combined with the incompetence and corruption that have found its way from the central government to rural officials, many of the recent songs that come out of these areas carry antiregime sentiment openly, including several tracks featured on *Seven Climes Vol. 1.*

IRAN OUTSIDE IN

There is a real danger that the high number of extremely talented Iranian artists living in the diaspora (whether voluntarily or because they were forced to leave) will distort attempts to discuss the present-day situation of music and its social implications inside Iran. But it's also true that the cost of so many decades of constant struggle has been extremely high—there has been more struggle with more negative consequences than is the case with most any other country in the MENA region or most other Muslim-majority countries, both from the repressive nature of the regime and the equally harmful US-led sanctions regime that was again put in place during the Trump Administration. As rapper Navid Sadr put it:

> Hip hop is like a beaten kid who doesn't talk to anyone anymore. Despite all the technology and remote access, there's a big wall separating artists, all because of some misplaced pride and extreme categorizations. Most of the rappers who have left Iran did it because they couldn't bear the pressure and the atmosphere anymore, but it's as if by exiting Iran, they exited the hip hop scene too. This created a sense of bitter hopelessness among everyone especially the generation who came after these first-generation artists, which of course can be easily solved by one-on-one communication. But that's only possible if everyone still has the love and passion they had back in the day.

Ali Azhari, for one, has certainly lost little of the passion he had when Mark first met him not long after his breakthrough song "Baptize" was put up on the Internet. Like his good friend and fellow shredder Farzad Golpayegani's, his talent as a guitarist was from the start matched by a strong visual artistic vision. But while Farzad's work from the start has been focused on Surrealist painting when not working professionally as a graphic artist, Ali has always been a filmmaker, and in the years since Mark first met him he has won prestigious international fellowships to study his craft, which ultimately took him to his present home, in Northern Cyprus, where he's lived since 2018. But it's his musical trajectory that is most interesting here, and in a way mirrors, however distortedly, that of his former bandmate Ali Sana'ei.

Ali Sana'ei, once he arrived in Los Angeles, was able to parley his unique talents on the bass and knowledge of Iranian music to become one of the most sought after bass players in the diaspora Persian music scene, working with Googoosh for almost three years before leaving her band to focus on a solo career focused not on metal, "which is where my heart still belongs," but on Iranian pop, where he might actually make a living.

There was no chance that Ali Azheri would ever start writing Iranian pop songs. However, that doesn't mean he's stayed completely inside the metal genre. Indeed, since settling in Northern Cyprus, Ali has sought to combine his filmmaking, art, and photography with music, but most recently he has been moving away from metal proper toward far more experimental ambient music, which for him is ultimately not so far removed from hardcore or extreme metal. Or at least is close enough when he looks at the scene now:

> To be honest with you, like everywhere else in the region it seems the metal scene is shrinking with the emergence of more deep house, electronic music. Eventually you give in and do electronic music. Even Trent Reznor has done it, or Jeff Waters from [the Canadian metal band] Annihilator back in the mid-1990s when he was broke and couldn't afford a full band or full studio so started using drum machines, just like we did back in the day. Even in the free world the same shit happens. And, really, if you listen to it right, "Baptize" in a way is electronica, just of a metal type.

With that in mind, in September 2019 Ali Azhari put on his own one-man show at the ARUCAD Art Space in Lefkoşa, Northern Cyprus, titled *Durağanlığın Tınısı* ("Resonating Inertia"), which combined the work of a local photographer, Hanifa Teymoorian, with a sound installation composed and recorded by Ali. This is part of a larger work in which each song is paired with a photograph taken by a friend.

Unlike either Ali Sana'ei or Farzad Golpayegani, however, Ali Azhari regularly returns to Tehran. Despite being one of the most directly provocative musicians of the metal era in Iran—readers of *Heavy Metal Islam* will recall Ali wearing a T-shirt boldly declaring that "Your god is dead" while we walked around Tehran on a sunny day—Ali was somehow able to return home unmolested several times a year to visit family and friends before the pandemic, making sure to play with younger metal artists while home to keep tabs on the scene he had helped create. Speaking with Mark right before the pandemic slammed into Iran in early 2020, he explained, "Whenever I go to Iran they talk to me and tell me how inspired they were and how they looked at us as role models and inspired them to compose. So although many of us are out of the country, some of us still go back when we can or stay in touch through social media. And it's clear that the music itself is really good, whatever might be happening with the possibility of shows."

Ali's experiences offer an important example of the dynamics of the metal scene today—as much as that is possible—because he is both out and in, and because he has the history of the scene written into his skin yet is abreast of the most recent developments. Thinking about his first "hit," "Baptize," he's not sure how much it would change if he wrote it today: "When I wrote 'Baptize' I was just a kid, so perhaps I'd change the lyrics a bit, but really has anything actually changed in last twenty years? Not really. It hasn't changed in the last two thousand years since people were first baptized by force, so the message would be the same. And however much my skills as a filmmaker have—hopefully—improved since we made that video I'm still happy with what the video was for the time it was made and its visualization and ideas. I only wish I'd had some hi-def cameras although the lower-quality helped create the right atmosphere in fact. Actually, nowadays when I make commercials and short films we naturally shoot hi-def but I often wind up making it look more Super-8, more gritty and even ugly afterward, like the aesthetic of 'Baptize.'"

Could Ali ever imagine releasing a song like "Baptize" today?

I've recorded over 100 songs that I've never released because the time isn't right. It doesn't make sense to release something that is going to go to the trash because people can't listen or find it online, and for me recording is actually just a small part of producing metal. The huge chunk is live shows and gigs, to connect to people. So when I'm in Iran I jam a lot. I go find a friend and find a basement somewhere and jam. Ironically, though, the other guitarist in Arthimoth when we recorded "Baptize," Alireza Saidian, left soon after its release for Canada and I didn't see him for fifteen years. And then, all of a sudden he moved to Northern Cyprus so now we're together again.

With "Baptize" Arthimoth forever enshrined themselves as one of the most badass metal bands of all time, certainly among the very elite in the MENA region, because of the stakes involved and the directness of the critique of the system (imagine if Black Sabbath were a Soviet band and released "War Pigs" at the height of the Afghan war—*and got away with it*). If we tweak genres a bit, another Iranian band comes into view, one every bit as original but a lot more quirky and fun. That band would be Abjeez (slang for "sisters" in Persian), a world pop fusion group (or "Persian World Pop," as the *New York Times* defined it in a profile of the group in 2012) defined by its Persian-inflected ska/reggae sound. Established in 2005 by Iranian-born sisters Melody and Safoura Safavi, the duo was forced to leave their home country during the Iran-Iraq war, in 1986, and spent much of their childhood and adolescence in Sweden immersed in the Stockholm music scene.

During more than fifteen years together Abjeez has become renowned across Europe, the US, and the MENA for its innovative musical as well as visual aesthetic. Their music is defined by creativity, fun, and serious musicianship, all of which are illustrated in the track and video for "Eddeaa," released in 2007, their best-known song, which means "pretension" in Persian. Over a ska-reggae beat that evokes the early Police and a stunning video, the sisters weave an audiovisual collage of sounds, grooves, and sights that is almost impossible to describe. With the sisters wearing miniskirts with chadors, and fashioned with unibrows done up in the traditional "Persian" style (simultaneously self-deprecating and celebratory), while the men in the group are dressed in various kinds of, it seems, late-nineteenth-century Qajar clothing, the sisters rail against "too much closeness" that "comes with harmful intervention," as well as against those who "claim to be cultured, educated, and wise" and who "play pure and innocent" while "behaving like thieves" and "looking down on your own."

"Eddeaa" is clearly a takedown of a kind of snobby and pretentious artist or art-lover whose "edgy arguments" mask an actual lack of knowledge or taste. In other words, it's a plea for authenticity at a moment when, as I explain below, it's under severe threat in Iran as much as in the West. This ability to touch on themes relevant to debates back home is likely a major reason why, although they've never played in Iran and haven't been home since 2003, Abjeez developed a strong following there. Indeed, Melody explained to Mark during one of their periodic conversations at a small Mexican restaurant in Ditmas Park, Brooklyn, that "most of our fan base is in Iran. They seem to be men between ages eighteen and forty. In the diaspora kids also like our music a lot; every time we have a show we get calls and emails from parents who want to bring their kids to the club."

This is not surprising. Even though the better part of their lives has been spent abroad and their music is immediately identifiable by its funky ska-tinged grooves, the overall sound is clearly influenced by home. So naturally they've harbored hopes to collaborate with artists back home. But here the separation of time and space does have an impact. "Safoura and I were thinking of collaborating with musicians in Iran. When we started Abjeez [two years after their last visit home] our intention was to bring diversity to Persian pop music in Iran. At the time there weren't many bands that played the type of music we did but today after fifteen years there are many wonderful bands so that's not an issue."

She continued, "More recently the idea came up again and I contacted some like-minded artists inside, but we concluded that because of safety concerns it wouldn't be possible; if they do something openly with us, they might get into trouble. But it's very hard to accept that artists can't work together." This sentiment points to one of the main problems faced by artists from Iran, as well as Egypt, Syria, and, more recently, Turkey. The political situation is so oppressive that any collaboration, even outside the country, puts whoever is still based in their home country at serious risk. Collaborations between diaspora artists, however, are only limited by taste, time, money, and distance. And so, inevitably perhaps, in 2007, two of the most avant-garde of Iranian musical artists, Abjeez and Mohsen Namjoo, were able to perform together in Amsterdam at the Rotterdam Film Festival, while the year before in Amsterdam they performed for the first and only time with Salome MC. Namjoo and Salome reunited once more a decade later, in 2018, at a Yale University symposium, "Popular Music and Society in Iran."

What's clear is how provocatively hybrid Iranian aesthetic culture has been. Anyone familiar with the Iranian film industry wouldn't be surprised at this claim, but the point is that while it's far less known and studied, contemporary Iranian music is equally as innovative and, considering the conditions in which it's forced to operate, just as high quality as well. Of course, every one of the countries discussed in this book has produced its share of innovative sounds and scenes, from Moroccan Gnawa funk to Pakistani Sufi metal. But in Iran the number of musical artists with an extremely advanced visual aesthetic—Abjeez, Farzad Golpayegani, Ali Azhari, and Salome MC, to name a few—is well beyond the norm across the region. (That the US government has no clue about this uniqueness was clear when they denied an artist's visa to members of Abjeez before their last tour, declaring that the group wasn't "culturally unique" enough to warrant such a designation.)

In 2020 a recording from a seminar held by a sociologist at Tehran University, Yusef Abazari, went viral, in which he expressed intense anger after an almost state-sponsored funeral held for a young pop musician, Morteza Pashaei, who'd died of cancer. His death was treated similarly to how a major pop or rock star's death would be treated in the United States. Prof. Abazari told his students that the fact that the Islamic government was inserting itself into the funeral of a middlebrow young pop singer was clearly meant to "depoliticize" young people (literally, "politicization project" [proje-i siaset zeda'i] in Persian, but clearly meaning depoliticization as it's understood in English), which was made easier in his view because people had been suffering from a kind of Stockholm syndrome since 2009 that made it much harder to actively oppose the state. Rather than attempting to censor and repress youth music, the government now uses it to form and change young people's musical and artistic tastes and co-opt or at least quiet them politically, without young fans having a clue.

Abazari's tirade in the seminar clearly channels Adorno, viewing pop music much the same way as the paragon of Critical Theory. Not surprisingly, his outburst caused very similar—and similarly intense—criticism to that suffered by Adorno in response. His adversaries went so far as to launch a "We Hate Yusef Abazari" ("Ma az yusef abazari mutanafarim") Facebook page, with other scholars and younger activists criticizing him as being an out-of-touch ivory tower intellectual for assuming that young fans couldn't be authentically grieving for Pashaei, or that all such pop music was merely an instrument of state-sponsored cooptation or depoliticization. One young journalist, Foad Shams, compared Abazari unfavorably with Marx in a Facebook post about the controversy, declaring that he could neither interpret nor change the world.

There is an even more insidious reason for the shift in attitude by sections of the government away from outright banning of the music. As one artist who's had communications with Ershad explained, "Once the Revolutionary Guards got into the picture, they realized that one of the best places they could wash their dirty money [allegedly from drugs and other officially illegal activities] was through music and culture. So they started producing their own 'alternative music'—not pop or Islamic pop, mind you. But rather they produced a more secretly ideological Namjoo, ideological Kiosk, and ideological Abjeez—the very artists the government had only recently pushed out of the country."

Aside from the problem of essentially mafia control of the still fragile music industry, in this dynamic the government creates ersatz copies of important artists that dilute the power of the original and more political music. Moreover, if they can ruin the border between cultural and commercial music and distort the difference between traditional or old school music and the progressive tastes of contemporary audiences, they can cause confusion between the artists in the public's mind. Doing so also has the benefit of making far more visible—and thus vulnerable—any groups that are still pushing for more direct social change.

Of course, pushing "authentic" artists out is easier than convincing the public to accept pale imitations. Such attempts fall flat, largely because the artists, whatever the individual skill and talent of the musicians and singers, sound far more like the Iranian equivalent of the state-sponsored rock bands of the Soviet Union than any kind of actual alternative, never mind "underground" music. There is simply no authenticity or originality, never mind convention-breaking, and certainly nothing that could be construed as socially or politically risqué or risky.

Babak Khiavchi explains further: "This has happened not only in the music scene but also in film and art, where large financial sponsorships and investments occur in support of independent art, which completely defies the meaning of alternative and independent. Ultimately history will tell if any of these sponsored creations will survive the test of time, but so far they have yet to produce anything groundbreaking or memorable."

This doesn't mean, however, that even seemingly apolitical music isn't political. As the metal fan who started *Iran Guitar Magazine,* his own Instagram magazine devoted to Iranian metal guitarists, put it to Mark, "You know, we are living in a dictatorship. We have no right to do our jobs, we are criminals. Every single day we're under attack by the government, by religious authorities. But we are trying to fight. We have our places, our underground studios." Even when they gather, the opposite of the generals and ayatollahs "gathered in their masses, just like witches at black masses, plotting destruction"—to quote a very apropos lyric by Black Sabbath—the music is just one reason for coming together. "This is not just about music. It's a human art. We are fighting but our weapon is music. Look at our logo on Instagram, the guitars are like weapons, the man is 'vahuman,' the man with good purpose from our ancient mythology."

In this case, the particular weapon, created right in time for the country-wide lockdown caused by the pandemic, was to create the "shredding" competitions mentioned above in the form of extended backing tracks over which many of Iran's top young metal guitarists would take turns recording themselves soloing and send to him (or he'd come and record them), at which point he edited them all together and released them on Instagram as videos with hashtags such as "igm_rockstars" and "igm_shredders" under the broader rubric of *Iran Guitar Magazine*.

"People are dying every day," he continued, "I was quarantined in my room for one year and for this project I decided to come out and meet people, go to their studios, and shoot. I put myself in danger with this but I think it is necessary. I can't stop or wait anymore. We need to send our voice to the world." The videos can get hundreds and even thousands of views, and considering the number of people who normally can come to a show—most of which are still in homes and basements to begin with—this level of exposure marks a great advance over what the scene had at its disposal a decade ago.

Indeed, between the videos, Instagram, and Telegram groups and other social media, a good young musician can reach tens of thousands of fans with little effort, and judging by the shredding videos—a perfect counterpart to the "rap battle" videos that have taken over hip hop scenes across the region, and the world, today—these musicians are extremely well trained, professional, and creative, with a level of sophistication and even pop sensibility like that of their peers in Lebanon or Pakistan that calls to mind the kind of fluid, melodic death metal with hints of Persian melodies pioneered by artists like Farzad Golpayegani and Ali Sana'ei fifteen years earlier. This number of artists involved in the videos also points to how much bigger the scene has become today, which, according to several younger metal musicians, has grown to the point where the number of bands in all styles of Iranian metal far outstrips venues and opportunities to play.

IN BETWEEN IN THE UPSIDE DOWN

With the central role women and their public appearance continue to play in official Islamic Republican discourse and in opposition to it (whether in the arts, in the legal sphere, or on the streets), it's not surprising that one of the most powerful examples of the intersection of power metal and cultural politics in Iran today runs through the thirty-something drummer Shirin Vaezi. Born in 1987 in Tehran, Shirin started classical piano at six but turned to drums at twenty, becoming fluent enough at the craft to become a full-time musician at age twenty-seven. "I've been playing in different projects with female pop bands, Latin jazz and fusion bands, and collaborated with some other pop musicians. But my main interest and occupation are the progressive/djent metal band called 'AtriA,'" Shirin explained not long after Mark was introduced to her by guitarist Ali Azhari.

"I've always been a huge fan of metal music and got my full focus on it, hence I see myself more as a metal drummer but I usually try to keep the balance to be able to improve my drumming in different styles. That's the main reason I never quit side projects and enjoy playing in different bands and genres." Shirin's eclecticness would be out of place in many other MENA countries, where the devotion to metal by musicians can often be more singular. But in countries like Iran and Pakistan mastery of a variety of styles is more the rule than the exception. As Shirin continues, "I've never been an old school metal fan so I kept myself busy with more contemporary bands such as Tool, Meshuggah, Opeth, Slipknot, Necrophgist, and many more in the early years of my listening to metal. Fellsilent, Periphery, Animals as Leaders, and modern djent metal bands are my favorite right now, as they satisfy my love of metal/jazz/electronic music at the same time."

As Shirin unfolded her history with metal, especially during the period from 2008 through the mid-point of the last decade, it quickly became clear just how little things had changed for artists in Iran, and just how hard it remains to be honestly metal in Iran today, at a moment when across the region protests are again building to a crescendo:

> Some of us knew and we tried to mold parts of this genre that could lead us to be judged as rebels and tried our best to be gentle and gracious in every performance to meet the Ershad requirements for having a gig and to respect the people who could make this happen after nearly forty years of prohibition. But many young musicians couldn't accept the fact that every change has to wait to be settled and if they want to get the whole of what they want, they'll have to wait for it to come.... This was new to everyone and some couldn't take it, and could not serve the purpose of this positive movement, which enabled more than three hundred shows in three years. They couldn't keep it slow and expected Iran to become a country with a full metal scene.

It's worth noting here that while the up-and-coming members of the scene were pushing faster than their relative lack of power would have suggested was prudent, this impatience was, according to Shirin, not shared by the few women in the metal scene, who, having constantly to judge when it is possible to push the boundaries of the acceptable, were more circumspect than their male peers, and were particularly mindful of the chances the opening of the scene presented them: "Definitely yes! Women are coming out of their caves one by one and it's been normalized in social media to listen to metal music." Describing a situation similar to the role played by social media in softening attitudes toward once problematic themes and images in Moroccan music, she continued explaining that "Of course, there has been a huge change in music taste and social media is always a big help. I'm truly happy that I could make a change and show women that it's possible! Even when the whole surrounding is against you. I'm still going through a lot and people are seeing it. . . . This makes them want to believe in themselves even more. . . . I haven't seen a female metal drummer other than myself in Iran yet but other instrumentalists and vocalists are growing every day and that's really a good point."

Unfortunately, the relatively small numbers made it hard to have much of an impact on the broader relationship between the metal scene and the Ershad, which was, not surprisingly, even more opposed to female metal musicians—never mind singers—than male ones. Her last WhatsApp message to Mark well sums up the present—and continuous—situation facing all musicians in Iran: "I wish we could have cherished the chance that was given and didn't make it go to waste. [But] as I'm writing you all the metal bands and even rock bands are banned and I could say we have reached the rock bottom again. We all have to wait for a chance to have a gig maybe in a couple of years."

SIX

Pakistan

SHREDDING THE FUNK FROM THE VALLEYS TO THE SEA

Composed by Mark LeVine and Haniya Aslam, arranged by Mekaal Hasan, produced by Mark, Haniya, and Mekaal

We all started off as metalheads. That's where you get your skills from, just like in the past it would have been the sitar, tabla, and other traditional instruments.

—ZAIN AHSAN,
Poor Rich Boy

Right here is the birth of Sufi Metal \m/

—*YouTube commentator on the song "Ya Ali,"
by the Mekaal Hasan Band, 2018*

People are programmed to like certain music and it's repeated all the time . . . so it's hard to break through.

—*Frustrated metal musician in Karachi, now making his
living as an indie artist and producer*

THE INTERNET AND PAKISTAN'S
JANUS-FACED HISTORY

"The story has flipped from a decade ago; the problem is that you're no longer judged by the work you do, but by what program you're on." So explained Zain Ahsan, guitarist for the Lahore-based indie rock band Poor Rich Boy, as we sat in the guest quarters of Pakistani guitar pioneer Mekaal Hasan, next door to his iconic studio, drinking tea. "And if you're not on the three main shows—Coke, Pepsi, and Nescafé—people don't think you're doing anything that matters, even if you are."

"A decade ago," Zain continued, Pakistani artists "created music from the ground up, like Mekaal's band." As we saw in *Heavy Metal Islam*, the Mekaal Hasan Band defined the genre of Sufi metal and rock over the last twenty years, and more or less every rock and jazz(y) musician who's mattered in this time has come through his studio and his home since then. Zain was only the most recent of dozens of Pakistan's best artists, and judging by the warm reception Mekaal's mother and brother gave to him, it's clear he's no stranger to the family's Lahore compound, an intellectual and musical respite from the sonic, political, and even atmospheric assault of one of the world's most intensely vibrant yet intense cities.

As the Pakistan chapter of *Heavy Metal Islam* explained, at the turn of the present century these videos, the end product of the fantastical new possibilities opened up by inexpensive digital recording, distribution, and consumption technologies, were sent by artists to the numerous video channels, "and if it went viral they'd be big," Mekaal explained. But now it's reversed, top down, corporatized. "Now bands don't release their own stuff but rather wait to get on *Pepsi Battle of the Bands*. It's a cycle: the corporations swoop onto the exploding scene and whatever they can't monetize they crush."

This, in a nutshell, is the quandary facing Pakistani musicians today, and its one Mark had already been hearing from Mekaal for years, since his last visit to Pakistan. For artists like Zain, who, when not leading Poor Rich Boy and performing with several other bands, is a music teacher, the hope remains that "whatever is coming up from the grassroots always bubbles through eventually," but there's little doubt that there will be a lot of casualties along the way. Of course, in a country with so many problems—compounded during Mark's last visit by an intensified Indian occupation of Kashmir on one side and the hastening advance of the Taliban across Afghanistan on the other—the struggles of rock musicians to get gigs and promote their music might seem unimportant, even petty. But they tell us a lot about how Pakistan has changed since *Heavy Metal Islam* was first published, and how it might address the numerous challenges it faces going forward.

In retrospect, the mid-2000s seem to most artists over a certain age (in this case, about thirty-five) a veritable golden era for Pakistani rock, and especially metal (hip hop had barely made a dent then). "Mark, you were there at the right time," Mekaal explained while we sipped chai in his studio, which had been completely rebuilt since Mark had last visited, although the live room still remains among the best anywhere. Few people know the ups and downs of the Pakistani music scene better than Mekaal, one of Pakistan's

OG metalheads, who turned into a Berklee-trained composer and guitar virtuoso who, more than most people, exemplifies the combination of traditional north Indian, progressive jazz, and hard rock styles that gives Pakistani rock its immediately recognizable sound. Given the A-list of musicians and singers he's worked with for over a generation, Mekaal remains one of the best-placed people to confirm the sentiment expressed years ago by the late Junaid Jamshed, one of Pakistan's first true rock stars, the founding singer of the pioneering rock group Vital Signs, who left music to follow a religious calling and became one of the most important public religious figures in the country. In Jamshed's view, what made Pakistani music so special was the "raw talent which has come out of [the country] without the backing of any institution."

"Music was at its peak for us as musicians back in the mid-late 2000s, even if the political situation was shit," Mekaal continued after contemplating his late friend's words. "But now the interest in hearing great music, which should have expanded since then, has gone down. Of course, I might be a bitter old musician," he admitted later, laughing, after they'd moved to his den later that evening. "But the central idea for this 'remix' if not rewriting of your chapter from *Heavy Metal Islam* has to be how the country's perspectives on music have evolved—or rather devolved; or at least changed. And at least for some of us, the change hasn't been good."

Being a musician has always been a hard life, regardless of where or when one's doing it. The challenges faced by Pakistani artists and musicians will ring familiar to struggling musicians not just in Cairo and Casablanca, but in London and New York as well, even for the few who are lucky enough to make a living doing it. But Pakistan's history tells a different story in terms of the role of musicians in the broader society. For centuries musical virtuosity was one of the most prized skills a north Indian could possess; families sent children at the tenderest of ages to study at the feet of the great sitar, sarod, bansuri (north Indian flute), and tabla masters. The situation fell largely out of the musicians' control in the decade after 2008, driven by political, geostrategic, technological, and cultural factors in equal measure. Indeed, what was already one of the more confusing rock scenes in the broader Muslim world became even harder to read in this period.

In most every other country discussed in this book, there is a broadly shared sentiment by participants in the scenes about where things stand, what the challenges are, and what is the wider state of the industry. Iran shows a bit of generational conflict, but in Pakistan it's even more evident. There is no doubt if you go to YouTube that Pakistan has some of the most well-produced, original, and beautiful rock and pop music, and what might be called "Sufi rock" as well, in the world today, just as it did a decade ago. Yet at the same time there is a clear divide that is both generational and economic between those who have been able to participate in and take advantage of the profoundly changed production, distribution, and consumption environment in Pakistan today versus ten years ago, and those who for whatever reason, whether by choice or by marginalization, are on the outside looking in.

The numbers are staggering. Just looking at one program on one platform—*Coke Studio* on YouTube: the songs "Tera Woh Pyar" by Momina Mustehsan and Asim Azharaand and "Tu Kuja Man Kuja" by Shiraz Uppal and Rafaqat Ali Khan have gotten over 140 million views each, while "Afreen Afreen" by Rahat Fateh Ali Khan and Momina Mustehsan has gotten over 330 million views and counting in late 2021. And then there are music videos, such as "Baari," by Bilal Saeed and Momina Mustehsan, which has racked up seventy million views, even though, as Haniya explains, "it's an independent release. None of us rock/indie people has even heard of him, and he'll cross a hundred million [views] easy." The presence of a big star like Momina only accounts for part of the success.

So an outsider might watch *Coke Studio* (the Pakistani music program that is among the most popular shows in the country) and see amazing collaborations between some of Pakistan's leading pop, rock, and traditional Sufi artists. Arif Lohar and Meesha Shafi doing the Alam Lohar folk hit "Alif Allah Chambey Di Booty," Saieen Zahoor and Sanam Marvi doing "Rabba Ho," and Saieen Zahoor with the band Noori doing the bone-tingling "Aik Alif" can easily leave one imagining, like the tens and even hundreds of millions of other viewers of these shows online, that whatever their feelings about Coke, Pepsi, or Nescafé (the other major sponsor of musical programs on television) as drink companies, they've at least partially redeemed themselves by providing such powerful platforms for music. But for most of the musicians discussed in *Heavy Metal Islam,* the situation is quite different.

Groups like Mekaal Hasan Band and Faraz Anwar (both during the time of his group Mizraab and after he went solo) had already been creating these kinds of musical singularities a decade earlier, including on *Coke Studio* and *Pepsi Battle of the Bands* multiple times, so they were a part of this phenomenon; in fact at one point they *were* the phenomenon, albeit without the current level of fanfare and big production budgets. And yet today they spend much of their time without the possibility of sustainably creating or performing their music.

FIGURE 24. Faraz Anwar performing at *Coke Studio* Pakistan, season 10, 2017. Photo by Insiya Syed.

For every groundbreaking collaboration, there are far more problematic—some say insidious—factors at work that are rendering the Pakistani musical economy toxic to a large share of the musical community. What becomes apparent ten years out is that a generational and economic divide has opened between those who have been able to take advantage of the developments of the last decade and those who have been pushed toward the margins.

POLITICS AND MUSIC MOVING IN
OPPOSITE DIRECTIONS

Pakistan's political, social, and economic history during the last ten years is as self-contradictory as the music, punctuated by the killing of Osama bin Laden, a wave of suicide bombings and other attacks that left hundreds dead, massive floods that killed thousands, and blackouts that left millions without power. The year 2008 certainly started well, with elections installing a new president after the military dictator Pervaiz Musharraf stepped down. But the year ended as badly as it began well, with terrorist attacks in Mumbai in late November organized by Pakistani militants that killed 164 people.

Instead of spurring a widespread crackdown on militants, however, the government began 2009 by signing a truce with the Taliban that accepted the imposition of the Taliban's version of "Islamic law" in the Swat Valley—which, before the Afghan war and rise of Islamist militancy, was considered "the Switzerland of Central Asia." Rather than stopping attacks, however, 2009 became one of the worst years in memory for terrorism, with numerous massive suicide bombings and killings. The violence continued in 2010 after the Parliament approved wide-ranging constitutional reforms, in particular with the assassination of two major supporters of reforming the infamous Blasphemy Law in the wake of the conviction of a Christian woman, Asia Bibi, for blasphemy on what were clearly trumped-up charges (while ultimately acquitted twice on appeal, Bibi was prevented from leaving Pakistan by the government till May 2019 for fear that her release would spark mass violence by religious groups).

But all this was only the lead-up to the main show of the year: the killing of Osama bin Laden on May 2, 2011. Strangely, the killing didn't lead to a major upswing in violence, at least in part because it was clear that the Pakistani government, who'd been shielding the Al-Qa'eda leader for years near a military base only fifty kilometers from the capital of Islamabad, was most likely not involved in the US Special Forces operation. Perhaps more important than a momentary spasm of violence, the event ramped up political tensions within the country, which were made worse in the wake of the attempted assassination of the girls' education promoter Malala Yousafzai, who was shot in the head and almost killed, causing an international uproar that only hardened positions across the increasing wide cultural divide in the country.

In the ensuing years ongoing political turmoil was highlighted by acts of spectacular violence such as the school massacre by the Taliban in Peshawar in December 2014 that killed nearly 150 people, most of them children of senior military personnel. In response, military forces finally cleared the Taliban out of most of the northern part of the country. The next year, the government secretly acquitted eight of the ten gunmen who had shot Malala Yousafzai, while in the following years the Islamic State, no friend to the Taliban, began penetrating the country from Afghanistan and launching attacks on Sufi shrines and similar targets. Ironically, the scope and devastation of the school attack actually had the countervailing effect of forcing the government to begin a nationwide military/security operation against militants, which most artists credit with making the country secure enough to begin holding concerts more regularly. Certainly, when visiting after twelve years, it was impossible for Mark not to feel the far more relaxed atmosphere all across the country, even during the holy days of Ashura, when Shi'a Pakistanis have often suffered large-scale attacks. But the harshness of the crackdown also led to the rise of a new civil rights movement in the Pashtun areas of the country, which has produced its own, still amateurish pop music.

Extremism and violence have been only a part of Pakistan's story in the last decade, and in many ways not the most important one. Economically and culturally the situation has not been quite so dismal and in some ways has clearly improved. While Pakistan's Human Development Index rank remained abysmal, around 154th in 2020, its actual index number in fact went up over 10 percent during the decade. More important, the country's overall GDP more than doubled, even as its population rose only by 20 percent. The landmark Protection against Harassment of Women at the Workplace bill was passed in 2010. The first fully democratically elected presidency was completed and power was peacefully transferred to another party in 2013. Major infrastructure projects were also undertaken, from new roads to a Chinese-built port and a major gas pipeline from Iran.

Moreover, while the psychological impact of all the violence, and particularly its impact on the live music scene, would be hard to overstate, the number of people killed from terrorism, even in the midst of the worst violence, remained exceedingly low in a country of two hundred million people; the total number of violent deaths as a percentage of the population was about .66 percent, lower than the .7 percent for the US during the same period. Indeed, during Mark's first visit friends didn't want to venture with him deep into the Northwest Frontier Province because of the Taliban presence, and they warned him that if he got into the wrong taxi he'd be "Daniel Pearled" in Karachi or Lahore, but now all anyone could talk about was their recent trips to the Pakistan's spectacular north, which once again is becoming a major international adventure tourism destination.

Though the political, geostrategic, and economic evolution of Pakistan has been, to say the least, confusing, its cultural and technological landscape remains even harder to pin down. The country has always been crisscrossed by ethnic, religious, and cultural chasms, and, perhaps widest of all, class. Not surprisingly, the rise of the Internet and social media opened new pathways for communication while exacerbating old tensions, becoming a veritable "war zone for competing narratives," as the newspaper *Dawn* put it in early 2019, as ultranationalist and religious trolls, as in most other countries, used Facebook, WhatsApp, and other media to spread hatred and suspicion between citizens.

Even in its far less pernicious function as a means of spreading music, the ubiquity and power of social media take their toll. As Mekaal explains, "Today you have to be seen everywhere, you have to be on every form of social media at all times—Twitter, Facebook, Instagram. No end. There's no time to take your time and do something right." And even if you have the time, with the growing power of corporatized music in Pakistan it's impossible to create freely and outside their control, as they control not only what is on television today but also what gets booked live in the major venues. Nevertheless, though the business end of music is more difficult than it was a decade ago, creatively artists have never been as well trained, original, and able to create innovatively as they have been today. Most every decent musician today has either a professional-caliber home studio or access to a world-class professional production studio, with equipment the equal of the best studios in New York or LA.

If your "drum room" has a raisable ceiling to tweak the natural reverb and your Logic Pro X DAW is run through twenty-four tracks of Rupert Neve preamps, you have definitely arrived. Such was the setup at Alif Studio in Karachi, where Mark and singer Arieb Azhar, whom he had first met in Islamabad a dozen years before, ran into a very familiar-looking and -sounding guitarist named Zishan Mansoor. After a few confused seconds putting names to faces, Mark and Zishan realized that they had met and even jammed at a wild party in Islamabad described in *Heavy Metal Islam,* where Zishan's then band was performing covers of Guns N' Roses and other metal bands while the children of Pakistan's elite partied themselves into oblivion. It was hard to imagine that night that a dozen years later all three would find themselves in one of the nicest studios on the planet, on the other end of the country. But since that time, Zishan's band, Malang Party, had achieved a good measure of success, appearing on *Coke Studio* in 2015, after which the then still dread-locked Zishan earned comparisons with Bob Marley, particularly for his most popular song, "Dil Jale" (he's cropped his hair close to the scalp since).

When Mark first entered the large guest room upstairs in the studio complex, Zishan was soloing over a Robben Ford song he'd been playing on his computer. His playing had the same character as it did a decade ago, though it was more polished melodically. But then he played his new song "Ziyarat" for Arieb and Mark to listen to, which was far more acoustic and dreamy. Asked to sum up all that's changed for him since their first meeting on that makeshift stage in an Islamabad villa, he explained that it was the influence of so many more influences, "from jazz to afrobeat, funk, soul, blues, and rock, to some modern UK jazz music. As important has been the availability and improvements in recording studios in the country, which has allowed us to record much more meticulously than ever before." In a way, Pakistan is going through a moment similar to the US and UK rock scenes from the late 1960s, epitomized by bands like the Beatles, Pink Floyd, Led Zeppelin, Miles Davis, and others who began experimenting with emerging multitrack technologies, effects, and synthesizers to create unprecedentedly sophisticated and complex productions. But that technological leap occurred at a moment when there was also a cultural and corporate ecosystem that encouraged and profited from such avant-garde creativity. Whether a similar ecosystem would be sustainable in Pakistan or anywhere today remains to be seen.

COKE AND SANITY

"Yes, music is the question." So declared Omer Khan, singer for Poor Rich Boy, whose authentically quirky cross-cultural mash-up of instruments, sounds, and styles has earned them a relatively small but devoted following in Pakistan, and invitations to perform in Europe and even the Kennedy Center and SXSW in the United States. He recalled Junoon guitarist Salman Ahmad's declaration to Mark in *Heavy Metal Islam* that he put down his stethoscope in favor of his guitar because he thought the latter could heal more people than the former. In Omer Madinati's view, that sentiment still rang true. It seems that a decade later Pakistanis haven't lost the palliative desire for music to heal what, as is the case with most every other country on Earth today, is a hopelessly schizophrenic society.

But what is the answer, or at least the treatment regimen, as it were? Omer's point was that the very premise and experience of music have changed in the last decade. Specifically, by 2008 many of the smaller independent labels that had enabled the exuberant explosion of Pakistani rock and pop had closed, with the exception of labels run by two of the biggest TV networks in Pakistan. Even worse, television channels like Geo's Fire Records and ARY's the Musik Records, which were far more commercially oriented, had become the dominant players in the industry. And even with stars like Atif Aslam and Ali Azmat (lead singer of Junoon) and more successful indie artists like Zeb and Haniya (whose beautiful folk-inflected groovy indie

FIGURE 25. Haniya Aslam, Lahore, 2012. Photo by Izabella Demavlys.

Urdu rock won the duo millions of fans on *Coke Studio* with tracks like "Bibi Sanam," from 2010) releasing important albums, they couldn't complete the process by staging concerts because of the deteriorating security situation, which devastated the relationship between artists and fans, which has, regardless of location, remained so crucial to incubating and supporting independent, youth-centered music scenes.

Perhaps the most important development in Pakistani music—and, in some ways, global music because of its worldwide impact—was the launching of *Coke Studio* in Pakistan in 2008, based on the model of the first *Coke Studio* in Brazil the year before. As the Pakistani paper *Dawn* put it, *Coke Studio* not only helped unify the Pakistani music industry toward one project, but, under the brilliant ear of former Vital Signs keyboardist and producer Rohail Hyatt, helped solidify the kind of "Sufi sheen" that characterized the often mesmerizing collaborations between leading traditional and pop, rock, and metal artists that came to be immediately recognizable as the *Coke Studio* sound. Two collaborations in particular, "Alif Allah Chambey Di Booty," with pop artist Meesha Shafi and the great Punjabi folk singer Arif Lohar (which has over fifty million views, one of the highest ever for *Coke Studio*), and "Aik Alif," written from a poem by the eighteenth-century poet Bulleh Shah and performed by the renown Sufi singer Saieen Zahoor and the rock duo Noori (which has upward of fifteen million views), demonstrate the sheer force, originality, and spirit of the sound Hyatt created.

Coke Studio single-handedly changed the Pakistani music scene. Joined by *Pepsi Battle of the Bands* and then *Nescafé Basement,* the three programs created a new star-making system in the country. You could be relatively or even completely unknown one day and, just by appearing on one of the shows, the next day your song and video will be marketed everywhere. Not surprisingly, the "caffeine companies" reshaped the sound and look of Pakistani music as well as its business model. Today, these programs remain the lenses through which not just Pakistanis but the wider world experience Pakistani music, with *Coke* the undisputed leader, *Pepsi* with a smaller audience because it's more into breaking new talent, and *Nescafé* in the "basement" with the more indie-sounding groups who, sooner or later, break through to the mainstream.

Interestingly, when Pakistan Reddit asked users what they'd like to see on the next season of *Coke Studio* (2019) the most requested item, along with a Junoon reunion (which would in fact happen in late 2018, just not on *Coke Studio*), was more metal. And indeed, while only achieving a few million views (relatively few by comparison), episodes featuring Mekaal Hasan, Faraz Anwar, Aaroh lead singer Farooq Ahmed, and other groups from the "classic" era covered in *Heavy Metal Islam* are among the program's most musically powerful (and are also nostalgic for many thirty- and forty-something Pakistanis).

This innovation was so musically and visually successful (in the look and high production values of the show compared to the DIY videos of the first generation of groups) and so commercially successful that Coke created similar "studios" in India, Morocco, and even across the Arab world broadly (with *Coke bil-Arabi*), all featuring artists from across the Arab world engaging in similar styles and kinds of collaborations. But hours spent watching most of the episodes of these other franchises confirm that there is something uniquely infectious about Pakistani music—whether traditional and Sufi or contemporary and extreme—that has enabled collaborations that have a degree of originality, power, and often sheer joy that simply is not reached by any other *Coke Studio.*

As a result of its popularity, *Coke Studio* established *Coke Studio Gigs,* which brought artists from the show as well as local talent to universities across the country "for the fans." But it also wasn't afraid to push some very fraught social boundaries—not just positioning popular music and even popular music mixed with religious music to the entirety of the country during a time when religious militancy and violence were at their peak, but even going so far as to highlight the participation of trans artists on the show, as happened in 2019 when it was announced to great fanfare that the eleventh season would feature singers Naghma and Lucky, under the slogan "One Nation, One Spirit, One Sound." As if to outdo itself, *Coke Studio* 2020 began with another all-star collaboration of leading female singers (including Sanam Marvi, Fariha Pervez, Zara Madani, Wajiha Naqvi, and Sehar Gul Khan), in which Meesha Shafi even "rapped."

As mentioned above, *Coke Studio* was joined by other music-related programs sponsored by the caffeinated drink companies. In fact, *Pepsi Battle of the Bands* first premiered six years before the launch of *Coke Studio;* the winner of season 1 (in 2002) was Aaroh, whose groundbreaking "Sufi metal" sound was discussed at length in *Heavy Metal Islam,* while the metal band Entity Paradigm (also known as EP) was runner-up and the Mekaal Hasan Band was third. Despite the success and popularity of the first year, Pepsi chose not to do another season for fifteen years, until the show's return in 2017. A third season took place in 2018 and a fourth in 2019. The finale of season 4 was won by the band Auj, another Karachi band straddling the musical space between highly commercialized Hindustani pop and harder-edged rock (other songs are reminiscent of Bad Company or Foreigner). Perhaps more interesting than their victory were the stars who performed at the finale, which included Meesha Shafi and an all-star performance with "iconic" pop and qawwali stars that was right out of the *Coke Studio* playbook. It has also recently started a rap battle series as well, picking up on the global trend of corporations sponsoring, commercializing, and—not surprisingly—removing any political valence from battle rap.

Pepsi is fundamentally different than *Coke*—the shows more so than the soft drinks—because it featured new(er) bands performing for judges rather than established acts collaborating in one-offs in a closed studio. But its cultural impact, the solidification of a particular Pakistani rock aesthetic outside of Bollywood or Lollywood sounds, was clear. Unfortunately, the quality of the bands, with the exception of a few of the yearly winners such as Kashmir and Badnaam, was diminished after the first season, when all three top finalists went on to become major forces in the Pakistani musical universe. To many musicians, even of the present generation, this says a lot about the deleterious impact of the "star system" encouraged by the "fizzy water" and caffeine companies' takeover of the music industry.

The third major program, *Nescafé Basement,* had its first season in 2012 and from the start has been geared specifically toward finding underground and largely unknown young musicians and bands, with the goal of "tak[ing] their individuality and music from humble jam sessions to mainstream audiences." *Nescafé Basement* is so named because in fact it is in the basement of the Nescafé headquarters in Lahore. As the *Tribune* newspaper described it in 2013, the space "blossomed into a neat musical retreat where aspiring musicians of different backgrounds and age groups gather to create nothing but inspired tunes and compositions." Being a successful independent musician, Entity Paradigm guitarist and songwriter Xulfi (born Xulfiqar Jabbar Khan) naturally knew what to put in his personal musicians' cave to bring out the best in the talented but young and largely inexperienced musicians and artists he recruited to record and perform there with the house band of similarly successful musicians.

Clearly the need for such spaces remains; Haniya Aslam (of Zeb and Haniya) believes that of the three "caffeine" programs the *Basement* is the only one that fulfills its promise to encourage and develop new talent. In good measure this is no doubt due to the show's musical director, Xulfi, who, like his counterpart at *Coke,* Rohail Hyatt, has become a Svengali of the music industry, crafting unlikely commercial hits out of previously underground artists and styles. So it's not surprising that the number of musicians who applied to be mentored on the show jumped from ninety-eight the first season to approximately thirteen hundred the second year. All for nineteen spots.

Xulfi has a different take than some of the other artists discussed here. Sitting in the control room of one of his three studios (this one in the basement of his home in the Defense zone of Lahore), he attenuated Mark's lament about the "death-by-corporatization" of Pakistani rock, explaining that corporations were more the jackals or hyenas feeding on the carcass of the musical animal that had already met its end: "In fact, the scene had died a couple of years before Coke, Pepsi, and Nescafé took over. It wasn't them who forced the dozen video channels out of business. Rather it was the rise of Pakistani TV dramas, which took over as the primary programs people wanted to watch. Then came the wave of violence that more or less shut down the live music scene completely." It was then that the corporations moved in and offered the perfect replacement for both videos and live music—bands recorded live with the air of newness and mystery around them.

But what the *Basement* has done is allow these young musicians and artists to not just train with the best professional musicians in Pakistan, but also record numerous tracks. But even though the focus has been on young musicians, the show has at least in one case discovered a bona fide star in the waiting, when it brought together the Soch Band with then eight-year-old qawwali prodigy Hadiya Hashmi for an epic rendition of the Sufi chant "Bol Hu" at the start of the 2019 season. The performance created the same state of *sama'*—or listening ecstasy (the term is the same in Arabic, Persian, and Urdu)—as the best *Coke Studio* Sufi/qawwali-rock collaborations. But even on more mundane episodes, the aesthetic and goal of bringing in young musicians without the gimmick of competition provide *Nescafé Basement* with a certain frisson that transcends its far more expensive-looking and -sounding caffeinated counterparts.

In this regard, the band Kashmir presents an interesting counterpoint to several of the views of the many who are highly critical of the present system ("Kashmir sounded better than Karachi," bassist Usman Sadiqi explained to Mark when he asked about the inspiration for the choice of name). The 2017 winner of *Pepsi Battle of the Bands,* Kashmir and bands like it have had a very different experience. Since their victory they have managed to gig regularly across the country, with five to six gigs at colleges most months, plus being asked to do jingles and other small projects, all of which has allowed all the band members to make livings as musicians and quit their day jobs. Yet it's equally clear that their success in working regularly is a function also of their being relatively new, young, and, therefore, far cheaper than it would be for these same colleges or other venues to hire the Mekaal Hasan Band or a similarly more established act. As always, the music business remains a young(er) man's or woman's game if you're not lucky enough to achieve a level of superstardom that guarantees you many other income streams.

It's not surprising that young Pakistani musicians are able to navigate so expertly between multiple genres and styles across several cultures. Even the previous generation of musicians had to learn other styles in what Ahmer Naqvi, music journalist and former COO of the "Spotify of Pakistan," Patari, describes as "physical form": "Back in the day there was a lack of access to 'world musics' because music came in physical form [cassettes, CDs] so they had to get it physically, so you had to make a lot of effort to get it. But now, amazingly, the entire history of human musical production is available online at the touch of a button. Because of this, as [in the series of documentaries on underground artists] Patari Tabeer has shown, even a small amount of money can make a difference given all the means available to obtain and create music." Another, perhaps paradoxical component is that the worsening security situation in the later 2000s and early 2010s made the so-called "caffeine programs" more attractive. Ahmer explained: "In the vacuum [created by the bad security situation] came these programs, where it was safe to enjoy music from the comfort of one's home. And it was already edited, looked good, was well produced, etc.; so it became really easy to produce and consume this kind of music. But, of course, this scenario is not at all good for rock 'n' roll."

But if you're not fully vested in one of the shows as a producer, bandleader, or regular member of the house bands, the downsides do weigh heavily. As one well-known musician who's worked with all three programs (and who asked not to be identified) explained, whatever good they're doing for a few artists and sidemen and women, ultimately they're "not making music better, they're making it worse. At the end of the day it's Coke, Pepsi, and Nescafé, so they're marketing and branding. They require a certain kind of sound. There are a lot of people sitting at the top of Pepsi in Pakistan and they have no musical ability; they don't know anything; yet they'll never give full leverage to a music producer." Ahmer Naqvi similarly explains that even if they're not just interested in doing a slightly Sufi version of Bolly/Lollywood music, "The guys who run the caffeine companies are not the kids who listen to the new music; they're our age; so they're more interested in bringing back the bands they grew up on like Aaroh and so on rather than sponsoring really new music."

Zain Ahsan of Poor Rich Boy concurs that the dynamics of the "caffeinated" programs leave little room for actual "indie" rock—of which there is a surprising amount of very good examples—to penetrate into the Pakistani mainstream, even if many indie rockers play in the house bands of these programs as their day gigs: "The music they want to listen and dance to is not the music I want to make. Hence, I have Poor Rich Boy, which is all about my aesthetics, and I can do what I want."

But doing what one wants comes at a big price in terms of freedom to create and make some sort of living, especially as the Pakistani music industry has entered an era than can best be described as "musical feudalism," one that for artists is even more deleterious than the true era of feudalism. At least in the precolonial era, wealthy patrons were the ones who chose musicians, and they chose the best and most virtuosic ones they could find and gave them great prestige. Coke only cares about selling Coke. Today the patron is a money-seeking corporation, for whom the artist is merely a tool for selling its wares or itself because it is a commodity. "Music has become as disposable as fizzy water," Ahmer Naqvi explained ruefully.

POLITICS' PRESENT ABSENCE

It's true that in comparison to the music scenes in most other countries we've looked at, Pakistan's music scene is strongly apolitical, although the burgeoning hip hop scenes (which we discuss below) are certainly changing that dynamic. One reason for this disengagement with politics is likely that the country had such a strong progressive political poetic tradition, which after 1971 and the breakup with Bangladesh was harshly repressed, first for political reasons under the Bhutto regime and then for cultural and religious reasons as well under Zia. Over the ensuing decades—similar to Americans, Zain Ahsan (who spent several years going to high school in Arizona) surmises—Pakistanis became unable to process all the inherent contradictions of their situation.

The Pakistani music scene, at least on television, is dominated by the caffeine conglomerates—Nescafé, after all, is just a brand of Nestlé, the biggest food and beverage company on Earth. But as in most hipsterized quarters of major global cities, the underground is now being served an even fresher, or "truer," blend of rock with the creation of True Brew, a combination record label and performance space in Lahore that has become the true space for underground and avant-garde music in the city, and on the Pakistani Internet. Started by Zain Peerzada and producer Jamal Rahman, an almost twenty-year veteran of the city's underground and experimental scene, the label was established in 2012 and as of 2019 it has over seventeen hundred subscribers each on YouTube and SoundCloud. The idea is spreading, with other venues, such as the Demo Music Room opening in Karachi, which bands are using to record live and interactive performances. Of course, these pale in comparison with *Coke Studio,* which has over 6.5 million YouTube subscribers and tens of millions of views on its most popular videos.

While Rahman and Peerzada have worked with mainstream, metal, and indie stars like Atif Aslam, Zeb and Haniya, EP, and Overload, and also on some well-known film scores and soundtracks, the heart of True Brew is its work with young artists who are unestablished or just rising, which allows them to not only record at the first-class studio but perform live streaming for webisodes, which viewed as a whole present a unique archive of the rising generation of Pakistani musicians and musical artists. As Rahman told the *Express Tribune* at the start of the enterprise in 2012, "Music is meant to be heard in a live environment; that's where you really make a connection with the audience."

Ironically, even with True Brew, metal is always lurking in the background of most people's appreciation for the project. Thus when Pakistani sociologist and journalist Farhad Mirza talked with one of the bands featured in Rahman's grassroots music festival, Storm in a Teacup, he couldn't help beginning with the admission that "if my memory serves me well, the cultural choices allocated to a teenager in those times [the late 1990s and early 2000s] were limited to your favorite metal band and somebody else's favorite metal band. . . . If you wanted to be slightly cerebral, then you had to listen to bands like Tool and Dream Theater. Everything else was effeminate, and hence, lame. There was a need to assert masculinity through the rhythmic angst of metal music." But even here the reality, as Mirza notes, was that in the present context the new scenes, and the patronage by experienced musicians like Zain and Jamal, or, at the more corporate level, Xulfi and Hyatt, are offering young artists a really unprecedented chance to build their craft and work with some of the most talented musical personalities, artists, and producers in the country. None of this means that all but the most fortunate of them will wind up making a living playing music, the way some of the best-known first-generation metal and rock players did, but perhaps that is no longer a viable goal in the contemporary musical ecosystem. Only time will tell.

SPOTIFY AND METAL

All four of the caffeine shows, each of which is drawing on and in musicians from a different part of the Pakistani music ecosystem, owe their popularity to that moment, around 2008, when Pakistan achieved what we term "high metal": the sophisticated, eclectic blend of Sufi melodies, metal riffs, and distorted guitars with sophisticated arrangements and pop production or sheen that has come to define the Pakistani "sound." Not surprisingly but disappointingly, Javed Bashir, lead singer of the Mekaal Hasan Band, chose the moment of the band's greatest success to depart for a solo career, while Meesha Shafi went from screaming brutal vocals to Desi/Bollywood super-star, as an actress and solo artist. Both have made some of the most watched *Coke Studio* collaborations, with tens of millions of views each.

But as we've already seen, the larger ecosystem that enabled the success up to this point was changing rapidly and unpredictably at the very moment this gen-eration achieved its greatest success. Recording and distribution practices once again changed rapidly, as they had in the previous decade with the arrival of high-quality digital recording software and the Internet. As Mekaal explains it,

> Around 2008, bands were making records; they'd come in and record albums at the studio. But then, very quickly, the whole idea of making a collection of songs into an album disappeared here, just as in the US. Those bands that didn't have money just used home studios, which got better with cheaper technology. But they didn't have the level of professionalization and equip-ment to really pull off the same level of production. So, for example, in 2007 I did four major records—Zeb and Haniya, Ali Azmat, Jal, and Noori; only two of those major artists have put out a full album since then, because soon after *Coke Studio* started, the whole scene changed. It became all about going on that program and albums became more or less irrelevant. Now I just get people calling me for mixes for singles or to record drums.

This change in the political and aesthetic economies of music-making at the margins (i.e., outside the pop/Lollywood system) reflected a broader change in the dynamics and substance of the music. In general, most artists we've discussed working in these genres agree that the decade before 2008 had a lot more independent music coming into the mainstream, with musi-cians self-funding their own music and videos. Few if any bands had sponsor-ships of any significance; most made their own records and their own videos; and the reasons that these recordings and videos got attention was that the Internet wasn't as big a sensation yet so people were genuinely interested in seeing what the kids came up with.

> Once the Internet and social media platforms kicked in, it shaped things in a very different way, especially because there hasn't been a proper live scene

FIGURE 26. Mekaal Hasan, photographed in Lahore, 2019. Photo by Aabroo Hashmi.

to support independent music. In Pakistan you can make videos and music at home and upload them, but if you're not playing live then your direct connection to people suffers; you can't have the kind of organic fan base that was starting to develop when *Heavy Metal Islam* was published.

As Haniya, Mekaal, and so many other musicians repeat, the lack of a live music system for independent artists has profoundly shaped—many would say distorted—the larger musical ecosystem. Today when people make new songs and videos, they no longer can send them to an independent video channel that has a built-in audience; rather they must upload them onto YouTube and then pay to "push" them so they can reach a big enough potential audience to have a chance to catch on. Ten years ago no one would have thought they'd have to invest money into a video beyond the cost of producing it. That was the label's responsibility if it bought the music. Now the labels and the channels are gone, so the entire component of getting music out there has been taken away. In its place are corporations, who realized at this time that music was a marketable commodity oriented to youth and that they could tap into the interests of Pakistanis everywhere, including the diaspora, as well as those in India and Bangladesh, through it.

Today there is in fact a corporate-sponsored live scene of sorts, one that is tied to the improving security situation in the country. At its heart is a growing number of food festivals that feature music, sponsored and branded by one fizzy drink corporation or the other. Standalone concerts, however, have comparatively higher ticket prices or are by invitation only, with tickets given out to corporate clients and executives and their friends, rather than the general public. The festivals "are funded by the same corporations making fizzy or caffeine drinks," Haniya explains. "They control who appears, how they're presented, and now most of the festivals are tied to food, with music ultimately as a backdrop in many cases."

How has the country's metal scene in particular fared during this period? As in so many other places metal in Pakistan was a sanctuary, a way for fans to address the numerous challenges they faced in daily life—both its exoticness and its relevance to the realities that so many young people faced every day helped make it popular. Even though a lot of the musicians who were attracted to metal were from upper-middle-class or wealthy families, metal still became a symbol of resistance against a stifling system from which many of their own families might have benefited, at least in some ways. One hard/grindcore group, Multinational Corporations, well summed up the sentiment of most Pakistani metal bands in their song "Salaab" ("Flood"), the title

taken from future prime minister Imran Khan's description of his party's rise
to prominence in the mass protests of 2014,

> Years have gone by, nothing seems to change
> Locked up in this cage while our spirits, they rage
> Face to face with fate, intoxicated on hate
> Time to break free, time to take control?
> Fuck your revolution, Fuck your inquilaab
> Badal apni soch,
> phir aye ga salaab
> [If you change your mindset, then the real flood will come]

HIGH-OCTANE METAL UNDER THE HOOD

As this book was being written, Spotify made a discovery that was shocking
(at least to them): metal fans were the streaming service's users who were
most loyal to their music, far more so than any other genre's fans. Needless
to say, Pakistani metal fans, and musicians, are equally loyal to their brands
of metal, but because that metal is so hybrid and elastic, it's much easier to
remain loyal to metal and still enjoy listening to and performing other, even
more traditional styles. Moroccan metalheads are the other group with tastes
as eclectic. Indeed, one of first things that one notices when studying metal
in the Muslim world is that the poles of the Muslim world, Morocco and
Pakistan, share a similar aesthetic, no doubt influenced by the power of traditional Sufi music, which is extremely malleable and amenable to adaptation
for the more earthy and earthly goals of rock music.

Even the hardest songs have always had a kind of beauty, or soul, to them
that comes straight from the intersection of North Indian Hindustani and
Persian traditional music. We can trace this "soul," or *rooh*, back more than
half a millennium to the music of Amir Khusrau and the Chisti Sufi order,
which first fused the South Asian and Persian (and, through it, Arabic) styles
of devotional and virtuosic music together. It's the same "intermediate
sphere" (to borrow a term from ethnomusicologist Peter Manuel) between
flat-out rock and highly elevated Sufi music that inspired Junoon, and more
recently pop stars like Atif Aslam, whose earlier songs and band were not
afraid to feature heavy guitars and riffs along with his qawwali-inflected
voice. (He fulfilled a lifelong ambition when he recorded and performed
with members of the original Guns N' Roses in 2010.) So it's not surprising

that, as in Iran, the metal in Pakistan, even when it's brutal and extreme, cannot escape the soulful core of the broader tradition.

In 2009, CNN did a special report, "Underground Musicians Aim to Change Pakistan's Image," that explained how natural metal seemed in a country as tense and torn as Pakistan, describing the scene at one show where headbanging spread from the stage to the crowd "like a virus," creating "the real Pakistan" as opposed to the "terrorists or mullahs" who'd given it such a bad name. The country's "economic liberalization program" was credited with helping jump-start the music because it encouraged the opening of the private TV stations that would play their videos and radio stations that would play their music (an accurate assessment, as Mark explored in the Pakistan chapter of *Heavy Metal Islam*). And indeed, a wealth of bands, many of whom existed prior to 2008 but were very much still in the often deep underground in the second third of the decade, began to flower as the decade drew to a close, right in time for the establishment of a local metal label, Gas Mask Holocaust. Epitomizing this trend was Entity Paradigm, whose first, celebrated album was coproduced by Mekaal, and which became one of the biggest rock bands in the country. The pioneering metal band Dusk, founded by Faraz Anwar, also achieved success, even as Anwar created a more commercial sounding group, Mizraab, whose hit "Ujalon Main" remains one of the defining songs of the era. For their part, more hardcore and extreme groups like Communal Grave, Autopsy Gothic, and Kosmos continued, and some of the oldest bands, like Black Warrant, soldiered on a few years more before going on seemingly permanent hiatus around 2012.

On the other hand, Entity Paradigm, one of the first full-on "rock" bands in Pakistan with a metal edge, reunited in 2009 to great acclaim after a several-year hiatus, although they've since released only one major track, the powerful and heavy single "Shor Macha" ("Shout Loud") in 2009. Similarly, Overload has not recorded a new album since 2009, although it's worth noting that it has the distinction of being not only one of the most unique-sounding metal bands anywhere, not just for its "Sufi" aesthetic featuring the Dhol—a heavy drum played on both sides—as a primary instrument, but also because it's where the now world-renowned singer Meesha Shafi got her start as front woman for this funkiest of Pakistani metal groups. More recently, Overload's drummer, Farhad Humayun, has become a well-known solo singer in his own right while occasionally organizing live jams that are recorded for the public under the title *Levis Riot Studios*.

By 2012 the newspaper *Pakistan Today* would write that "within two generations, we have gone from solid classical crooning to bouncy pop and moved on to gut-wrenching, metallic sounds that anyone from 15 years ago would be loath to endure." It was clear that as musical tastes were changing so was the musical vocabulary and the skill set of the artists. Simply put, whereas in the first decade or so there were a handful of virtuoso standouts like Mekaal Hasan and Faraz Anwar, in the last decade there's been an explosion of talent, as the Internet in particular has made it far easier to teach oneself to play at an almost virtuosic level.

This was perhaps epitomized best by a progressive metal band that emerged in the last decade, Takatak. Founded in 2010 in Lahore and with Mekaal Hasan close by, from the start Takatak revealed a clear level of skill that set a very high bar for the near-term future of the metal scene. Described as the very "quintessence of Pakistani metal" and the virtuosos of "djent/progrcore," Takatak, one reviewer declared, could even "play alongside the likes of Lamb of God and probably steal a few of its fans by the time they are done." Indeed, the well-known metal magazine *Metal Injection* named their album *Acrophase* one of the best of 2020.

The power of the band was clear even early on, as an early live show caught on video at the Guitar School (owned by Junoon frontman Ali Azmat) in which they're playing Lamb of God's "Faded Line" shows the band's rising power bubbling up through the still raw surface. The band kept growing and becoming more sophisticated, till the point where their release in early 2021, "Backseat," combines metalcore and progressive metal with even more syncopation and harmonized brutal vocals to stand out with the leading bands globally, a feat made more powerful thanks to the retro-styled high-quality video for the song. Listening to it was a perfect catharsis for the very shitty year that had just ended.

As Haniya explained in thinking about the metal scene, "The Internet and social media are crucial, as the younger generation grew up listening to so much online and got so good at reverse engineering, figuring out how anything is done. And now with the software—people are composing on iPads! But even here a band like Takatak is unique, because the level of musicianship is so high. It's no wonder the members almost all work as session musicians."

Ironically, while for Haniya the members of Takatak's work as session musicians is a badge of honor for one of the country's best bands, for the band itself it's very much out of necessity rather than professional ambition. As

Mekaal explains it, "The reality is that despite the great bands the metal scene didn't pick up after its late 2000s crest. Today there is Takatak, but it's very difficult to see them live and they don't have the huge online base to pull in income that way. So these great musicians become sidemen or session players for pop stars who have media and marketing and do well-paid corporate shows. Or they suffer despite their talent and even genius." As Zain Peerzada, lead guitarist of Takatak, lamented to Mark, "Look at Mekaal's flute player Papu. He's one of the world masters of the flute, and he's approaching 60 and still driving a motorcycle; he can't afford a car."

On the far other side, commercially successful artists are getting more and more removed from these struggles. As Mekaal continues, "You have to realize these big artists no longer do noncorporate shows; they never have to worry about organizing their own shows, selling tickets, etc., and they get spoiled by these invite-only or very expensive shows, and the intimate relationship between artists and fans that is at the core of metal and rock is lost. Meanwhile the mega stars become so big largely because of their media-savvy approach and how much corporations think they're worth."

Zain Peerzada seconds Mekaal's diagnosis of the situation. "Everyone looks up to metal chops—that's the marker of virtuosity as a musician." But that doesn't explain what happened to the scene itself. After a lot of back and forth on the subject, Zain explained that the initial success of bands like Junoon—which weren't strictly metal but had distorted guitars and riff-based songs—and more proper metal bands like Dusk, who'd toured Europe, inspired the younger generation: "So when we started playing together in school we played battle of the bands in Lahore, were doing metal covers, getting better, and then hooked up with the bass player from another great band, Odyssey, M. W. Khan, who's since become a very successful producer in LA, and he produced our first songs before Mekaal took over. But even though we started with a sound like Lamb of God because our singer sounded like Randy Blythe, we moved toward a more progressive sound with more weird and difficult arrangements; so we lost the singer and became an instrumental band." Tragically, Zain's father passed away the day the band was supposed to start recording their first album and it wound up taking three years to finish. Even then, when the first video came out members of the Indian metal band Skyharbour saw its premier at the Music Mela (festival) in Lahore, and wound up mixing their next song, "Master Beast."

It's not just extreme metal that's persevering. As the Kominas's Basim Usmani put it in a *Guardian* music blog in 2011, "Youths from Punjab to

Balochistan are turning out relevant, Pakistani takes on everything from punk, to crust and black metal." But not surprisingly, the majority of the bands who were considered praiseworthy by Usmani at the start of the decade have long since faded from view, with perhaps the band Foreskin the most important band to be more or less still around today. What's clear, however, is that, even in more remote corners of the country such as Balochistan, metal is, if not exactly thriving, then still very much making its presence known in a wide variety of flavors and aesthetics. But even with a growing number of bands, shows are often extremely small, many in rehearsal rooms or other small repurposed rooms that hold only two or three dozen fans at most. The atmosphere is exactly as it has always been at truly underground DIY punk, hardcore, and metal shows—exuberant and raw, largely male, with unison headbanging and a sense of camaraderie that belies the sometimes sterile surroundings in which the shows take place.

The problem is that music really can't stand still; it has to keep cresting to develop. "It was like a wave, but with a short amplitude," Zain reflected. "Not as big as we thought it would become. Another great artist, Hassan Omar, was in Foreskin, was putting on shows in backyards, rooftops wherever, and that's the only shows we'd do besides this guitar school that was ultimately owned by Ali Azmat from Junoon."

During this period metal in particularly completely retreated in the public eye. Indeed, while *Coke Studio* has featured the kind of "Sufi metal" sound discussed above, that sound became less common over time and the edgier sounds, distorted guitars, and more aggressive music on Pakistan's flagship music show receded. While *Pepsi* and *Nescafé* still feature more rock since they are focused on the rock-centric "battle of the bands" narrative, the political economy of the corporate music ecosystem means that the bands on *Pepsi* don't necessarily have songs or experience; rather, people start forming bands at the start of every year to try to get on it, and disband if they don't make it (sometimes re-forming for auditions in subsequent years depending on the feedback). What this means is that bands are not usually driven organically to be creative or perform. These problems would be circumvented if there were a healthy live scene, but without it, it's impossible to have the organic connections and growth that are at the heart of rock 'n' roll, never mind the more virtuosic kind of musical symbiosis involved in metal (hip hop, as we've discussed several times in the book, does not have this problem since it's not about live performances and doesn't require group virtuosity, and all the economic, time, and space requirements that accompany it).

Poor Rich Boy's Zain Ahsan explains that, especially in light of the limitations of Pakistan's political and economic circumstances, "the scene just sort of fizzled." While for some it was simply about the girls ("It's so hard to get girls to go to metal shows, so I thought, why should I do that?" one music journalist explained to Mark), Zain sees it as more of an issue of maturity: "It was a high school phase and then they moved on because most people would start to think it was corny. The problem is that even if most bands were shitty, had they stayed with it the music could have become more polished." What also became a problem was that the people who were into underground music—that sort of educated, middle and upper class that today is into indie rock—were the people into metal. But a lot of people who were doing metal became indie artists like Poor Rich Boy, or got into Deep House and other kinds of electro, a dynamic similar to what happened in Egypt, Palestine, and Lebanon, as we've seen. And so Takatak only plays around one show every two years because it simply doesn't make sense to do more. "We don't have big crowds. People want to dance to EDM and Indian/Bollywood music."

This problem couldn't be more of a shame. Listen to a song like Takatak's "Jibraatka" off the EP *Out of Something,* released in 2017, and you hear a band that is at the top of its form, which, in fact, could easily share the stage with Lamb of God or other top European and American bands. But unlike Arab and Turkish bands, who can reach Europe for tours and festivals for relatively little money, Pakistani bands have a much harder time breaking through outside the country, even as they remain marginalized in Pakistan. Takatak members even formed a second group, Karakoram (the name taken from a mountain range and gorgeous yet deadly mountain highway connecting Pakistan and China), with vocals to have more of commercial potential. And musically it worked, as the music sounds like what the Foo Fighters would sound like if they were twenty years younger, ten times rawer, much more creative, and had nothing to lose.

When you listen to Karakoram's first major song, "Toofan," it becomes clear that whatever technical gaps might have been there in Pakistani music a decade ago are long gone. If Lebanon's The Kordz spent over a year searching for the best producer and had to go to Canada to get a proper sound a decade ago, Karakoram sounds as fully produced as any top European or American band purely with local talent and studios. Equally important, the younger, rawer, and more DIY bands from across the country, such as Venom Vault, Depletion, Black Hour, Corpsepyre, and Inferner, also sound as authentically relevant as their counterparts anywhere else. But as Foreskin's singer Hassan Amin put it in an interview in 2013 with the webzine *Global Metal Apocalypse,* "When the gigs died out [in the late 2000s] they died out too."

Pakistan's many music scenes point to a crucial change in the dynamics of extreme music across the MENA and broader Muslim world. Whereas in the 1990s and 2000s the metal and hip hop scenes were like canaries in a coal mine for understanding the larger view of rulers and societies at large toward political as well as social freedom, in the last decade most countries have seen a more liberal attitude develop toward these musics, both by governments and within society; yet they operate in contexts where, besides Tunisia, governments are monitoring social media far more heavily than before, dampening the ability of alternative/extreme music scenes to engage in political music. Indeed, Salman Ahmad traveled across Pakistan to convince mullahs that music isn't against Islam, but that act seems quaint today. This isn't to deny that there aren't ultraconservatives and extremists who want to prevent (even violently) any kind of music beyond a cappella "nasheeds" praising the Prophet Muhammad; rather, it's that these debates are more or less settled in the mainstream of Pakistani culture, whatever the fantasies of Salafis.

And, far less positively, there's so much violence on an everyday level that cultural events are no longer a high-value target for militants. As Zain Ahsan explains, "In truth, the whole opposition to the music thing was never that big a deal. I never really knew anyone who got threatened. Now a lot of festivals have started as well as EDM events—we've even had Major Lazer and Diplo in Islamabad! The underground stuff is happening through cafes, open mics, and through setting up floating event agencies that will find venues to present events." Just as it used to happen in the NYC club culture, "it's about the promoter, not the venue. People follow the promoter and the artists, regardless of where."

Even as most of the artists here express similar levels of frustration vis-à-vis their ability to penetrate the mainstream in terms of the massive numbers of views regularly achieved by pop stars like Atif Aslam and the high-paying corporate gigs, films, and commercials that come with it, there is also a sense among many that the situation is beginning to improve. As Zain Peerzada put it, "Right now the scene is rejuvenating, we have more talented musicians than ever before." As proof, he calls up a video of a young progressive fusion group called Wisdom Salad, which sounds like nothing if not a kind of baby, Desi version of Snarky Puppy, replete with heavy synth and guitars and crazy time signatures.

Despite all this creativity Haniya, who when Mark met her in 2007 was a fresh-faced intern at Mekaal Hasan's studio and is now one of the most recognizable voices and talented producers and postproduction specialists in Pakistan, is not sure about the future. During a long evening of dinner and music with her, Sajid Gharfoor of Sajid, Zeeshan, and his brother Sarmad (one of the top producers and a rising film composer in Islamabad) that took us to a small but delicious restaurant and then her newly refurbished studio in the Defense Housing Authority, it was clear that Pakistan's most creative musicians are struggling to achieve a balance between talent, originality, and commercialism. "All the creativity of the scene is at the ground's end," she explained after debuting a beautiful new song of hers on acoustic guitar as we sat in her living room.

> But at the top it's a different story. Yes, it's amazing how they blend this stuff together with the Sufi rock or metal sound; but ultimately they keep doing covers that everyone grew up listening to. They're not expanding the sound to new horizons, instead of using more original stuff—original poetry and so on. Sadly, people are scared to express themselves in Pakistan; there's self-censorship now, not by the state, but internally; it's seeped down into everyone. You have to choose your words or you can wind up dead. And so what should be expressed in the underground scene, at least in indie, rock, and metal, isn't, because even they want to be picked up by Coke, or if you're younger Pepsi and Nescafé. How then are you supposed to make an edgy song or call it like it is politically when the corporation will not take you if you do?

Haniya's question rings true whether you're listening to Kashmir (the band, not the song) at an underproduced festival in the majestic Hunza Valley in the Himalayan foothills, or in one of the spectacular new recording studios in Karachi, two thousand kilometers to the south. Talking with Sajid, whose recordings with Zeeshan Parwaz still, for Mark, constitute some of the most original and ahead-of-its-time hybrids of rock and electronica of this millennium, you realize how hard it is to both stay in the avant-garde musically and make a living as an artist. After half a decade in Canada the former law professor returned to Pakistan, but instead of going home to Peshawar, he moved in with his brother Sarmad, whose own career as a musician, composer, and producer took off in the meantime, first as a guitarist for pop idol Atif Aslam and more recently as a soundtrack and film score composer for Pakistan.

Similar to the dynamic in the US, while Sajid's focus on songwriting and singing has meant that there's not much he can do in the business apart from his periodic releases of music (either solo or with Zeeshan), Sarmad, like Zeeshan, is continuously busy with one project or another. (Zeeshan, whose talents as a video director were already apparent on Sajid and Zeeshan's early videos, has become one of the top videographers in the country after getting a degree in filmmaking in Vancouver.) The other major issue that becomes clear in spending time with so many diverse artists is that the dividing line is, at least to some degree, technology and access to a good recording studio, as those artists who are most busy are those who have the means, ability, and desire not just to produce their own work but to work constantly with other artists, especially those who in some way are working on one of the main shows, such as *Coke Studio, Pepsi Battle of the Bands,* or *Nescafé Basement,* as well as on commercials and soundtracks of various sorts, usually in studios that equal or even surpass most noncorporate studios in the United States today.

POOR RICH MUSIC

Pakistan has what is undoubtedly one of the most interesting indie music scenes on the planet. This is not surprising, given the richness of Pakistani music and culture more broadly. Poor Rich Boy is perhaps the epitome of the indie trend in Pakistan: wide acclaim outside the country but, despite significant exposure on mainstream Pakistani TV, a limited impact at home. The band is a world music impresario's dream: "Lahore's answer to the Smiths . . . conjur[ing] the strangeness of everyday life in a society where expressing one's inner world can be both a cathartic and subtly rebellious act," as *The National* put it in 2017. Fluent in English, and blending together Pakistani and Hindustani styles with Americana, the band members bring a wide range of experiences and interests, both musical and intellectual (the lead guitarist records Sindhi folks songs, the bass player is a lawyer and sociology teacher, and the drummer was a carpenter). Yet even after a celebrated appearance at Center Stage and a subsequent invitation to SXSW in 2015, once they returned home they were back to playing "bookshops and ice-cream parlours." Unfortunately, Zain explained to *The National* in the same story, "there aren't many opportunities for paid shows for indie musicians in Pakistan."

Haniya, an old friend of Zain's (they both learned to engineer in good measure at Mekaal's studio), agrees: "Today it's much harder, unless doing corporate work and jingles. It's very hard to get work . . . but not so different from the US. At least here it's a small enough scene so that you can reach even the top musicians, but in the US and even in Canada there's no way to even dream about collaborating with them." As Haniya poignantly recounts: "We [Zeb and Haniya] did this great Center Stage tour in the US, which was a big deal. And yet when we returned home, there was no work. We saw the same thing happen with Poor Rich Boy—I watched them live streaming from the Kennedy Center and felt so much pain because I knew what would happen when they got home." Later, she joked that most of their money, like hers, during Zeb and Haniya's Center Stage tour, was probably spent "on sushi and gear."

To some degree, one can see a situation where metal, indie, and hip hop are no longer "alternative" or even very "underground," as they do not have the same kind of subcultural identities, experiences, and political implications as they did before. The defining "alternative" music in most countries across the region seems to have shifted toward various forms of electronic and indie music—true indie in the sense that it's outside the system of commodified musical production, distribution, and consumption. In Egypt we see this in both the *mahraganat*/electro-sha'bi scene as well as the experimental electronic music scene, which is among the most creative anywhere. Given that the highly original music of Peshawar's Sajid and Zeeshan's *One Light Year at Snail Speed* remains one of the seminal electro-rock albums of the millennium, it shouldn't be surprising that Pakistan is seeing the rapid growth of an EDM scene that is not simply a copy of either Euro-American-style EDM or its Bollywood version. But it is the indie rock scene in Pakistan that is the most interesting in terms of its place in the larger Pakistani musical universe sonically as well as culturally.

One thing driving the indie/alternative/electro scene in Pakistan is that the traditional music is already so complex and hybrid, with interwoven melodies and rhythms, that fans are ready for more adventurous sounds coming from rock 'n' roll. The strong history of Sufi-inspired music in Pakistan makes most public performances verge on the ecstatic, which also opens up the possibility for new aesthetic and artistic experiences as well (which is, needless to say, one reason hardcore religious Muslims are so against Sufism).

Of course, as any struggling band will confirm, this situation is not unique to Pakistan. And in fact, as Arieb Azhar pointed out in a conversation not long after he and Mark had first reunited in Karachi, "You can't ignore the growing festival scene in Pakistan. Though still tiny compared to the size of the country, it's the only thing that provides an alternate platform for musicians besides Coke, Pepsi, and Nescafé, and in fact Coke and Pepsi have selected several of their acts after listening to them perform live at festivals." While the festivals more or less stopped after the terrorist wave in 2008, a new era of festivals began with the Islamabad Music Mela, which he cofounded in 2014 and curated for three years. In 2015 the Lahooti Melo was established in Hyderabad and the Lahore Music Meet was established in Lahore. In 2014 Sabeen Mahmud also established the Creative Karachi Festival (which happened again in 2016 and 2019), followed by the I Am Karachi Festival in 2015 (which ran for two years before closing for lack of funds) and Arieb's own Art Langar. It's just that regardless of how many festivals there are, it still remains very hard to make a living consistently.

But it remains just as hard to get consistent, paying gigs in New York as it is in Lahore for most rock bands. But there is a major difference, as Haniya elaborated a few days later, when we renewed the conversation. "First of all," she reflected,

> the bands and music we're talking about take up a very narrow slice of the Pakistani music spectrum. Every weekend all over Pakistan there's live music, at weddings, Ghazzals, parties, Sufi gatherings, and so on. And it's not just that there's no money, as happens in most scenes for newer or noncommercial bands. It's the frequency issue. The fact that even when bands are making no money in Toronto or New York, they can gig multiple times a month and develop themselves, their music, and their crowd. Here, despite the great efforts of people like Jamal Rahman and True Brew in Lahore, or Arieb Azhar and T2F [The Second Floor] in Karachi, there remain too few places for rock, metal, and alternative/indie bands, or any other noncommercial style of music, to perform.

Rutaba Yaqub, one of the fastest rising indie artists in Pakistan, brings in yet another crucial dimension to the dynamics of the scene: the role of the Pakistani diaspora in germinating and nourishing the eclectic scenes we've discussed. Over a decade ago, it was already clear that being outside Pakistan was a formative component of the experiences that produced the first generation of Sufi metal and rock artists like Salman Ahmad and Mekaal Hasan, who spent formative years learning their craft in the US. As we'll see below, some of the most important hip hop artists in Pakistan started off rapping in the US, where they spent large parts of their childhood. Rutaba, however, was raised in Saudi Arabia by Pakistani parents who'd moved to the Kingdom for work. She only moved home for college because there were so few decent college opportunities for women there. As she describes her music, "My sense of belonging, my sound, when it comes to music is . . . twisted and disfigured. Every song is just a reminder for me that I'm constantly evolving."

The evolution might have had strange twists and turns, but Rutaba's roots are not far from the norm. As she explains, it was very hard to be a musician there, especially as a woman, and she spent most of her time listening to music from home and watching the many video channels from Pakistan that could be viewed in Saudi Arabia, grooving to Aaroh, EP, and the other top bands of this era. Interestingly, she explains, she never got into metal because that wasn't the kind of music that was on the video channels. On the other hand, she did hear a fair amount of Lebanese and Jordanian metal, which she'd find on SoundCloud, until she went home for her university studies. "I was living alone in my second year. I started singing and exploring my musical side, doing events at university, specifically at the campus Music Society at the University of Central Punjab, which organized shows and jams and would even do competitions with clubs from other universities, where everyone's doing mostly rock or Sufi rock, and that's how I got started."

Rather than fall into the Sufi mode, which, in her (no doubt correct) view, had become completely overdone—"with all the bands just sounding the same with the same chord progressions and vocal style, so why bother?"— Rutaba got into more experimental, progressive rock, synth pop, and electronic music. Then she met members of the band Roots, who were, as she describes it, "a kind of a math band," so they had to reconfigure to have vocals. "We sent a demo to audition for *Pepsi Battle of the Bands* for its second season—just like Mekaal described it :-)—and because part of the band was in Lahore and the rest in Karachi we actually first met as a group in the Karachi airport the day before the live televised audition. We had twenty-four hours to get three songs together; no one slept that night!"

Once again, the metal DNA of even indie music becomes clear. (In the US, the two are different genres, with little in common.) Indeed, it's impossible not to notice when you listen, for example, to their cover of Vital Signs's "Mera Dil Nahi" on the *Battle of the Bands,* replete with tapping and Rush-like time changes and rapid-fire drumming and a bass player simultaneously playing synths. But the problem isn't so much lack of opportunities for Rutaba's band as it is age. "My band is young, 20–21, and everyone is in college or medical school in different cities. So everyone is so busy it's hard to get together." Because of this, even programs that would be perfect for them such as True Brew, but that require an hour's worth of original material to perform, remained out of reach, so Rutaba auditioned on her own for *Nescafé Basement*. The rest, as the saying goes, is history.

After being discovered by none other than Xulfi, she did her first show in 2015 and she's been participating in *Nescafé Basement* while also working as artist liaison with Patari and collaborating with much more established artists like Meesha Shafi (who clearly, from her effusive praise of the band, fell in love with Roots when she was a judge during their 2017 *Pepsi* run), Xulfi, and Talal Qureshi. In particular, her collaboration with Meesha is noteworthy because when she was starting out as an explicitly indie artist, Meesha was too close to a mainstream singer—the Pakistan equivalent, in function if not sound, to Lebanese pop diva Nancy Ajram. And yet, there she was on the big stage at *Battle of the Bands* with none other than Meesha praising her voice and performance.

A similar story occurred with Janoobi Khargosh, the stage name for musician Waleed Ahmed. He has a retro yet infective synth-pop sound that, like so many other Pakistani indie artists, goes hand in hand with a very strong visual conceptual sense, and has produced videos that are stand-alone films rather than mere visual reflections of the music. As for Poor Rich Boy, despite its clear debt to eighties British new wave, Zain Ahsan's early love of Metallica and Pantera and other classic heavy and blues rock groups meant that Ahmed began his musical life as a full-on metal acolyte, whose first two albums were far closer to death/black metal than new wave or retro indie.

The current generation of bands are truly so broad in their sound and orientations that it's impossible to describe the majority of them with any justice to their complexity and originality. If Poor Rich Boy is the spearhead of the genre, groups like Gentle Robot, Ali Suhail, Natasha Noorani, Natasha Ejaz, the Biryani Brothers, Keeray Makoray, and Janoobi Khargosh are creating folky indie rock, much of it in English and with beautifully shot or animated videos, which can easily stand against any of their counterparts coming out of the US, the UK, or anywhere else for that matter. The experimental electronic group Nawksh, the intensely Oriental trance rock of Saakin, and the prog hard jazz rock of Wisdom Salad raise profound questions about the nature of "traditional" or "local" musics and of "cultural appropriation," an accusation often thrown at Euro-American artists who have borrowed, riffed off of, ripped off, and sampled all kinds of traditional and often religious music from faraway cultures without context. This is an important issue for (ethno)musicologists and musical ethicists to consider, but it doesn't actually have much currency in Pakistan and, as important, doesn't impact the ability of these artists to pay the rent. What is clear from almost every one of these artists, even in the most respected and known of these genres, is that it's nearly impossible to make a living doing these types of music today, even for those who are regularly appearing on one of the big shows. Everyone has some sort of day job, especially because for much of the last decade they couldn't play live because of the political situation, which ultimately led most of the acts to go on indefinite hiatus or simply disband and move on, however brilliant their music was while it lasted, as happened to bands such as Communal Grave and Odyssey, who were very well known at the height of their popularity. Even Faraz Anwar has had to fall back on his training as a civil engineer as he keeps releasing music. And Faraz, Mekaal Hasan, and other leading musicians have moved into the online tutorial, master class, and lesson business, which completes the circle that began several decades ago when they perfected their craft through mail-ordering VHS tapes made by guitarists that were advertised in music magazines.

If Poor Rich Boy is the height of indie bandom, the singer, actor, director, and otherwise talented Mooroo (aka Taimoor Salahuddin) stands out today as perhaps the country's most unique, original, and multifaceted artist. Since 2011, when he released his first song, "Patakhi Larki," Mooroo has made a series of songs and videos that defy comparison to most any other artists working globally. Not only is he an excellent singer with a face whose expressiveness is made for the camera, he's equally, if not more, talented on the other side, envisioning, shooting, and editing videos, and as a vlogger himself. Indeed, it was here that he first made his mark as an artist, after returning to Pakistan from film school in the US.

It's hard to know, in fact, whether Mooroo is a singer who makes videos or a filmmaker who sings. Clearly the two are inseparable for him, whether it's the clear critique of social class on "Patakhi Larki" (where Mooroo plays a peon in love with a beautiful woman who's forced to watch her evolving romance with a wealthy suitor) or the equally hilarious and even more biting commentary of his short film *Kebaab Mein Haddi* (which satirizes the incredible disparities in wealth in Pakistan by focusing on the relationship between a middle-class mother and son and their housekeepers). But beyond the politics, whether he is imitating American doo-wop in "Patakhi Larki" or alternatively folksy and soaring singing in "Self Made Man" (yet another song built into a short film that touchingly critiques the class disparities in Pakistan, which he clearly knows firsthand), Mooroo in fact represents the paradigm for how artists today manage to create a viable career in Pakistan.

Sadly, that paradigm seems very hard for either more established artists working more purely in music or most younger artists to emulate. How many people can sing, rap, film, vlog, and relentlessly create in a variety of media at an equally high level in each of them? Zeeshan Parvaz is perhaps the earliest example of someone who was equally brilliant as a video director and a composer/musician; other examples are few and far between in the last decade. Of course, the singing, dancing, and acting star is a standard Bollywood and Lollywood construct (much as it once was in America and remains for a few artists like Justin Timberlake today). They have an entire Holly/Bolly/Lollywood system to support them. For most artists without these resources, the need to branch out and be so multifaceted inevitably gets in the way of being a virtuoso artist in any one field.

PATARI AND THE RISE OF HIP HOP

The question facing the metal and more broadly rock (which in Pakistan is majority indie) scenes is, today, essentially how to take the caffeine, as it were, from Coke, Pepsi, and Nescafé and use it to energize the musical economy without being forced to add in the artificial sweeteners and accompanying empty musical calories that make it so aesthetically toxic. Can this come from below, from the DIY instinct at the heart of the scene, or has the corporate system become so powerful that even the most well-planned attempts quickly become overly commercialized, hurting the very artists they were supposed to help? Perhaps more adventurous and ostensibly noncommercial endeavors like Patari Tabeer will ultimately tell the tale, as no one has criticized the intention or the ability to take unknown talented young artists and bring them the public recognition they clearly deserve.

Patari Tabeer and its parent venture, Patari (which has about twenty-five hundred Pakistani artists signed on and upwards of several hundred thousand registered users), are at the center of the explosion of hip hop across the Pakistani mainstream. Former COO Ahmer Naqvi's personal history with music sheds light on the roots of the streaming concept:

> In my generation, when you wanted to do music you had to ask your parents
> to buy you a cheap guitar or keyboard, the cheapest things you could buy if
> you wanted to start to play. But now we have kids who don't even know how
> to play anything but have learned Fruity Loops, Ableton, etc. and have a very
> diverse sense of how to do music, all due to the Internet and everything that

came with it. But sadly, despite this explosion of talent and possibilities, we still have a situation here where the industry as a whole is not managing to get much music produced and put out there widely to the public. So Patari was all about getting content to Pakistanis as efficiently as possible.

Ahmer brought in the terminology of start-ups that is all the rage in Pakistani business culture, as it is everywhere else.

Moreover, he understood that with the culture of live performances increasingly decimated by the violence and economic issues, there was little way for musicians to make money outside the lucky few who could do jingles, film, or television soundtracks. In these circumstances Patari sought to "make the entire ecosystem sustainable, since it can't be sustained just on passion without getting paid. If we wanted to make music and money we had to help musicians, to give artists the space to create something where they'd have creative control and get paid."

The reasons that this was so important were financial as much as artistic. There simply wasn't enough content for the service: "We had a platform for music but not enough music! So we had a platform and had a bunch of indie artists, but the way we monetized it was very convoluted because corporations make their own songs now. So we started getting contracts as a digital PR or creative agency. So for the *Battle of the Bands,* we essentially helped them create a database of bands, whom to contact, and so on."

At the same time, working with Patari, it was clear that the narrative of the bands in the era of social media had become as important as the music. "How do we make something that would make the *New York Times, al-Jazeera,* and the *Guardian* report on it?" asks Ahmer. Yet equally important was the realization that, in Ahmer's words, "there is a huge inefficiency in the Pakistani music industry in that it's not getting out all the amazing artists the country has to offer, so the same music is making it to the mainstream over and over. It's time for new stuff." And that's partly how Patari Tabeer, "one of the most impactful local music projects" in the Pakistani music industry, according to journalist Aamna Isani, came to be, with the goal of finding music largely, if not completely, unknown outside its locale, music clearly unique, by artists who had a narrative that was compelling enough to attract international media attention.

In a sense, the Pakistani hip hop scene when it was "discovered" by the mainstream industry and culture was like the metal scene before, having already existed for a long time with its own subculture and following. Of the six tracks that were released as part of the Tabeer project, two of them were directly related to hip hop: Abid Brohi, the "tea-seller from Sibbi" (a poor and often violent city in Balochistan), and Dynoman, a rapper from Lyari (a similarly poor neighborhood in Karachi), who along with the other four singers were put together with top-flight producers, recording videos and documentaries about the artists and their lives, and using the platform offered by Patari to spread the music as far and wide as possible.

The fact that hip hop has long been rooted in Pakistani soil even if underground, or at least out of the way (that is, not part of the Peshawar-Islamabad-Lahore-Karachi axis), explains why, once people in the industry went looking for it, it was discovered without much trouble. The raw and often rude hip hop of the Pakistani backstreets outside the main cities was not just fresh; as Rutaba explained it to Mark, "We put it on Tabeer because we thought it something completely different than the Sufi rock we're listening to, and hip hop is something that is so important. We put Abid with the electronic duo Somewhat Super because that combined two different genres that really weren't mainstream to create something new and unheard of. The funniest part of the collaboration was that without knowing it we were both already working with him, and so once we saw that, the collaboration became natural."

As soon as "Sibbi Song" broke and started becoming massive, Patari Tabeer started getting a lot of submissions from underground rappers looking to go mainstream. "It all kind of just happened," Rutaba exclaimed, still in seeming disbelief at how it all played out. Many new rappers have hit the scene. Abid was and remains one of Pakistan's greatest hip hop artists, but he's by no means the first or the only one today. While Brohi has been dubbed the "Pakistani Tupac" and the "King of Pakistani Rap" and has done many high-profile shows and appearances, as of early 2019 he only had twenty-seven Twitter followers (although his Instagram page had 4,375). The low number of followers helps keep the grassroots image of the enterprise.

Abid wouldn't have become a rapper, or at least certainly not a great one, without the inspiration of the OG rapper Bohemia, who is not merely one of Pakistan's first rappers of any significance but also the only one up to this point to appear on *Coke Studio*. A Karachi native, Bohemia moved to the US when he was thirteen, ultimately living in Oakland, where his hip hop career began amid the same kind of inner-city poverty and violence that he'd seen in Pakistan. Bohemia's American stylings and social conscience, encouraged by his association with producer Shah One, earned him a deal with Universal Music Group and proved infectious to the Pakistani hip hop scene beyond just Abid, as his experiences of violence in Oakland helped his own lyrics, while focused often on the US inner city, to resonate back home at a time when violence was more endemic than ever.

Of the hundreds of aspiring top-level rappers active across Pakistan, there are at least half a dozen who are at the highest level. Montreal-born, Karachi-raised, and half-Chinese Chen-K is one of them, with at least half a dozen videos averaging a million views each on YouTube. Not surprisingly, given its universal ubiquity in recent years, his music tends toward the kind of mumble rap style that has become ubiquitous in the US and across Africa and the Middle East, except that, unlike most mumble rappers, he actually articulates his words well, while also focusing on very political subjects, nowhere more so than in his version of Childish Gambino's now seminal "This Is America," which was titled "Pakistan." The video is much slower than the American original and has language that not only invokes Islam but directly takes on the hypocrisy and violence of the Pakistani system in ways few rock or metal songs have ever done, regardless of how "Sufi" they might have been.

In early 2019 he released another powerfully political rap, "Asli Hip Hop," which is categorized as a "Dis 18+" track (i.e., a "diss" track focused on adult themes) because he goes after a lot of rappers that he felt were "promoting sex, drugs, alcohol, money, and all the other things which [are] destroying our culture and damaging the moral values of our society." Not surprisingly, given the topic, as the video proceeds—like his other videos, this one is shot very simply, with one camera in a close-up shot in a single room—his face and hands become increasingly covered in blood (Pakistani hip hop is nothing if not unsubtle). In his explanation of the video Chen-K calls for more "ASLI hip hop": that is, rap that is more rooted in social realities and local norms and values, listing a number of Pakistani rappers that he feels are on the right path, such as Xpolymer Dar, Sunny Khan Durrani, and Faris Shafi.

Chen-K was clearly expecting a lot of negative responses, and indeed the local hip hop community treated it very much as a diss track, putting up "reaction" videos on YouTube, which in fact had more views than the video itself at the time of writing. One leading Pakistani "analyst," Farrukh Shabbir, from the website Pakistani Reactions blurted out with an incredulous laugh as he rubbed his face in bewilderment, "What the fuck did I just watch?!" when the video finished, before explaining that "like a great chess player," Chen-K had anticipated and responded to every defense of the rappers he's dissing within the track and responded to them as well in his rhymes. "Chen-K is not really a rapper, he's a poet. He's not rhyming words, he's

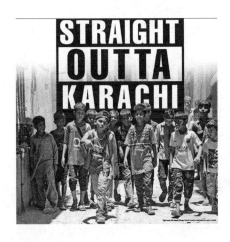

FIGURE 27. Internet image featuring local children, playing off NWA's famous *Straight Outta Compton* artwork, created to support the Lyari Underground (L.U.G.) crew in Karachi.

rhyming ideas," an assessment that's completely clear from the flow even if you don't really understand the lyrics.

Lyari Underground, also known as L.U.G., is another rising, rapid-fire, Balochi-English hip hop force in Pakistan. Its story is as inspiring as Abid's (thus their inclusion in the Patari Tabeer program). The members of the group heard rap when it first arrived in Karachi and wanted to do it themselves but had no one to help them learn how to record or perform hip hop. So they looked up everything they could online about how to do so, got a simple mic (the kind you use on your phone or computer to talk to someone), and began recording only with these implements. These simple recording tools match the poverty of life in Lyari, where racism against Balochis remains strong, and paved streets, decent sanitation, and even a good football coach are usually beyond reach, as the song they recorded for Tabeer, "The Players of Lyari," about their neighborhood's football team and its struggles, makes clear.

By the time Ahmer discovered them a few years later, however, they were already quite sophisticated. In that sense, perhaps they didn't really need Patari Tabeer to take them to the mainstream; there was every likelihood that the arrival in the Pakistani mainstream of rap, like hip hop globally, was a foregone conclusion. All that was needed was rappers with enough personality, charisma, and talent to break through. Yet at the same time, the fact that the Abid Brohi and Lyari rappers are dark-skinned, likely of African descent, and thus from the bottom of society made them the objects of continued racism and attacks across the country. This was made clear when they performed at a major show at the Alhamra during the yearly Lahore Music Mela.

Despite the invitation and being the stars of the show, everywhere they went they were followed or asked for identification and they wouldn't be let alone, all because they are of "Afro-Pakistani" descent. In this sense, the presence of Afro-Pakistanis in the heart of the music industry is in fact very political; for that reason, when working-class hip hop artists, especially those from marginalized and minority populations, record songs that even subtly challenge the existing political narratives, it in fact has more impact than rich or upper-class musicians making an overtly political song that is not well liked, Ahmer believes.

Rappers Faris Shafi and Mooroo are the other major rappers shaping the local scene, reaching a level visually, sonically, and politically that competes with the best hip hop globally. Faris in particular uses his natural charisma to make biting criticisms of the corruption and violence of the government that would otherwise be hard to get away with. In particular, his duet in 2012 with Mooroo in "Awaam" showed how powerfully malleable Pakistani hip hop, like its counterparts worldwide, can be in the larger pop music scene, and no doubt cemented his reputation as one of the most eloquent lyricists and rappers in the Pakistani and broader Desi scenes. This was given fresh evidence most recently when Faris collaborated with Talal Qureshi for an amazing jam in 2018 for the BBC Asian Network. With Qureshi on the decks and Faris free-styling, it was a rare electronica-meets-hip hop moment that shows quite likely one of the most important future directions of Pakistani music, given the creative dominance of hip hop and electronica across the board today inside Pakistan and globally.

BETWEEN THE VALLEYS

Mark's trips to Pakistan tend to move north to south. They begin in Islamabad and Peshawar; he then drives down to Lahore, and flies to Karachi, one of the biggest cities in Asia and indeed the world, sadly and in many ways unfairly infamous for its overcrowding, chaos, crime, and pollution. These are all there to be sure, but the city is also home to amazing cultural associations, universities, artists, and intellectuals of all kinds. And for the middle and wealthier classes, much of the worst parts of life in Karachi can be kept at bay, as in so many other urban locations. With *Coke Studio* and so many other great studios and venues, it's not surprising that Karachi was where, after so many acrimonious years apart, Junoon chose to reunite with a huge concert, even though two of the three band members are based in Lahore. Or that Faraz Anwar refuses to leave despite all the problems that remain living there.

But if Karachi remains the beating (if often bleeding) heart of Pakistani popular musical culture, the other end of the country, the northern regions from the Hindu Kush and Swat Valley to the Himalayas have come equally alive in the last few years after years locked in a deadly spiral of violence. Today, Pakistanis and foreigners are again able to travel more or less freely from Swat Valley to Hunza, Chitral to Gilgit, a region that is absolutely one of the most spectacular places on Earth—like the Rockies or the Alps, only three thousand meters higher, with (thankfully still) far more snow, and valleys and views that defy description. Think the Dead or U2 at Redrocks and you get the idea of the feeling of witnessing a transcendent performance with the Himalayas as your backdrop. What's more, the dozens of local communities, many of whom have lived there for thousands of years and have unique linguistic, cultural, religious, and musical practices, offer a treasure trove of inspiring traditional folk music and dance.

Indeed, the music of these regions is so unique and powerful that *Coke Studio* sent its modular unit, *Coke Studio Explorer,* all the way north to explore and share it with the rest of the country. The *Explorer* crew headed to the Kalash Valley in Chitral, whose inhabitants follow an ancient form of Hinduism, to "discover an all-female Indigenous act" (the use of the term "Indigenous" is particularly interesting here, as it both recognizes how different their culture is from the hegemonic Muslim culture of Pakistan and exoticizes the musicians to make the story more interesting). What happened when they got there was telling about the relationship between "Sufi" and "traditional" music that has been a calling card of *Coke Studio* and the needs and natural inclination toward the commercialization of everyone who comes through the *Studio.* In this case the producers, Ali Hamza and Zohaib Qazi, came to record a young duo, Pareek. (One member of the group, Ariana, changed her name from Farsi in honor of her idol, Ariana Grande.) The group had garnered a lot of attention for their beautiful renditions of classic local folk songs.

The episode itself was quite laudable, showing the rest of Pakistan the lives and beautiful surroundings of the two girls who were being profiled. But the interesting thing, as Chitral native Irfan Ali Haj pointed out to me, was that the producers naturally tried to force the music, which is naturally in 7/8 or other odd meters, into a 4/4 beat. The video even shows them forcefully counting to the girls in 4/4 to get them to sing in time. After they finished recording, in a beautiful wooden elevated structure at the foothills of the enormous mountains, they declare that "it was a very trance, EDM type of beat. A very hipster 2018 beat." For the girls, however, it was the wrong beat for their music, which elsewhere had been recorded at the natural 7/8 tempo. As Haj explains, the attempt to force the girls to perform in 4/4 was a violation of the kind of complex rhythms that have for centuries defined this music. "They can't play with a click track and even tempos, rhythms, and pitches. The music is almost entirely improvised; it doesn't work this way," he declared as he WhatsApp'ed me a few versions of the traditional song they'd sung done in the normal way for the region. It was only when Arieb Azhar—who is one of the country's most knowledgeable and devoted students of regional Sufi and tribal music in Pakistan—invited Chitrali musicians to perform at one of his "Artlangers" festivals in Islamabad (before he moved to Karachi in 2019) that they could play in their own, far more spontaneous manner, and not have to cater to what *Coke Studio,* however well intentioned, thought its audience would want to hear.

A dozen years ago the uniqueness of Pakistani music first became apparent to Mark as he was driving through the northern outskirts of Peshawar with Sajid and Zeeshan, whose music, videos, and business model were heralding a new level of sophisticated hybridity that over the coming years would come to define the pop avant-garde globally. Today the north is no longer terra incognita for Pakistanis or even foreigners, and, like everyone else, musicians are heading up the Karakoram Highway to see what unique beauty and adventures they can find. Achieving the right balance between the country's powerful musical history and its hugely burdensome political present, between the aesthetic power of the "strange beats" and the simple commercial pleasures of Atif Aslam, is likely the key to determining just how powerful the idea of music as a force for healing and change remains in Pakistan.

By Way of an Epilogue

THE JOYS OF RESISTANCE

Written and produced by Pierre Hecker, Mark LeVine, Nahid Siamdoust, and Jeremy Wallach

It's important for musicians to keep doing metal in countries like ours where it's not safe and very dangerous. Because music in general and metal especially is a great way to express yourself and have your message abroad and be heard, because in these countries everyone is at war and metal is a war that we are taking and fighting for our freedom. . . . If not us, who? If not now, when?

—IRAQI METAL ARTIST MIR CYAXARES,
Dark Phantom, We Are Warriors, *2019*

These bands—the effort they put in is tremendous. It's not like in Europe, where bands can just jump in a van and play on weekends, easily go from one country to another. Here, you have to pay huge amounts just to get out of the country.

—ANTHONY KAOTEON, *interview, Vice.com, February 2018*

The Revolution was a moment of . . . joy. But the overjoy of the revolution gave us illusions that we'd won and that we were stronger than we actually were.

—MAHIENOUR EL-MASSRY, *Egyptian human rights lawyer (imprisoned for most of the writing of this epilogue)*

THERE IS, AS A RULE, never a good time to end a book about the contemporary Middle East and larger Muslim world. Without fail, something is going to happen—war, mass refugee crises, a giant explosion, a national uprising (or eleven uprisings), a pandemic—to challenge and potentially upend the narratives you've spent years constructing. And yet, from the perspective of the various forms of extreme youth music and movements in the Arab/ Muslim world explored in this book, none of the momentous events of these last dozen extremely eventful years has fundamentally altered or challenged our understanding of the prismatic power of music to explore broader social relations. In fact, it has become even clearer that music, through its creation, circulation, performance, and consumption, is itself a generator of powerful social relations and forms of power that interact with and can powerfully shape broader social and political dynamics in the societies we study.

In early 2020, after then-President Trump announced the Israel-UAE peace deal, Mark asked Orphaned Land lead singer Kobi Farhi if he'd be playing in Abu Dhabi or Dubai soon. His response was, "Sure, why not?" Meanwhile, the Iranian death metal pioneers Arsames had just escaped a fifteen-year prison sentence by crossing over into Turkey, where they remained in limbo during the year of the pandemic, waiting to learn if any European country would offer them political asylum. Their comrades in the band Confess, who similarly escaped lashes and long prison sentences after serving eighteen months in the hellish Evin prison, have just released their first album in seven years, *Revenge at All Costs,* in collaboration with some of the best thrashers in Norway, where they now safely reside.

In Vancouver, Massive Scar Era lead singer Cherine Amr was working on a solo album after a successful return home to Alexandria and Cairo, where she was joined by cofounder Nancy Mounir for several shows. Scarab was also working on a new disc, and they promised it would be grander than any of their previous releases. Across the Pacific in Jakarta, Voice of Baceprot, the young all-female metal band that had been taking the global music media by storm, was planning their next recordings and, presumably, like any band with that level of publicity, how to live up to the hype. And in Iraq, where half a decade before Emo fans had literally been marked for death, the rock and metal scene was celebrating a rejuvenation, even in the midst of the coronavirus pandemic, with two new live music spots opened and half a dozen new bands creating music as exuberant and inventive as any metal across the region.

Twenty-five years ago, when scholars began to study globalization in the MENA region in earnest, a primary theme was the—then—unquestioned hegemony of the American-led neoliberal order and the specific forms of cultural and economic integration it encouraged. Then came the terrorist attacks of September 11, 2001, the global "War on Terror," the US invasions of Afghanistan and Iraq, and a series of economic crises culminating in the global great recessions of the late 2000s, all of which challenged the optimistic narrative of the "Washington Consensus" model of neoliberal globalization, although with little if any impact on the ground. For their part, Arab/Muslim fears and critiques of "Cocacolonization" and "cultural invasion" by the "West," however justified the critique by those most antagonistic toward US-dominated globalization, missed the far more complex and multidirectional cultural diffusions between local and global forces, of which music and the arts more broadly were always at the forefront. Specifically, the growing sense of economic and political marginalization accompanied the emergence of unprecedented opportunities for greater participation in the global cultural ecumene of the *fin de millennium*.

This paradoxical situation accounts for what so many artists across the region have described as the "schizo" personality (in the words of Moroccan fusion rock band Hoba Hoba Spirit) of a new generation—*jil aj-jadid* in Arabic, *nasl-e jadid* or *nasl-e javan* in Persian, *Yeni Türkiye* in Turkish (there's not really an equivalent sociological or political term in Javanese today)—that had little if any stake in the emerging transnational economies in the region, and therefore had less incentive either to cooperate with increasingly out-of-touch, blatantly corrupt, and crassly repressive elites, or to blindly copy or follow so-called "Western" norms or products. What they did have a stake in, however, was the new technologies and cultural spaces outside of state control that were a necessary byproduct of neoliberal reforms, which they used to create their own subcultures, sometimes their own countercultures, and in a few cases their own revolutionary culture that would force a radical change to the region in the coming years.

Even as their economic and political marginalization continued, these same young people (joined by some not-so-young people who weren't too old, as the saying goes, to rock 'n' roll in its various incarnations) were at the forefront of a globalized, if not quite global, cultural renaissance through their embrace of transglobal musical styles. Of course, other young people were the vanguard of a very different kind of extreme youth culture, one grounded in closed, exclusivist, and "resistance" forms of identity that were the polar opposite in substance and intent to that of the EYM cultures discussed in this book. Uniting the two otherwise opposed groups was their early and expert adoption of the most important creative and communication technologies that defined contemporary globalization, as their peers did globally.

Cultural and political "creatives" often drew on homegrown and sometimes centuries-old discursive and musical traditions that gave their work purchase with a wider audience, showcasing the processes and possibilities of hybridity from the grassroots that has always been a core part of "globalization." What this book, like *Heavy Metal Islam,* Nahid's *Soundtrack of the Revolution: The Politics of Music in Iran,* Jeremy's *Modern Noise, Fluid Genres: Popular Music in Indonesia,* and Pierre's *Turkish Metal: Music, Meaning, and Morality in a Muslim Society,* among other recent books, has shown is that before the new generation was able to organize politically it had to (self-)organize culturally. It's undeniable that genres and scenes like heavy metal and hip hop became vectors for some of the most intense globalization of culture and political criticism in the region, or anywhere for that matter. Along with that came experiences and skills that would prove quite important in the struggles ahead.

The role of religion, and Islam in particular, in the dynamics of popular music in the Muslim-majority world has fundamentally changed since we and our colleagues began our research well over two decades ago. While extremist movements and a few governments might still oppose and periodically crack down on metal, hip hop, and other forms of nonreligious popular music, there's been a clear solidification of the sense among ordinary people that even more extreme-sounding forms of music are permissible as long as they don't advocate or involve clearly un-Islamic practices or beliefs. That is, metal, hip hop, and other forms of EYM have become normalized and accepted within most of the societies we've discussed to an even greater degree than they had in the previous decade. More broadly, governments have at various moments and to various degrees adopted a laissez-faire attitude toward what music young people listen to and play, but as protests heated up and members of the scenes were involved, sometimes at the center, more artists and fans have been censored, arrested, imprisoned, exiled, and even worse because of their actions across the MENA region, from Morocco to Iran. Where they have had more latitude, such as in Tunisia or Indonesia, it's among the best evidence of an arduous but at least partially successful transition toward a truly democratic system.

As longtime Iraqi metalhead and founder of Ideas Beyond Borders Faisal al-Mutar explained to Mark, "Metal remains one of the best metrics for measuring society's acceptance of difference. You can see it in the number of gigs, number of fans, if it's in mainstream venues, and so on. These scenes are in fact a very smart way of measuring the overall health of societies in the region." One could, of course, say something similar, if not the same, about hip hop, which in Iraq as in most other Middle Eastern countries is more

FIGURE 28. MahmOd Hamasi and his band Gudians performing at One Café, Baghdad, 2021. Courtesy of MahmOd Hamasi.

popular commercially than metal. As they did a decade ago, music scenes continue to serve as a canary in the coalmine for how societies are faring more broadly in the post-9/11 and post-uprisings era of extreme neoliberal globalization.

EXTREME MUSIC FROM A POSTCOLONIAL TO DECOLONIAL EDGE

Each of us has spent a significant share of our careers researching youth music, and particularly "harder" genres such as rock, metal, hip hop, punk, and hardcore, focusing on tracing and understanding the "roots" of these genres across the MENA and broader Muslim world. But—borrowing from anthropologist James Clifford—we are reminded of the ostensibly well-known but not often followed admonition to move beyond the sometimes obsessive focus on origins and "roots" and turn to the "routes" taken by these forms of cultural production as they become, themselves, "traveling cultures." And these routes are not just quite old; they can also be quite long. As historian Michael Denning demonstrated in his masterful *Noise Uprising,* a self-consciously global "vernacularization of music" was already occurring nearly a century ago with the spread of phonograph recordings and radio; they in turn fostered inter- and transnational musical cultures and identities during the colonial era that ultimately gave way to the global metal, rock, hip hop, and punk communities we research today, as well as "regional" popular music scenes such as Caribbean merengue, West African highlife, Arab sha'bi and Bhangra, which have long united people across national, ethnic, and religious borders.

"Rock 'n' roll" in its various forms discussed in our work (rock 'n' roll proper, heavy metal, hip hop, punk/hardcore, etc.) in the MENA and broader Muslim world is a specifically postcolonial phenomenon, as it emerged in the wake of formal processes of decolonization. But rock 'n' roll and specifically EYM can also and more accurately (or at least powerfully) be considered decolonial, emerging out of a deeper level of critique than the postcolonial desire to create identities and culture free of "foreign" influence. Depending on their social and political positioning vis-à-vis their broader society, "decolonial" music encourages, enables, and compels listeners (and, through the video form, viewers) to confront and take action against what decolonial theorists refer to as the ongoing "colonialities of power"—the hegemonic patriarchal and authoritarian political, social, and economic structures that continue to operate along many, if not most, of the same lines of power and domination that existed during the colonial era.

Of course, not every rock or EYM song, group, or scene is decolonial or even broadly antiauthoritarian; much of EYM either avoids politics or sometimes actually supports racist, misogynist, authoritarian, or uncritically consumerist identities or practices. We argue that metal, hip hop, punk, hardcore, electronica, and other forms of alternative or independent youth music become decolonial when the music is no longer attached to or experienced as a foreign import that is directly tied, aesthetically as well as politically and economically/commercially, to colonial systems of power, whether in the past or continuing to the present day. The question then arises as to when music moves from postcolonial to decolonial, and in so doing, from being merely subcultural to being countercultural and even revolutionary. One answer is that this transformation occurs when the music becomes "indigenized."

Recalling the importance of Indigenous perspectives discussed in the "author's note," becoming indigenized and becoming Indigenous comprise two different if sometimes intersecting processes. The first occurs when citizens or inhabitants of a society—or, in settler-colonial societies, actual

Indigenous members of the society—adopt specific forms of music and make them their own. The second, following from the first, is the gradual "indigenization" of these styles, meaning that an originally "foreign" genre of music becomes aesthetically embedded, popular, and self-sustaining enough in a local culture to reproduce itself through local musicians without constant new input from outside. As music indigenizes, it mutates from the forms that first entered the culture or country; like a virus, the new forms are harder to repress and expel by whatever "medicine" political and religious elites try to administer to cure fans of their "disease." The music has in fact moved beyond hybrid; even as people understand its origins as outside their home culture, it now feels at home. At the same time, like the Indigenous Australian "songspirals" mentioned in the author's note, in this process indigenization marks a process of planting and deepening roots and of creating new landscapes of identity and possibility for young people who remain otherwise marginalized from political, economic, and cultural power. It is from this combination of roots and routes that a decolonial critique *and* deployment of power become possible.

GLOBAL VILLAGE VAGABONDS

In the first decade of the new century, artists across the MENA region still felt the need, as Iraqi filmmaker and guitarist Oday Rasheed explained in the epilogue of *Heavy Metal Islam,* to remind their counterparts that Middle Eastern artists knew American and Western culture more broadly and far better than "we" knew their cultures—much to our detriment and, far more violently, theirs. Today such declarations no longer seem so necessary, even if far too many Americans and Europeans remain willfully ignorant about the cultures of the Muslim world. But as our own research has shown, not only have the music scenes across the MENA region and broader Muslim world— especially EYM—become among the most globalized cultural environments on Earth; more and more American and European fans today are aware of the global reach of these styles (not least because bands from the region regularly perform at Glastonbury, Roskilde, Wacken, SXSW, Bloodstock, Hellfest, and smaller international festivals). Moreover, artists from the Arab world, Africa, Iran, and South and Southeast Asia routinely collaborate with A-list American artists in various genres and even help to define the latest trends, while music magazines feature artists from these regions and even devote entire issues to MENA countries. In short, more than in the past we have come to a moment where musicians truly are "one race," as Manu Dibango described it, led by an elite of "global village vagabonds," as the South African anti-Apartheid poet, painter, and writer Breyten Breytenbach tellingly called the loose band of international artists, activists, and intellectuals who are pushing global culture forward, often despite itself.

METAL, HIP HOP, AND THE "WOMB OF REVOLUTION"

While metal, punk/hardcore, hip hop, and now trap have the hard and expressive edge that has made them so popular among young people the world over, they are by no means the only genres of music to capture and transfer that kind of energy. Indeed, as Jeremy has argued in his contribution to *The Bloomsbury Handbook of Rock Music Research,* while popular music scholarship has been increasingly criticized for underemphasizing the sociopolitical impact of rock music in the (formally) decolonized world, the creative artistry of rock musicians in the Global South has also been overlooked, meaning that a full recognition of *both* the political and artistic/aesthetic innovations and power of youth music has yet to be achieved. Nor has the ease with which all these forms of music have been hybridized, indigenized, and otherwise transformed been sufficiently explored. What is increasingly clear from our individual and collaborative research, however, is that such transformations in these scenes cannot be fully appreciated in isolation from one another; rather, as evidenced here, and in the work of scholars such as Stefano Barone in Tunisia and Thomas Burkhalter in Beirut, the development of individual youth music scenes needs to be explored as much in relation to one another as to their broader societies, since they intersect aesthetically, technologically, sociologically, and politically in so many ways.

As we were finishing this epilogue, Egyptian musician and activist Noor Ayman Nour sent Mark a new project he had developed with an international group of environmental scholars and activists to improve what they term "coproductive agility" in collaborative research and artistic creation. Explaining that "tensions often emerge when research and practice come together," the group's goal was to make that tension transformative rather than hindering the creative process, to "navigate differences in agile ways" through embedding new, collaborative, and nonhierarchical forms of knowledge into processes of coproduction. What's most relevant for our discussion is how the group utilized music as a medium for conveying its findings. Specifically, it created a "musical abstract" in the form of a YouTube video, with music composed and produced by Noor and the abstract sung by the lead author, Josephine Chambers, as well as graphics that point to how collaborative creation can question dominant, elevate marginalized, and navigate conflicting agendas.

Bringing artists into the heart of the research process with the explicit goal of upending hierarchies and enabling the voices—and music—of marginalized groups to be more prominently heard is precisely what is needed to empower art, activism, and research to come together more effectively and push one another to new levels of creativity. Using music and art to both develop and disseminate new ideas carried by newly amplified voices is crucial to this process, precisely when research, advocacy, and art increasingly take place in repressive and violent environments. Indeed, more than most genres, metal, hip hop, and EYM more broadly are, tragically but not surprisingly, nurtured and made more powerful by conflict and war, and so artists from these genres are best positioned to play a role in pushing these endeavors forward.

It's not hard in that regard to imagine how Syrian metal groups like Dark Phantom, Maysaloon, and Step to Eternity not only survive physically in the intense brutality of the Syrian government's war on its people (and the many miniwars that have sprouted from it) but have managed to turn the dark energy of the war into something that may not affirm life but does save it. On the other hand, it is undeniable that however effectively politically or sonically extreme forms of metal hold a mirror up to their societies, there remains a fatalism deeply embedded in many scenes that limits their translatability to activism. Here, it's worth noting, as Stefano Barone has shown in his comprehensive *Metal, Rap, and Electro in Post-Revolutionary Tunisia*, that the country that underwent what remains the region's only "successful" revolution to date saw its metal scene suffer a "striking . . . collapse," as the upper-middle-class prog metal that was overrepresented in the pre-2011 scene didn't match the mood of the generation behind the revolution, compared with more working-class genres like hip hop, grunge, and even stambeli. Jeremy Wallach notes a similar temporary weakening of the Indonesian metal underground during the decade following Suharto's resignation.

On the other hand, echoing the sentiments of an Iranian fan that metal in war-torn Tehran was like "a flower growing in the desert," Syrian musician Bahaa Nassar, founder of the group Step to Eternity, explains in the 2017 documentary *We Are Warriors* that even amid the violence and ruins of the

Syrian government's war on its people there was a great opportunity "to work harder and take the chances and the advantages of making life out of death. Making music that can tell the world our story and our way. Because none are really listening." Mir Cyaxares, of the Iraqi band Dark Phantom, agreed, asking (as quoted in one of the epigraphs to this chapter), "If not us, who? If not now, when?"

As with their Iranian and Lebanese comrades before them, for today's artists on the front lines of war metal is key to their survival and to retaining humanity not just in the midst of war, but when bombs and bullets literally crash through studio walls in the middle of rehearsals (as happened to leading Iraqi and more recently Syrian metal musicians during their countries' civil wars).

Perhaps the most famous musician associated with the Arab uprisings is El Général, a previously unknown MC whose song "Rais Lebled" (Arabic for "President of the Country") earned him global fame and was one of the most important cultural sources of the revolutionary energy that toppled Tunisia's long-serving ruler Zine El Abidine Ben Ali. Addressing the president like an abusive father in a grainy video that for someone steeped in hip hop aesthetics evokes images of the downtrodden neighborhoods where hip hop was born, El Général exclaims, "Mr. President, today I am speaking on behalf of myself and all the people who are suffering. . . . There are still people dying of hunger. People have become like animals." The barely controlled anger with which the lyrics are spit from El Général's mouth, along with the haunting minor piano line and the constantly out-of-focus video, creates a sense of dissonance and even aphasia that captures the affective experience of life for his generation. El Général's arrest at the start of the protests that became the Tunisian Revolution sent a signal to an entire generation that the Tunisian state treated their pleas for dignity and mercy with complete disdain.

El Général was by no means the only political rapper in Tunisia; indeed, the consensus among the country's hip hop community is that he was not as talented as many other rappers and musicians, such as Bendir Man and the Armada Bizerte crew, who also wrote dangerously political songs in the lead-up to the uprisings. At the same time, like their Egyptian counterparts (to whom they would send messages of support and advice almost as soon as Ben Ali was gone and the #Jan25 Uprising began), a broader cadre of young activists had honed their skills as hackers and clandestine organizers building the metal, hip hop, and other alternative music and cultural scenes in Tunisia in the previous decade. In the Tunisian case, these skills were used against the government once protests began, as activists from the metal scene (among others) hacked into police cameras meant to control the streets during protests and, locking out the security forces, used them to watch where the police were heading and then get the message to protesters before the police arrived. It was out of small victories like these as much as huge crowds of protesters that Ben Ali was forced from power.

Not surprisingly, a decade later Tunisia is home to one of the MENA's most self-reflexive artists, Znoos ("species" in Tunisian Arabic, often used as a derogatory reference to young people who deviate from societal norms). Working in the crossroads of hardcore punk and metal, Znoos's music is a direct retort to the majority of Tunisian society who take offense at those who refuse to conform to their conservative expectations. If there's any doubt about such a literal intention, the band's symbol is a traditional North African "khamsa," or hand against the evil eye, but with the middle finger raised unmistakably higher than normal.

As with the previous generation of political artists, the band's political lyrics and beautifully angry sound are "fueled by social and political injustices in post-revolutionary Tunisia" (as they describe it). Unlike the musical generals and foot soldiers of 2011, however, it's accompanied by an explicitly sophisticated critique and is more self-aware and reflexive than the more awkward "decolonial" arguments of, for example, the Hardzazat festival at the Maghreb's western end, in Morocco (discussed in chapter 1). As one of the band's deliberately anonymous members explained to Mark in an interview in October 2021 in Tunis, "We're doing music as a historical document. Our job is to counteract colonial narrative and the religious and patriarchal system still governing our country, but we're also having fun making music and expressing ourselves."

What makes Znoos such a unique project is that it captures the spirit of ferocious joy that was reflected in Tunisia's revolutionary music of a decade ago. Today the same power and purpose are at the heart of hip hop in Algeria and Sudan, where the music played an important role in the protests of 2018–19 that rocked both countries, which forced both countries' long-serving dictators from power and put their nations, however provisionally as of the time of writing, on the paths—albeit with many obstacles—toward some form of political liberalization, if not yet full democracy. Not surprisingly, the songs that became anthems of the protests, like the Algerian rapper Soolking's "Liberté" (Freedom) and female MC and filmmaker Raja Meziane's banger "Allo le Système," were in the style of trap. As interesting, the organized football fan clubs known as ultras, who played an outsized role in the #Jan25 protests in Egypt, as well as in Morocco, participated in the making of Soolking's "La Liberté," as members of Ouled El Bahdja, the supporters of the USM Alger Football Club, helped publicize the song and offered broader support to the protest movement, known as "Hirak." The YouTube views tell the story: three hundred million views (as of December 2021), more than almost every song of the MENA uprisings put together.

Meziane's lyrics for "Allo le Système" are as cutting as El Général's almost a decade previous. She declares, "$100 billion gone up in smoke and you still want more. . . . Today we are silent no more, we're scared no more. Today we want a people's republic, a democracy, not a monarchy" ("'alf milyar mashat fir-rih wa mazala tama'in . . . al-youm ma ra'na sakatin, ma rana kha'ifin. Jumhuriyyah bghainaha sha'abiyyah, dimuqratiyyah ma hiyya malakiyya"), but as the technology of music production has improved so much at the home-studio level, it sounds far phatter. It's clear that the enfeebled Bouteflika didn't have a chance against her. Unfortunately, "le Système" (the entirety of the country's military-political governing apparatus) proved to be a lot harder to wound.

In Sudan, rappers as well as other musicians, artists, writers, poets, and most every other type of cultural creative were involved in the ever-escalating protests that began in late 2018. One day would see rappers dropping poetry about the regime and the Revolution, and the next would see dozens of violinists playing well-known folk melodies in unison, while behind them various kinds of art were being produced. "All types of music are here" is how one woman put it in an al-Arabiyya interview at the height of the protests. As an article from the local news portal noonpost.com put it, "Revolutionary arts were born from the womb of the Sudanese Revolution [lit. movement]" (funun thawriyya wulidat min rahm al-hirak as-sudani).

One of the most powerful musical moments of the Sudanese Revolution was when Sudanese-Canadian rapper Ayman Mao flew into Khartoum, headed right for the main sit-in site outside the Army headquarters, jumped onstage, and, illuminated by thousands of mobile phones, performed his most famous song, "Dum" ("Blood"), while the audience screamed the refrain "Thawra!" ("Revolution!") after each line:

Live ammunition (Rassasa hayya!)/Revolution! (Thawra!)
And they tell you it's rubber [bullet] (Wa yagulu layk matata)/Revolution!
(Thawra!)

They're Janjaweed (Dayl Janjaweed)/Revolution! (Thawra!) . . .
Hallucination and fanboyism (Halwasa wa Hawwata)/ Revolution!
  Thawra! . . .
In my hand is a brick (Fi yedi balata)/Revolution! (Thawra!)
I strike corruption (Barjum al-fasad)/Revolution! (Thawra!")

FROM PAIN TO JOY

It is now almost a commonplace among music critics to compare EYM with
post-tonal modern and contemporary classical music. Yet, though these
intense and angry forms of music dominated the local scenes before and at
the start of the current wave of protests, a crucial change in the affective
quality of the music occurred once the revolutions commenced. It became
happy and even joyful, catchier, and with a warmer and more inviting and
listenable sound, at least for the period when the idea of a better future still
seemed possible. Whether it was the catchy hooks of many Tunisian and
Egyptian revolutionary songs or, more recently in the uprisings in Sudan and
Lebanon, the joyous and festival-like atmospheres featuring music and dancing that were constantly shared on social media, these were the perfect vehicles to free bodies from their submission to dire realities. Turkey and even
Iran too have been sites of joyous performance that assumed political significance in large part because of the imposition of highly conservative cultural
policies (in Iran's case, exacerbated by a half-century policy of grief and
sacrifice).

These dynamics are evident even in the midst of high levels of oppression.
We can see them in the exuberant performances of Palestinian musicians at
PMX even as Israeli troops were marauding a block or two away in Ramallah
and sniping at protesters in Gaza. We could see it in the soft glow of the early
evening sun on the steps of the Municipal Opera House on Tunis's Bourguiba
Boulevard, where a young singer, Emel Mathlouthi, channeled her favorite
bands, In Flames, Dark Tranquility, and The Gathering, to enrapture thousands of protesters with an a capella rendition of the folk song "Kelmti horra"
("My Voice Is Free"), capturing the resolve of the revolutionaries and the beauty
of the revolution that had unfolded before their eyes with a joy-filled smile.

More recently, such joy was manifest with particular intensity at a Cairo
concert in 2018 featuring *mahraganat* stars DJ Sadat and Islam Chipsy collaborating with several American "footwork" artists, including the Chicago-based

band Teklife (DJ Taye and Wass), with whom they also recorded the song "Ayez eh?" ("What Do You Want?"). What was most striking about the music was not how easily Midwestern footwork and Cairene *mahraganat* could blend together (not a surprise, since both genres have roots in a combination of techno and hip hop, and Sadat even described footwork as "*mahraganat* localized for a European audience"), but rather the sheer joy that was emanating like a massive aura from Sadat and Chipsy as they played, rapped, and danced with their American comrades during their joint concert at the American University of Cairo's Greek Campus downtown, meters from Tahrir Square and Muhammad Mahmoud Street, ground zero of the #Jan25 Uprising.

To watch the video of the concert on YouTube is to witness two explosively creative musical genres come together to create, however momentarily, an entirely new and auratic blending of music and dance, manifesting the joy that survives inside and even transcends the pain of the last half-decade of dictatorship and regime violence. As with gospel, blues, and so many forms of African American music (a connection specifically cited by DJ Taye in a minidocumentary about the collaboration), music's functioning as a transversal and revolutionary force couldn't be clearer on that stage. Even if political freedom is unimaginable for most Egyptians in the near future, on that stage with these artists and the lucky audience members, a space was created out of this spontaneous musical combustion where, at least for a moment, the revolutionary energy reemerged to remind all those present that the dream of January 25 had not been lost.

One can relate this sense of community and beauty to what Barry Shank in his book *The Political Force of Musical Beauty* describes as music's ability to "enact its own force, creating shared senses of the world. The experience of musical beauty confirms within its listeners the sense that this moment of listening has within it the promise of things being right, of pieces fitting together, of wholes emerging out of so much more than assembled riffs and rhythms." In other words, music can give hope, honoring Toni Cade Bambara's belief that great art can make revolution irresistible. How it does so varies but, as so well demonstrated when *mahraganat* met footwork, it most often involves the emancipatory potential of disruptive artistic collaboration—with so many sparks being generated, one will ultimately ignite the fire of revolt, and perhaps even revolution.

Indeed, building on the work of philosopher Jacques Rancière, we argue that the aesthetic pleasure and efficacy of music are a necessary first step toward any kind of emancipatory politics, pushing those who experience its aura toward new imaginations of freedom. To put it simply, a great song in the right political context can have a powerful impact on multiple audiences. And when a song is not (merely or only) angry but also expresses joy against the violence of the state, that expression is a vehicle both for resistance and of agency—and, through it, once the revolutionary moment has dissipated or has been crushed, it is a cathartic repository of memory that is both aesthetic and political.

THE AESTHETIC EMBEDDEDNESS OF ART, ACTIVISM, AND SCHOLARSHIP

Music can make you stronger, but can music change the world? On the one hand, an absurd or at least egotistical question (coming from a musician), to be sure. Only *people* change the world. To state otherwise is to commit the fallacy of reification—to bestow human agency on an abstract human creation. Yet the question persists, at least for those scholars who investigate popular music and society. Put another way: Does composing, performing, listening to, talking about music encourage people to fight for social change? Perhaps we need to approach the question differently. What exactly is it that music does? At its most potent—and this we have now observed numerous times in the last decades across the Muslim world, especially in places with authoritarian governance—it has the power to create publics. Music, through its most elemental components, such as lyrics or melodies, but also through more complex processes, such as affect, can empower and move people to gather and stand up for certain causes. It can bring together perfect strangers who in a simple melody or line of a song instantly recognize a world of meaning that no other form of cultural production can transmit with such ease. Furthermore, those strangers can easily partake in the enactment of a song through singing, clapping, or dancing, allowing for the performance of a particular public. Yet how do we measure and quantify music's affective power, never mind its effect on individuals, groups, and society at large?

Clearly, linear narratives and simple explanations bound by traditional theories or disciplinary boundaries won't prove satisfactory. And yet, as we enter the third decade of the twenty-first century, it is clear that scholarly projections regarding the emancipatory potential of popular culture are in need of revision. Haughtily dismissed as the soulless products of a capitalist industry, and then dismissed again as ideological forms deeply complicit in cultural hegemony, popular culture—whether it's inherently or only implicitly political—has nonetheless been responsible for seismic attitudinal shifts across the globe regarding race, sexuality, gender, democracy, and generational identity. Though global neoliberal capitalism has turned out to be as bad as advertised for a large share of the world's population, rock 'n' roll in its many forms has historically given young people trapped in authoritarian and even totalitarian regimes the tools and the motivation to reach outward. And while the previous assertion may sound like a cliché, one only has to study the ways in which oppressive governments have sought to silence and jail, and sometimes coopt and corrupt, musicians to confirm the importance and danger of their work.

Indeed, as evidenced particularly in Morocco, Saudi Arabia, and Iran, governments that previously had censored and repressed youth music, including EYM, have more recently attempted to coopt the styles, if not musicians, so that they can be used as sonic legitimation or persuasion vis-à-vis their citizens. In our hypermediated world, where so much of life takes place on social media, the power of music—whether live, recorded, via streaming and social media, or as videos and even memes—has become even more pronounced. The aura of a work of art now extends to the infinite ether, multiplied in numbers that were unfathomable in the pre-social-media age.

What is clear is that the music that can affect or at least encourage and support broader movements for social and political change will not be that of the lone composer sitting in the citadel, studio, or café creating music whose very impenetrability forces society to confront its demons and hypocrisies. Rather, the soundtrack of future protests will be messy, created by artists and activists in the muck and the mosh pit as well as DIY home studios, which is where those of us who study these scenes need to be ourselves. Our research needs to articulate the potential of this popular culture within political contexts, but also attend to the new ways of its mediation, whether on Instagram or TikTok, and by the time you're reading this, probably some app that is not yet known at the time of writing this sentence. While technological mediation might be a fast-moving field, the building blocks of what makes a piece of cultural production powerful are not.

IN TURKEY, THE END OF ONE ERA, BUT WILL THE NEW ONE BE STILLBORN?

The Egyptian, Tunisian, Libyan, and other economies of soon-to-be defunct regimes were left in dire shape by the combination of decades of kleptocratic rule by mafia families and their cronies and the crisis brought on by the revolts and revolutions. But not every country in the region experienced the same level of economic distress, and thus not all musicians faced threats to their ability to live a decent life similar to the one members of the Tunisian hip hop crew Armada Bizerte faced after the Revolution, two of whose members decided it was better to disappear in the middle of their first European tour and spend much of the next decade living as clandestinos in Italy and France than remain based in Tunisia as one of the country's most important revolutionary artists. Countries as far apart as Turkey and Indonesia enjoyed a more robust economy, and even the more underground musicians did not face the stark choice that led members of the group to remain illegally in Europe even at the expense of their musical futures. Turkey in particular saw a very different set of challenges to artists in the last decade, with an increasingly authoritarian and religiously oriented government and an Islamization of public outdoor life that saw many bars and clubs closed, alcohol sales restricted or banned, and religious structures in previously secular spaces. By the time the Gezi protests erupted in 2013 the goals of the Erdoğan government were far less benign, and far more dangerous for anyone in the secular cultural avant-garde, than originally imagined.

The Gezi uprising, which was at least partly inspired by the Arab uprisings and global Occupy Movement, had local as well as international roots. Lasting from late May till late August of 2013, it was initiated by a small group of environmentalists who protested the destruction of Istanbul's Gezi Park in the wake of the government's plans to rebuild an Ottoman-era military barracks that once stood on the site, as well as luxury condominiums and a new shopping mall. A symbol of the development-through-destruction being witnessed in most every major Turkish city, the destruction of such an iconic public space encouraged protests throughout the country.

Even though metal did not function as a driving force behind the protests, it certainly provided important means to challenge the government's authoritarian rule in the same manner as did many other forms of cultural resistance (including dance performances, protest songs, theater plays, public lectures, graffiti, comic books, stand-up comedy, TV game shows, and so on). Indeed, the events surrounding Gezi led some Turkish metalheads to conclude that extreme metal in Turkey couldn't and didn't discover its full identity except through the struggle against political Islam, which, in the words of one Ankara-based band interviewed by Pierre, "gave a great opportunity to [do] black metal" in Turkey because it forced people "to find their own sound."

Ultimately the police violently cleared Gezi in mid-June, protest encampments in other cities were cleared in the ensuing months, and protesters were prosecuted and imprisoned. The situation became even worse after the attempted coup d'état in 2016, which led to far harsher crackdowns by Erdoğan, not just on artists, but on intellectuals, scholars, and anyone else who challenged his increasingly autocratic rule.

The Gezi protests saw a significant involvement of both local and international artists. As Rafaella Bianchi's research on music in Gezi has demonstrated, the long historical precedent for political music in Turkey made a deep engagement with music in the protests inevitable, producing a "Gezi Spirit" rooted in music. Indeed, one of the first iconic images of the Gezi movement was that of musician Murat Öztürk of the street musician group Siya Siyabend, guitar slung over his shoulder, confronting police during the protests—a far less violent version of the Libyan guitar hero, but still more than a little foolhardy. In the first month about thirty new songs were specifically composed by famous groups active in the flourishing Turkish musical industry. Perhaps the most famous song to be created around it was "Tencere Tava Havası" ("Sound of Pots and Pans"), by the folk group Kardeş Türküler. Named after the well-known Turkish protest activity of banging pots and pans, the song accused the government not just of destroying the park but of selling out the territory for profit, taking one of the few green spaces left and converting it into "cinemas and squares, covered in shopping malls."

Another exemplar of the power of Gezi's music is "Eyvallah" by Duman, whose combination of stadium-rock arrangement, criticism of Erdoğan's justifications for using force against protesters, and call for the police to "Bring it on!" (the rough translation of the song's title) and declaration that "the streets belong to us, this nation is ours" (*"Meydanlar bizim unutmayın bu vatan bizim"*) made it a veritable "manifesto of resistance" against the violence and autocracy of the Erdoğan government. Even more metal-sounding and direct in its lyrical intention is the song "Direniş Çığlığı" ("Scream of Resistance") by the band Quantum. At least half a dozen other songs, from genres as eclectic as jazz and electronica, similarly took up the Gezi cause.

Even more elemental than pots and pans, groups spontaneously created music using the broken concrete, sheet metal, and pipes used to create barricades, beating out heavy beats on the metal with their hands and feet while chanting against the government, as when the rock/punk/ska singer Hakan Vreskala led a crowd in a rendition of his song "Dağılın Lan!" (released in

FIGURE 29. Still from video of Turkish musician Hakan Vreskala leading a crowd in a spontaneous rendition of the song "Dağılın Lan!" ("Get Lost, Punks!") near Taksim Square, Istanbul, 2013.

2011, roughly translated as "Get Lost, Punks!," a phrase cops shout at kids or protesters when they're trying to disperse them). Its lyrics begin, prophetically, by calling out that "Fascism everywhere is tyranny everywhere.... Get loose, let's breathe. Friends, enough; comrades, where are you stones, sticks, darbuka, on [your] shoulder" *("Her yanda faşizm her yerde zorba... Savulun ulan nefes alalım. Dostlar yetisin yoldaşlar nerdesiniz. Taşlar sopalar darbukalar omza")*.

As Hakan reflected to Mark in a conversation in January 2021,

That video shot in Taksim of "Dağılın Lan!" was actually a rehearsal. I'm a percussion teacher, so I went outside, and grabbed about fifteen people and told them what I wanted to do and they all agreed to follow me. I said, "Look, let's try this and if it works we'll perform it tomorrow. We started working on it and my friends started filming it just to see how it would look, but also CNN Turk and other news outlets were around and started filming too. And like everything in Gezi, it just took off. We ran home to edit it and by the time we got there it was already being broadcast and online from the news stations. So I was actually the last one sharing it from YouTube. It was such a beautiful time, I still remember, but now, while I live in Sweden, most of my friends are stuck with few options for the future.

Even major artists who didn't write music specifically for the protests (as their counterparts did in Egypt and Tunisia, for example) lent their support. For example, punk/metal/alternative pioneer Hayko Cepkin marched with protesters and spoke publicly and tweeted in support of them, while also supporting the "No" campaign (Hayır campaign) against the constitutional referendum in 2017. Other, even more popular stars, such as pop singer Tarkan, also participated in protests, although they were careful to avoid being photographed doing so.

Music was important enough to organizing and representing the protests that a movement known as Gezici Müzisyenler, or Gezi Musicians, formed as part of the protests. It channeled through the artists who participated in it, as organic intellectuals, the messages of nonviolent resistance, political militancy, and building a "culture of solidarity among musicians" based on the notion that "another world is possible" *("Başka bir dünya mümkün")*. At the same time, the protests afforded new opportunities for noncommercial artists to use the digital platforms and (at that point) uncensored social media platforms to circulate their music in a way that reached unprecedented numbers of people and established, however temporarily, grassroots control over spaces normally controlled by the state or capital.

Although it would be an exaggeration to speak of metal as a political power during the protests, as in Tunis and Egypt countless metalheads individually participated in the protest. Turkish metalheads also used Iron Maiden's Istanbul concert on July 26, 2013, as an opportunity to protest the government's wide-scale repressive action against peaceful protesters (perhaps the most peaceful political protests in modern Turkish history, in fact). In the videos for the songs they are even more direct, with images in Murder King's video for "Demokrasi" directly linking the violence of Gezi to the country's military coups. Metal wasn't the cause of Gezi, but there is certainly no better sonic metaphor for the struggle it represented than the songs of bands such as Murder King. And indeed, when, at a concert not long after the worst of the violence, Bruce Dickinson, in solidarity with the Turkish fans, recast the band's famous song "Fear of the Dark" into "Fear of the Park," emotions ran high.

The positive feelings experienced and expressed by protesters dissipated as the authorities pushed protesters out of the Park and other protest sites during the summer of 2013. For the metal scene in particular, the loss of Gezi and other protest sites merely added to the woes caused by the systematic destruction of Istanbul's central nightlife hub in Beyoğlu, which was home to numerous rock and metal bars, small concert venues, record shops, and even rehearsal studios, and the broader pushing out of the city's once lively subcultural scenes. And yet, despite the severe diminishment of what could be termed its "analog infrastructure," the Turkish metal underground has survived thanks to a strong communications network that includes print and online fanzines like *Delikasap* and *Headbang* that have created a strong collective memory and living archive of the scene.

Unfortunately, however, not all bands who challenged the system, directly or otherwise, fared so well. The celebrated activist folk group Grup Yorum, who, in addition to performing collectively, since 1985 has edited a cultural magazine and run a community center in Istanbul, has been regularly censored, banned, and harassed, and has seen members arrested and imprisoned for its critical lyrics. In 2019 after being banned from performing for two consecutive years and more arrests of band members, members Helin Bölek and Ibrahim Gökçek were themselves imprisoned, during which they began a hunger strike, which, tragically, led in April and May of the next year to their deaths. And despite international support from well-known artists and governments for their case, the Turkish government has not eased up on its attacks on political artists, including musicians, filmmakers, and other cultural creatives.

Hip hop has had a different but equally fraught trajectory in Turkey. In part thanks to its "outsider" origins among the Turkish diaspora in the 1980s, Turkish rappers from the start understood their function as speaking "for those who have been silenced.... We resist by making our art" (as rapper Slang explained in a interview with *Vice* in 2017).

The zenith of political hip hop was reached in September 2019, when Turkish rappers released two songs on the same day that were highly critical of the Turkish government. The first, titled "Olay" ("The Incident") by Ezhel, which was accompanied by an official video clip with images of Gezi and other government violence as well as the body of young Alan Kurdi (the Syrian refugee boy whose body washed up on Turkish shores), Donald Trump, and other seemingly incongruous images, focused on the intensity of government corruption and the paranoia it leads to, and how easily it becomes normalized. But Olay's ten million YouTube views by mid-2021 was dwarfed by the almost fifty million views achieved by another song, "Susamam" ("I Can't Stay Silent"), a collaboration between eighteen rappers. At an astonishing fifteen minutes in length, with each artist more intensely accusatory than the last, it directly attacked the government and the Turkish public for being silent about the ongoing violence, oppression, and injustice across the country. Political commentator Can Okar termed the music a "political earthquake," explaining almost immediately after the songs' release: "These rappers are creating a mind-numbing critique of a dystopia that speech can't really cover in the same way. Violence against women, nepotism, industrialized education and concretized cities, jailed journalists and a silent people who bear responsibility. . . . Just wow."

What is crucial about these songs and videos is not just their lyrical content or musical aesthetics. Rather, these videos, which have the advantage of being ultimately uncensorable as they exist in a highly permeable digital landscape with limitless ways to reach Turks even if the government censors major media platforms, demonstrate that until or unless Erdoğan deploys a level of social media surveillance and policing similar to that of Sisi or other brutally authoritarian leaders, the digital circulation and consumption of highly political art and music can make an important—if clearly limited—contribution to keeping the flame of dissent alive under conditions where at the official and even public level there remains little appetite for it.

THE INDONESIAN MIRACLE?

Most every country in the Muslim-majority world is today still experiencing some form of struggle for democracy, dignity, and sustainable development, if it's not under too harsh an autocratic rule to allow even the struggle to occur. Tunisia had been one exception to this trend, but it continues to suffer from the severe economic struggles that led to an autogolpe, or "self-coup," by President Kais Saied in 2021, which might well doom its democratic experiment. One of the only countries where the transition to democracy and at least a modicum of freedom, dignity, and social justice seems relatively secure is Indonesia, the world's largest Muslim nation. Beginning with President Soeharto's resignation in 1998, the country has undergone a "reform," or "Reformasi," period that today has put metal at the center of the political landscape, with over twenty-two hundred metal bands across the archipelago out of a population of 270 million (in contrast, with 1.5 billion people, China has somewhere between three hundred and five hundred).

Twenty-three years later, among the most unique features of the Indonesian revolution is that its most important soundtrack comprised death metal, punk, and hardcore. For its part, hip hop was slower to catch on; it wasn't until 2012 or so that grassroots hip hop really took off in Indonesia. The story of underground rock music in Indonesia's momentous political transition is more established and by now familiar to scholars of popular culture: grassroots organizing and media production skills acquired in order to produce independent music became potent tools of political resistance; radical ideologies were imported into Indonesian student culture via music zines from abroad; and, most crucially, underground rock provided the soundtrack, the affective context, for the struggle—it gave a sense of what revolution *feels like*.

After Soeharto's dramatic resignation on May 21, 1998, in response to sustained student-led protests, there was a veritable explosion of underground bands representing multiple genres or streams *(aliran)*, from industrial to old-school hardcore to Britpop. Many of these bands sang about politics now that it was completely safe to decry the brutality of the Soeharto regime. Bands continue to do so vociferously to this day, and antimilitary, pro-grassroots-mobilization themes abound even in subgenres such as death, stoner, and black metal that tend to be less "political" in other nations.

Yet in February 2019, the Indonesian music community received a nasty jolt. A bill was introduced in the People's Representative Council (the Indonesian equivalent to the US House of Representatives) that would regulate musical expression, seek to purge music of "negative foreign influences," and professionalize the production and promotion of music. These measures specifically seemed to target members of Indonesia's vast underground music scene, who not only play "foreign-influenced" music but rely upon networks of nonprofessional, noncredentialed participants, as all independent music scenes do. Indonesia's musicians and industry figures responded quickly: in a matter of days, an online petition calling for the bill to be rejected received over a quarter of a million signatures.

Luminaries in the music world spoke out in the national press, voicing intense opposition to the proposed law, which was deemed unnecessary, inhibitory, and draconian. Not surprisingly, the list of objectors included prominent punk and metal musicians, including Jerinx from Superman Is

Dead, Arian13 from Seringai, and the country's most prominent metaller, Eben Burgerkill, whose relentless drive, musicianship, and international tours had raised the global profile of the entire Indonesian underground rock scene. (His sudden passing in September 2021 at age forty-six would devastate the Indonesian music community.) As feminist musician/activist Kartika Jahja pointed out in an interview with ABC Australia, the real motivations behind this sudden attempt at censorship were not difficult to interpret: grassroots musicians' support had been crucial to the success of Indonesia's incumbent president, Joko Widodo (known by all as Jokowi), who faced reelection in April. Running against Jokowi for the second time was Prabowo Subianto, a military strongman supported by religious fundamentalists and other opponents of pluralist democracy.

Jokowi is an avowed heavy metal fan and surprisingly proficient guitarist; one of his acts as governor of Jakarta (the post he held before becoming president) was bringing Metallica back to the city after a twenty-year hiatus. The concert took place in August 2013 and this time there were no riots (unlike the infamous conflagrations of 1993). The show was opened by Seringai, who was joined onstage by members of DeadSquad and Burgerkill. It was a proud day for homegrown Indonesian metal, and the scene has continued to flourish. After Jokowi won reelection handily, the music bill was withdrawn. Yet the forces of repression, remnants of the despotic Soeharto era in league with Islamic fundamentalists, have not given up their decades-long war on Indonesian metal, hardcore, and underground hip hop.

The Indonesian underground rock scene has enjoyed over thirty years of growth, but it is now threatened by the rise of political Islam of a similar sort to that which has stunted music scenes and the development of democratic institutions in the MENA region for decades. Indeed, the relative unimportance of Islamism and the strong link between rock and liberal politics have, until now, strongly characterized the Indonesian case. As much as any music scene discussed in this book, Indonesian popular music's promotion of progressive politics has a long history, one made possible by the fact that the secular authoritarian government that ruled Indonesia from 1966 to 1998, though occasionally responsive to restive Islamic hardliners concerned about infidels, was aggressively pro-Western, welcoming foreign direct investment, economic expertise, and Western cultural imports. And so unlike in many other Muslim countries rock, metal, jazz, punk, and hip hop all found a welcome home in the archipelago nation.

To this day, it is unclear why the central government never cracked down on underground music, which seems to have succeeded in radicalizing a significant portion of young people, turning them against both the military regime *and* the religious fundamentalists, just as it did in Tunisia, Turkey, Egypt, and many other places in Southeast Asia and the MENA regions. Indeed, this remained the case even after the Islamist government of the semiautonomous Aceh province arrested sixty-four punks at a concert in 2011, shaved their mohawks, and sent them to a reeducation camp for "moral rehabilitation," causing an international outcry.

Vocalist Arian Tigabelas of the "kings of Indonesian metal" (as *Vice* described them), Seringai, suggested to Jeremy at a 2017 lecture that the brutal "cookie-monster"-style vocals of extreme metal and hardcore may have helped conceal the message of the lyrics, as it did in many other scenes. Certainly this was salient, though most groups at the time also released their own DIY cassettes that included printed, uncensored lyric sheets.

One reason for the absence of crackdowns is perhaps the all-encompassing nature of hardcore (and hardcore metal) communities, which are as much ways of life, philosophy, and politics as they are styles of music. In his landmark study *Global Punk: Resistance and Rebellion in Everyday Life,* Kevin Dunn argues that punk's promise of resistance and autonomy from oppressive mainstream society is fulfilled by the grassroots networks of DIY punk scenes that now encircle the globe. In addition to its DIY model of grassroots organization, which continues to inform global nongovernmental organizations and political campaigns, punk culture's critique allowed young people to see beyond their temporal-spatial and ideological limitations, wherever the music and culture have taken hold.

Punk's willingness to question the status quo and defy settled opinion (including its own subculture's consensus) can take unexpected turns. Few predicted the twenty-first-century rise of Indonesian punk bands with a strident Islamist message, which occurred despite the much-publicized religiously motivated police harassment and imprisonment of Indonesian punks in Aceh province in December 2011. Spearheaded by metal groups Tengkorak and Purgatory, the One-Finger Metal (Metal Satu Jari) movement, combining Islamic piety with metallic riffs, peaked around 2011 and subsequently declined. Islamic punk, on the other hand, gained momentum with groups such as Punk Muslim. The number of punks in the Islamic versus older leftist mold remains a subject of contention, but it's clear that each has their own ethics of social justice, communal struggle, and liberation at the heart of their identities. Both religious and leftist punk communities remain important cultural-political actors in Indonesia in ways that their counterparts could only dream of in Morocco or other scenes in the MENA.

EYM, ISLAM, AND GENDER

While the novelty of Islamist punk has waned in recent years, feminist interventions are a common and important part of the punk/hardcore scenes in Indonesia, as they are globally. As Belfast-based punk scholar and musician Jim Donaghey has shown in detail, despite ongoing sexism in the punk scene and concerted repression by conservative social groups and the government, these scenes have opened important cultural as well as political platforms for feminism to reach the wider Indonesian society. Metal has experienced a similar, if not always as explicitly political, dynamic, most recently related to Voice of Baceprot (loosely translated, *baceprot* means "chatterbox"), the now world-renowned trio of teenage hijab-wearing shredders who play a unique combination of thrash metal, nu-metal, and thrash-funk.

Originally from the tiny village of Singajaya in rural West Java, the members of Voice of Baceprot (hereafter VoB), singer/guitarist Firdda Kurnia (aka Marsya), bassist Nidi Rahmawati (aka Widi), and drummer Euis Siti Aisyah (aka Sitti), have been celebrated for their instrumental proficiency and their ability to "uproot ... gender and religious stereotypes," in the words of an article published in *The Week*. "For us, metal is media to show our critical voices," Kurnia explained to the article's author. "Metal music matches with the determination in our souls." Beyond its spiritual power, however, playing metal is seen by the band as a kind of resistance against the still-powerful conservative elements of their society, including authority figures who stymie the ability of young women to get educated (which they tackle in their song "School Revolution"), distract people from dealing with pressing issues such as climate change (the subject of their song "The Enemy of Earth Is You"), and even molest female students ("[Not] Public Property," an incendiary song written in reaction to a scandal at an Indonesian madrasah).

VoB has received a great deal of attention from Western media outlets, but in fact headscarf-wearing Muslim women playing heavy metal aren't that unusual in Indonesia. Vocalist Asri Yuniar (Achie) of Gugat, virtuoso

FIGURE 30. Voice of Baceprot performing at a graduation ceremony in Garut, Indonesia, May 2017. Photo by Yuddy Cahya.

guitarist Meliana Siti Sumartini (aka MelSickScreamoAnnie), and drummer Siti Nurjanah of Soul of Slamming are some of the best-known figures currently in the scene. Moreover, the vast Indonesian punk and metal scenes are places where countless women of varying degrees of adherence to Islamic practice (and female members of non-Muslim minorities) have found avenues of self-expression.

In a display of nationalism hard to imagine coming from any other metal scene surveyed in this book, on Indonesia's 2020 Independence Day VoB released a new song, "Merdeka: Kami Satu Indonesia Untuk Dunia" ("Independence: We Are One Indonesia for the World"), celebrating their country. The lyrics, in part, declare:

Good morning world, we are the sons and daughters of Indonesia.
Who will not be afraid to speak, and cry for freedom.
Behold we, O world, standing firm on the beloved land.
That will never be separated, even if we are different.

Here we are, the generation of change.
Here we are, the civilization-building generation.
This is us, a generation that will never give up on our promise to our motherland.

The difference in themes and intention compared with other scenes, particularly in the MENA, is striking. Rather than mobilizing resistance, this music mobilizes the energy of youth to build the society that is created *after* that rare occasion when resistance succeeded and a democratic system is in place. Without the need to focus on or vent frustration at political oppression, the band can focus on more "normal" problems faced by teenagers globally, such as students feeling "lost and detached from their hopes and dreams for the sake of following rigid school rules," and larger messages of "freedom and independence as a woman," as the band explained in an interview with *Metal Hammer* magazine in early 2021.

Worth noting is the role of secular nationalism here—Indonesia is a religiously observant country, but non-Muslim minorities are included *by definition* in Indonesian nationalist rhetoric and the country has been noted for its relative tolerance and inclusivity. Following democratization, there has been a rise both in exclusivist religious extremism and in calls for greater regional autonomy and respect for ethnic, sexual, racial, and religious minorities who have been marginalized by past nation-building projects.

No doubt because of this positivity in attitude and, not surprisingly, the relatively wholesome and empowering image of young women asserting themselves while remaining "true" to their identity, Nobel Peace Prize–winner Malala Yousafzai became a fan, and her "Malala Fund" donated money to the band's projects, with Malala explaining in an Instagram post on February 11, 2020 (nine years to the day after Egyptian President Mubarak was forced from power, coincidentally): "Firdda, Eusi and Widi—the members of @voiceofbaceprot, an all-girl heavy metal band from Indonesia—believe that music is the best way to address the issues they witness in their country and around the world. They fell in love with heavy metal after their teacher (and now band manager) played them the song 'Toxicity' by System of a Down." As she continued through her @malalafund account, "Upon hearing it, we seemed to find something that was very compatible with our noisy and critical personalities," no doubt owing in part to the fact that VoB formed when the girls were a year younger than the age at which Malala was shot by the Taliban.

In fact Malala's timing was spot on: not long after (and perhaps because of) her gesture of support, VoB was attacked again by religious conservatives, including calls to break up the band and death threats. As lead singer and guitarist Firdda Kurnia explained to the *South China Morning Post,* religious critics declared that they should remove their headscarves while playing metal, as "it was heresy [literally, acting like an infidel] to wear a headscarf while playing metal music." Echoing the words of so many metalheads from Maghreb to the Java Sea, she continued, "Metal is just a kind of music for us. We do music but we did not stop praying; we continue to wear the headscarf, as we do not leave our other [religious] obligations." And the band has taken a courageously dismissive attitude toward the threats. "We were a bit scared at first," guitarist Kurnia explained in the *Metal Hammer* interview, "but we just put our heads down and focused back on our music. As the cliché goes, what doesn't kill us makes us stronger."

Underground rock music culture was an agent of political radicalization in Indonesia just as it had been in the West. It has also been indigenized to a surprising degree, melding with populist traditions of mutual self-help, social criticism, and communalism in ways only deep cultural and historical understanding of the Indonesian context can reveal. Compared with those in other countries in the Muslim world (including neighboring Malaysia, also home to a massive underground scene), Indonesian underground rock fans have had to deal with less government and religious harassment. They are part of what international relations experts consider the healthiest democracy in Southeast Asia, yet their freedom of expression is constantly threatened, as the emergence of the music censorship bill illustrates. The bill also serves as a reminder of the undeniable link between music and politics in Indonesia.

THE RETURN OF THE ANALOG IN A DIGITAL WORLD

We imagine that it is clear by now how complex and contradictory are the lives of EYM artists, fans, and scenes across the MENA and broader Muslim world. Indeed, the number of contradictions and dissonances in their lives and politics is often greater than in the music they produce. Art and politics are not merely "aesthetically embedded" or implicated in relation to each other; they are productively contradictory and microtonally ambivalent in the realities they produce, inhabit, and intersect. Such complexity reinforces the importance of developing more creative and robust paradigms for collaborative research, not merely with "local" researchers, but with the local producers of knowledge—artists themselves—and under conditions of censorship and surveillance where such collaboration can involve risks of arrest, imprisonment, or worse.

Indeed, the pandemic itself demonstrates these points with great clarity. To take one example, in a YouTube interview posted in February 2021 with the online music magazine *SceneNoise,* Egyptian synth artist and producer Ahmed Kubbara revealed the inherent dichotomies characterizing the new political and technology economies of the contemporary youth music scenes in Egypt. Specifically, he explained that "I think we're living in one of the most exciting times in Egyptian or Middle Eastern music. Around the [region] there are [few] places to play live. . . . It's kind of leveled the playing field because you put your music online and people listen to it. There's not the thing of how many people am I going to play to."

Kubbara's comment, made in the midst of the pandemic in Cairo, points to the heightened opportunities for the digital production, circulation, and consumption of music, particularly in a country like Egypt in the midst of a pandemic. Indeed, more than the lack of opportunities to perform live, that ability to record and circulate one's music anywhere for free has truly leveled the playing field for younger or lesser-known and even unknown artists, especially those trying to reach an audience outside their home country. At the same time, because of the amount of time musicians of every stripe need to practice and improve their art, there are certainly worse things than being stuck in your bedroom for over a year with nothing much to do besides practice, write songs, record, and, crucially, constantly share your music and collaborate with other musicians.

On the other hand, the "common subcultural consciousness" out of which more countercultural and directly political identities often emerge has clearly suffered during the pandemic because of the difficulties of meeting in person and developing or maintaining close personal relationships, upon which solidarity must be built when the stakes are this high—whether musically or politically. It's very hard to acquire, process, and reinforce common experiences, never mind maintain group solidarity and cohesiveness against antagonistic social and political forces, when you can't get together in person to play or listen to music. Moreover, while in the case of nonpolitical artists in Egypt and other authoritarian countries where culture is at present not heavily policed and the Internet and social media offer expanded opportunities for online creation, connections, and collaboration, in countries like Iran and Turkey today, there is much more online surveillance and even policing of artists' creative activities.

The coronavirus pandemic made already complex and contradictory scenes much more so. Among the many impacts of the pandemic for music scenes and those who study and write about them has been the inability for even scholars fortunate enough to live in and with the communities they research to do fieldwork (WhatsApp and Zoom calls are no substitute for physical presence, and most definitely do not have any of the upsides of virtual/digital musical production, circulation, and consumption). This makes it very hard even for scholars working with and in their home cultures and societies to obtain accurate and reliable data and knowledge about the clearly important and in some cases quite significant changes caused by the pandemic on the musical as well as broader political and social systems.

What this reality has brought home is the foundational need to move beyond linear narratives—temporal, causal, ideological/political, or musical—and singular voices, that is, the voice of the author who is at some basic level separate from the people, communities, and cultures being studied. Equally important is the need to refuse any kind of determinism, in which the problems and even nightmares of the recent past or the present moment lead to assumptions about futures that have yet to be created (the growth of the Iraqi metal scene in the midst of such political violence and a pandemic crackdown is but one example of how unexpectedly things can change and why it remains so important to pay attention to art).

So the online spaces Kubbara celebrates are often conditioned by state regulations and have become more securitized and thus limited in their value as spaces of true musical, never mind political, freedom—indeed, as we hope is clear, it's impossible to have the former without the latter. In one way, in fact, it's as if we've returned to the analog era, as the ability to surveil and securitize online spaces means that today in many respects it's safer to meet face to face (which, of course, became largely impossible during the pandemic) than online. Even if apolitical music can circulate online without arousing much suspicion, many members of EYM scenes increasingly restrain themselves from expressing any potentially controversial opinions and have even closed down WhatsApp and Facebook groups because they're afraid of government infiltration. On the other hand, even for a community as surveilled as Iranian EYM fans, young people live in a world that is so thoroughly transnational, facilitated by so many social and other media platforms, that the boundaries between diaspora and home are extremely porous and seep into the musical ecosphere from numerous hard-to-trace points in the mediaverse.

But Kubbara is certainly correct that the pandemic has been momentous for all kinds of developments in the region even in this short period. In Iran, for example, the fact that music continues to travel online even as it disappeared for much of 2020 and 2021 (Iran was among the countries first hit by Covid-19 and was hit much worse) has changed the nature of musical experience. The number of Instagram live events, for example, has dramatically increased since the start of the pandemic, as has the experience, described in chapter 5, of collaborative shredding over and then sharing of jam tracks. So have similar collaborations over Clubhouse and Telegram, where even well-known artists are now regularly interacting with fans.

But even these more purely musical gatherings have an attendant politics: Who gets to play and who gets to listen? Which social media platforms are used and why? So while there was an embodied space and community of sound and performance and for the moment that's gone, people are thinking about what it meant, and what the new types of online performance might mean for the way music will be performed when people can take up that space again.

This again raises the issue of Turner's notion of *communitas*. Nelson Varas-Díaz and Niall Scott's edited collection *Heavy Metal Music and the Communal Experience* and Mika Elovaara and Brian Bardine's *Connecting Metal to Culture: Unity in Disparity* both argue that even among EYM scenes metal is unusual, if not unique, in its emphatic fixation on the communal experience, its prioritization of community over consensus, of "unity in disparity." In that regard, like other intense music scenes, the metal scene can be quite *takfiri*—literally damning, or condemning as an infidel—about what is legitimately or truly "metal," in terms of not just music but also specific styles of dress as well as personal and communal practices, such as drinking alcohol, having long hair, wearing specific T-shirts, and so on. Someone who doesn't have long hair or drink *raki* (Turkey) or beer (Egypt) or smoke kief (hash-spiked hand-rolled cigarettes in the Maghreb) might well be considered a poseur across the region, even as metal scenes bridge ideological gaps and scene participants from conflicting political and even religious orientations meet at concerts, talk, and even hug one another.

Other EYM scenes have their own dynamics of community. But as the last decade has shown, the very experience of community has changed with the emergence of new technologies, new kinds and directions of population flows, the growing importance of diasporization in music-making, and the technologies to make boundary-breaking and community-making music not just possible but "irresistible." And so it's even less accurate today than it was previously to conceptualize music communities within national boundaries; diaspora communities, many of them increasingly created through forced migrations and even refugeehood—Iraq's Acrassicauda, Iran's Arsames, and Syria's Maysaloon, as well as rappers like Moroccan MC l7a9d epitomizing this trend—create new music scenes partly rooted in their homelands but

Libya's Fighting Guitar Hero

5,272 views • Mar 29, 2012   30   15   SHARE   SAVE   ...

FIGURE 31. Still from meme video, meme made of photo taken by photographer Aris Messinis of singer/guitarist Masoud Biswir playing during the battle of Sirte during the Libyan civil war, October 2011.

also fused with new aesthetic, cultural, and even ideological components that boomerang back from the diaspora. These flows and transformations create a different kind of consciousness of the music and the communities that partake in it, and increasingly include exiled and refugee artists from other communities as well.

And the meaning and process of solidarity can change dramatically over time and space. Metal and punk became political in Indonesia when there was a common, consensus worldview (opposition to Soeharto), but there's a lot less political energy in the scene today and differences in political opinion among people are much more quietly expressed. On the other hand, in Turkey the tensions with an increasingly religious authoritarian government have repoliticized EYM to an unprecedented degree, creating a greater need for solidarity. Less directly political but equally telling, Turkish musicians, like their Lebanese counterparts, extended significant solidarity to Syrian artists when they began arriving in large numbers during the Civil War, but much of that wore out as the relative lack of development of the Syrian scene and professionalization of Syrian musicians became evident (hip hop artists integrated more easily despite the language barriers because the Syrian scene was far more developed). Finally, in Iran, the competing security, surveillance, and policing structures that monitor young people and their cultures have often tended to ease the pressure on music while harshly policing any hint of political intention or content.

After more than four decades of EYM, and rock music in all its incarnations, being created, recorded, performed, circulated, and consumed across the Middle East and larger Muslim world, music's ability to enrage and inspire, give hope and cause fear, create new solidarities and communities, and provoke extreme responses remains as powerful as it was when the first metal albums and hip hop cassettes began to make their way into the region. But with each new iteration and experience, new band and style, the power of the young people behind the music to tell their own stories and the urgency to listen to their voices become more difficult to ignore. Extreme youth music, like other forms of intense artistic expression, remains a bullet and a bullhorn, raising awareness and alarm about the ever-graver threats to societies by brutally oppressive and unendingly corrupt regimes, and shooting down the propaganda and false consciousness deployed—along with the violence and coercion—to maintain their control over the largest and potentially most powerful group within most every country from Morocco to Indonesia: young people, who have the greatest interest in bringing about truly revolutionary changes in the way their societies, and the global political and economic system more broadly, are governed.

Even as too many governments, supported by powerful patrons, have for the moment managed to crush most opposition to their rule, and the pandemic, border closures, and ever-greater surveillance have made it harder than ever to travel, ever more innovative and powerful music continues to be created, circulated, and consumed, offering hope and strength to a generation, too many of whose members came of age with freedom and justice on the horizon, only to see them ripped away by governments, as well as a global system, that require their continued subjugation and marginalization to survive. As Pedram, the drummer of Afghanistan's only metal band, District Unknown, put it in the documentary *Rockabul*, "If we are not making music, we are dead."

The growing tolerance, if not acceptance, of even extreme youth music by societies and governments who only a few years ago were actively hostile to them, and the successful, if still challenging, democratic transitions in countries like Indonesia and—to the extent it still qualifies—Tunisia, and tentatively in the Sudan and Algeria, remind us that people can win rights and even take the power to govern themselves from the most brutal regimes. The experience of the last dozen years equally shows that music and art more broadly will remain crucial to that struggle. It might not be two minutes to midnight everywhere yet, but the metronome is ticking toward the coda, the temperature is rising fast, and the music is getting louder, harder, funkier, and wilder with each passing year. If a metalhead could become president of Indonesia, the same can someday happen in Egypt, Turkey, Iran, or Syria—and we can hope perhaps one day in the United States too.

. . .

During the eighteen years encompassing *Heavy Metal Islam* and now *We'll Play till We Die,* I have had the privilege of meeting some of the most talented, innovative, and courageous musicians in the world. Nothing has been more inspiring than standing in a classroom in Kabul watching the girls of Miraculous Love Kids, a music school in Kabul started by LA-based metal guitarist and producer Lanny Cordola, learning the riff to "Seven Nation Army." For five years, Lanny managed to use rock music and guitar lessons to educate, feed, and even house upwards of two hundred students and their families—right up until the moment the Taliban cruised into Kabul and destroyed the school, along with the dreams of millions of young Afghans, especially girls and women. Despite the threats to their freedom and even lives, and with many still in hiding at the time of writing, the MLKs continue to dream of using their guitars to change Afghanistan, and the world. No musicians embody the title of this book, and the beauty and hope of music, more than they do. More information at miraculouslovekids.org.

REFERENCES BY CHAPTER

Please note: I have not put any links or sources for the musical artists that are discussed in the book. All but the most obscure musician or artist today have a social media presence and their music is available on multiple platforms. Every artist mentioned in this book has their music available on YouTube, Instagram/Facebook, Bandcamp, SoundCloud, Spotify, iTunes, Patari, or other platforms, usually in multiple formats and with multiple versions. The best source for learning about the state of the art in heavy metal studies is the journal *Metal Music Studies,* edited by Niall Scott and Nelson Varas-Díaz. The best source for finding any heavy metal group is Encyclopedia Metallum, available at www.metal-archives.com. The longest-running and most deeply researched blog on popular music in the Arab world is University of Arkansas anthropologist Ted Swedenburg's blog, *Hawgblawg,* at http://swedenburg.blogspot.com. If you can't find an artist or musician mentioned in this book, please contact me.

AUTHOR'S NOTE

Adorno, Theodor. *The Culture Industry: Selected Essays on Mass Culture.* London: Routledge, 2001.

———. *Essays on Music.* Berkeley: University of California Press, 2002.

Attali, Jacques. *Noise: The Political Economy of Music.* Minneapolis: University of Minnesota Press, 1985.

Bambara, Toni Cade. "An Interview with Toni Cade Bambara." In *Conversations with Toni Bambara,* edited by Thabiti Lewis, 35–47. Jackson: University Press of Mississippi, 2012.

Behrens, Roger. *Adorno-ABC.* Leipzig: Reclam Verlag, 2003.

Benjamin, Walter. "The Work of Art in the Age of Mechanical Reproduction." 1936. Online English translation of essay at Marxists.org, www.marxists.org/reference /subject/philosophy/works/ge/benjamin.htm.

Berlant, Lauren. *The Female Complaint.* Durham, NC: Duke University Press, 2008.

Campos Fonseca, Susan. "Noise, Sonic Experimentation, and Interior Coloniality in Costa Rica." In *Experimentalisms in Practice: Music Perspectives from Latin America,* edited by Ana R. Alonso-Minutti, Eduardo Herrera, and Alejandro L. Madrid, 161–88. Oxford: Oxford University Press, 2018.

Castells, Manuel. *The Power of Identity.* London: Blackwell, 1996.

Davis, Angela Y. *Blues Legacies and Black Feminism.* New York: Vintage, 1998.

Dibango, Manu. *Three Kilos of Coffee: An Autobiography.* Chicago: University of Chicago Press, 1994.

Donaghey, Jim. "Punk and Feminism in Indonesia." *Cultural Studies* 35, no. 1 (2021): 136–61.

Gay'wu Group of Women. *Songspirals: Sharing Women's Wisdom of Country through Songlines.* Sydney, Australia: Allen & Unwin, 2019.

Gramsci, Antonio. *The Prison Notebooks.* New York: Columbia University Press, 2011.

Harcourt, Bernard. "The Late Frankfurt School on Theory and Praxis (Circa 1970)." *Critique & Praxis* 13, no. 13 (December 16, 2018). http://blogs.law.columbia.edu/praxis1313/the-late-frankfurt-school-on-theory-and-praxis/?unapproved=2413&moderation-hash=e1eee9e8964f347470a05bb666d0b353#comment-2413.

Horkheimer, Max. "On the Sociology of Class Relations." *nonsite.org,* 8, no. 18 (2016): 1–63. Originally published in 1943. http://nonsite.org/the-tank/max-horkhei-mer-and-the-sociology-of-class-relations.

Lassiter, Luke Eric. *The Chicago Guide to Collaborative Ethnography.* Chicago: University of Chicago Press, 2005.

LeVine, Mark. "From Neoliberalism to Necrocapitalism in 20 Years." *al-Jazeera,* July 15, 2020. www.aljazeera.com/opinions/2020/7/15/from-neoliberalism-to-necrocapitalism-in-20-years.

———. *Heavy Metal Islam: Rock, Resistance and the Struggle for the Soul of Islam.* New York: Random House, 2008; new edition, Berkeley: University of California Press, 2022.

———. "Music and the Aura of Revolution." *International Journal of Middle East Studies* 44, no. 4 (2012): 794–97.

———. "New Hybridities of Arab Musical Intifadas." *Jadaliyya,* October 29, 2011. www.jadaliyya.com/Details/24562.

———. *Why They Don't Hate Us: Lifting the Veil on the Axis of Evil.* Oxford: Oneworld Publications, 2005.

Lipsitz, George. *Dangerous Crossroads.* London: Verso, 1997.

Mbembe, Achille. *Necropolitics.* Durham, NC: Duke University Press, 2019.

Oliver-Velez, Denise. Interviewed in *Summer of Soul,* dir. Ahmir Thompson, Searchlight Pictures, 2021.

Robinson, Dylan. *Hungry Listening: Resonant Theory for Indigenous Sound Studies.* Minneapolis: University of Minnesota Press, 2020.

Saleh, Sherif. "Living in Songs." Translated by Enas El-Torky. *Arablit.org*, May 3, 2021. https://arablit.org/2021/05/03/short-fiction-living-in-songs.

Shank, Barry. *The Political Force of Musical Beauty*. Durham, NC: Duke University Press, 2014.

Smith, Linda Tuhiwai. *Decolonizing Methodologies: Research and Indigenous Peoples*. 3rd ed. London: Zed, 2021.

Strathausen, Carsten. "Benjamin's Aura and the Broken Heart of Modernity." In *Benjamin's Blind Spot: Walter Benjamin and the Premature Death of Aura*, edited by Lise Patt et al. Los Angeles: Institute of Cultural Inquiry, 2001.

Thompson, Edward P. "Notes on Exterminism, the Last Stage of Civilization." *New Left Review* 1, no. 121 (May/June 1980). https://newleftreview.org/issues/i121/articles/edward-thompson-notes-on-exterminism-the-last-stage-of-civilization.

Tilly, Charles. "War Making and State Making as Organized Crime." In *Bringing the State Back In*, edited by Peter Evans, Dietrich Rueschemeyer, and Theda Skocpol. Cambridge: Cambridge University Press, 1985.

Wedeen, Lisa. *Authoritarian Apprehensions: Ideology, Judgement, and Mourning in Syria*. Chicago: University of Chicago Press, 2019.

Yunkaporta, Tyson. *Sand Talk: How Indigenous Thinking Can Save the World*. New York: HarperCollins, 2020.

INTRODUCTION

Abadi, Houda. "Celebrating El Haqed's Freedom: Soundtracking Resistance." *Jadaliyya*, April 2, 2013. www.jadaliyya.com/Details/28362/Celebrating-El-Haqed%E2%80%99s-Freedom-Soundtracking-Resistance.

Adorno, Theodor. *Mahler: A Musical Physiognomy*. Translated by Edmund Jephcott. Chicago: University of Chicago Press, 1992.

Beinin, Joel. "Arab Workers and the Struggle for Democracy." *Jacobin*, May 10, 2020. www.jacobinmag.com/2020/05/arab-spring-workers-struggle-democracy-unions.

Buck, Joan Juliet. "Asma al-Assad: A Rose in the Desert." *Vogue*, March 2011. https://gawker.com/asma-al-assad-a-rose-in-the-desert-1265002284.

Frase, Peter. *Four Futures Visions of the World after Capitalism*. London: Verso, 2018.

LaBelle, Brandon. *Sonic Agency: Sound and Emergent Forms of Resistance*. London: Goldsmiths Press, 2018.

MTV Arabia. "Metal," promotional commercial, 2008. www.youtube.com/watch?v=sfsG-6RTa7g.

Turner, Bryan S. "The Enclave Society: Towards a Sociology of Immobility." *European Journal of Social Theory* 10, no. 2 (2007):287–303.

Wallach, Jeremy, and Alexandra Levine. "'I want you to support local metal': A Theory of Metal Scene Formation." *Popular Music History* 6, nos. 1–2 (2011): 116–34.

Bayat, Asef. *Revolution without Revolutionaries: Making Sense of the Arab Spring.* Palo Alto, CA: Stanford University Press, 2017.

Belghazi, Taieb. "Festivalization of Urban Space in Morocco." *Critique: Critical Middle Eastern Studies* 15, no. 1 (2006): 97–107.

Bennani-Chraïbi, M., and M. Jeghllaly. "La dynamique protestataire du movement du 20 Février à Casablanca." *Revue Française de Science Politque,* no. 62 (2012): 867–94.

Bestley, Russ, Mike Dines, Matt Grimes, and Paula Guerra, eds. *Punk Identities, Punk Utopias: Global Punk and Media.* Bristol, UK: Intellect, 2021.

Bhabha, Homi. *Of Mimicry and Man: The Ambivalence of Colonial Discourse.* Berkeley: University of California Press, 1997.

Bohlman, Philip. *World Music: A Very Short Introduction.* Oxford: Oxford University Press, 2002.

Bouhmouch, Nadir. *My Makhzen and Me.* 2012. https://vimeo.com/36997532.

Boum, Aomar. "Festivalizing Dissent in Morocco." *Middle East Report,* no. 263 (Summer 2012). https://merip.org/2012/05/festivalizing-dissent-in-morocco.

Caubet, Dominique. "De la 'Nayda' à l'après 20 Février au Maroc, écrire en darija2: Textes d'une jeunesse . . . " In *Cultures et jeunes adultes en région Méditerranée: Circulations, pratiques et soft power,* edited by Abdelfettah Benchenna, Hélène Bourdeloie, and Zineb Majdouli. Paris: L'Harmattan, 2019.

———. *Dima Punk.* Documentary on the Moroccan punk scene. Panorama des cinemas du maghreb, 2021.

———. "DIY in Morocco from the Mid 90's to 2015: Back to the Roots?" In *Keep It Simple, Make It Fast: An Approach to Underground Music Scenes,* vol. 2, edited by Paula Guerra and Tania Moreira. Porto: University of Porto and Instituto Politécnico de Tomar, 2016.

Caubet, Dominique, and Amine Hamma. *Jil lklam: Poètes urbains.* Casablanca: Editions du Sirocco, 2016.

Crowley, Michael. "The Deep State Is Real." *Politico.com,* September/October 2017. www.politico.com/magazine/story/2017/09/05/deep-state-real-cia-fbi-intelligence-215537.

Daadaoui, Mohamed. *Moroccan Monarchy and the Islamist Challenge.* London: Palgrave, 2011.

Dunn, Kevin. *Global Punk: Resistance and Rebellion in Everyday Life.* New York: Bloomsbury, 2016.

Heydemann, Steven. "Syria and the Future of Authoritarianism." *Journal of Democracy* 24, no. 4 (2013): 59–73.

Hinnebusch, Raymond. "Syria: From 'Authoritarian Upgrading' to Revolution?" *International Affairs* 88, no. 1 (January 2012): 95–113.

Kiwan, Nadia. "Moroccan Multiplicities." *Cahiers d'études africaines,* no. 216 (2014). Online version from 2017: http://journals.openedition.org/etudesafricaines/17905.

LeVine, Mark. "Moving Closer to God: The Master Musicians of Joujouaka." *Songlines,* no. 172 (November 2021): 44–51.

Mekouar, Merouan. "Nayda: Morocco's Musical Revolution." *Foreign Policy,* August 27, 2010. https://foreignpolicy.com/2010/08/27/nayda-moroccos-musical-revolution.

Moreno Almeida, Cristina. "Critical Reflections on Rap Music in Contemporary Morocco: Urban Youth Culture, between and beyond State's Cooptation and Dissent." PhD thesis, SOAS, University of London, 2015.

Moulay Driss El Maarouf. "Po(o)pular Culture: Measuring the 'Shit' in Moroccan Music Festivals." *Journal of African Cultural Studies* 28, no. 3 (2016): 327–42. http://dx.doi.org/10.1080/13696815.2016.1160826.

Patton, Raymond. *Punk Crisis: The Global Punk Rock Revolution.* Oxford: Oxford University Press, 2018.

Quintella, Pedro, and Paula Guerra, eds. *Punk, Fanzines and DIY Cultures in a Global World: Fast, Furious and Xerox.* London: Palgrave, 2021.

Rachidi, Ilhem. "Au Maroc, ces foyers de contestation qui ne s'éteignent pas." *OrientXXI,* April 17, 2018. https://orientxxi.info/magazine/au-maroc-ces-foyers-de-contestation-qui-ne-s-eteignent-pas,2396.

CHAPTER 2—EGYPT

Abdallah, Ahmed, dir. *Microphone.* United Artistic Group/Film Clinic, 2010.

Armbrust, Walter. *Martyrs and Tricksters: An Ethnography of the Egyptian Revolution.* Princeton, NJ: Princeton University Press, 2019.

Boraie, Sherif. *Wall Talk: Graffiti of the Egyptian Revolution.* Cairo: AUC Press, 2012.

Burkhalter, Thomas, Kay Dickinson, and Benjamin J. Harbert, eds. *The Arab Avant-Garde: Music, Politics, Modernity.* Middletown, CT: Wesleyan University Press, 2013.

Close, Ronnie. *Cairo's Ultras: Resistance and Revolution in Egypt's Football Culture.* Cairo: American University of Cairo Press, 2019.

ElNabawi, Maha. "ReTuning Egyptian Dance Music." *Mada Masr,* October 10, 2013. www.madamasr.com/en/2013/10/10/feature/culture/retuning-egyptian-dance-music.

El Tarzi, Salma. *Underground/On the Surface (Ele Beheb Rabena Yerfaa Edoh lefook).* Aker Productions, 2013.

Elshamy, Mosa'ab. "Guardians of Joy." October 8, 2014. www.youtube.com/watch?v=byW6__1znMo.

Ghadbian, Weyam. "Egyptian Band Massar Egbari: On Turning 10 and Staying Indie, and How Art Can Change Society." *Mideast Tunes,* undated. https://blog.mideastunes.com/post/139160543424/egyptian-band-massar-egbari-on-turning-10-and.

Hanan, Fayed. "Mahraganat: Egyptian Ghetto Meets Western Electronic." *Egypt Today,* October 9, 2018. www.egypttoday.com/Article/4/58662/Mahraganat-Egyptian-ghetto-meets-Western-electronic.

Jawad, Ferida. "Sadat's Dance Moves to Tek Life and Islam Chipsy." Facebook.com, March 23, 2018. www.facebook.com/ferida.jawad/videos/10156276924627803.

Karawya, Fayrouz. "Black Theama Hits the Mainstream." *Egypt Independent,* August 5, 2010. www.egyptindependent.com/black-theama-hits-mainstream.

Meddeb, Hind, dir. *Electro-Chaabi.* IPS, 2013.

Noujain, Jehane, dir. *The Square (al-Midan).* Gathr Films, 2013.

Rossi, Sabine. "In Rage Die Heavy Metal-Frontfrau in Ägypten." *Deine Korrespondentin,* July 27, 2016. www.deine-korrespondentin.de/in-ragedie-heavy-metal-frontfrau-in-aegypten/.

Swedenburg, Ted. "Egypt's Music of Protest from Sayyid Darwish to DJ Haha." *Middle East Report,* no. 265 (Winter 2012). www.merip.org/mer/mer265/egypts-music-protest.

Ultras Ahlawy. "Oh Council of Bastards" (Ya maglis, ya ibn haram), recorded in front of the Egyptian Parliament, April 2012. https://www.youtube.com/watch?v=3XvnIOzX64I.

Weis, Ellen. *Egyptian Hip-Hop: Expressions from the Underground.* Cairo: American University of Cairo Press, 2013.

CHAPTER 3—PALESTINE/ISRAEL

Arrigoni, Vittorio. *Gaza: Stay Human.* Markfield, UK: Kube, 2010.

Belkind, Nili. *Music in Conflict: Palestine, Israel and the Politics of Aesthetic Production.* London: Routledge, 2020.

Cohen, Roger. "A Rap Song Lays Bare Israel's Jewish-Arab Fracture—and Goes Viral." *New York Times,* July 21, 2021. www.nytimes.com/2021/07/21/world/middleeast/israel-palestinian-rap-video.html.

Gaza Youth Breaks Out (GYBO). "Manifesto 1.0." December 2010. https://gazaybo.wordpress.com/manifesto-0-1.

Harman, Danna. "How an Incendiary Rapper Became a Symbol for Israel's Angry Far Right." *Haaretz,* May 18, 2016. www.haaretz.com/israel-news/culture/.premium-incendiary-rapper-becomes-symbol-for-israels-angry-far-right-1.5384172.

Kahn-Harris, Keith. *Extreme Metal: Music and Culture on the Edge.* London: Bloomsbury Academic, 2007.

LeVine, Mark. "At Midnight in Jenin, the Smell of Resistance." *al-Jazeera America,* March 21, 2015. http://america.aljazeera.com/opinions/2015/3/at-midnight-in-jenin-the-smell-of-resistance.html.

LeVine, Mark, and Bryan Reynolds. "Staging the Occupation in Nabi Saleh." *Tikkun,* February 22, 2016. www.tikkun.org/staging-the-occupation-in-nabi-saleh.

Palestine Music Expo. www.palestinemusicexpo.com/about.

Ratner, David. "Rap, Racism, and Visibility: Black Music as a Mediator of Young Israeli-Ethiopians' Experience of Being 'Black' in a 'White' Society." *African and Black Diaspora: An International Journal* 12, no. 1 (2019): 94–108.

Salloum, Jackie Reem, dir. *Slingshot Hip Hop*. Fresh Booza Productions, 2008.

Shalev, Ben. "Ethiopian Musicians 'Marked' as Black Are Now Making Their Mark in Israel." *Haaretz*, April 10, 2018. www.haaretz.com/israel-news/culture/. premium-ethiopian-israelis-making-mark-in-music-1.5437778.

———. "The Ethiopian Music Scene in Israel Begins to Take Center Stage." *Haaretz*, October 2, 2018. www.haaretz.com/israel-news/.premium.MAGAZINE-say-it-loud-these-musicians-are-black-and-they-re-proud-1.6511428.

Walled Off Hotel, Bethlehem. http://walledoffhotel.com.

CHAPTER 4—LEBANON

Allers, Jackson. "Caught in the Middle: Beirut's Alt Music Scene." *Red Bull Music Academy,* June 28, 2012. https://daily.redbullmusicacademy.com/2012/06/beirut-scene.

Kassir, Samir. *Dimuqratiya suriya wa-istiqlal lubnan (Syria's Democracy Lebanon's Independence)*. Beirut: Dar al-Nahar, 2004.

Khoury, Elias. "Lubnan min al-intifada ila-l-thawra." *al-Quds al-Arabi,* October 28, 2019. https://www.alquds.co.uk/%D9%84%D8%A8%D9%86%D8%A7%D9%86-%D9%85%D9%86-%D8%A7%D9%84%D8%A7%D9%86%D8%AA%D9%81%D8%A7%D8%B6%D8%A9-%D8%A5%D9%84%D9%89-%D8%A7%D9%84%D8%AB%D9%88%D8%B1%D8%A9.

Mrad, Yara. "A Glimpse behind the Curtains: Sharif Sehnaoui Talks Irtijal and Beyond." *Revolver,* October 16, 2018. https://projectrevolver.org/features /interviews/glimpse-behind-curtains-sharif-sehanoui-talks-irtijal-beyond.

CHAPTER 5—IRAN

Eckerström, Pasqualina, and Titus Hjelm, "The Unintended Consequences of State-Enforced Orthodoxy: 'Blasphemous' Metal Music as Secondary Deviation in Iran." Unpublished article manuscript.

Ghobadi, Bahman. *No One Knows about Persian Cats [Kasi az Gorbehaye Irani Khabar Nadareh]*. Wild Bunch, 2009.

Goli, Shabnam. "Voices of a Rebellious Generation: Cultural and Political Resistance in Iran's Underground Rock Music." PhD diss., University of Florida, 2014.

Milani, Abbas, and Larry Diamond, eds. *Politics and Culture in Contemporary Iran: Challenging the Status Quo*. Boulder, CO: Lynne Reiner, 2015.

Rohde, Andi. "I Went to a Heavy Metal Festival—IN IRAN!" YouTube, April 23, 2018. www.youtube.com/watch?v=uA7rKLRuvqg&t=10s.

Coke Studio Pakistan. www.cokestudio.com.pk/season2020/index.html?WT
.cl=1&WT.mn=Home.

Khalil, Tayyab. *Rockistan: History of the Most Turbulent Music Genre in Pakistan.*
Islamabad: Daastan Publications, 2021.

Nescafé Basement. YouTube channel, www.youtube.com/channel
/UC9Nx8Ep_41tfGbuZtqJ4Yyg.

Patari Music platform. https://patari.pk/home/new.

Pepsi Battle of the Bands. YouTube channel, www.youtube.com/channel
/UCQXd4P5-_QDdK9nnW7GT7_g.

Shahid, Kunwar Khuldune. "Pakistan's Rock 'n Roll Resurgence." *Diplomat,*
December 20, 2019. https://thediplomat.com/2019/12/pakistans-rockn-roll-
resurgence.

Usmani, Basim. "Noise from the New Pakistani Underground." *Guardian,* July 1,
2011.www.theguardian.com/music/musicblog/2011/jul/01/pakistani-underground-
punk-music-scene.

EPILOGUE

Achterberg, Abdal Rahman, dir. *We Are Warriors.* Metalheads Corporation, 2019.
Available on YouTube, www.youtube.com/watch?v=aF-_n3yCjpY.

ANF News Desk. "When Music Resists Violence." October 6, 2013. https://
anfenglish.com/culture/when-music-resists-violence-8241.

Barone, Stefano. *Metal, Rap and Electro in Post-Revolutionary Tunisia: A Fragile
Underground.* London: Routledge, 2019.

Burkhalter, Thomas. *Local Music Scenes and Globalization: Transnational Platforms
in Beirut.* London: Routledge, 2013.

Clifford, James. *Routes: Travel and Translation in the Late Twentieth Century.*
Cambridge, MA: Harvard University Press, 1997.

Denning, Michael. *Noise Uprising: The Audiopolitics of a World Musical Revolution,*
London: Verso, 2015.

Donaghey, Jim. "Punk and Feminism in Indonesia." *Cultural Studies* 35, no. 1 (2021):
136–61.

Elovaara, Mika, and Brian Bardine, eds. *Connecting Metal to Culture: Unity in Disparity.* Bristol, UK: Intellect, 2017.

Erkara, Busra. "How a Gen Z Rap Group from Istanbul Became the Definitive
Voice of Turkish Youth." *Vice.com,* April 7, 2017, 9:24am. https://i-d.vice.com
/en_us/article/kzwawa/how-a-gen-z-rap-group-from-istanbul-became-the-
definitive-voice-of-turkish-youth.

Hecker, Pierre. *Turkish Metal: Music, Meaning, and Morality in a Muslim Society.*
London: Routledge, 2012.

Hintz, Lisel. "Here's How Pop Culture Woke Turkey's Disillusioned Opposition on Friday." *Washington Post,* September 10, 2019. www.washingtonpost.com /politics/2019/09/10/how-rap-is-making-changes-turkey.

Hjelm, Titus, Keith Kahn-Harris, and Mark LeVine, eds. *Heavy Metal: Controversies and Counterculture.* London: Equinox, 2013.

Jenzen, Olu, Itir Erhart, Hande Eslen-Ziya, Derya Güçdemir, Umut Korkut, and Aidan McGarry. "Music Videos as Protest Communication: The Gezi Park Protest on YouTube." In *The Aesthetics of Global Protest: Visual Culture and Communication,* edited by Aidan McGarry, Itir Erhart, Hande Eslen-Ziya, Olu Jenzen, and Umut Korkut, 211–32. Amsterdam: Amsterdam University Press, 2020.

Kadıoğlu, Duru Su, and Ceren Sözeri Özdalb. "From the Streets to the Mainstream: Popularization of Turkish Rap Music." *Turkish Studies* (2020): 1–18.

Leivers, Dannii. "Voice of Baceprot Are the Metal Band the World Needs Right Now." *Loudersound.com,* March 8, 2021. www.loudersound.com/features/voice-of-baceprot-interview-indonesian-metal-band?fbclid=IwAR3WGZYGf27SLrJ WK7Sf6L_xNcqVo8onLBNF_moybdY33vrzaxryKYJwpkY.

Patton, Marcie J. "Generation Y in Gezi Park." *Middle East Report,* no. 268 (Fall 2013).

Rancière, Jacques. *Aesthetics and Its Discontents.* London: Polity, 2009.

Sayfa, Ana. "Onlar Bir Kültüre Hayat Verdi: Türk Metal Müzik Sahnesinin Öncüsü 21 Grup." *One Dio,* November 27, 2016. http://cf-source.onedio.com /haber/onlar-bir-kulture-hayat-verdi-turk-metal-muzik-sahnesinin-oncusu-21-grup-741436.

Scenenoise. "Artist Spotlight: Kubbara, Egypt's Modular Synth Maestro." February 14, 2021. www.youtube.com/watch?v=UwSyOrE1aYo.

Scott, Niall, and Nelson Varas-Diaz, eds. *Heavy Metal Music and the Communal Experience.* Boulder, CO: Lexington, 2016.

Shank, Barry. *The Political Force of Musical Beauty.* Durham, NC: Duke University Press, 2014.

Siamdoust, Nahid. *Soundtrack of the Revolution: The Politics of Music in Iran.* Palo Alto, CA: Stanford University Press, 2017.

Wallach, Jeremy. *Modern Noise, Fluid Genres Popular Music in Indonesia, 1997–2001.* Madison: University of Wisconsin Press, 2008.

CONTRIBUTORS

JACKSON ALLERS is an archivist, storyteller, reporter, filmmaker, and editor focusing on the subcultures of his surroundings in the United States, Kosovo, Lebanon, and other places. For the last ten years, Jackson has been based in Beirut, reporting on politics and the independent musical trends in the major and grassroots international media of the Arab world and is a central force behind the Beirut Groove Collective. https://twitter.com/ajacksonjoint?lang=en.

ANONYMOUS 1 & 2, cocomposers of the Egypt chapter, are female and male longtime members of the Egyptian underground and alternative music scenes. Their names are withheld because of the ever-intensifying and brutal oppression of any artist, writer, academic, or intellectual who dares to challenge or criticize the Egyptian government.

HANIYA ASLAM is a critically acclaimed Pakistani-Canadian composer and sound designer. After a decade-long career as one-half of acclaimed duo Zeb and Haniya, she now runs her music and audio-post studio Citrus Audio from Islamabad, Pakistan. Citrusaudio.ca.

MEKAAL HASAN, an alumnus of the famed Berklee College of Music, is a musician and producer known for his work with his band the Mekaal Hasan Band as well as his production and engineering work for Pakistani and international artists, including Atif Aslam, Rahat Fateh Ali Khan, Noori, EP, Ali Azmat, Zeb and Haniya, Pete Locket, Zoe Rahman, Nana Tsiboe, and Shez Raja. He has also produced several festivals, including the I Am Karachi Festival and the Koblumpi Festival. https://youtube.com/c/mekaalhasanband1.

ABED HATHOUT is a music entrepreneur, composer, and Arabic music expert. He started his music career as founder and guitarist of Khalas Arabic Rock Orchestra, winner of the *Metal Hammer* & Orange Golden Gods Award for Best Global Metal Band, and has composed and produced for television and film, New-Age Music, and artists like DAM, Bashar Murad, Lina Makoul, and many more. He is also the cofounder of the Palestine Music Expo (PMX). @abedhat.

PIERRE HECKER is a Senior Researcher and Lecturer at the Centre for Near and Middle Eastern Studies (CNMS) at Philipps-University Marburg, Germany. He is the author of the book *Turkish Metal: Music, Meaning, and Morality in a Muslim Society* (Ashgate, 2012; Routledge, 2016), and coeditor, with Ivo Furman and Kaya Akyıldız, of *The Politics of Culture in Contemporary Turkey* (Edinburgh University Press, 2021). He currently works on atheism and nonreligion in Turkey. https://uni-marburg.academia.edu/PierreHecker.

SALOME MC is an Iranian rapper, producer, educator, and multimedia artist currently living in Seattle. She is the first woman to make hip hop music in her country, as both a rapper and a music producer. www.instagram.com/salomemcee.

SAMEH "SAZ" ZAKOUT is a native of Ramla, Palestine/Israel. Rhyming in Arabic, Hebrew, and English and widely hailed for his beatbox technique, SAZ has been featured in *Rolling Stone* and on CNN, and has toured extensively in Europe and the United States, and across Palestine and Israel. www.instagram.com/alsaz.

NAHID SIAMDOUST is an anthropologist and cultural historian whose work focuses primarily on the intersection between politics and various modes of cultural production and media forms in Iran and the wider Middle East. After a career as an Iran and Middle East journalist for *Der Spiegel, Time,* the *LA Times,* and *al-Jazeera English,* Nahid completed her PhD at St. Antony's College, Oxford, after which she held teaching and postdoctoral positions at NYU, Yale, and Harvard. Her first book, *Soundtrack of the Revolution: The Politics of Music in Iran,* was published by Stanford University Press in 2017.

JEREMY WALLACH is Professor of Popular Culture at Bowling Green State University in Ohio. A scholar of popular music and globalization, he is the author of *Modern Noise, Fluid Genres: Popular Music in Indonesia, 1997–2001* (University of Wisconsin Press, 2008), and coeditor, with Harris M. Berger and Paul D. Greene, of *Metal Rules the Globe: Heavy Metal Music around the World* (Duke University Press, 2011). www.jeremywallach.com.

INDEX

Aaroh, 219, 220, 223, 240
Abd el-Fattah, Alaa, 60, 61, 92, 93
Abdo, Mohamed, 64
Abjeez, 202, 203, 204, 205
Ableton, 243
Abouz, Houda (aka Khtek), 25
Abyusif, 87
ACCES Africa (music festival), 36
Acrophase, 231
Adorno, Theodor, xx, xxii–xxv, xxix, 204;
    as "first punk rocker," xxv
Africa, xv, 35, 37, 94, 96, 141, 246, 257
African, 40–41, 57, 91, 94, 107, 109, 247,
    256, 261, 264
African American (music), 264
Afrobeat, 134
Afro-Mizrahi, 109
Afro-Pakistani, 248
Aghakhanian, Behrooz, 189
Ahl Sina, 86
Ahmad, Salman, 150, 217, 235, 239
Ahmed, Waleed, 241
Ahmedinejad, Ahmed, 175, 176, 178
Ahsan, Zain, 209–10, 223–24, 224, 234,
    235, 237, 241
Alaa 50 (aka Alaa 50 Cent), 75, 79, 81
al-Akhareen, 148–50
al-Aqsa Intifada, 60, 96
Albarn, Damon, 4
Algeria, 23, 56, 73, 261, 285; Algerian hip
    hop/rappers, 261–62; Le Pouvoir (the
    Algerian ruling system), 140; Rai
    (see raï)

Alif, 154, 212, 216, 219
Allers, Jackson, 132
Alternative Matter, 84
Amazigh, 21, 29, 38
Amazon Music, 188
American, xxiv, xxviii, 2, 11, 35, 57, 64, 71,
    72, 75, 76, 87, 108, 109, 117, 127, 133, 147,
    152, 162, 184, 193, 196, 197, 234, 242, 245,
    246, 252, 257, 263, 264. *See also* United
    States
Amharic soul (music), 109
Amin, Hassan, 235
Amnesty International, 163
Antar, Muhammad, 114, 115
Anwar, Faraz, 11, 212, 213, 219, 230, 231, 242,
    249
Aoun, Michel, 140
Arabian Knightz, xxv, 11, 57, 58, 63, 69, 70,
    81, 82, 83
Arab Idol, 105
Arab League All-Stars, 82
Arab Spring, 14, 16, 33, 37, 42, 47, 48, 100,
    113, 114, 134, 136, 139
Arab uprisings, 2, 15, 18, 50, 52, 53, 69, 112,
    113, 126, 135, 148, 150, 152, 153, 175, 181,
    260, 267
Ardebili, Farbod, 172
Arian 13, 274
Arrigoni, Vittorio (Vik), 113–14
Arsames, 187, 252, 282
Arthimoth, 171, 202
Asfalt, 57, 63
Ashkenazi (Jew), 108, 109

Haaretz (newspaper), 106, 109

Hadag Nahash, 108

Haddad, Emmanuel, 138

Haddad, JP, 10, 168

Haddad, Raymond (Rimon), 103

Hamas, 113, 115, 123, 124, 129

Hamasi, MahmOd, 255

Hamdan, Yasmine, 118, 121, 137, 139

Hamdan, Zeid, 65, 137, 139, 141, 142

Hamma, Amine, 35

Hamzeh, Moe, 11, 132–36, 145–47, 156, 167

hardcore, xii, 2, 4, 6, 24, 26, 35, 37, 40, 41, 76, 82, 159, 200, 230, 233, 255, 256, 258, 273, 274, 275, 276; decolonial hardcore, 37; punk hardcore, xx, 27, 76, 82, 233, 255, 256, 258, 261, 273, 276

Hariri, Rafiq, 134–36

Hariri, Saad, 139–40, 167

Harman, Chris, 60

Hasan, Mekaal, 11, 209–12, 216, 219, 220, 222, 226–32, 236–40, 242

Hathout, Abed, 96, 97, 103, 104, 117

Hayır campaign ("No" campaign), 270

headbang(ing), 24, 54, 55, 65, 81, 122, 171, 230, 233, 271

heavy metal, xii, xiv, xv, xxiii, xxiv, xxvi, xxvii, 2, 4, 5, 6, 16, 17, 24, 82, 84; black metal, 77, 159, 161, 273; brutal, extreme, and death metal, xxv, xxxi, 53, 72, 75, 80, 85, 95, 98, 99, 132, 159, 174, 200,; class basis of, 73; as culturally "foreign," 79; djent, 207; emo-metal, 53; female metal and rock musicians, xxvii, 5, 24, 27, 53, 88, 89, 90, 157, 158, 187, 208; global metal, 145, 159, 256; hair metal, 72; heavy metal pioneers (of Birmingham), 1; metalcore, 231; metalheads, xii, xxiii, xxvi, xxviii, xxxi, xxxii, 7, 9, 22, 30, 43, 50, 52, 53, 54, 56, 58, 59, 62, 65, 81, 84, 85, 93, 122, 132, 160, 165, 166, 180, 183, 197, 229, 267, 270; metal horns, 3; metal-*mahraganat* mash-up/fusion, 84, 85, 88; nu-metal, 276; "Oriental" or Arabic metal, 53, 55, 86, 94, 98, 104, 144, 145, 147, 194; progressive metal, 105, 231; and rock scenes and communities, 23, 24, 26, 27, 28, 35, 36, 51, 70, 72, 76, 103, 142; "Satanic" metal/Devil worship, xxxii, 3,

13, 14, 23, 54, 163, 169; Sufi metal, 204, 210, 220, 233, 239; surpassed by hip hop in popularity, 42, 69, 86; and technology, 83; underground metal, 102, 238; as "womb of revolution," 258

Heavy Metal Islam, xi, xii, xiii, xiv, xv, xvii, xix, xx, xxiii, xxiv, xxv, xxvi, xxvii, 6, 8, 9, 18, 24, 31, 38, 53, 55, 57, 60, 84, 92, 96, 105, 110, 132, 134, 135, 163, 170, 171, 195, 201, 210, 211, 212, 216, 217, 219, 220, 228, 230, 254, 257

Hecker, Pierre, 251, 254, 267

Hellfest (festival), 257

Hezb El Rock, 165, 166

Hezbollah, 134, 135, 136, 137, 140, 163, 164, 165

Hichkas, 184, 192, 197

highlife (West African), 256

hijab-wearing metalheads, xii, 4, 5, 24, 25, 50, 54, 55, 276

Hipgah (Iranian music website), 189

hip hop, xiv, xv-xvii, xx, xxiv–xvi, 2–6, 11, 15–17, 19, 22, 24, 26, 29, 30, 35, 37, 40, 42, 43, 45, 57, 58, 62, 64–65, 67–70, 72–77, 80–83, 85, 87, 91, 93, 95, 97–99, 103–12, 114–16, 119, 122, 127, 133, 142–44, 147–49, 152, 153, 155–56, 170–71, 182, 183–84, 186–91, 194–99, 206, 210, 224, 233, 235, 238, 239, 243–48, 254–56, 258–61, 264, 267, 271, 273, 274, 284; battle raps, 82, 84, 221; dissident/revolutionary rapper(s), 15, 29–30, 33–35, 37, 41, 44–45, 46, 57, 58, 59, 63, 68, 69, 282; female MCs/rappers, 5, 24, 25, 91, 108; gangsta rap, xx, 57, 166, 174; gay rappers, 115; hip hop *à l'américaine,* 141; hip hop heads, 41; proregime (Morocco), 26, 32, 35, 45; rapper(s), xx, 5, 11, 17, 23–25, 29, 32, 79–80, 81, 82, 84, 91, 107, 109, 115, 127, 131, 138, 148, 149, 174, 180, 183–87, 190, 195–99, 245–48, 260, 262; trap, 5, 41–43, 59, 84, 258, 261; West Coast hip hop, 75

Hirak (political movement): in Algeria, 262; in Morocco, 43, 46

H-Kayne, 16, 17, 29, 32

Hoba Hoba Spirit, 20, 22, 32, 35–36, 253

Hong Kong, 7

Peerzada, Zain, 224, 225, 232, 235
Pepsi, 76, 209, 210, 212, 219–23, 233, 236, 237, 239, 240–41, 243
Pepsi Battle of the Bands, 210, 212, 219, 220, 222, 237, 240–41, 244
Peshawar, 135, 214, 236, 238, 245, 248, 250
Pink Floyd, 197, 217
Pitt, Brad, 3
Plant, Robert, 32, 48, 147, 154
Plastic Beach (album), 4
Plastic People (of the Universe), 1
PMX, 96, 103, 104, 105, 109, 117–28, 263
Political Force of Musical Beauty, The (book by Barry Shank), xvi, 264
Poor Rich Boy, 209–10, 217, 223–24, 234, 237–38, 241–42
praxis, xxii, xxix, 7, 17
Project for the Elimination of Underground Music, 174
Prophet and the Proletariat, The (book by Chris Harman), 61
Public Enemy, 62, 68
punk, xiv, xv, xvi, xvii, xx, xxiv, xxv, xxvi, xxviii, xxx, 2, 4, 6, 10, 35, 36, 37, 76, 81, 82, 160, 233, 255, 256, 258, 268, 273, 274, 275, 276, 277, 283; hardcore punk (*see* hardcore); punk aesthetic, 33, 38; punks, 41, 270, 275

Quantum, 268
Qureshi, Talal, 241, 248

Radio Javan, 192
Rage Against the Machine, 68
Rahbary, Arash, 170, 182, 192
Rahman, Jamal, 224–25, 239
raï, 73
"Rais Lebled" (song), 260
Ramallah Underground, 119, 127, 136
rap. *See* hip hop
Rasheed, Oday, 257
Ratner, David, 109, 110
Rayess Bek, 136, 139
Red Bull, 71, 136, 141
Red Bull Music Academy, 136, 141
Refat, Mahmoud, 81, 85, 87, 90, 91, 152
refugees, 8–9, 98, 137–38, 150
Refugees of Rap, 35

Restiamo Umani (book by Vittorio Arrigoni), 113
Revolutionary Artists Corner, 67, 68
revolutionary culture, xxi, xxiv, 15, 57, 253
Revolutionary Socialists, 60, 61
Revolver Magazine, 133
Reynolds, Bryan, xxi
Rifian: protests, 36, 45; rappers, 46
Robinson, Dylan, xxviii
Rock Era Magazine, 94
Rockabul (festival), 284
Rohde, Andi, xxxiv, 171, 172
Rothstein, Jed, xii, xiii, xxxi, xxxiv, 55
Rouhani, Hassan, 185, 186, 189
Rumi, xxxii
Ruptured, 142, 152

Saakin, 241
Sadat, 73–75, 79, 81, 83, 263, 264
Sadr, Navid, 196, 199
Saeed, 212
Safavi, Melody and Safoura (Abjeez), 202
Sajid, 236, 237, 238, 250
Sajid and Zeeshan, 237, 238, 250
Salafis, 70, 235
Saleh, Maryam, 65, 69, 77, 78
Saleh, Sherif, xxxi
Salloum, Jackie, 112
Salome MC, 11, 35, 170, 179, 181, 182, 184, 185–86, 192, 193, 194, 195, 196–97, 198–99, 203, 204
Sana'ei, Ali, 183, 193, 201, 206
Sassi-Sa'aron, Yossi, 98, 99, 103, 104, 105
Satanism, xiv, 37, 51, 52, 54, 74, 85, 159
Saudi Arabia, 1, 4, 63, 140, 190, 239, 240, 266
Sawi Culture Wheel, 53, 72
Sayed, Sammy, 10, 62, 78, 94
Saz (Sameh Zakout), xxxiii, 97, 110, 122, 123, 131
Scandinavia, xv, 80
Scarab, xxv, 10, 53, 60, 86, 87, 94, 144, 252
Scene Noise, 75, 94
Scott, Niall, 282
Scrambled Eggs, 137, 142
Sehnaoui, Sharif, 132
Seringai, 274, 275
sha'bi (music), 104, 122; electro-sha'bi, 127

transversal (power in music and politics), xxii, 5, 68, 95, 264

trap. *See under* hip hop

Troll, xxxi, 54, 55, 56, 59

True Brew (Pakistani music program), 224, 225, 239, 240

Trump, Donald, 17, 119, 130, 186, 187, 188, 189, 199, 252, 271

Tuhiwai-Smith, Linda, xxx

Tunisia, xxv, 7, 14, 58, 63, 71, 113, 133, 181, 235, 254, 258–61, 267, 270, 272, 275, 285

Turkey, xxv, 17, 19, 114, 203, 252, 263, 267, 268, 271, 275, 280–85; Turkish hip hop/rappers, 271–72; Turkish metal, 254, 267, 270, 271

Twitter (and tweeting), 178, 216, 245, 270

Ultras, 50, 68

United States, 56, 68, 81, 110, 137, 173, 191, 193, 204, 217, 237, 285

Universal Music Group, 245

Usmani, Basim, 232, 233

Vaezi, Shirin, 207, 208

Varas-Díaz, Nelson, 282

velayat-e faqih, 177

Vice (magazine), 81, 251, 271, 275

viscerallectric (power of music), xxi, 68

Voice of Baceprot (VoB), xiii, 5, 252, 276, 277, 278

Vreskala, Hakan, 268, 269

Wacken (festival)146, 157, 160, 257

Wallach, Jeremy, 251

Walled Off Hotel, 116–17, 118, 119

Warner Music, 11

Watar Band, 120, 121, 122, 124, 125

We Are Warriors (film), 251, 259

Wedeen, Lisa, xviii

Wegz, 74

West Bank, 96–98, 114, 118, 125–27

WhatsApp, 43, 128, 208, 216, 250, 281

Widodo, Joko (Jokowi), 274

Wighat Nazar, 57, 63

Wild, Ulrich, 146

Wonder, Stevie, 32

Wisdom Salad, 235, 241

World Festival of Sacred Music, 21, 36

World Metal Congress, 10, 144, 161, 168

world music, 21, 133, 155

Wretched of the Earth, The (book by Frantz Fanon), 56

Wu-Tang Clan, 132

Xulfi (Xulfiqar Jabbar Khan), 221, 225, 241

Yaqub, Rutaba, 239

Yas, 181

Y-Crew, 57, 60

Yemen, 9, 14, 136, 152

Your Prince Harming, 53

Yousafzai, Malala, 214, 278

Youssef, Bassem, 76

You Stink!, 138, 139

youth, xiii, xxxii, 18, 23, 31, 52, 57, 61, 78, 113, 115, 128, 147, 151, 152, 154, 186–88, 190, 198, 228, 232, 278; leftist and Islamist, 29; "metal youth" (*shbab al-metal*), 50; music, culture, and scenes, xx, 4, 8, 16, 18, 23, 30, 33, 42, 59, 63, 64, 65, 71, 77, 84, 103, 106, 109, 173, 179, 181, 182, 187, 191, 204, 218, 255, 256, 258, 266, 280; revolutionary, 61, 71, 175, 176, 181, 186. *See also* Extreme Youth Music (EYM)

YouTube, 11, 26, 28, 30, 33, 43, 44, 45, 46, 63, 66, 74, 75, 76, 82, 84, 88, 93, 128, 154, 169, 178, 187, 209, 212, 224, 225, 228, 246, 259, 262, 264, 270, 272, 279

Yunkaporta, Tyson, xxviii

Zahoor, Saieen, 212, 219

Zamalek, 54, 87

Zandi, Shaya, 195, 196

Zapatistas, xxvi

Zine, Reda, xxiii, 1, 8, 16, 33, 72, 84, 260

Zionism/Zionist, 51, 98, 107, 108, 109, 111, 112

Zirzamin, 179

Zix, 157

Znoos, 261

Zoroastrian themes, 171

Founded in 1893,
UNIVERSITY OF CALIFORNIA PRESS
publishes bold, progressive books and journals
on topics in the arts, humanities, social sciences,
and natural sciences—with a focus on social
justice issues—that inspire thought and action
among readers worldwide.

The UC PRESS FOUNDATION
raises funds to uphold the press's vital role
as an independent, nonprofit publisher, and
receives philanthropic support from a wide
range of individuals and institutions—and from
committed readers like you. To learn more, visit
ucpress.edu/supportus.